THE BEST IN

DIAGRAMMATIC

GRAPHICS

DOING IT BY THE NUMBERS

"GEE, IF ONLY I HAD KNOWN..."

Someone once said that life is always viewed backwards, but it must be lived forward.
These statistics may help improve your hindsight in the year 2012.

1972 Volkswagen
Beetle convertible
1972 COST: $2,375
VALUE TODAY:
$6,600

Tax-sheltered stock mutual fund
such as an IRA or a 401(k) account
1972 COST: $1,000
VALUE TODAY:
$8,171

Stock mutual fund
1972 COST: $1,000
VALUE TODAY:
$5,474

Tax-sheltered stock mutual fund with
50% matching employer contribution
1972 COST: $1,000
VALUE TODAY:
$12,256

Series E U.S. savings bond
1972 COST: $1,000
VALUE TODAY:
$3,046

American Flyer Model locomotive,
Burlington Rt. L2002
1972 COST: $30
VALUE TODAY:
$185

14k gold wedding band
1972 COST: $40
VALUE TODAY:
$20

1909S VDB U.S. penny
1972 COST: $200
VALUE TODAY:
$1,450

THE BEST IN

DIAGRAMMATIC

GRAPHICS

NIGEL HOLMES

ROTOVISION

A QUARTO BOOK

Published by ROTOVISION SA
Route Suisse 9
CH-1295 Mies
Switzerland

ISBN 2-88046-192-8

This book was designed and produced by
Quarto Publishing plc
6 Blundell Street
London N7 9BH

Creative Director: Richard Dewing
Designer: Steve Miller
Project Editor: Stefanie Foster
Picture Researcher: Michele Faram
Editorial Assistant: Anna Briffa

Typeset in Great Britain by
Central Southern Typesetters, Eastbourne
Manufactured in Hong Kong by Regent Publishing Services Limited
Printed in Hong Kong by Leefung-Asco Printers Ltd

Contents

Introduction

In the world of information design there is a gulf between the information and the design. That gulf is there because graphic designers rarely create or find the raw material that forms the basic content of their ultimate designs. Indeed, the designer is often the last person to be involved in the information: he or she is asked to *display* material of a factual nature, seldom to understand it. The trouble is, some designers in this field find nothing wrong with such a situation. They can happily "design" without the responsibility of explaining. They can bring their art expertise into play as a surface sheen to make the numbers look nicer. They are more interested in enticing readers to look at the design than in informing them.

If, as some would have it, we are really in the middle of an information explosion, shouldn't we expect the role of the information designer to be an important one? All that information buzzes around us like so many

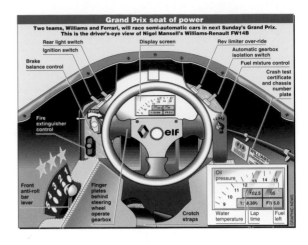

stinging insects, and we cannot get away from it. We begin to fear statistics, and one result of this fear is that we do not ask enough questions. Whose point of view is represented in this or that map? How much research went into this diagram or that chart? How were the questions worded in such and such a poll? Fear makes us accept facts as the truth.

Whether or not we are in the middle of an information explosion, we are certainly in the middle of a data flood, and that's worse. It is worse because data has not yet become information. By itself data does not inform – it is merely a list. A list of numbers, statistics and facts, all unedited and unruly. The good information designer can bring to a data flood exactly what most of us seek: meaning. This is done first by editing, then by understanding and finally by presenting the data so that its meaning is revealed to the particular audience reading it. The reader is *informed.*

The computer is the tool of choice for the creation and production of most graphics today. This has two results. The first is good: money and time are saved in the production, correction and reproduction of what

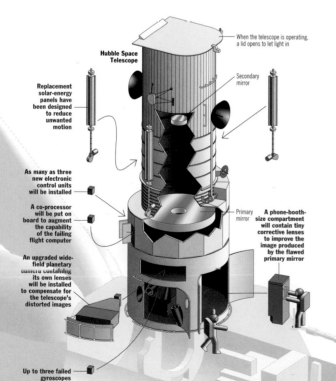

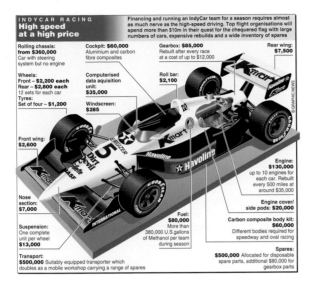

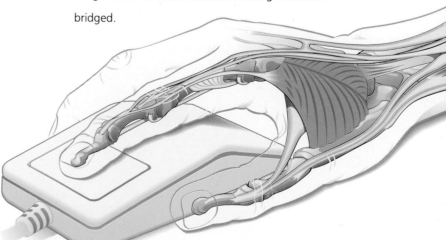

The history of statistical graphics is a comparatively short one. In 1786, William Playfair, a Scottish draughtsman, showed that the visualization of numbers and statistics was a good way of helping people to understand what they meant. He invented the fever chart, the bar graph and, later, the pie chart. These three forms are the basis of chartmaking today. The beginning of maps and diagrams is much older and can be thought of as originating with the gestures of early man as he indicated to fellow cavemen the location of likely food or the nearest shelter. The pointing finger, and its graphic cousin the arrow, remain potent tools in signage and descriptions today. Inside the caves permanant graphic signs remain: it is still debated whether the pictures of animals there were visual catalogues, recognition devices or merely decoration. Whatever their original intent, the paintings inform us about man's knowledge in those times and as such are the forerunners of the messages that we call diagrams today.

used to be called artwork. The second is bad: designers can hide behind the technical gloss a computer gives to their work that absolves them of the necessity of knowing what they are doing. Nowhere is this more obvious than in the field of diagrammatic graphics. Technical expertise on the computer has become a substitute for real explanation. The computer artist looked at the work, and it looked good. The editor or client looked at the work, and it look good. The reader looked at the page and on it was a good-looking diagram. Who is to judge (and worse, who cares) whether any of them *understood* it? In this world, design equals looks. So when the gulf between information and design is added to the computer's graphic pyrotechnics, the point of the finished piece is often lost.

This book is an attempt to show that this scenario is not always the case. Here, artists do successfully combine a picture with a set of facts in a way that entices the audience and informs them, too. Here, artists do use computers to reveal the meaning hidden inside a dense group of numbers. Here, artists are not just showing off with their latest electronic toys.

We have progressed from realistic pictures on cave walls and now know that abstractions can represent numbers, processes or animals. But abstract or not, *pictures* are what designers still produce when they set about the work of explaining something. Charts and diagrams *are* pictures — pictures of information. Keeping the picture from overwhelming the information it represents is the problem that diagram designers face with every job. With each new project, the gulf between information and design has to be bridged.

Diagrams

News diagrams help to explain to the readers of daily papers and weekly news magazines the events of the day or the week before. As such, they are generally created under tight time constraints and with information that is being updated as the artist works. The mind of a particular kind of journalistic news junkie is required to cope with this way of working. The tension between research, aesthetics and deadline – the content of the work, what it looks like and when it will be ready – is what pumps the adrenalin of such people. They thrive under pressure. From the fire at Windsor Castle to the burning of Kuwait's oil fields, this is visual reporting in the old tradition. From the in-space repairs to the Hubble Space Telescope orbiting 125 miles above us to a very earth-bound IRA attack on the Prime Minister's residence at 10 Downing Street, these artists make it possible to see things that cannot be adequately described in words.

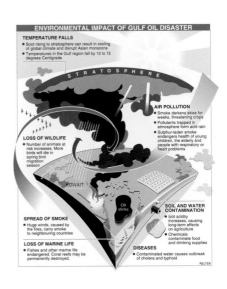

Sport is a natural for visual explanations, and it seems that our appetites are never sated. Whether it's how the game is played or how the results compare with those of previous years readers want to know more. Our capacity for studying the minutiae of a tennis player's competitive record is boundless. Newspapers and magazines, especially during the Olympics, are filled with wonderful images of swimmers, yachtsmen, fencers and archers. The large spaces that publications give to this kind of display is an indication of the importance that diagrammatic graphics have attained in recent years. Readers love these displays — as a result of reader demand, many papers in the US and Japan even reprint them and sell them as posters. Such sports coverage is not limited to special occasions such as the Olympics: here you will see Grand Prix racing, ice hockey, baseball and football. The pieces are packed with well-researched information and are rich in graphic detail. They are the visual equivalent of a complete written feature and can be read as such.

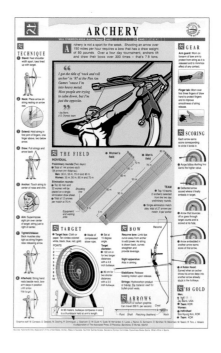

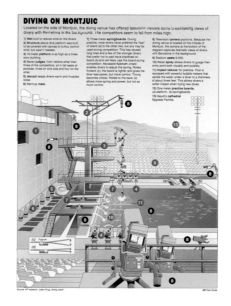

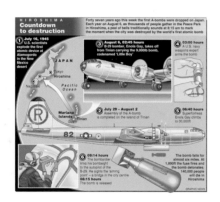

Military diagrams first appeared in earnest when the *Illustrated London News* sent artists to the Crimean War in the middle of the 19th century. Their drawings were sent back to London, where they were painstakingly engraved on wood (with many engravers working simultaneously on the image, in separate pieces) and were finally reproduced weeks after the events they depicted. We are spoiled today by the instant transmission of images, and it is hard to imagine the effect that such pictures would have had then. Yet there remains today a facet of those early artist-as-report efforts: during both the Falklands War of 1982 and the Gulf War of 1991 so few photographs were made available to the press that the graphics departments of most news organizations were called upon to supply readers with visual images of the battles. Maps, of course, have always done this (for the battle commanders, if no one else), but now maps were joined by drawings of the machinery of war. Planes swooped down on Baghdad and tanks rolled into Kuwait on top of the maps.

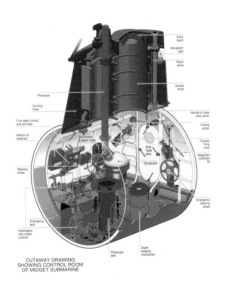

CUTAWAY DRAWING
SHOWING CONTROL ROOM
OF MIDGET SUBMARINE

History, too, is well-served by diagrammatic graphics. Here you will see cutaways of World War II submarines or a countdown to Hiroshima, drawn nearly 50 years after the events. These are more thoughtful and considered images than are the rough-and-tumble products of news deadlines.

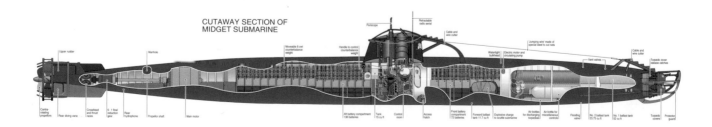

CUTAWAY SECTION OF
MIDGET SUBMARINE

Process diagrams are representations of all manner of things, from the structure of a cell to the procedure a patient goes through before and during a medical operation. While some of these pieces may be based around a central picture, most are more than that: they take the reader through a series of steps that ultimately add up to a fuller understanding of the procedure or scientific idea. Here we can find out about quarks or the problem with the ozone layer, we can take a look at fly fishing and how to save water, we can learn about the important functions of the brain, or what is happening inside the wrist while we type on a computer keyboard.

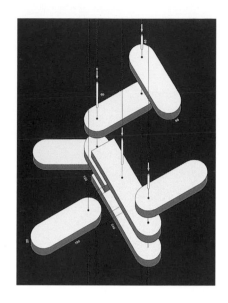

Print is a static medium, one that cannot call on the moving image to help explain a sequence. The images on these pages go as far as the medium can without breaking into animation. The reader's reward for that limitation, however, is that the picture is there to be studied again and again, at the reader's own pace. The page can be turned, and turned back. Much is made of the coming of multimedia to the business of diagramming, and come it will. But the calm of the printed page, most especially for complex subject matter, ensures that we will look at images like these long after we have been entertained by the bells and whistles of new technology.

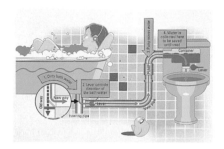

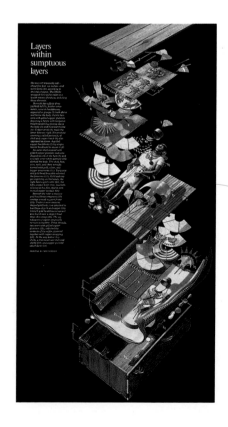

Layers within sumptuous layers

The Repair Plans

DESIGN: Joe Lertola, USA

PUBLISHER/CLIENT: *Time* magazine

DATE OF 1ST PUBLICATION/USE: 22 March 1993

DESIGN RATIONALE: To show planned repairs to the Hubble
Space Telescope. The diagram provides a detailed illustration of
the telescope and colour-keys all the replacement parts in red.

CREDIT: Researcher, Debby Wells.

THE REPAIR PLANS

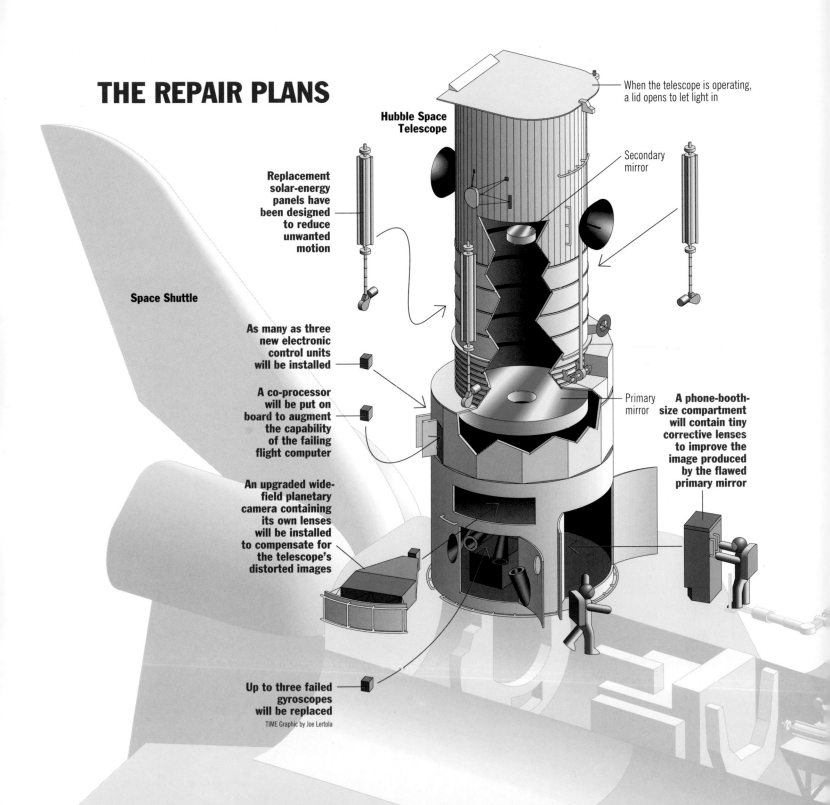

Hubble Space
Telescope

When the telescope is operating,
a lid opens to let light in

Secondary
mirror

Replacement
solar-energy
panels have
been designed
to reduce
unwanted
motion

Space Shuttle

As many as three
new electronic
control units
will be installed

A co-processor
will be put on
board to augment
the capability
of the failing
flight computer

An upgraded wide-
field planetary
camera containing
its own lenses
will be installed
to compensate for
the telescope's
distorted images

Primary
mirror

A phone-booth-
size compartment
will contain tiny
corrective lenses
to improve the
image produced
by the flawed
primary mirror

Up to three failed
gyroscopes
will be replaced

TIME Graphic by Joe Lertola

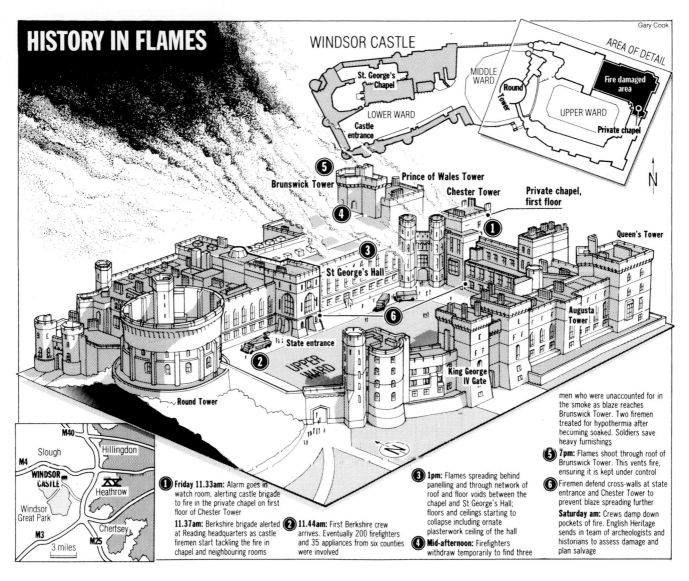

HISTORY IN FLAMES

WINDSOR CASTLE

Gary Cook

AREA OF DETAIL

St. George's Chapel

MIDDLE WARD

LOWER WARD

Castle entrance

Round Tower

UPPER WARD

Fire damaged area

Private chapel

N

⑤ Brunswick Tower

Prince of Wales Tower

Chester Tower

Private chapel, first floor

④

①

Queen's Tower

③

St George's Hall

Augusta Tower

⑥

State entrance

②

UPPER WARD

King George IV Gate

Round Tower

Slough

M40

Hillingdon

M4

WINDSOR CASTLE

Heathrow

Windsor Great Park

M3

Chertsey

M25

3 miles

① **Friday 11.33am:** Alarm goes in watch room, alerting castle brigade to fire in the private chapel on first floor of Chester Tower

11.37am: Berkshire brigade alerted at Reading headquarters as castle firemen start tackling the fire in chapel and neighbouring rooms

② **11.44am:** First Berkshire crew arrives. Eventually 200 firefighters and 35 appliances from six counties were involved

③ **1pm:** Flames spreading behind panelling and through network of roof and floor voids between the chapel and St George's Hall; floors and ceilings starting to collapse including ornate plasterwork ceiling of the hall

④ **Mid-afternoon:** Firefighters withdraw temporarily to find three

men who were unaccounted for in the smoke as blaze reaches Brunswick Tower. Two firemen treated for hypothermia after becoming soaked. Soldiers save heavy furnishings

⑤ **7pm:** Flames shoot through roof of Brunswick Tower. This vents fire, ensuring it is kept under control

⑥ Firemen defend cross-walls at state entrance and Chester Tower to prevent blaze spreading further

Saturday am: Crews damp down pockets of fire. English Heritage sends in team of archeologists and historians to assess damage and plan salvage

History in Flames

DESIGN: Gary Cook, UK

PUBLISHER/CLIENT: *Sunday Times*

DATE OF 1ST PUBLICATION/USE: 22 November 1992

DESIGN RATIONALE: An aerial section of Windsor Castle locating the fire within the building, with a flat plan and location map. The diagram was required to show the timescale, the extent of the fire and the location of Windsor.

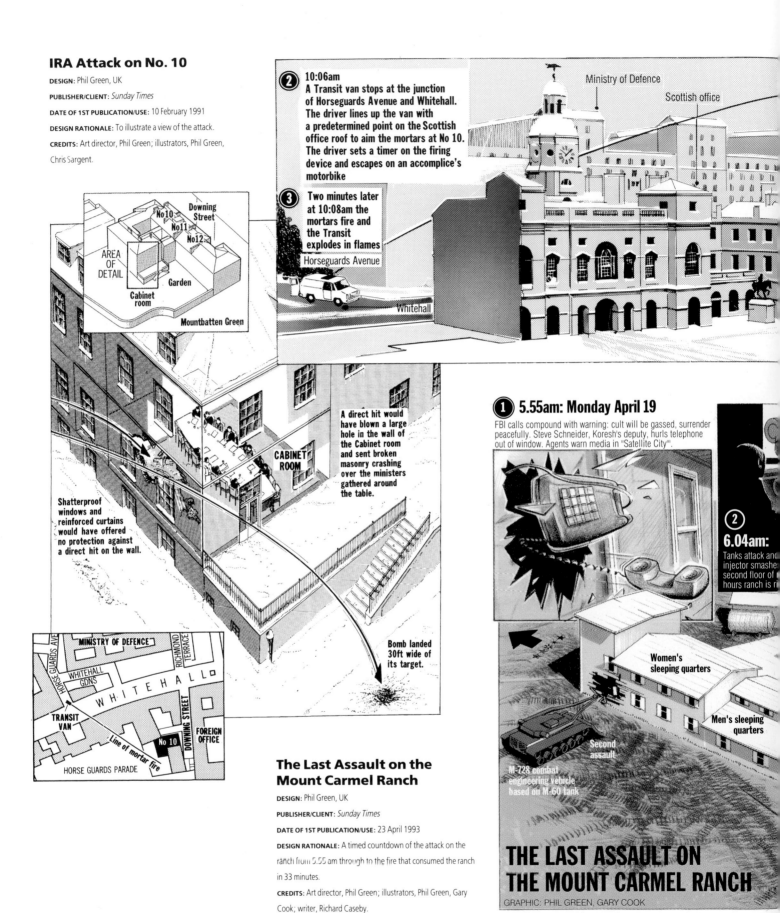

IRA Attack on No. 10

DESIGN: Phil Green, UK

PUBLISHER/CLIENT: *Sunday Times*

DATE OF 1ST PUBLICATION/USE: 10 February 1991

DESIGN RATIONALE: To illustrate a view of the attack.

CREDITS: Art director, Phil Green; illustrators, Phil Green, Chris Sargent.

2
10:06am
A Transit van stops at the junction of Horseguards Avenue and Whitehall. The driver lines up the van with a predetermined point on the Scottish office roof to aim the mortars at No 10. The driver sets a timer on the firing device and escapes on an accomplice's motorbike

3
Two minutes later at 10:08am the mortars fire and the Transit explodes in flames

Horseguards Avenue

Whitehall

Ministry of Defence

Scottish office

No10
No11
No12

Downing Street

AREA OF DETAIL

Garden

Cabinet room

Mountbatten Green

A direct hit would have blown a large hole in the wall of the Cabinet room and sent broken masonry crashing over the ministers gathered around the table.

CABINET ROOM

Shatterproof windows and reinforced curtains would have offered no protection against a direct hit on the wall.

Bomb landed 30ft wide of its target.

MINISTRY OF DEFENCE

RICHMOND TERRACE

WHITEHALL GDNS

WHITEHALL

HORSE GUARDS AVE

TRANSIT VAN

Line of mortar fire

No 10

DOWNING STREET

FOREIGN OFFICE

HORSE GUARDS PARADE

The Last Assault on the Mount Carmel Ranch

DESIGN: Phil Green, UK

PUBLISHER/CLIENT: *Sunday Times*

DATE OF 1ST PUBLICATION/USE: 23 April 1993

DESIGN RATIONALE: A timed countdown of the attack on the ranch from 5.55 am through to the fire that consumed the ranch in 33 minutes.

CREDITS: Art director, Phil Green; illustrators, Phil Green, Gary Cook; writer, Richard Caseby.

1 5.55am: Monday April 19
FBI calls compound with warning: cult will be gassed, surrender peacefully. Steve Schneider, Koresh's deputy, hurls telephone out of window. Agents warn media in "Satellite City".

2 6.04am:
Tanks attack and injector smashes second floor of r hours ranch is ri

Women's sleeping quarters

Men's sleeping quarters

Second assault

M-728 combat engineering vehicle based on M-60 tank

THE LAST ASSAULT ON THE MOUNT CARMEL RANCH

GRAPHIC: PHIL GREEN, GARY COOK

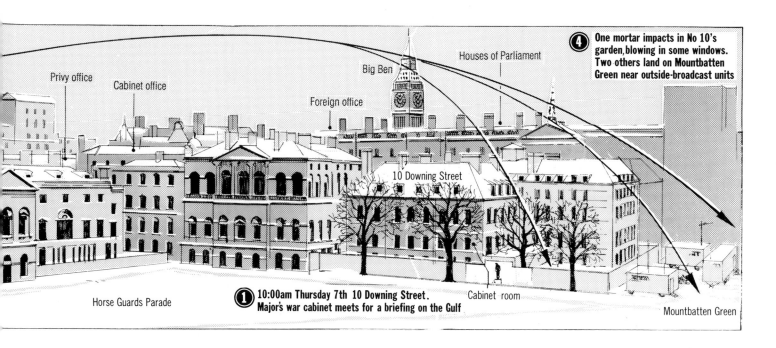

Killing Kuwait's Oil Fires

DESIGN: Duncan Mil, UK

PUBLISHER/CLIENT: Graphic News

DATE OF 1ST PUBLICATION/USE: 5 August 1992

DESIGN RATIONALE: Capping a blazing oil well in Kuwait following the Iraqi withdrawal after the Gulf War.

CREDITS: Art director, Duncan Mil; illustrators, Duncan Mil, Russell Lewis; writer/researcher, Julie Hacking.

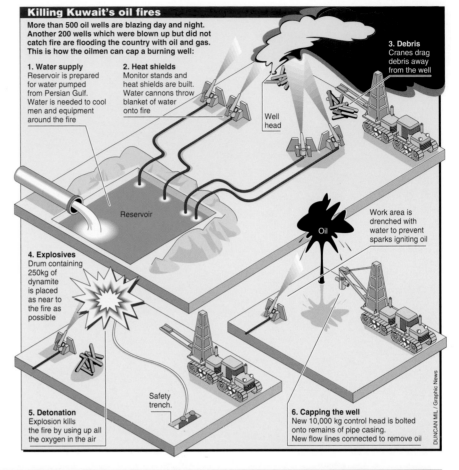

Killing Kuwait's oil fires

More than 500 oil wells are blazing day and night. Another 200 wells which were blown up but did not catch fire are flooding the country with oil and gas. This is how the oilmen can cap a burning well:

1. Water supply
Reservoir is prepared for water pumped from Persian Gulf. Water is needed to cool men and equipment around the fire

2. Heat shields
Monitor stands and heat shields are built. Water cannons throw blanket of water onto fire

3. Debris
Cranes drag debris away from the well

Well head

Reservoir

Oil

Work area is drenched with water to prevent sparks igniting oil

4. Explosives
Drum containing 250kg of dynamite is placed as near to the fire as possible

5. Detonation
Explosion kills the fire by using up all the oxygen in the air

Safety trench.

6. Capping the well
New 10,000 kg control head is bolted onto remains of pipe casing. New flow lines connected to remove oil

DUNCAN MIL. / Graphic News

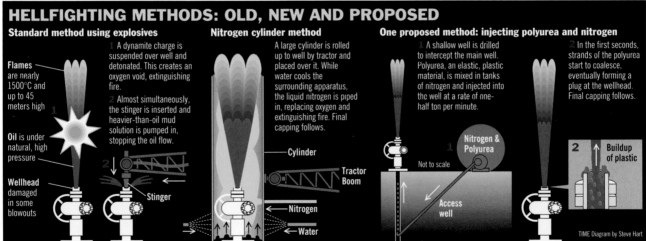

HELLFIGHTING METHODS: OLD, NEW AND PROPOSED

Standard method using explosives

Flames are nearly 1500°C and up to 45 meters high

Oil is under natural, high pressure

Wellhead damaged in some blowouts

1 A dynamite charge is suspended over well and detonated. This creates an oxygen void, extinguishing fire.

2 Almost simultaneously, the stinger is inserted and heavier-than-oil mud solution is pumped in, stopping the oil flow.

Stinger

Nitrogen cylinder method

A large cylinder is rolled up to well by tractor and placed over it. While water cools the surrounding apparatus, the liquid nitrogen is piped in, replacing oxygen and extinguishing fire. Final capping follows.

Cylinder

Tractor Boom

Nitrogen

Water

One proposed method: injecting polyurea and nitrogen

1 A shallow well is drilled to intercept the main well. Polyurea, an elastic, plastic material, is mixed in tanks of nitrogen and injected into the well at a rate of one-half ton per minute.

2 In the first seconds, strands of the polyurea start to coalesce, eventually forming a plug at the wellhead. Final capping follows.

Nitrogen & Polyurea

Not to scale

Access well

2 **Buildup of plastic**

TIME Diagram by Steve Hart

Oil Fire Fighting Methods

DESIGN: Steve Hart, USA

PUBLISHER/CLIENT: *Time* magazine

DATE OF 1ST PUBLICATION/USE: 11 May 1991

DESIGN RATIONALE: Diagrams of fighting oil fires, showing two conventional methods and one new one.

CREDITS: Art director, Rudy Hoglund; illustrator, Steve Hart; researcher, Debby Wells.

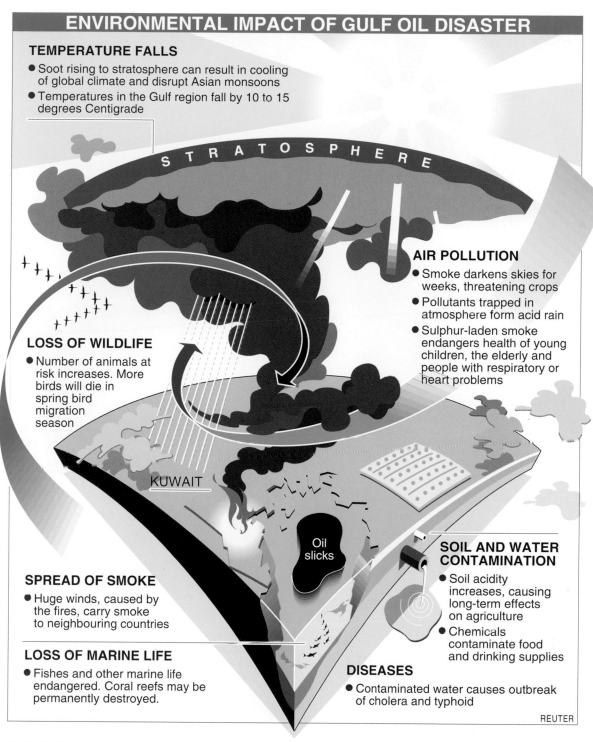

ENVIRONMENTAL IMPACT OF GULF OIL DISASTER

TEMPERATURE FALLS
- Soot rising to stratosphere can result in cooling of global climate and disrupt Asian monsoons
- Temperatures in the Gulf region fall by 10 to 15 degrees Centigrade

S T R A T O S P H E R E

AIR POLLUTION
- Smoke darkens skies for weeks, threatening crops
- Pollutants trapped in atmosphere form acid rain
- Sulphur-laden smoke endangers health of young children, the elderly and people with respiratory or heart problems

LOSS OF WILDLIFE
- Number of animals at risk increases. More birds will die in spring bird migration season

KUWAIT

Oil slicks

SOIL AND WATER CONTAMINATION
- Soil acidity increases, causing long-term effects on agriculture
- Chemicals contaminate food and drinking supplies

SPREAD OF SMOKE
- Huge winds, caused by the fires, carry smoke to neighbouring countries

LOSS OF MARINE LIFE
- Fishes and other marine life endangered. Coral reefs may be permanently destroyed.

DISEASES
- Contaminated water causes outbreak of cholera and typhoid

REUTER

Gulf Oil Disaster

DESIGN: Chan Chee Kin, Singapore

PUBLISHER/CLIENT: Reuter News Graphics Service

DATE OF 1ST PUBLICATION/USE: 3 February 1991

DESIGN RATIONALE: A visual explanation of the effect and impact of the Gulf War oil disaster on the environment. Dramatic alteration of scale enabled graphics journalist Chan Chee Kin to concentrate on cause and effect issues.

AROUND THE WORLD IN 20 DAYS

It may look like a double bubble, but Earthwinds is the first free-flying balloon system designed to circle the world. Pilot/adventurer Larry Newman, who has crossed the Atlantic and Pacific oceans in conventional helium balloons, hopes to begin his around-the-world adventure later this month. Depending on the speed and direction of the jet stream, the non-stop flight could take two to three weeks and cover 19,000 miles or more.

Earthwinds, possible flight route

The balloon will be launched from Akron, Ohio. Earthwinds should reach its floating altitude of 35,000 to 40,000 feet within two hours after taking off. The balloon will move along in the jet stream. At the end of the flight, which may take 12 to 21 days, the crew may land anywhere east of Akron's longitude, 81 degrees west.

Region of violent thunderstorms: Storms can rise above the level where the balloon will fly.

The Earth as viewed from the North Pole

USSR
Africa
Pacific Ocean
Atlantic Ocean
North America

Potential winter storm area: Hazardous to the crew if they need to land.

Potential winter storm area: Hazardous to the crew if they need to land.

A discription of the crew

Larry Newman first flew solo when he was 12 years old in California. By the time he was 18, he had a commercial pilot's license. At 23, he was flying Learjets. A few years later, he owned one — having turned a hobbyist's interest in hang gliders and ultralight aircraft into a multimillion-dollar business. At 44, he flies Boeing 757s for America West Airlines. Despite the deeply discounted fares he gets as a professional pilot, he still charges expenses for the Earthwinds project on a VISA card that gives frequent flier miles. He's already got enough for two more trips around the world. His wife, Lynne, is the coordinator of the growing Earthwinds support staff.

Vladimir Dzhanibekov circled the world as a Soviet cosmonaut, having logged more than 20 weeks in space in five missions since 1978, often in quarters far more confining than those aboard the Earthwinds capsule. He was an air force flight instructor before he joined the cosmonaut corps in 1970. Mr. Dzanibekov has twice been named a hero of the Soviet Union. He has also been awarded the Order of Lenin, Order of the Red Star and other medals. Now 49, he serves as chief of the cosmonaut training department. He has a wife and two daughters.

Don Moses was the last member of the crew chosen for the around-the-world flight, but may be the most indispensable. Mr. Newman persuaded him to help design and build the Earthwinds capsule. He will be expected to keep all of the equipment on board running while the balloon is aloft. Born in California, Mr. Moses, now 45, spent much of his adult life in Hawaii as a commercial boat builder and sightseeing guide. Mr. Newman said he was prepared to sacrifice fuel and other supplies to make room for him as a crew member.

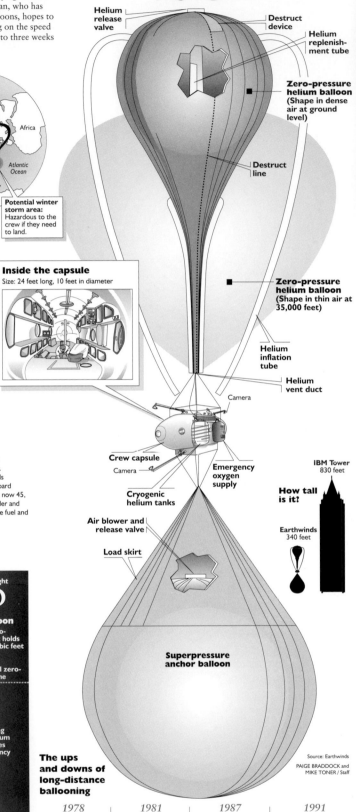

Helium release valve

Destruct device

Helium replenishment tube

Zero-pressure helium balloon (Shape in dense air at ground level)

Destruct line

Inside the capsule
Size: 24 feet long, 10 feet in diameter

Zero-pressure helium balloon (Shape in thin air at 35,000 feet)

Helium inflation tube

Helium vent duct

Camera

Crew capsule
Camera

Emergency oxygen supply

Cryogenic helium tanks

Air blower and release valve

Load skirt

Superpressure anchor balloon

How tall is it?

IBM Tower 830 feet

Earthwinds 340 feet

Source: Earthwinds

PAIGE BRADDOCK and MIKE TONER / Staff

How Earthwinds works

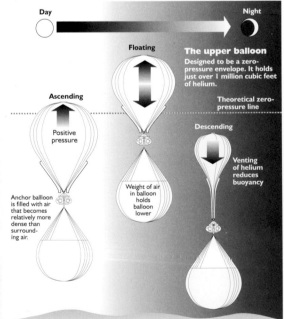

Day
Night

Floating

Ascending

The upper balloon
Designed to be a zero-pressure envelope. It holds just over 1 million cubic feet of helium.

Theoretical zero-pressure line

Positive pressure

Descending

Venting of helium reduces buoyancy

Weight of air in balloon holds balloon lower

Anchor balloon is filled with air that becomes relatively more dense than surrounding air.

The anchor balloon

An air-filled superpressure anchor balloon becomes lighter or heavier with changes in altitude, providing a helium balloon with a "variable ballast" that never runs out. A powerful electric fan can pressurize the anchor balloon with air, while a valve permits the pressure to be released.

The ups and downs of long-distance ballooning

1978
3,233 miles from Maine to Paris; 5 days, 17 hours.

Larry Newman and two other veteran balloonists cross the Atlantic in a helium balloon. Thirteen balloonists have tried and failed since 1873. The Double Eagle II makes the journey only after the crew jettisons emergency gear and equipment to keep the balloon aloft.

1981
5,209 miles from Japan to California; 3 days, 12 hours.

Mr. Newman and three others make the first balloon crossing of the Pacific Ocean. Ice accumulation threatens the flight of Double Eagle V most of the way. The first landing attempt, in heavy rains in the coastal mountains of California, has to be aborted.

1987
2,788 miles from Maine to near Limavady Ireland; 1 day, 7 hours and 40 min.

Richard Branson and Per Lindstrand attempt to cross the Atlantic in a hot air balloon. The Virgin Atlantic Flyer is forced to set down in heavy seas one mile off the coast of Scotland, after touching down briefly in Ireland. Purists say the wet landing disqualifies the flight as an ocean crossing.

1991
5,879 miles from Japan to Canada; 1 day, 22 hours, 3 min.

Mr. Branson and Lindstrand fly a hot air balloon across the Pacific, but accidentally jettison one-third of the Pacific Flyer's propane fuel. Strong winds come to their aid, pushing them eastward at a record speed of nearly 200 miles an hour. Aiming for Utah, the balloonists land instead on a frozen lake in northern Canada.

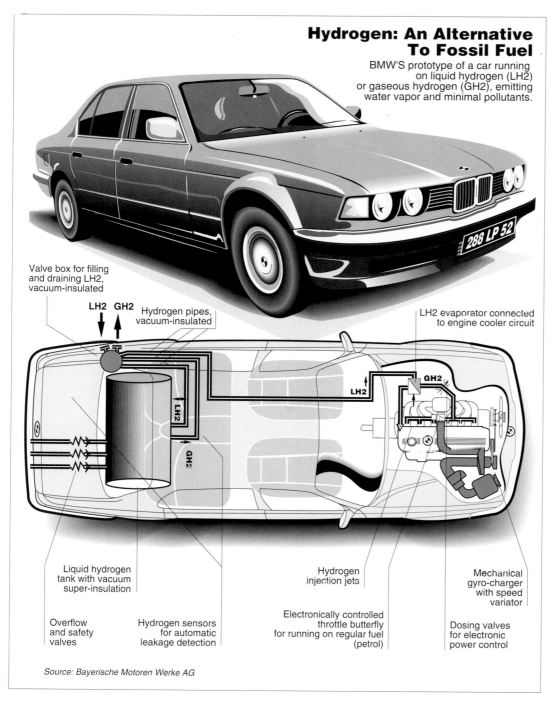

Hydrogen: An Alternative To Fossil Fuel

BMW'S prototype of a car running
on liquid hydrogen (LH2)
or gaseous hydrogen (GH2), emitting
water vapor and minimal pollutants.

Valve box for filling
and draining LH2,
vacuum-insulated

LH2 GH2

Hydrogen pipes,
vacuum-insulated

LH2 evaporator connected
to engine cooler circuit

LH2

GH2

LH2

GH2

Liquid hydrogen
tank with vacuum
super-insulation

Hydrogen
injection jets

Mechanical
gyro-charger
with speed
variator

Overflow
and safety
valves

Hydrogen sensors
for automatic
leakage detection

Electronically controlled
throttle butterfly
for running on regular fuel
(petrol)

Dosing valves
for electronic
power control

Source: Bayerische Motoren Werke AG

Hydrogen as Fossil Fuel Alternative

DESIGN: Richard Yeend, UK

PUBLISHER/CLIENT: *International Herald Tribune*

DATE OF 1ST PUBLICATION/USE: September 1989

DESIGN RATIONALE: To illustrate the hydrogen-powered BMW. A section front for an *IHT* technical supplement.

CREDITS: Art director, Richard Yeend; illustrator, Phillippe Launay.

Around the World in 20 Days

DESIGN: Paige Braddock, USA

PUBLISHER/CLIENT: *Atlanta Journal*

DATE OF 1ST PUBLICATION/USE: May 1992

DESIGN RATIONALE: To illustrate a new design in balloon technology – a double balloon, designed so that the bottom balloon acts as ballast.

CREDITS: Art director, Tony Defeira; illustrator, Paige Braddock; writer, Mike Toner; researchers, Paige Braddock, Mike Toner.

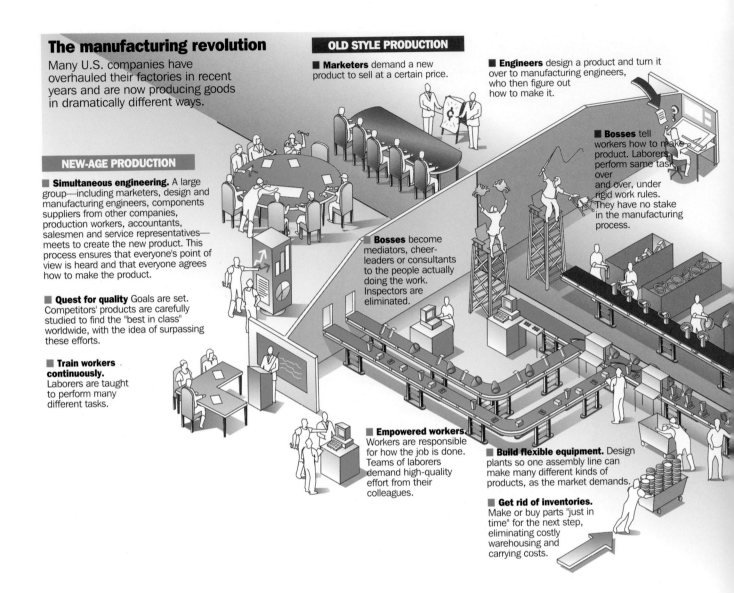

The manufacturing revolution

Many U.S. companies have overhauled their factories in recent years and are now producing goods in dramatically different ways.

OLD STYLE PRODUCTION

■ **Marketers** demand a new product to sell at a certain price.

■ **Engineers** design a product and turn it over to manufacturing engineers, who then figure out how to make it.

NEW-AGE PRODUCTION

■ **Simultaneous engineering.** A large group—including marketers, design and manufacturing engineers, components suppliers from other companies, production workers, accountants, salesmen and service representatives—meets to create the new product. This process ensures that everyone's point of view is heard and that everyone agrees how to make the product.

■ **Quest for quality** Goals are set. Competitors' products are carefully studied to find the "best in class" worldwide, with the idea of surpassing these efforts.

■ **Train workers continuously.** Laborers are taught to perform many different tasks.

■ **Bosses** tell workers how to make product. Laborers perform same task over and over, under rigid work rules. They have no stake in the manufacturing process.

■ **Bosses** become mediators, cheer-leaders or consultants to the people actually doing the work. Inspectors are eliminated.

■ **Empowered workers.** Workers are responsible for how the job is done. Teams of laborers demand high-quality effort from their colleagues.

■ **Build flexible equipment.** Design plants so one assembly line can make many different kinds of products, as the market demands.

■ **Get rid of inventories.** Make or buy parts "just in time" for the next step, eliminating costly warehousing and carrying costs.

The Manufacturing Revolution

DESIGN: Dave Merrill, USA

PUBLISHER/CLIENT: *US News & World Report*

DATE OF 1ST PUBLICATION/USE: 22 October, 1990

DESIGN RATIONALE: A graphic representation of the assembly line of the future. A side-by-side comparison shows how the elements of the old-style production teams differ from the elements of 1990s management ideas of quality control, simultaneous engineering and empowered workers.

CREDITS: Art director, Rob Covey; illustrator, Dave Merrill; writer/researcher, William Cook.

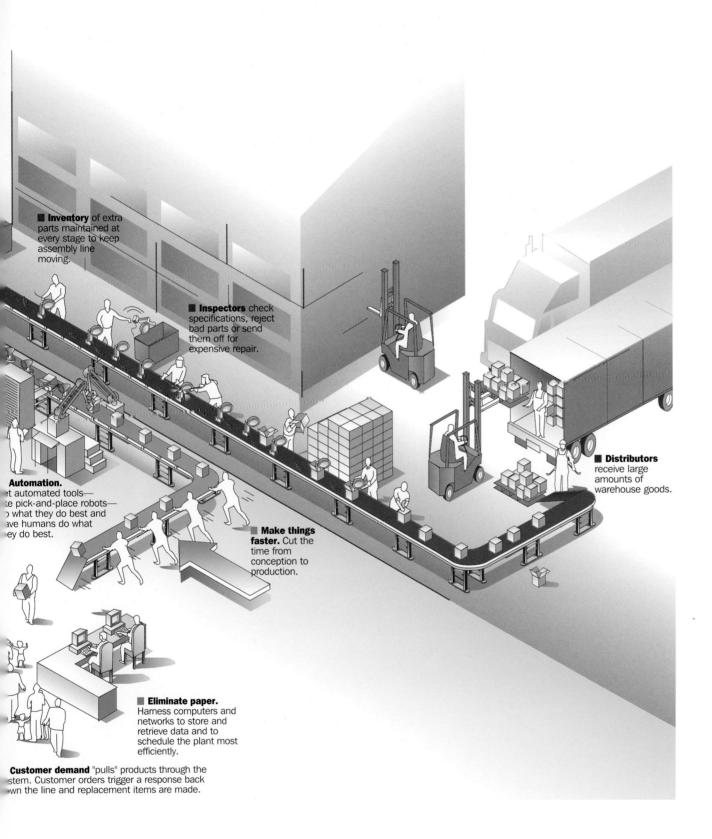

■ **Inventory** of extra parts maintained at every stage to keep assembly line moving.

■ **Inspectors** check specifications, reject bad parts or send them off for expensive repair.

■ **Distributors** receive large amounts of warehouse goods.

Automation.
et automated tools—
e pick-and-place robots—
o what they do best and
ave humans do what
ey do best.

■ **Make things faster.** Cut the time from conception to production.

■ **Eliminate paper.** Harness computers and networks to store and retrieve data and to schedule the plant most efficiently.

Customer demand "pulls" products through the stem. Customer orders trigger a response back wn the line and replacement items are made.

The Corruption of Italy

DESIGN: Nobuko Edotsune, Japan

PUBLISHER/CLIENT: Asahi Shimbun, *AERA* magazine

DATE OF 1ST PUBLICATION/USE: March 1993

DESIGN RATIONALE: The diagram illustrates famous Italian financiers, political parties and others under suspicion of bribery, as well as illustrating all Italian political parties.

Iraqgate

DESIGN: Dave Merrill, USA

PUBLISHER/CLIENT: *US News & World Report*

DATE OF 1ST PUBLICATION/USE: 16 March 1992

DESIGN RATIONALE: The diagram shows the complex path of arms money in what is commonly referred to as the Iraqgate scandal in the US. Banks, governments and officials are symbolically or iconographically illustrated, and the reader simply follows the money trail to determine the role of each party in this scandal.

CREDITS: Art director, Rob Covey; illustrator, Dave Merrill; writer/researcher, Steve Budiansky.

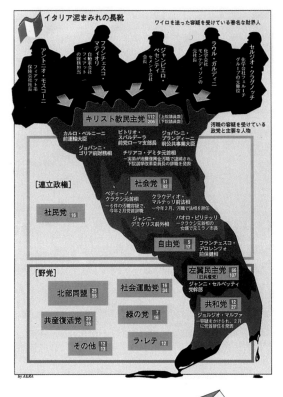

Money machine: The Iraqi diversion

Deprived of other sources of loan money, Baghdad borrowed money to purchase U.S. farm goods at artificially inflated prices and used the excess profits to pay for weapons research and procurement. The U.S. Agriculture Department guaranteed the loans to Iraq. When Saddam Hussein's Army invaded Kuwait, Washington was stuck with more than $2 billion in bad loans. U.S. taxpayers must now repay them.

① Iraq. Seeks approval to participate in U.S. Department of Agriculture program guaranteeing repayment of loans for purchase of American farm products.

② Washington. Between 1983 and 1990, approves more than $5 billion in loan guarantees for Iraqi commodities purchases under the Agriculture Department program.

③ Intermediaries. Coordinating with the government of Iraq, grain dealers and shippers agree to sell American commodities at prices considerably above market rates.

④ Bankers. Accept the Agriculture Department loan guarantees and approve millions of dollars in loans for the commodities purchases.

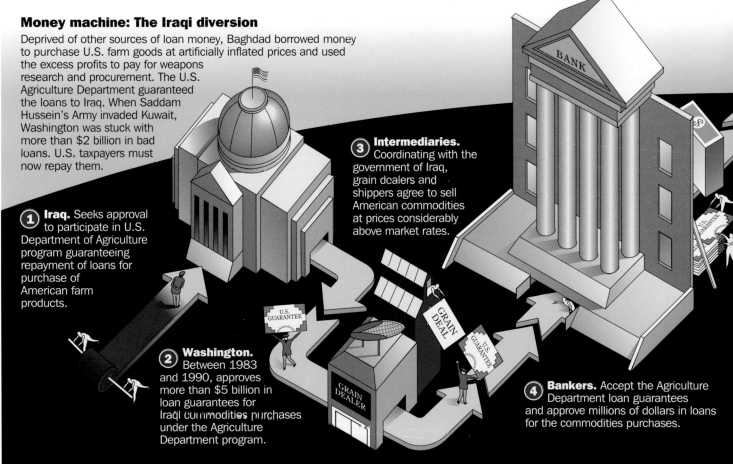

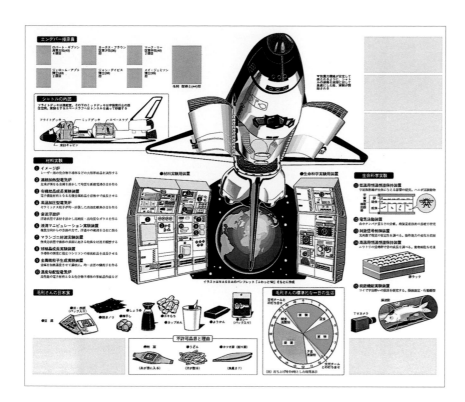

Space Shuttle

DESIGN: Sankei Design, Japan

PUBLISHER/CLIENT: *Sankei Shinbun* in *Scope* series

DATE OF 1ST PUBLICATION/USE: 18 January 1991 –
25 March 1993

DESIGN RATIONALE: To illustrate data concerning
everyday news.

CREDITS: Art director, Katsuhiko Nakazawa, Kazuhiro Morita;
photographer, *Sankei Shinbun*; illustrator, Sankei Design;
writer, *Sankei Shinbun*, Tokusyu-Han.

DAVID S. MERRILL—*USN&WR*

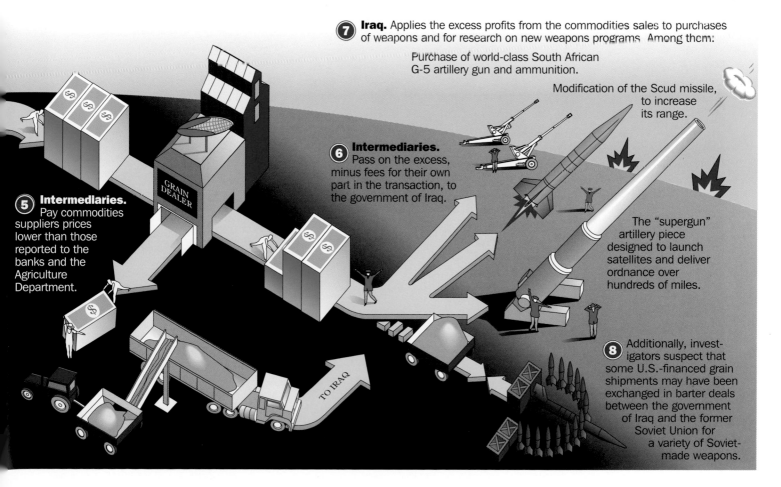

7 Iraq. Applies the excess profits from the commodities sales to purchases of weapons and for research on new weapons programs. Among them:

Purchase of world-class South African G-5 artillery gun and ammunition.

Modification of the Scud missile, to increase its range.

6 Intermediaries. Pass on the excess, minus fees for their own part in the transaction, to the government of Iraq.

5 Intermediaries. Pay commodities suppliers prices lower than those reported to the banks and the Agriculture Department.

GRAIN DEALER

TO IRAQ

The "supergun" artillery piece designed to launch satellites and deliver ordnance over hundreds of miles.

8 Additionally, investigators suspect that some U.S.-financed grain shipments may have been exchanged in barter deals between the government of Iraq and the former Soviet Union for a variety of Soviet-made weapons.

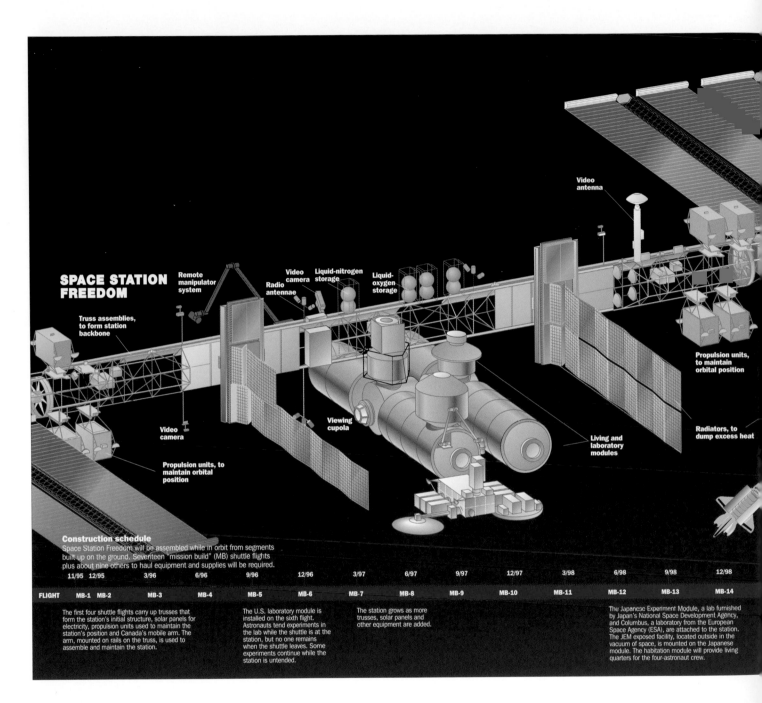

SPACE STATION FREEDOM

Remote manipulator system

Video camera

Radio antennae

Liquid-nitrogen storage

Liquid-oxygen storage

Video antenna

Truss assemblies, to form station backbone

Video camera

Propulsion units, to maintain orbital position

Viewing cupola

Living and laboratory modules

Propulsion units, to maintain orbital position

Radiators, to dump excess heat

Construction schedule

Space Station Freedom will be assembled while in orbit from segments built up on the ground. Seventeen "mission build" (MB) shuttle flights plus about nine others to haul equipment and supplies will be required.

	11/95	12/95	3/96	6/96	9/96	12/96	3/97	6/97	9/97	12/97	3/98	6/98	9/98	12/98
FLIGHT	MB-1	MB-2	MB-3	MB-4	MB-5	MB-6	MB-7	MB-8	MB-9	MB-10	MB-11	MB-12	MB-13	MB-14

The first four shuttle flights carry up trusses that form the station's initial structure, solar panels for electricity, propulsion units used to maintain the station's position and Canada's mobile arm. The arm, mounted on rails on the truss, is used to assemble and maintain the station.

The U.S. laboratory module is installed on the sixth flight. Astronauts tend experiments in the lab while the shuttle is at the station, but no one remains when the shuttle leaves. Some experiments continue while the station is untended.

The station grows as more trusses, solar panels and other equipment are added.

The Japanese Experiment Module, a lab furnished by Japan's National Space Development Agency, and Columbus, a laboratory from the European Space Agency (ESA), are attached to the station. The JEM exposed facility, located outside in the vacuum of space, is mounted on the Japanese module. The habitation module will provide living quarters for the four-astronaut crew.

Life in Space

DESIGN: Matt Zang, USA

PUBLISHER/CLIENT: *US News & World Report*

DATE OF 1ST PUBLICATION/USE: 25 May 1992

DESIGN RATIONALE: To show a comprehensive view of the new budget-plagued US, European, Japanese and Canadian space station Freedom. The work is a classic cutaway technical illustration and is a great example of how the Macintosh, with its duplication of rotation and scaling functions, can ease the burden of large technical illustration.

CREDITS: Art director, Rob Covey; illustrator, Matt Zang; writer/researcher, William Cook.

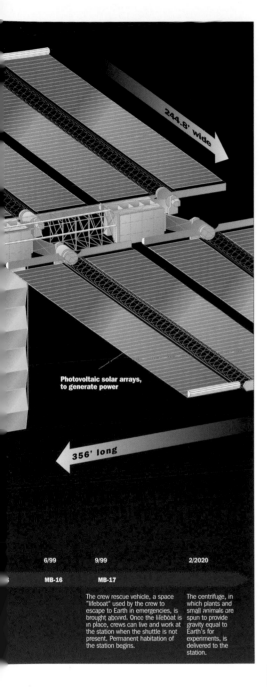

Photovoltaic solar arrays,
to generate power

244.8' wide

356' long

| 6/99 | 9/99 | 2/2020 |
| MB-16 | MB-17 | |

The crew rescue vehicle, a space "lifeboat" used by the crew to escape to Earth in emergencies, is brought aboard. Once the lifeboat is in place, crews can live and work at the station when the shuttle is not present. Permanent habitation of the station begins.

The centrifuge, in which plants and small animals are spun to provide gravity equal to Earth's for experiments, is delivered to the station.

The Sinking of the *Titanic*

DESIGN: Steven Stankiewicz, USA

PUBLISHER/CLIENT: McGraw-Hill Publishing

DATE OF 1ST PUBLICATION/USE: August 1992

DESIGN RATIONALE: The illustration shows the break-up and descent of the pieces of the *Titanic* in their relative positions from ocean surface to floor.

CREDITS: Art director, Leonard Vigliarolo; illustrator, Steven Stankiewicz.

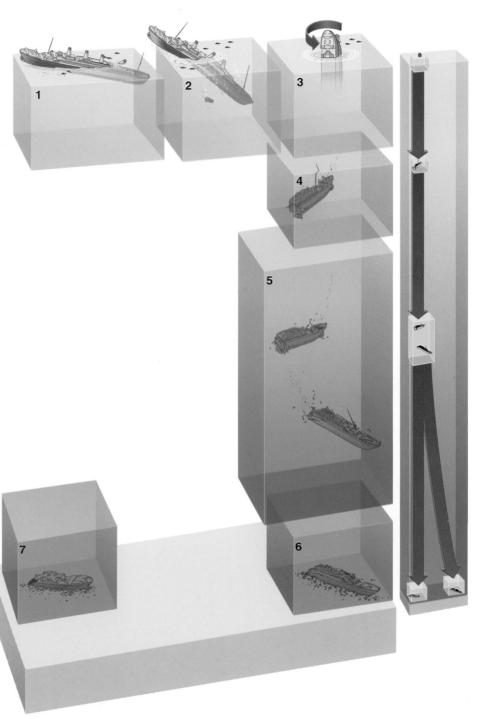

Pit Stop

DESIGN: John Grimwade, UK

PUBLISHER/CLIENT: *Fast Lane*

DATE OF 1ST PUBLICATION/USE: 1991

DESIGN RATIONALE: Anatomy of a pit stop in the Indianapolis 500. The graphic was supported by a detailed description of each stage to give a tight analysis of very fast activity.

CREDITS: Art director, Larry Hask.

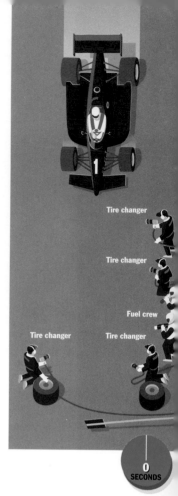

Tire changer

Tire changer

Fuel crew

Tire changer

Tire changer

0 SECONDS

Indycar Costs

DESIGN: Duncan Mil, UK

PUBLISHER/CLIENT: Graphic News

DATE OF 1ST PUBLICATION/USE: 19 March 1993

DESIGN RATIONALE: To give a breakdown of the cost of Indycar parts – wheels, engines, body mouldings, etc – and team financing.

CREDITS: Art director, Duncan Mil; illustrators, Duncan Mil, Russell Lewis; writer/researcher, Julie Hacking.

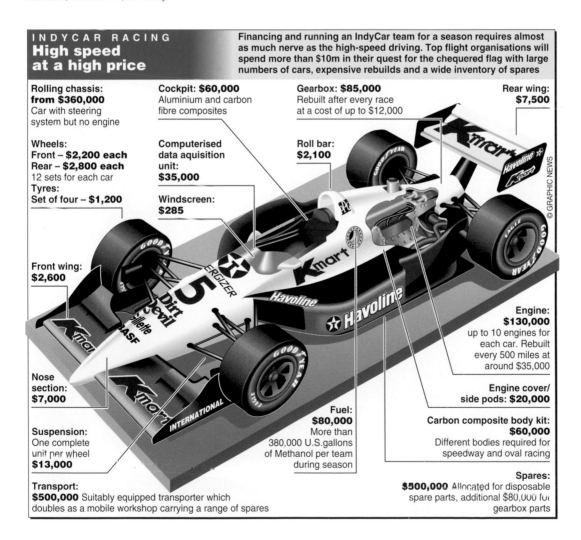

INDYCAR RACING
High speed at a high price

Financing and running an IndyCar team for a season requires almost as much nerve as the high-speed driving. Top flight organisations will spend more than $10m in their quest for the chequered flag with large numbers of cars, expensive rebuilds and a wide inventory of spares

Rolling chassis: from $360,000 Car with steering system but no engine

Wheels: Front – $2,200 each Rear – $2,800 each 12 sets for each car
Tyres: Set of four – $1,200

Front wing: $2,600

Nose section: $7,000

Suspension: One complete unit per wheel **$13,000**

Transport: $500,000 Suitably equipped transporter which doubles as a mobile workshop carrying a range of spares

Cockpit: $60,000 Aluminium and carbon fibre composites

Computerised data aquisition unit: $35,000

Windscreen: $285

Gearbox: $85,000 Rebuilt after every race at a cost of up to $12,000

Roll bar: $2,100

Fuel: $80,000 More than 380,000 U.S.gallons of Methanol per team during season

Rear wing: $7,500

Engine: $130,000 up to 10 engines for each car. Rebuilt every 500 miles at around $35,000

Engine cover/ side pods: $20,000

Carbon composite body kit: $60,000 Different bodies required for speedway and oval racing

Spares: $500,000 Allocated for disposable spare parts, additional $80,000 for gearbox parts

© GRAPHIC NEWS

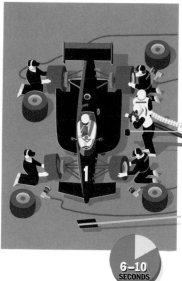

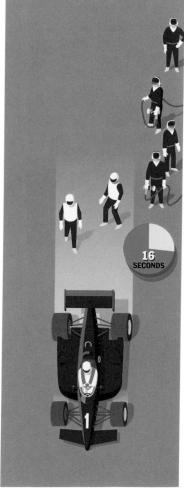

1–5 SECONDS

6–10 SECONDS

11–15 SECONDS

16 SECONDS

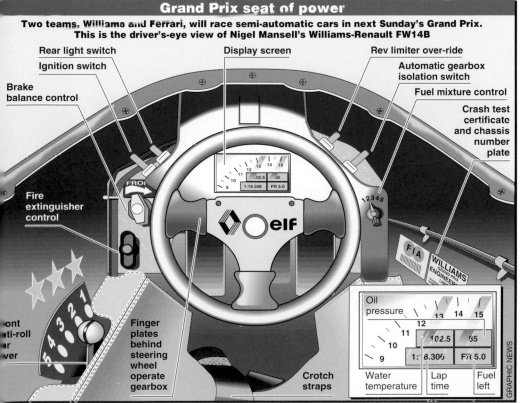

Grand Prix seat of power

Two teams, Williams and Ferrari, will race semi-automatic cars in next Sunday's Grand Prix. This is the driver's-eye view of Nigel Mansell's Williams-Renault FW14B

Rear light switch

Ignition switch

Display screen

Rev limiter over-ride

Automatic gearbox isolation switch

Brake balance control

Fuel mixture control

Crash test certificate and chassis number plate

Fire extinguisher control

Finger plates behind steering wheel operate gearbox

Crotch straps

Oil pressure		13	14	15
12				
11	102.5	35
10		
9	1:18.306	FR 5.0
Water temperature	Lap time	Fuel left

GRAPHIC NEWS

Williams Cockpit

DESIGN: Duncan Mil, UK

PUBLISHER/CLIENT: Graphic News

DATE OF 1ST PUBLICATION/USE: 19 March 1992

DESIGN RATIONALE: To show a driver's view of the cockpit of the Williams Formula 1 car in the year Williams and Nigel Mansell won the World Championship.

CREDITS: Art director, Duncan Mil; illustrators, Duncan Mil, Russell Lewis; writer/researcher, Julie Hacking.

Hockey!

DESIGN: Chris Morris, Kelly Frankeny, USA

PUBLISHER/CLIENT: *San Francisco Examiner*

DATE OF 1ST PUBLICATION/USE: 1 October 1991

DESIGN RATIONALE: The illustration was intended to explain hockey to an audience of receptive new fans as a team was moving to the Bay Area. The hockey rink, positions of players, equipment and penalties are explained.

CREDITS: Art director, Kelly Frankeny; illustrator, Chris Morris

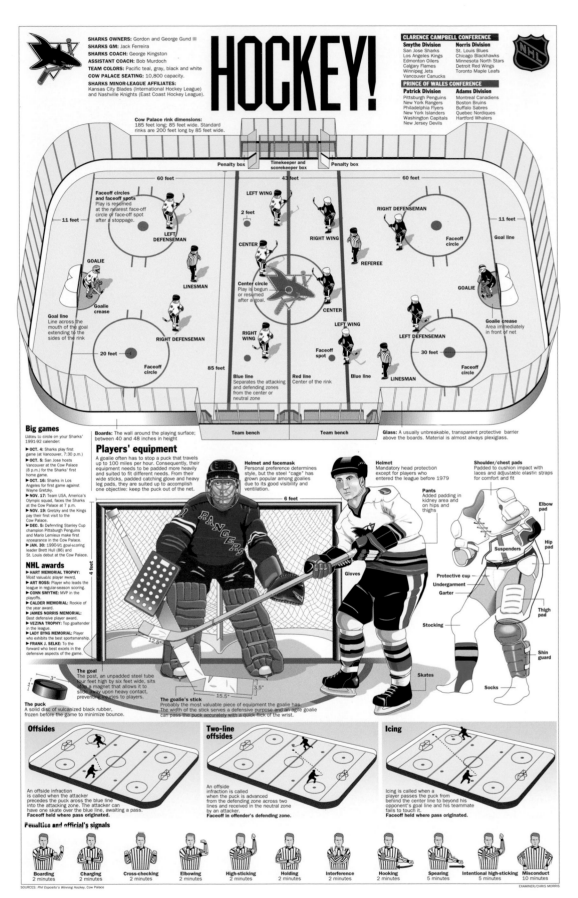

HOCKEY!

SHARKS OWNERS: Gordon and George Gund III
SHARKS GM: Jack Ferreira
SHARKS COACH: George Kingston
ASSISTANT COACH: Bob Murdoch
TEAM COLORS: Pacific teal, gray, black and white
COW PALACE SEATING: 10,800 capacity.
SHARKS MINOR-LEAGUE AFFILIATES:
Kansas City Blades (International Hockey League)
and Nashville Knights (East Coast Hockey League).

CLARENCE CAMPBELL CONFERENCE

Smythe Division
San Jose Sharks
Los Angeles Kings
Edmonton Oilers
Calgary Flames
Winnipeg Jets
Vancouver Canucks

Norris Division
St. Louis Blues
Chicago Blackhawks
Minnesota North Stars
Detroit Red Wings
Toronto Maple Leafs

PRINCE OF WALES CONFERENCE

Patrick Division
Pittsburgh Penguins
New York Rangers
Philadelphia Flyers
New York Islanders
Washington Capitals
New Jersey Devils

Adams Division
Montreal Canadiens
Boston Bruins
Buffalo Sabres
Quebec Nordiques
Hartford Whalers

Cow Palace rink dimensions:
185 feet long; 85 feet wide. Standard rinks are 200 feet long by 85 feet wide.

Penalty box — Timekeeper and scorekeeper box — Penalty box

Faceoff circles and faceoff spots Play is resumed at the nearest face-off circle or face-off spot after a stoppage.

Center circle Play is begun or resumed after a goal.

Goal line Line across the mouth of the goal extending to the sides of the rink

Goalie crease

Blue line Separates the attacking and defending zones from the center or neutral zone

Red line Center of the rink

Goalie crease Area immediately in front of net

Positions: LEFT WING, RIGHT DEFENSEMAN, LEFT DEFENSEMAN, CENTER, RIGHT WING, REFEREE, GOALIE, LINESMAN, RIGHT DEFENSEMAN, LEFT WING, CENTER, RIGHT WING, Faceoff circle, Faceoff spot, Goal line

Measurements: 60 feet, 43 feet, 60 feet, 11 feet, 2 feet, 11 feet, 20 feet, 30 feet, 85 feet

Boards: The wall around the playing surface; between 40 and 48 inches in height

Glass: A usually unbreakable, transparent protective barrier above the boards. Material is almost always plexiglass.

Team bench — Team bench

Big games

Dates to circle on your Sharks' 1991-92 calendar:

► **OCT. 4:** Sharks play first game (at Vancouver, 7:30 p.m.)
► **OCT. 5:** San Jose hosts Vancouver at the Cow Palace (8 p.m.) for the Sharks' first home game.
► **OCT. 16:** Sharks in Los Angeles for first game against Wayne Gretzky.
► **NOV. 17:** Team USA, America's Olympic squad, faces the Sharks at the Cow Palace at 7 p.m.
► **NOV. 19:** Gretzky and the Kings pay their first visit to the Cow Palace.
► **DEC. 5:** Defending Stanley Cup champion Pittsburgh Penguins and Mario Lemieux make first appearance in the Cow Palace.
► **JAN. 30:** 1990-91 goal-scoring leader Brett Hull (86) and St. Louis debut at the Cow Palace.

NHL awards

► **HART MEMORIAL TROPHY:** Most valuable player award.
► **ART ROSS:** Player who leads the league in regular-season scoring.
► **CONN SMYTHE:** MVP in the playoffs.
► **CALDER MEMORIAL:** Rookie of the year award.
► **JAMES NORRIS MEMORIAL:** Best defensive player award.
► **VEZINA TROPHY:** Top goaltender in the league.
► **LADY BYNG MEMORIAL:** Player who exhibits the best sportsmanship.
► **FRANK J. SELKE:** To the forward who best excels in the defensive aspects of the game.

Players' equipment

A goalie often has to stop a puck that travels up to 100 miles per hour. Consequently, their equipment needs to be padded more heavily and suited to fit different needs. From their wide sticks, padded catching glove and heavy leg pads, they are suited up to accomplish one objective: keep the puck out of the net.

Helmet and facemask Personal preference determines style, but the steel "cage" has grown popular among goalies due to its good visibility and ventilation.

Helmet Mandatory head protection except for players who entered the league before 1979

Pants Added padding in kidney area and on hips and thighs

Shoulder/chest pads Padded to cushion impact with laces and adjustable elastic straps for comfort and fit

Gloves

Elbow pad, Suspenders, Hip pad, Protective cup, Undergarment, Garter, Stocking, Thigh pad, Shin guard, Skates, Socks

The goal The post, an unpadded steel tube four feet high by six feet wide, sits atop a magnet that allows it to slide away upon heavy contact, preventing injuries to players.

The puck A solid disc of vulcanized black rubber, frozen before the game to minimize bounce.

The goalie's stick Probably the most valuable piece of equipment the goalie has. The width of the stick serves a defensive purpose, and an agile goalie can pass the puck accurately with a quick flick of the wrist.

Measurements: 6 feet, 4 feet, 12.5", 15.5", 3.5", 3", 1"

Offsides

An offside infraction is called when the attacker precedes the puck across the blue line into the attacking zone. The attacker can have one skate over the blue line, awaiting a pass. **Faceoff held where pass originated.**

Two-line offsides

An offside infraction is called when the puck is advanced from the defending zone across two lines and received in the neutral zone by an attacker. **Faceoff in offender's defending zone.**

Icing

Icing is called when a player passes the puck from behind the center line to beyond his opponent's goal line and his teammate fails to touch it. **Faceoff held where pass originated.**

Penalties and official's signals

Boarding	Charging	Cross-checking	Elbowing	High-sticking	Holding	Interference	Hooking	Spearing	Intentional high-sticking	Misconduct
2 minutes	2 minutes	2 minutes	2 minutes	2 minutes	2 minutes	2 minutes	2 minutes	5 minutes	5 minutes	10 minutes

SOURCES: Phil Esposito's Winning Hockey, Cow Palace

EXAMINER/CHRIS MORRIS

The simple but complex 'Triangle'

The Chicago Bulls' successful offense combines the high-powered talent and experience of its two-time NBA championship team with a strategy emphasizing speed and unpredictability. Their unique playing style results, in part, from a reluctance by coach Phil Jackson to use set plays. Instead, they often rely on many variations of what has come to be called the triangle offense, sometimes known as the triple-post offense.

The theory behind the practice

For Bulls assistant coach "Tex" Winter, the center is the apex of the way the Bulls' offense operates. The offense takes advantage of the way the defense is playing, finding the defense's weaknesses and exploiting them. If B.J. Armstrong, for example, is playing, the Bulls take advantage of his skills. His presence changes the complexion of the passing to enhance his shooting. Michael Jordan is so fast the defense can't react quickly enough to his one-on-one moves, so the offensive strategy strives to isolate him and avoid double team pressure. All the players are important, but the Bulls try to keep driving lanes open for smaller outside players. Following is the underlying theory that has helped bring two consecutive championships to the Bulls:

1. Penetrate the defense.
 A. Take good percentage shots – define good shots for each player.
 B. Stress inside power game. Play for three-point power play.
 C. Break down all defenses. Full-court presses to double teams.
2. Utilize a full-court game, with end-to-end play. Skills must be learned at fast-break pace. Know optimum speed and work to increase it. Transition basketball starts on defense. Look to run!
3. Provide proper floor spacing of 15-18 feet, creating operating room and clearing area on the court. It keeps the defense occupied on and off the ball.
4. Establish player and ball movement with a purpose. There is only one ball and five players. All things being equal, a player is without the ball 80% of the time.
5. Establish strong rebound position and good defensive balance on all shots.
6. Provide the player who has the ball an opportunity to pass the ball to any of his teammates. The offense should provide for a counter to the defense.
7. Utilize the abilities of the individual players. Must create high percentage shots for best shooters, rebound opportunities for bounders, driving opportunities for best drivers, etc. Affords the opportunity to play out a format rather than be restricted to a definite set play.

The working positions

▲ Players position themselves in a 2-2-1 offensive set initially with center in.
▲ The floor spacing should be 15-18 feet between players. This helps to spread the defense and at the same time allows for quick, accurate passing. A pass of 15-18 feet is easier to control with less risk of an interception.

▲ The guards are approximately 15 feet apart and just beyond the 3-point arc. The forwards are in an area opposite the free-throw line extended, and just far enough from the side line for a teammate to go to the outside. The forwards are in this area for several reasons:
1. So the guard-to-forward pass is not appreciably longer than the 15 feet desired.

2. So the forward can establish a 45-degree passing and cutting angle between himself and the basket.
3. So the corner area is cleared, thereby creating operating room for passing, cutting, faking and driving.
4. So the guard cutting to the outside has more room and a better cutting angle to the basket.
5. So the ball can be easily passed into the center.
6. See methods described below.

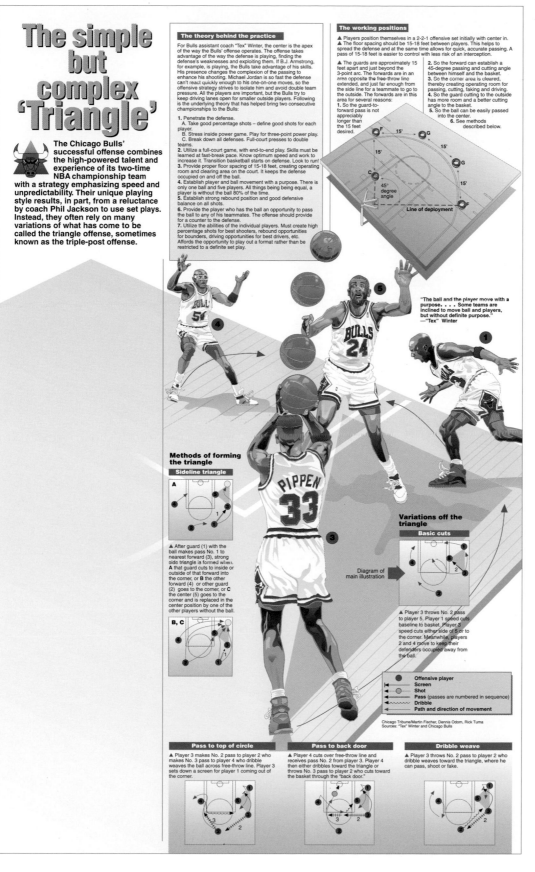

"The ball and the player move with a purpose. . . . Some teams are inclined to move ball and players, but without definite purpose."
—"Tex" Winter

Methods of forming the triangle

Sideline triangle

▲ After guard (1) with the ball makes pass No. 1 to nearest forward (3), strong side triangle is formed when: **A** that guard cuts to inside or outside of that forward into the corner, or **B** the other forward (4) or other guard (2) goes to the corner, or **C** the center (5) goes to the corner and is replaced in the center position by one of the other players without the ball.

Variations off the triangle

Basic cuts

Diagram of main illustration

▲ Player 3 throws No. 2 pass to player 5. Player 1 speed cuts baseline to basket. Player 3 speed cuts either side of 5 or to the corner. Meanwhile, players 2 and 4 move to keep their defenders occupied away from the ball.

●	Offensive player	
○	Screen	
	Shot	
	Pass (passes are numbered in sequence)	
	Dribble	
	Path and direction of movement	

Chicago Tribune/Martin Fischer, Dennis Odom, Rick Tuma
Sources: "Tex" Winter and Chicago Bulls

Pass to top of circle

▲ Player 3 makes No. 2 pass to player 2 who makes No. 3 pass to player 4 who dribble weaves the ball across free-throw line. Player 3 sets down a screen for player 1 coming out of the corner.

Pass to back door

▲ Player 4 cuts over free-throw line and receives pass No. 2 from player 3. Player 4 then either dribbles toward the triangle or throws No. 3 pass to player 2 who cuts toward the basket through the "back door."

Dribble weave

▲ Player 3 throws No. 2 pass to player 2 who dribble weaves toward the triangle, where he can pass, shoot or fake.

Triangle Offense

PUBLISHER/CLIENT:

Chicago Tribune

DATE OF 1ST PUBLICATION/USE:

25 January 1993

DESIGN RATIONALE: To illustrate The Chicago Bulls' offense tactics.

CREDITS: Art director, Stacy Seveat; illustrators, Rick Tuma, Dennis Odorn; researchers, Martin Fischer, Dennis Odorn.

Olympic Archery

DESIGN: The Associated Press (US)/*El Mundo* (Spain)/*El Periodico* (Spain)

PUBLISHER/CLIENT: Member and subscriber newspapers of the Associated Press worldwide

DATE OF 1ST PUBLICATION/USE: Prior to and during the Barcelona Olympics 1992

DESIGN RATIONALE: Illustrates and explains diagrammatically the Olympic archery field, techniques and equipment.

CREDITS: Art directors, Karl Gude, Robert Dominguez, AP; Jeff Goertzen, *El Periodico;* Mario Tascón, *El Mundo;* illustrator, Andrew Lucas; technical illustrators M. Carrasco, M. Doelling, R. Dominguez, J. Goertzen, K. Gude, M. Hernandez, J. Nunoz, G. Sampredo, D. Sanchez, R. Toro, J. Velasco; writer, Dorsey Weber Gude; researchers, Dawn Desilets, Mary Stevenson.

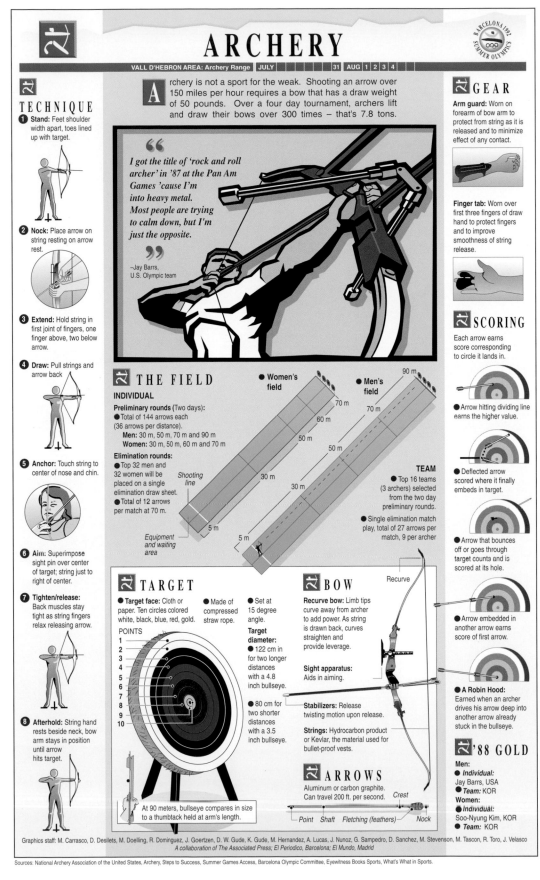

YACHTING

PARC DE MAR AREA: Nova Icaria Yacht Basin | JULY | | 27 | 28 | 29 | 30 | | AUG | 1 | 2 | 3 | 4 | 5 | 6 | |

BOATS

Boats in each class are made exactly alike, therefore the best sailor, not the best boat, wins. There are 10 regattas and eight classes of boats. Each country can enter one boat in each regatta.

● Division II Sailboard
Men and new for women

Crew: 1 **Length:** 12 ft.
Sailors stand on boat, holding sail. Requires great strength.

● Finn
Men

Crew: 1 **Length:** 14 ft. 9 in.
Very responsive boat requires great athleticism and concentration.

● Europe
New event. Women only

Crew: 1 **Length:** 11 ft.
Sharp competition encouraged by precision handling.

● 470
Men and women

Crew: 2 **Length:** 15 ft. 5 in.
Boat responds immediately to body movements.

O lympic yachting events usually take place far offshore and hundreds of miles from the host city. But this year, the race courses are set in Mediterranean waters just off the shore of Barcelona, within range of landlubber spectators.

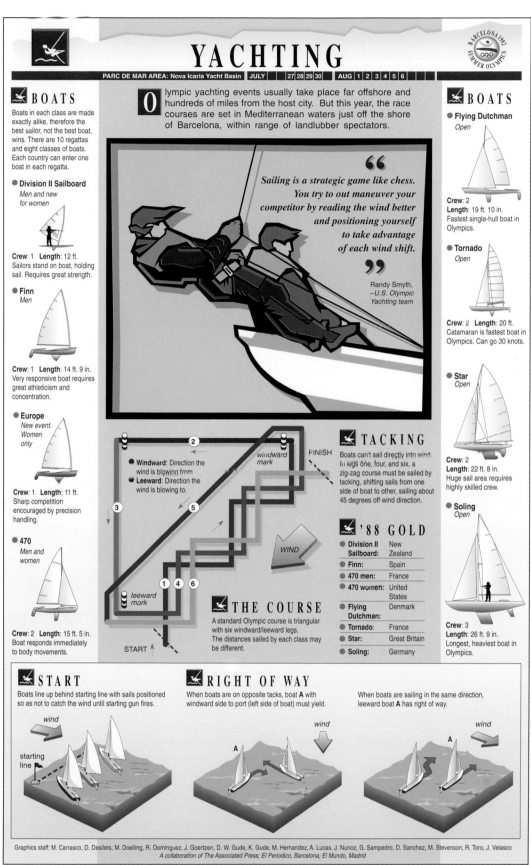

" Sailing is a strategic game like chess. You try to out maneuver your competitor by reading the wind better and positioning yourself to take advantage of each wind shift. "

Randy Smyth,
–U.S. Olympic Yachting team

BOATS

● Flying Dutchman
Open

Crew: 2
Length: 19 ft. 10 in.
Fastest single-hull boat in Olympics.

● Tornado
Open

Crew: 2 **Length:** 20 ft.
Catamaran is fastest boat in Olympics. Can go 30 knots.

● Star
Open

Crew: 2
Length: 22 ft. 8 in.
Huge sail area requires highly skilled crew.

● Soling
Open

Crew: 3
Length: 26 ft. 9 in.
Longest, heaviest boat in Olympics.

TACKING

Boats can't sail directly into wind. In legs one, four, and six, a zig-zag course must be sailed by tacking, shifting sails from one side of boat to other, sailing about 45 degrees off wind direction.

● **Windward:** Direction the wind is blowing from
● **Leeward:** Direction the wind is blowing to

windward mark FINISH

leeward mark

WIND

START

'88 GOLD

● Division II Sailboard:	New Zealand
● Finn:	Spain
● 470 men:	France
● 470 women:	United States
● Flying Dutchman:	Denmark
● Tornado:	France
● Star:	Great Britain
● Soling:	Germany

THE COURSE

A standard Olympic course is triangular with six windward/leeward legs. The distances sailed by each class may be different.

START

Boats line up behind starting line with sails positioned so as not to catch the wind until starting gun fires.

wind

starting line

RIGHT OF WAY

When boats are on opposite tacks, boat **A** with windward side to port (left side of boat) must yield.

wind

When boats are sailing in the same direction, leeward boat **A** has right of way.

wind

Graphics staff: M. Carrasco, D. Desilets, M. Doelling, R. Dominguez, J. Goertzen, D. W. Gude, K. Gude, M. Hernandez, A. Lucas, J. Nunoz, G. Sampedro, D. Sanchez, M. Stevenson, R. Toro, J. Velasco
A collaboration of The Associated Press; El Periodico, Barcelona; El Mundo, Madrid

Sources: AhlerSmith Inc., Summer Games Access, Barcelona Olympic Organizing Committee, What's What in Sports

Olympic Yachting

DESIGN: The Associated Press (US)/*El Mundo* (Spain)/*El Periodico* (Spain)

PUBLISHER/CLIENT: Member and subscriber newspapers of the Associated Press worldwide

DATE OF 1ST PUBLICATION/USE: Prior to and during the Barcelona Olympics 1992

DESIGN RATIONALE: Illustrates and explains diagrammatically the Olympic yachting course, boats and techniques.

CREDITS: Art directors, Karl Gude, Robert Dominguez, AP; Jeff Goertzen, *El Periodico;* Mario Tascón, *El Mundo;* illustrator, Andrew Lucas; technical illustrators M. Carrasco, M. Doelling, R. Dominguez, J. Goertzen, K. Gude, M. Hernandez, J. Nunoz, G. Sampredo, D. Sanchez, R. Toro, J. Velasco, writer, Dorsey Weber Gude; researchers, Dawn Desilets, Mary Stevenson.

Diving on Montjuic

DESIGN: The Associated Press, USA

PUBLISHER/CLIENT: Member and subscriber newspapers of the Associated Press worldwide

DATE OF 1ST PUBLICATION/USE: Created on-site during the Barcelona Olympics 1992

DESIGN RATIONALE: Illustrates the Olympic diving venue.

CREDITS: Art director, Karl Gude; illustrator, Karl Gude; writer, Karl Gude; researcher, Karl Gude.

DIVING ON MONTJUIC

Located on the side of Montjuic, the diving venue has offered television viewers some breathtaking views of divers with Barcelona in the background. The competitors seem to fall from miles high.

1) **Wall** built to reduce wind on the divers.
2) **Structure** above dive platform was built to be covered with canvas to furthur control wind, but wasn't needed.
3) 10-meter **platform** is as high as a three story building.
4) Seven **judges**, from nations other than those of the competitors, sit in tall seats at poolside, three on one side and four on the other.
5) **Jacuzzi** keeps divers warm and muscles loose.
6) Warmup **mats**.

7) Three-meter **springboards**. During practice, most divers have prefered the "feel" of board *(a)* to the other two, but any may be used during competition. This has caused long lines and a few of the stronger divers that prefer not to wait have practiced on board *(b)* and will likely use this board during competition. Moveable **fulcrum** *(inset)* enables divers to adjust the spring. Rolled forward *(c)*, the board is tighter and gives the diver less power, but more control. Timing becomes critical. Rolled to the back *(d)* allows more spring and power, but not as much control.

8) Television **camera** positions. Because the diving venue is located on the hillside of Montjuic, the camera at the bottom of the diagram captures dramatic views of divers with Barcelona in the background.
9) Stadium **seats** 6,500.
10) Water **spray** allows divers to guage their entry point both visually and auidibly.
11) **Impact reduce**r for practice. Pool is equipped with powerful bubble makers that aerate the water under a diver to a thickness of about three feet. This allows divers a softer impact when trying new dives.
12) One meter **practice boards**, *(a)* platform, *(b)* springboards
13) Gaudi's **cathedral** Sagrada Familia.

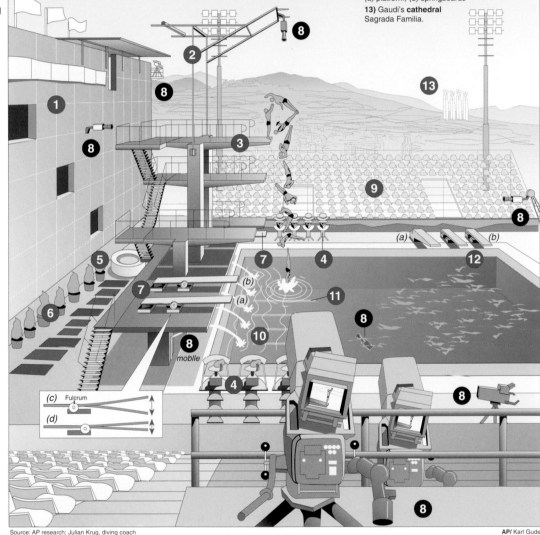

Source: AP research; Julian Krug, diving coach

AP/ Karl Gude

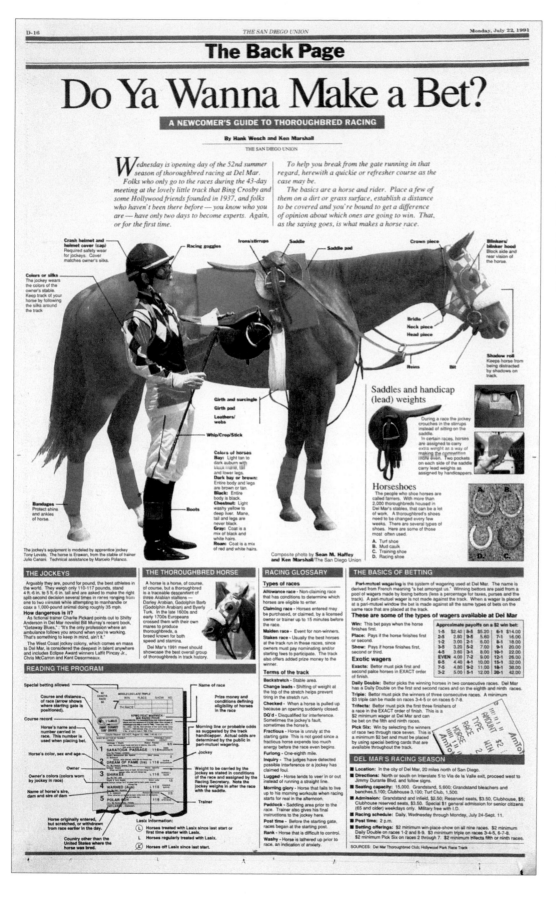

Do Ya Wanna Make a Bet?

DESIGN: Ken Marshall, USA

PUBLISHER/CLIENT: *San Diego Union-Tribune*

DATE OF 1ST PUBLICATION/USE: 22 July 1991

DESIGN RATIONALE: The page ran on the opening day of the thoroughbred racing season to explain the basics of the sport and betting for novice fans.

CREDITS: Art director, Ken Marshall; photographer, Sean M. Haffey; illustrator, Ken Marshall; writers and researchers, Ken Marshall, Hank Wesch.

Tracking a Baseball

DESIGN: Peter C. T. Elsworth, UK

PUBLISHER/CLIENT:

New York Times

DATE OF 1ST PUBLICATION/USE:

28 April 1991

DESIGN RATIONALE: The illustration shows how a 3-C graphics program can track a baseball after it leaves the pitcher's hand – its speed, angle along horizontal and vertical planes, the view from the pitcher's mound and from the batter. The design won the 1992 award for three-dimensional graphic design from the Society of Newspaper Design.

CREDITS: Art director, Greg Ryan. Copyright © 1991 *The New York Times*. Reprinted by permission.

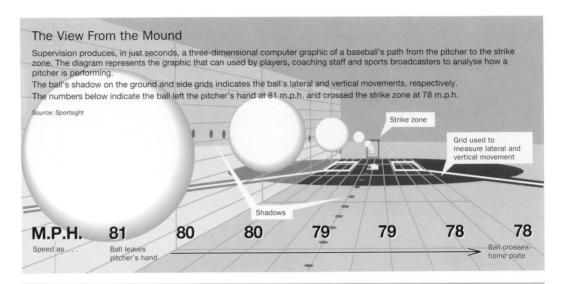

The View From the Mound

Supervision produces, in just seconds, a three-dimensional computer graphic of a baseball's path from the pitcher to the strike zone. The diagram represents the graphic that can used by players, coaching staff and sports broadcasters to analyse how a pitcher is performing.

The ball's shadow on the ground and side grids indicates the ball's lateral and vertical movements, respectively.

The numbers below indicate the ball left the pitcher's hand at 81 m.p.h. and crossed the strike zone at 78 m.p.h.

Source: Sportsight

Strike zone

Grid used to measure lateral and vertical movement

Shadows

M.P.H. **81** **80** **80** **79** **79** **78** **78**

Speed as . . .   Ball leaves pitcher's hand   Ball crosses home plate

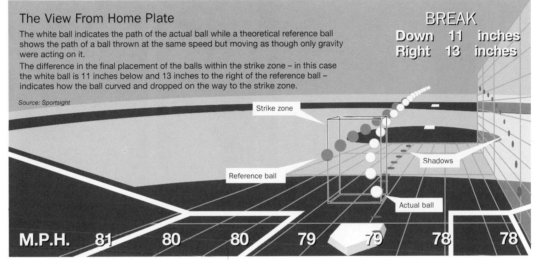

The View From Home Plate

The white ball indicates the path of the actual ball while a theoretical reference ball shows the path of a ball thrown at the same speed but moving as though only gravity were acting on it.

The difference in the final placement of the balls within the strike zone – in this case the white ball is 11 inches below and 13 inches to the right of the reference ball – indicates how the ball curved and dropped on the way to the strike zone.

Source: Sportsight

BREAK
Down   11   inches
Right   13   inches

Strike zone

Reference ball

Shadows

Actual ball

M.P.H. **81** **80** **80** **79** **79** **78** **78**

Football Punt

DESIGN: John Grimwade, UK

PUBLISHER/CLIENT: *Sports Illustrated for Kids*

DATE OF 1ST PUBLICATION/USE: 1991

DESIGN RATIONALE: Intended for children, this simple but accurate diagram shows how to punt a football with tips from the pros.

CREDITS: Art directors, Rocco Alberico, Sarah Micklem.

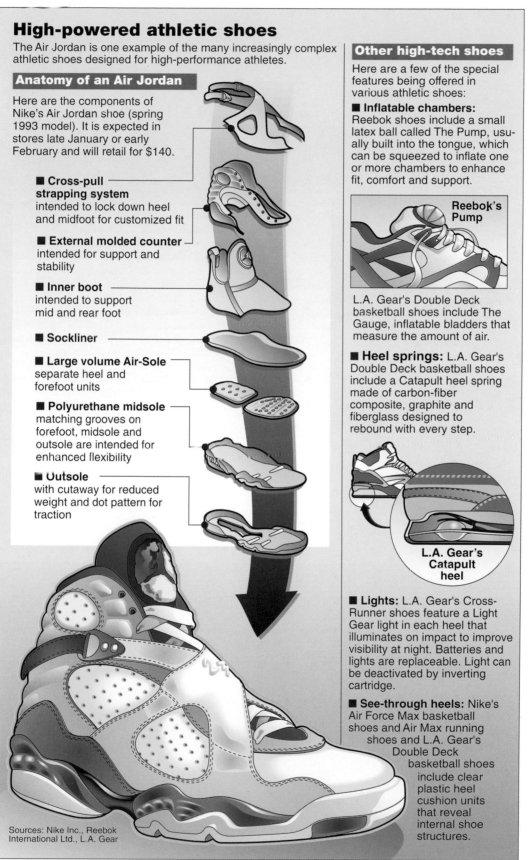

High-powered athletic shoes

The Air Jordan is one example of the many increasingly complex athletic shoes designed for high-performance athletes.

Anatomy of an Air Jordan

Here are the components of Nike's Air Jordan shoe (spring 1993 model). It is expected in stores late January or early February and will retail for $140.

- **Cross-pull strapping system** intended to lock down heel and midfoot for customized fit

- **External molded counter** intended for support and stability

- **Inner boot** intended to support mid and rear foot

- **Sockliner**

- **Large volume Air-Sole** separate heel and forefoot units

- **Polyurethane midsole** matching grooves on forefoot, midsole and outsole are intended for enhanced flexibility

- **Outsole** with cutaway for reduced weight and dot pattern for traction

Sources: Nike Inc., Reebok International Ltd., L.A. Gear

Other high-tech shoes

Here are a few of the special features being offered in various athletic shoes:

- **Inflatable chambers:** Reebok shoes include a small latex ball called The Pump, usually built into the tongue, which can be squeezed to inflate one or more chambers to enhance fit, comfort and support.

Reebok's Pump

L.A. Gear's Double Deck basketball shoes include The Gauge, inflatable bladders that measure the amount of air.

- **Heel springs:** L.A. Gear's Double Deck basketball shoes include a Catapult heel spring made of carbon-fiber composite, graphite and fiberglass designed to rebound with every step.

L.A. Gear's Catapult heel

- **Lights:** L.A. Gear's Cross-Runner shoes feature a Light Gear light in each heel that illuminates on impact to improve visibility at night. Batteries and lights are replaceable. Light can be deactivated by inverting cartridge.

- **See-through heels:** Nike's Air Force Max basketball shoes and Air Max running shoes and L.A. Gear's Double Deck basketball shoes include clear plastic heel cushion units that reveal internal shoe structures.

Chicago Tribune/Steve Little/Martin Fischer

High-powered Athletic Shoes

DESIGN: Steve Little, USA

PUBLISHER/CLIENT: *Chicago Tribune*

DATE OF 1ST PUBLICATION/USE: 8 February 1993

DESIGN RATIONALE: An exploded view of a Nike Air Jordan Athletic shoe, endorsed by a local celebrity, together with descriptions of other shoe accoutrements.

CREDITS: Illustrator, Steve Little; researcher, Martin Fischer.

Judo

DESIGN: Hiroyuki Kimura,
Sachiko Hagiwara, Hiroko
Enomoto, Yuko Minoura, Takeshi
Kamoi, Japan

PUBLISHER/CLIENT: Asahi
Shimbun, *AERA* magazine

DATE OF 1ST PUBLICATION/USE:
14 July 1992

DESIGN RATIONALE: A diagram
for the Barcelona Olympic Games
to show the rules and moves of
judo.

CREDITS: Art director,
Hiroyuki Kimura.

Fencing

DESIGN: Hiroyuki Kimura,
Sachiko Hagiwara, Hiroko
Enomoto, Yuko Minoura, Takeshi
Kamoi, Japan

PUBLISHER/CLIENT: Asahi
Shimbun, *AERA* magazine

DATE OF 1ST PUBLICATION/USE:
9 June 1992

DESIGN RATIONALE: A diagram
for the Barcelona Olympic Games
to show the rules and history of
fencing.

CREDITS: Art director,
Hiroyuki Kimura.

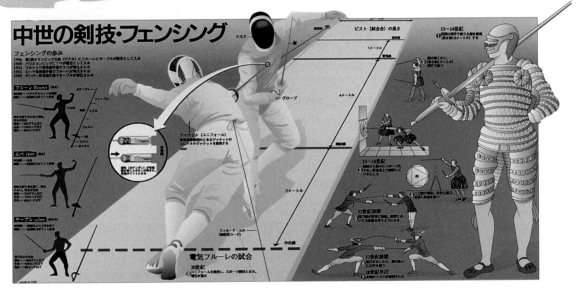

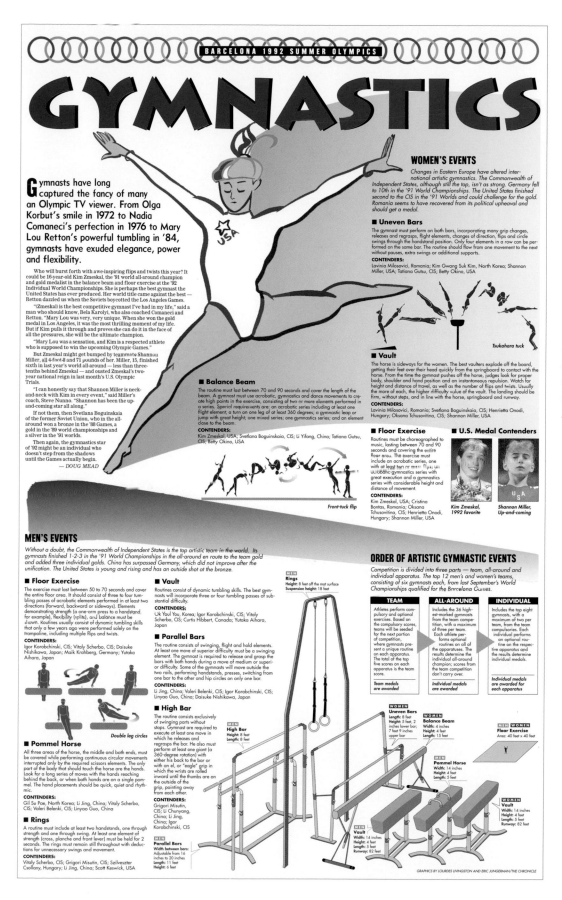

BARCELONA 1992 SUMMER OLYMPICS

GYMNASTICS

Gymnasts have long captured the fancy of many an Olympic TV viewer. From Olga Korbut's smile in 1972 to Nadia Comaneci's perfection in 1976 to Mary Lou Retton's powerful tumbling in '84, gymnasts have exuded elegance, power and flexibility.

Who will burst forth with awe-inspiring flips and twists this year? It could be 16-year-old Kim Zmeskal, the '91 world all-around champion and gold medalist in the balance beam and floor exercise at the '92 Individual World Championships. She is perhaps the best gymnast the United States has ever produced. Her world title came against the best — Retton dazzled us when the Soviets boycotted the Los Angeles Games.

"(Zmeskal) is the best competitive gymnast I've had in my life," said a man who should know, Bela Karolyi, who also coached Comaneci and Retton. "Mary Lou was very, very unique. When she won the gold medal in Los Angeles, it was the most thrilling moment of my life. But if Kim pulls it through and proves she can do it in the face of all the pressures, she will be the ultimate champion.

"Mary Lou was a sensation, and Kim is a respected athlete who is supposed to win the upcoming Olympic Games."

But Zmeskal might get bumped by teammate Shannon Miller, all 4-foot-8 and 71 pounds of her. Miller, 15, finished sixth in last year's world all-around — less than three-tenths behind Zmeskal — and ousted Zmeskal's two-year national reign in last month's U.S. Olympic Trials.

"I can honestly say that Shannon Miller is neck-and-neck with Kim in every event," said Miller's coach, Steve Nunno. "Shannon has been the up-and-coming star all along."

If not them, then Svetlana Boguinskaia of the former Soviet Union, who in the all-around won a bronze in the '88 Games, a gold in the '89 world championships and a silver in the '91 worlds.

Then again, the gymnastics star of '92 might be an individual who doesn't step from the shadows until the Games actually begin.

— DOUG MEAD

WOMEN'S EVENTS

Changes in Eastern Europe have altered international artistic gymnastics. The Commonwealth of Independent States, although still the top, isn't as strong. Germany fell to 10th in the '91 World Championships. The United States finished second to the CIS in the '91 Worlds and could challenge for the gold. Romania seems to have recovered from its political upheaval and should get a medal.

■ Uneven Bars
The gymnast must perform on both bars, incorporating many grip changes, releases and regrasps, flight elements, changes of direction, flips and circle swings through the handstand position. Only four elements in a row can be performed on the same bar. The routine should flow from one movement to the next without pauses, extra swings or additional supports.

CONTENDERS:
Lavinia Milosovici, Romania; Kim Gwang Suk Kim, North Korea; Shannon Miller, USA; Tatiana Gutsu, CIS; Betty Okino, USA

Tsukahara tuck

■ Vault
The horse is sideways for the women. The best vaulters explode off the board, getting their feet over their head quickly from the springboard to contact with the horse. From the time the gymnast pushes off the horse, judges look for proper body, shoulder and hand position and an instantaneous repulsion. Watch for height and distance of travel, as well as the number of flips and twists. Usually the more of each, the higher difficulty value of the vault. The landing should be firm, without steps, and in line with the horse, springboard and runway.

CONTENDERS:
Lavinia Milosovici, Romania; Svetlana Boguinskaia, CIS; Henrietta Onodi, Hungary; Oksana Tchusovitina, CIS; Shannon Miller, USA

■ Floor Exercise
Routines must be choreographed to music, lasting between 70 and 90 seconds and covering the entire floor area. The exercise must include an acrobatic series, one with at least two or more flips, an acrobatic-gymnastics series with great execution and a gymnastics series with considerable height and distance of movement.

CONTENDERS:
Kim Zmeskal, USA; Cristina Bontas, Romania; Oksana Tchusovitina, CIS; Henrietta Onodi, Hungary; Shannon Miller, USA

■ Balance Beam
The routine must last between 70 and 90 seconds and cover the length of the beam. A gymnast must use acrobatic, gymnastics and dance movements to create high points in the exercise, consisting of two or more elements performed in a series. Special requirements are: an acrobatic series including at least one flight element; a turn on one leg of at least 360 degrees; a gymnastic leap or jump with great height; one mixed series; one gymnastics series; and an element close to the beam.

CONTENDERS:
Kim Zmeskal, USA; Svetlana Boguinskaia, CIS; Li Yifang, China; Tatiana Gutsu, CIS; Betty Okino, USA

Front-tuck flip

■ U.S. Medal Contenders

Kim Zmeskal, 1992 favorite

Shannon Miller, Up-and-coming

MEN'S EVENTS

Without a doubt, the Commonwealth of Independent States is the top artistic team in the world. Its gymnasts finished 1-2-3 in the '91 World Championships in the all-around en route to the team gold and added three individual golds. China has surpassed Germany, which did not improve after the unification. The United States is young and rising and has an outside shot at the bronze.

■ Floor Exercise
The exercise must last between 50 to 70 seconds and cover the entire floor area. It should consist of three to four tumbling passes of acrobatic elements performed in at least two directions (forward, backward or sideways). Elements demonstrating strength (a one-arm press to a handstand, for example), flexibility (splits), and balance must be shown. Routines usually consist of dynamic tumbling skills that only a few years ago were performed solely on the trampoline, including multiple flips and twists.

CONTENDERS:
Igor Korobchinski, CIS; Vitaly Scherbo, CIS; Daisuke Nishikawa, Japan; Maik Krahberg, Germany; Yutaka Aihara, Japan

■ Pommel Horse
All three areas of the horse, the middle and both ends, must be covered while performing continuous circular movements interrupted only by the required scissors elements. The only part of the body that should touch the horse are the hands. Look for a long series of moves with the hands reaching behind the back, or when both hands are on a single pommel. The hand placements should be quick, quiet and rhythmic.

CONTENDERS:
Gil Su Pae, North Korea; Li Jing, China; Vitaly Scherbo, CIS; Valeri Belenki, CIS; Linyao Guo, China

■ Rings
A routine must include at least two handstands, one through strength and one through swing. At least one element of strength (cross, planche and front lever) must be held for 2 seconds. The rings must remain still throughout with deductions for unnecessary swings and movement.

CONTENDERS:
Vitaly Scherbo, CIS; Grigori Misutin, CIS; Szilveszter Csollany, Hungary; Li Jing, China; Scott Keswick, USA

Double leg circles

■ Vault
Routines consist of dynamic tumbling skills. The best gymnasts will incorporate three or four tumbling passes of substantial difficulty.

CONTENDERS:
Uk Yaul You, Korea; Igor Korobchinski, CIS; Vitaly Scherbo, CIS; Curtis Hibbert, Canada; Yutaka Aihara, Japan

■ Parallel Bars
The routine consists of swinging, flight and hold elements. At least one move of superior difficulty must be a swinging element. The gymnast is required to release and grasp the bars with both hands during a move of medium or superior difficulty. Some of the gymnasts will move outside the two rails, performing handstands, presses, switching from one bar to the other and hip circles on only one bar.

CONTENDERS:
Li Jing, China; Valeri Belenki, CIS; Igor Korobchinski, CIS; Linyao Guo, China; Daisuke Nishikawa, Japan

■ High Bar
The routine consists exclusively of swinging parts without stops. Gymnast are required to execute at least one move in which he releases and regrasps the bar. He also must perform at least one giant (a 360-degree rotation) with either his back to the bar or with an el, or "eagle" grip in which the wrists are rolled inward until the thumbs are on the outside of the grip, pointing away from each other.

CONTENDERS:
Grigori Misutin, CIS; Li Chunyang, China; Li Jing, China; Igor Korobchinski, CIS

ORDER OF ARTISTIC GYMNASTIC EVENTS

Competition is divided into three parts — team, all-around and individual apparatus. The top 12 men's and women's teams, consisting of six gymnasts each, from last September's World Championships qualified for the Barcelona Games.

TEAM	ALL-AROUND	INDIVIDUAL
Athletes perform compulsory and optional exercises. Based on the compulsory scores, teams will be seeded for the next portion of competition, where gymnasts present a unique routine on each apparatus. The total of the top five scores on each apparatus is the team score.	Includes the 36 highest-marked gymnasts from the team competition, with a maximum of three per team. Each athlete performs optional routines on all of the apparatus. The results determine the individual all-around champion; scores from the team competition don't carry over.	Includes the top eight gymnasts, with a maximum of two per team, from the team compulsories. Each individual performs an optional routine on the respective apparatus and the results determine individual medals.
Team medals are awarded	*Individual medals are awarded*	*Individual medals are awarded for each apparatus*

MEN — Rings
Height: 8 feet off the mat surface
Suspension height: 18 feet

WOMEN — Uneven Bars
Length: 8 feet
Height: 5 feet, 2 inches lower bar; 7 feet 9 inches upper bar

MEN — High Bar
Height: 8 feet
Length: 8 feet

WOMEN — Balance Beam
Width: 4 inches
Height: 4 feet
Length: 15 feet

MEN WOMEN — Floor Exercise
Area: 40 feet x 40 feet

WOMEN — Pommel Horse
Width: 14 inches
Height: 4 feet
Length: 5 feet

MEN — Parallel Bars
Width between bars: Adjustable from 16 inches to 20 inches
Length: 11 feet
Height: 6 feet

MEN — Vault
Width: 14 inches
Height: 4 feet
Length: 5 feet
Runway: 82 feet

WOMEN — Vault
Width: 14 inches
Height: 4 feet
Length: 5 feet
Runway: 82 feet

GRAPHICS BY LOURDES LIVINGSTON AND ERIC JUNGERMAN/THE CHRONICLE

Gymnastics

DESIGN: Lourdes Livingstone, Eric Jungerman, USA

PUBLISHER/CLIENT: *San Francisco Chronicle*

DATE OF 1ST PUBLICATION/USE: 21 July 1992

DESIGN RATIONALE: The full-page graphic was one of a series illustrating various Olympic sports that appeared in the newspaper in advance of the summer games in Barcelona 1992. The purpose of this one was to provide an overview of upcoming gymnastic events for men and women, including diagrams of the equipment used, descriptions of various moves, scoring methods and profiles on the top athletes to watch.

CREDITS: Graphics editor, Steve Outing; illustrator, Lourdes Livingstone; designer, Eric Jungerman.

Submarine Cutaway

DESIGN: Peter Sullivan, UK

PUBLISHER/CLIENT: *Battle Surface*, Random House, Australia

DATE OF 1ST PUBLICATION/USE: 1992

DESIGN RATIONALE: Cutaway of a Japanese Midget Submarine control tower. As the subject had never been drawn before in such detail, it had to be researched completely from scratch.

CREDITS: Researchers, Peter Sullivan, David Jenkins (author of *Battle Surface*).

CUTAWAY SECTION OF
MIDGET SUBMARINE

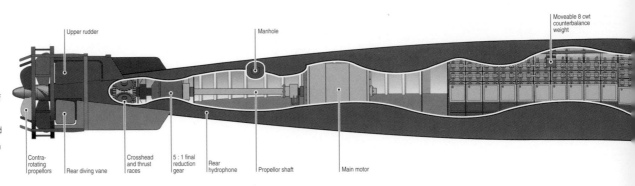

Upper rudder · Manhole · Moveable 8 cwt counterbalance weight

Contra-rotating propellors · Rear diving vane · Crosshead and thrust races · 5 : 1 final reduction gear · Rear hydrophone · Propellor shaft · Main motor

Submarine Control

DESIGN: Peter Sullivan, UK

PUBLISHER/CLIENT: *Battle Surface*, Random House, Australia

DATE OF 1ST PUBLICATION/USE: 1992

DESIGN RATIONALE: Cutaway of a Japanese Midget Submarine control tower. As the subject had never been drawn before in such detail, it had to be researched completely from scratch.

CREDITS: Researchers, Peter Sullivan, David Jenkins (author of *Battle Surface*).

Entry hatch

Navigation light

Radio aerial

Access chute

Periscope

Conning tower

Handle to raise radio aerial

Fine depth control and ammeter

Meters for batteries

Folding ladder

Clinometer & depth meter

Torpedo firing lever

Bulk head door

Steering wheel

Gyroscope

Watertight bulkhead 30

Emergency tank

Hydroplane and rudder controls

Emergency steering wheel

Periscope well

Depth keeping mechanism

CUTAWAY DRAWING
SHOWING CONTROL ROOM
OF MIDGET SUBMARINE

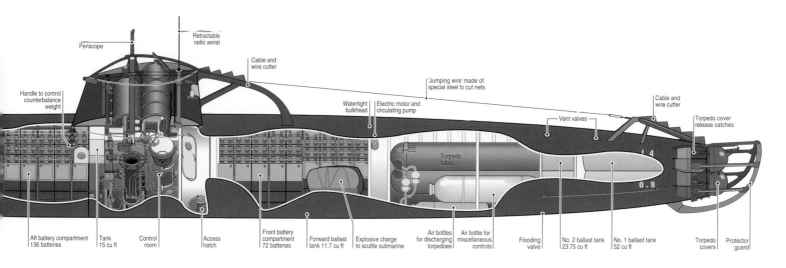

Periscope

Retractable
radio aerial

Cable and
wire cutter

'Jumping wire' made of
special steel to cut nets

Handle to control
counterbalance
weight

Watertight
bulkhead

Electric motor and
circulating pump

Vent valves

Cable and
wire cutter

Torpedo cover
release catches

Torpedo
tubes

| Aft battery compartment 136 batteries | Tank 15 cu ft | Control room | Access hatch | Front battery compartment 72 batteries | Forward ballast tank 11.7 cu ft | Explosive charge to scuttle submarine | Air bottles for discharging torpedoes | Air bottle for miscellaneous controls | Flooding valve | No. 2 ballast tank 23.75 cu ft | No. 1 ballast tank 52 cu ft | Torpedo covers | Protector guard |

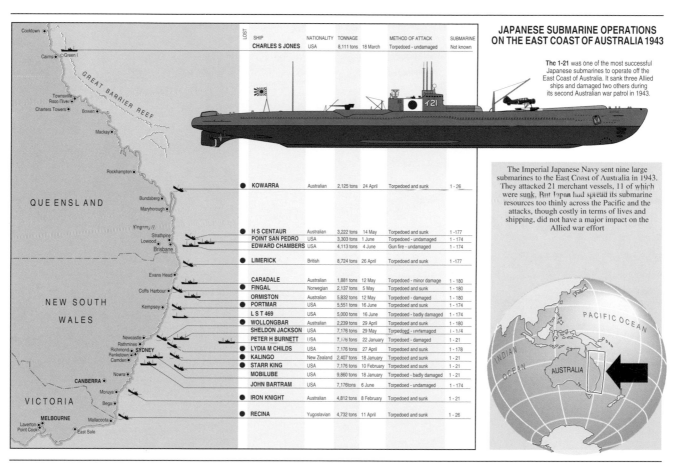

JAPANESE SUBMARINE OPERATIONS ON THE EAST COAST OF AUSTRALIA 1943

The I-21 was one of the most successful Japanese submarines to operate off the East Coast of Australia. It sank three Allied ships and damaged two others during its second Australian war patrol in 1943.

The Imperial Japanese Navy sent nine large submarines to the East Coast of Australia in 1943. They attacked 21 merchant vessels, 11 of which were sunk. But Japan had spread its submarine resources too thinly across the Pacific and the attacks, though costly in terms of lives and shipping, did not have a major impact on the Allied war effort

LOST	SHIP	NATIONALITY	TONNAGE		METHOD OF ATTACK	SUBMARINE
	CHARLES S JONES	USA	8,111 tons	18 March	Torpedoed - undamaged	Not known
●	KOWARRA	Australian	2,125 tons	24 April	Torpedoed and sunk	1 - 26
●	H S CENTAUR	Australian	3,222 tons	14 May	Torpedoed and sunk	1 - 177
	POINT SAN PEDRO	USA	3,303 tons	1 June	Torpedoed - undamaged	1 - 174
	EDWARD CHAMBERS	USA	4,113 tons	4 June	Gun fire - undamaged	1 - 174
●	LIMERICK	British	8,724 tons	26 April	Torpedoed and sunk	1 - 177
	CARADALE	Australian	1,881 tons	12 May	Torpedoed - minor damage	1 - 180
●	FINGAL	Norwegian	2,137 tons	5 May	Torpedoed and sunk	1 - 180
	ORMISTON	Australian	5,832 tons	12 May	Torpedoed - damaged	1 - 180
●	PORTMAR	USA	5,551 tons	16 June	Torpedoed and sunk	1 - 174
	L S T 469		5,000 tons	16 June	Torpedoed - badly damaged	1 - 174
●	WOLLONGBAR	Australian	2,239 tons	29 April	Torpedoed and sunk	1 - 180
	SHELDON JACKSON	USA	7,176 tons	29 May	Torpedoed - undamaged	1 - 1/4
	PETER H BURNETT	USA	7,176 tons	22 January	Torpedoed - damaged	1 - 21
	LYDIA M CHILDS	USA	7,176 tons	27 April	Torpedoed and sunk	1 - 178
	KALINGO	New Zealand	2,407 tons	18 January	Torpedoed and sunk	1 - 21
	STARR KING	USA	7,176 tons	10 February	Torpedoed and sunk	1 - 21
	MOBILUBE	USA	9,860 tons	18 January	Torpedoed - badly damaged	1 - 21
	JOHN BARTRAM	USA	7,176tons	6 June	Torpedoed - undamaged	1 - 174
●	IRON KNIGHT	Australian	4,812 tons	8 February	Torpedoed and sunk	1 - 21
●	RECINA	Yugoslavian	4,732 tons	11 April	Torpedoed and sunk	1 - 26

Submarine Operations 1943

DESIGN: Peter Sullivan, UK

PUBLISHER/CLIENT: *Battle Surface*, Random House, Australia

DATE OF 1ST PUBLICATION/USE: 1992

DESIGN RATIONALE: Map of all Japanese submarine attacks on the East Coast of Australia. Together with a drawing of a submarine and a location indicator on a small globe, this map explained the story.

CREDITS: Researchers, Peter Sullivan, David Jenkins (author).

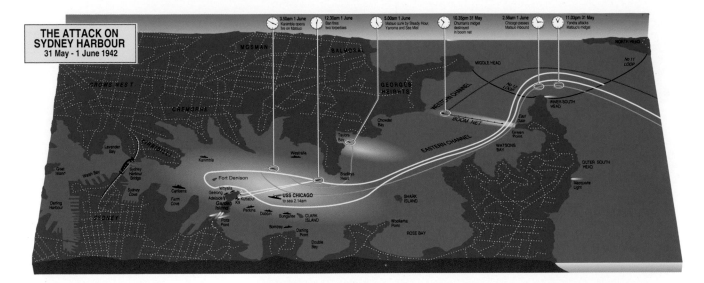

The Attack on Sydney Harbour

DESIGN: Peter Sullivan, UK

PUBLISHER/CLIENT: *Battle Surface*, Random House, Australia

DATE OF 1ST PUBLICATION/USE: 1992

DESIGN RATIONALE: A three-dimensional map in colour showing how Japanese midget submarines attacked shipping in Sydney Harbour in World War II. The attack was at night and this was shown by use of colour.

CREDITS: Researchers, Peter Sullivan, David Jenkins (author of *Battle Surface*).

Gulf Chemical Warfare

DESIGN: Duncan Mil, UK

PUBLISHER/CLIENT: Graphic News

DATE OF 1ST PUBLICATION/USE: 12 August 1990

DESIGN RATIONALE: Protecting RAF aircrew against chemical warfare in the Gulf War.

CREDITS: Art director, Duncan Mil; illustrators, Duncan Mil, Russell Lewis; writer/researcher, Julie Hacking.

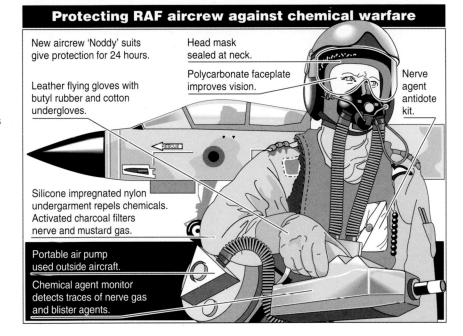

Panama Stealth

DESIGN: Duncan Mil, UK

PUBLISHER/CLIENT: Graphic News

DATE OF 1ST PUBLICATION/USE: 21 February 1989

DESIGN RATIONALE: A study of the Lockheed F-117A "Stealth" fighter as used during the Panama invasion in December 1989.

CREDITS: Art director, Duncan Mil; illustrators, Duncan Mil, Russell Lewis; writer/researcher, Julie Hacking.

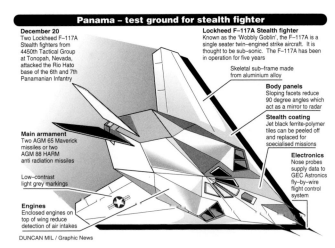

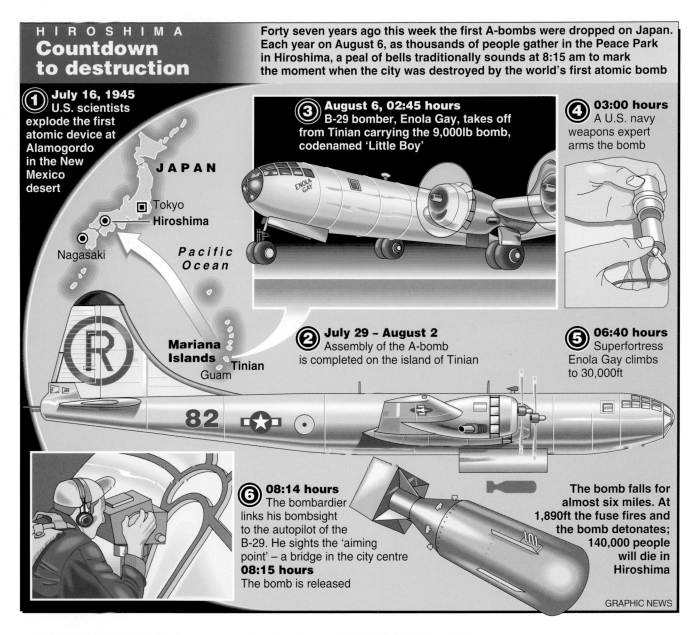

HIROSHIMA
Countdown to destruction

Forty seven years ago this week the first A-bombs were dropped on Japan. Each year on August 6, as thousands of people gather in the Peace Park in Hiroshima, a peal of bells traditionally sounds at 8:15 am to mark the moment when the city was destroyed by the world's first atomic bomb

① July 16, 1945 U.S. scientists explode the first atomic device at Alamogordo in the New Mexico desert

③ August 6, 02:45 hours B-29 bomber, Enola Gay, takes off from Tinian carrying the 9,000lb bomb, codenamed 'Little Boy'

④ 03:00 hours A U.S. navy weapons expert arms the bomb

JAPAN

Tokyo
Hiroshima

Nagasaki

Pacific Ocean

Mariana Islands
Tinian
Guam

② July 29 – August 2 Assembly of the A-bomb is completed on the island of Tinian

⑤ 06:40 hours Superfortress Enola Gay climbs to 30,000ft

⑥ 08:14 hours The bombardier links his bombsight to the autopilot of the B-29. He sights the 'aiming point' – a bridge in the city centre
08:15 hours The bomb is released

The bomb falls for almost six miles. At 1,890ft the fuse fires and the bomb detonates; 140,000 people will die in Hiroshima

GRAPHIC NEWS

THE STEALTH COUNTERATTACK

The immune system has trouble fighting the AIDS virus because of its stealth-like structure.

The vaccine can trigger the immune system to make new kinds of antibodies that may find and destroy the virus.

Vaccine

Immune system

AIDS virus (HIV)

Antibodies

TIME Diagram by Joe Lertola

Hiroshima

DESIGN: Duncan Mil, UK

PUBLISHER/CLIENT: Graphic News

DATE OF 1ST PUBLICATION/USE: 5 August 1992

DESIGN RATIONALE: A countdown of events leading to the dropping of the world's first atomic bomb.

CREDITS: Art director, Duncan Mil; illustrators, Duncan Mil, Russell Lewis; writer/researcher, Julie Hacking.

The Stealth Counterattack

DESIGN: Joe Lertola, USA

PUBLISHER/CLIENT: *Time* magazine

DATE OF 1ST PUBLICATION/USE: 24 June 1991

DESIGN RATIONALE: Uses a metaphor to show how a vaccine against the HIV virus might work.

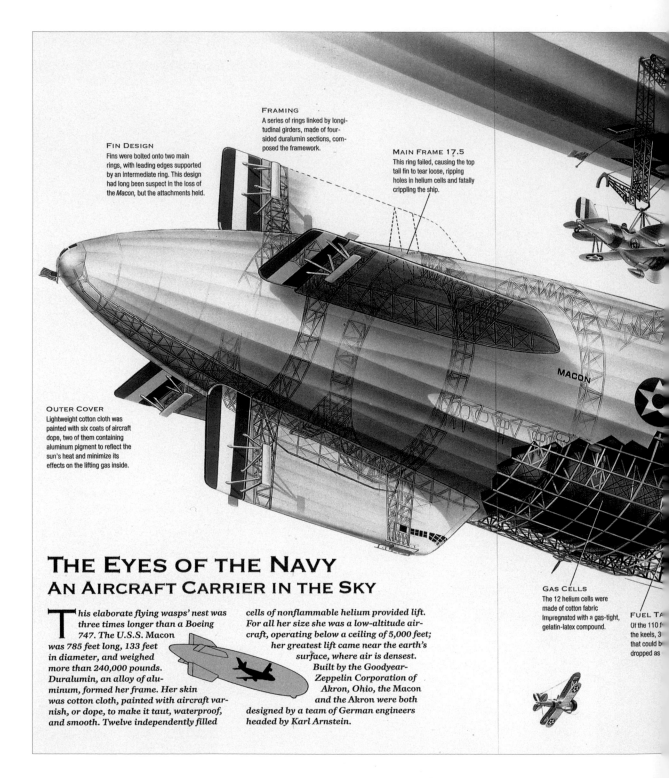

FIN DESIGN
Fins were bolted onto two main rings, with leading edges supported by an intermediate ring. This design had long been suspect in the loss of the *Macon*, but the attachments held.

FRAMING
A series of rings linked by longitudinal girders, made of four-sided duralumin sections, composed the framework.

MAIN FRAME 17.5
This ring failed, causing the top tail fin to tear loose, ripping holes in helium cells and fatally crippling the ship.

OUTER COVER
Lightweight cotton cloth was painted with six coats of aircraft dope, two of them containing aluminum pigment to reflect the sun's heat and minimize its effects on the lifting gas inside.

GAS CELLS
The 12 helium cells were made of cotton fabric impregnated with a gas-tight, gelatin-latex compound.

FUEL TA
Of the 110 f
the keels, 3
that could b
dropped as

THE EYES OF THE NAVY
AN AIRCRAFT CARRIER IN THE SKY

This elaborate flying wasps' nest was three times longer than a Boeing 747. The U.S.S. Macon was 785 feet long, 133 feet in diameter, and weighed more than 240,000 pounds. Duralumin, an alloy of aluminum, formed her frame. Her skin was cotton cloth, painted with aircraft varnish, or dope, to make it taut, waterproof, and smooth. Twelve independently filled cells of nonflammable helium provided lift. For all her size she was a low-altitude aircraft, operating below a ceiling of 5,000 feet; her greatest lift came near the earth's surface, where air is densest. Built by the Goodyear-Zeppelin Corporation of Akron, Ohio, the Macon and the Akron were both designed by a team of German engineers headed by Karl Arnstein.

Macon Cutaway

PUBLISHER/CLIENT: *National Geographic* magazine

DATE OF 1ST PUBLICATION/USE: January 1992

DESIGN RATIONALE: Cutaway diagram revealing the construction of the USS *Macon*.

CREDITS: Art director, Mark Holmes; illustrator, Richard Leech; researcher, David Woodell.

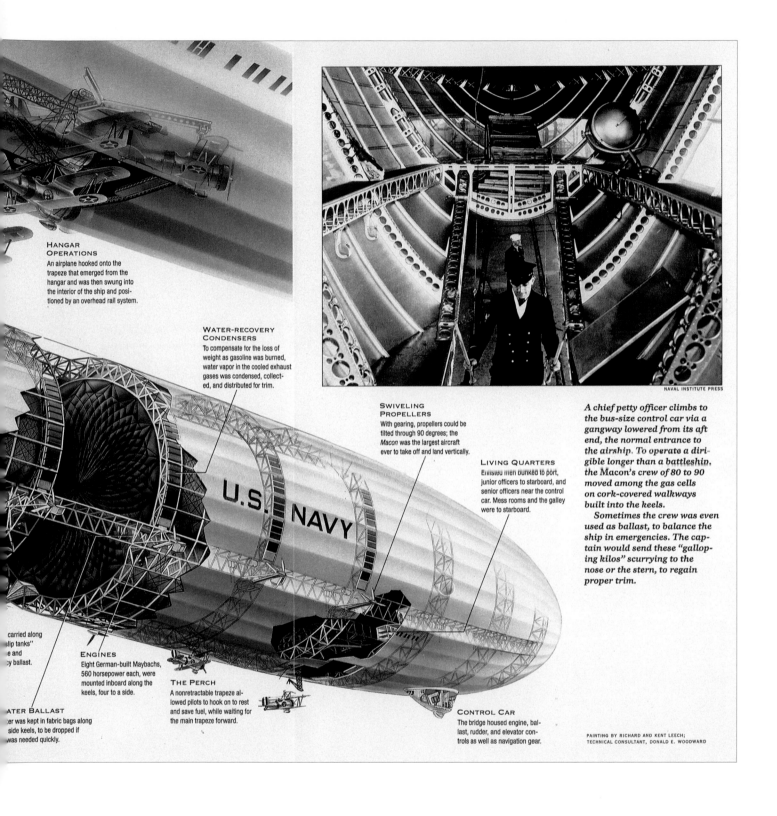

HANGAR OPERATIONS
An airplane hooked onto the trapeze that emerged from the hangar and was then swung into the interior of the ship and positioned by an overhead rail system.

WATER-RECOVERY CONDENSERS
To compensate for the loss of weight as gasoline was burned, water vapor in the cooled exhaust gases was condensed, collected, and distributed for trim.

SWIVELING PROPELLERS
With gearing, propellers could be tilted through 90 degrees; the *Macon* was the largest aircraft ever to take off and land vertically.

LIVING QUARTERS
Enlisted men bunked to port, junior officers to starboard, and senior officers near the control car. Mess rooms and the galley were to starboard.

carried along lip tanks'' e and y ballast.

ENGINES
Eight German-built Maybachs, 560 horsepower each, were mounted inboard along the keels, four to a side.

THE PERCH
A nonretractable trapeze allowed pilots to hook on to rest and save fuel, while waiting for the main trapeze forward.

ATER BALLAST
er was kept in fabric bags along side keels, to be dropped if was needed quickly.

CONTROL CAR
The bridge housed engine, ballast, rudder, and elevator controls as well as navigation gear.

NAVAL INSTITUTE PRESS

A chief petty officer climbs to the bus-size control car via a gangway lowered from its aft end, the normal entrance to the airship. To operate a dirigible longer than a battleship, the Macon's crew of 80 to 90 moved among the gas cells on cork-covered walkways built into the keels.

Sometimes the crew was even used as ballast, to balance the ship in emergencies. The captain would send these "galloping kilos" scurrying to the nose or the stern, to regain proper trim.

PAINTING BY RICHARD AND KENT LEECH; TECHNICAL CONSULTANT, DONALD E. WOODWARD

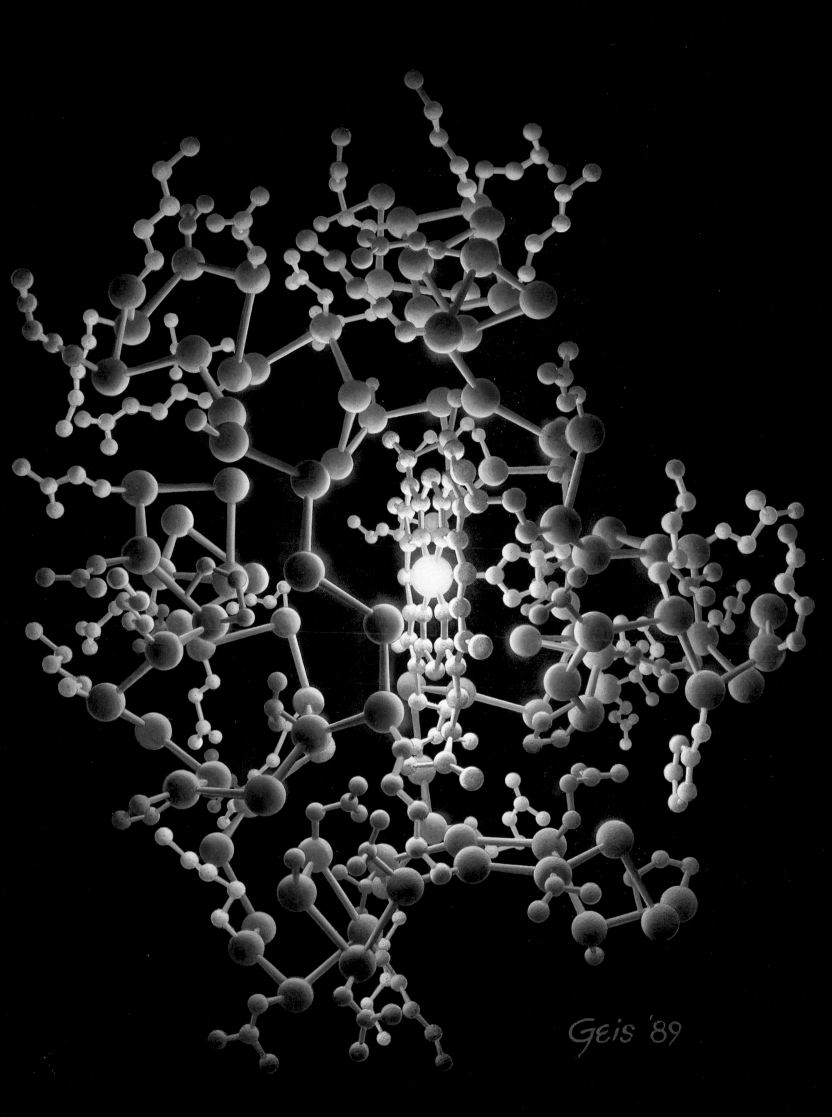

Geis '89

Three-dimensional Structure of Cytochrome-c

DESIGN: Irving Geis, USA

PUBLISHER/CLIENT: Saunders College Publishing Co., Philadelphia, USA; published in Biochemistry Textbook by Dr Mary K. Campbell

DATE OF 1ST PUBLICATION/USE: 1991

DESIGN RATIONALE: This illustrates the three-dimensional structure of the macromolecule Cytochrome-c, an electron transfer molecule that is part of the energy extraction system of living organisms. The painting portrays, in green, those sections of the molecule that are in contact with water in the cell. The central iron atom is the source of illumination in the painting.

CREDIT: Illustrator, Irving Geis.

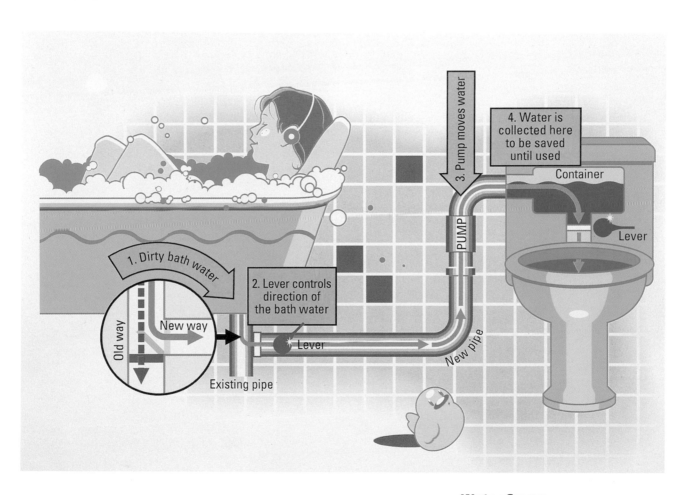

Water Saver

DESIGN: Eliot Bergman, USA

PUBLISHER/CLIENT: *Disney Adventures* magazine

DATE OF 1ST PUBLICATION/USE: 1993

DESIGN RATIONALE: The diagram is an interpretation of a contest winner's concept for saving water. *Disney Adventures* is a magazine for elementary school childen, so the diagram had to be fun and inviting as well as informative.

CREDITS: Art director, Juanita Kuan.

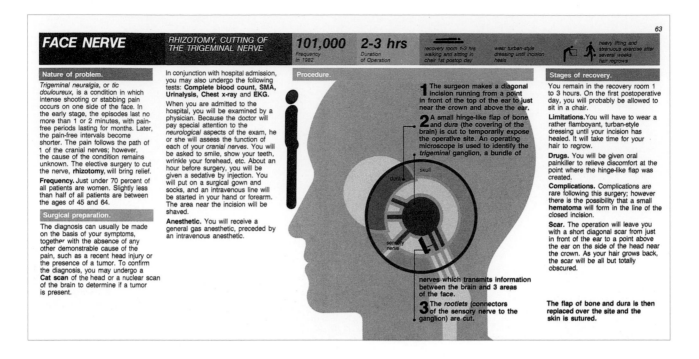

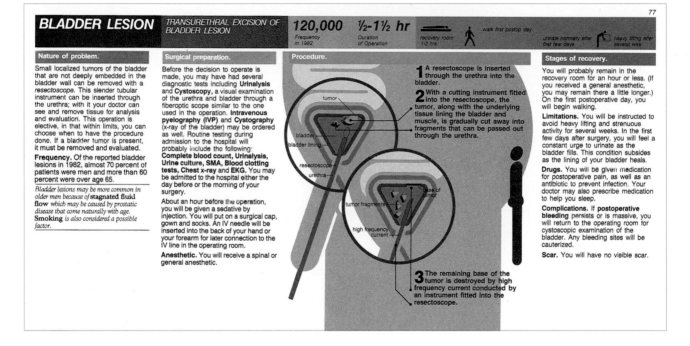

Medical Access
(surgical section)

DESIGN: Peter Bradford, USA

PUBLISHER/CLIENT: *Medical Access*/Access Press Inc.

DATE OF 1ST PUBLICATION/USE: 1989

DESIGN RATIONALE: The 32 most common surgical procedures are systematically described and diagrammed. Non-technical language is used to explain all stages of each operation, and step-by-step diagrams are used to clarify the surgery procedure.

The complexities of diagnostic tests and operations often confuse and intimidate patients: *Medical Access* was published to guide patients simply and clearly through common medical experiences.

CREDITS: Art directors, Peter Bradford, Richard Saul Wurman; illustrators, Lorraine Christiani, Peter Bradford; researchers, Ellen Lupton, Ellen O'Neill.

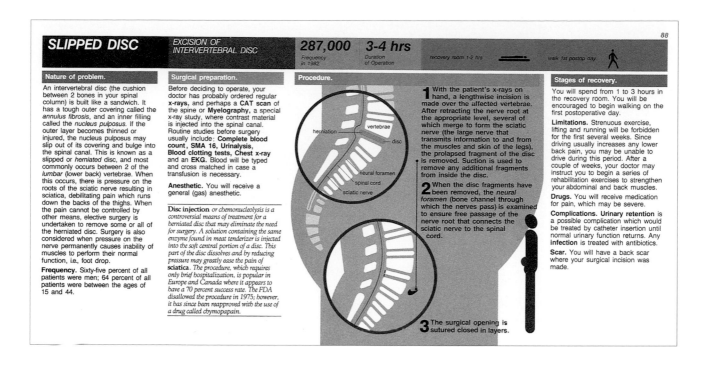

SLIPPED DISC

EXCISION OF INTERVERTEBRAL DISC

287,000 Frequency in 1982

3-4 hrs Duration of Operation

recovery room 1-2 hrs

walk 1st postop day

Nature of problem.

An intervertebral disc (the cushion between 2 bones in your spinal column) is built like a sandwich. It has a tough outer covering called the *annulus fibrosis*, and an inner filling called the *nucleus pulposus*. If the outer layer becomes thinned or injured, the nucleus pulposus may slip out of its covering and bulge into the spinal canal. This is known as a slipped or *herniated* disc, and most commonly occurs between 2 of the *lumbar* (lower back) vertebrae. When this occurs, there is pressure on the roots of the sciatic nerve resulting in sciatica, debilitating pain which runs down the backs of the thighs. When the pain cannot be controlled by other means, elective surgery is undertaken to remove some or all of the herniated disc. Surgery is also considered when pressure on the nerve permanently causes inability of muscles to perform their normal function, i.e. foot drop.

Frequency. Sixty-five percent of all patients were men; 64 percent of all patients were between the ages of 15 and 44.

Surgical preparation.

Before deciding to operate, your doctor has probably ordered regular **x-rays**, and perhaps a **CAT scan** of the spine or **Myelography**, a special x-ray study, where contrast material is injected into the spinal canal. Routine studies before surgery usually include: **Complete blood count, SMA 16, Urinalysis, Blood clotting tests, Chest x-ray** and an **EKG**. Blood will be typed and cross matched in case a transfusion is necessary.

Anesthetic. You will receive a general (gas) anesthetic.

Disc injection or chemonucleolysis is a controversial means of treatment for a herniated disc that may eliminate the need for surgery. A solution containing the same enzyme found in meat tenderizer is injected into the soft central portion of a disc. This part of the disc dissolves and by reducing pressure may greatly ease the pain of sciatica. The procedure, which requires only brief hospitalization, is popular in Europe and Canada where it appears to have a 70 percent success rate. The FDA disallowed the procedure in 1975; however, it has since been reapproved with the use of a drug called chymopapain.

Procedure.

herniation

vertebrae

disc

neural foramen

spinal cord

sciatic nerve

1 With the patient's x-rays on hand, a lengthwise incision is made over the affected vertebrae. After retracting the nerve root at the appropriate level, several of which merge to form the sciatic nerve (the large nerve that transmits information to and from the muscles and skin of the legs), the prolapsed fragment of the disc is removed. Suction is used to remove any additional fragments from inside the disc.

2 When the disc fragments have been removed, the *neural foramen* (bone channel through which the nerves pass) is examined to ensure free passage of the nerve root that connects the sciatic nerve to the spinal cord.

3 The surgical opening is sutured closed in layers.

Stages of recovery.

You will spend from 1 to 3 hours in the recovery room. You will be encouraged to begin walking on the first postoperative day.

Limitations. Strenuous exercise, lifting and running will be forbidden for the first several weeks. Since driving usually increases any lower back pain, you may be unable to drive during this period. After a couple of weeks, your doctor may instruct you to begin a series of rehabilitation exercises to strengthen your abdominal and back muscles.

Drugs. You will receive medication for pain, which may be severe.

Complications. Urinary retention is a possible complication which would be treated by catheter insertion until normal urinary function returns. Any **infection** is treated with antibiotics.

Scar. You will have a back scar where your surgical incision was made.

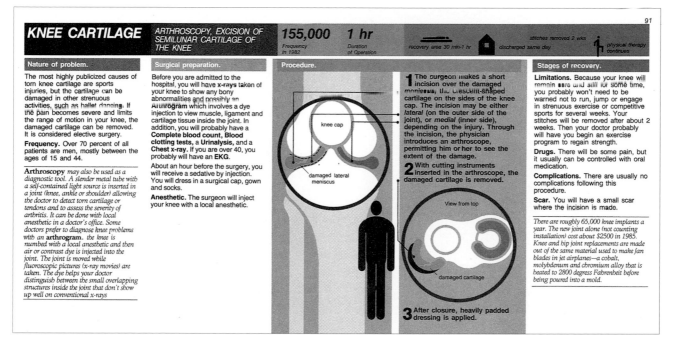

KNEE CARTILAGE

ARTHROSCOPY, EXCISION OF SEMILUNAR CARTILAGE OF THE KNEE

155,000 Frequency in 1982

1 hr Duration of Operation

recovery area 30 min-1 hr

discharged same day

stitches removed 2 wks

physical therapy continues

Nature of problem.

The most highly publicized causes of torn knee cartilage are sports injuries, but the cartilage can be damaged in other strenuous activities, such as ballet dancing. If the pain becomes severe and limits the range of motion in your knee, the damaged cartilage can be removed. It is considered elective surgery.

Frequency. Over 70 percent of all patients are men, mostly between the ages of 15 and 44.

Arthroscopy may also be used as a diagnostic tool. A slender metal tube with a self-contained light source is inserted in a joint (knee, ankle or shoulder) allowing the doctor to detect torn cartilage or tendons and to assess the severity of arthritis. It can be done with local anesthetic in a doctor's office. Some doctors prefer to diagnose knee problems with an arthrogram. the knee is numbed with a local anesthetic and then air or contrast dye is injected into the joint. The joint is moved while fluoroscopic pictures (x-ray movies) are taken. The dye helps your doctor distinguish between the small overlapping structures inside the joint that don't show up well on conventional x-rays

Surgical preparation.

Before you are admitted to the hospital, you will have **x-rays** taken of your knee to show any bony abnormalities and possibly an **Arthrogram** which involves a dye injection to view muscle, ligament and cartilage tissue inside the joint. In addition, you will probably have a **Complete blood count, Blood clotting tests,** a **Urinalysis,** and a **Chest x-ray.** If you are over 40, you probably will have an **EKG.**

About an hour before the surgery, you will receive a sedative by injection. You will dress in a surgical cap, gown and socks.

Anesthetic. The surgeon will inject your knee with a local anesthetic.

Procedure.

knee cap

damaged lateral meniscus

1 The surgeon makes a short incision over the damaged meniscus, the crescent-shaped cartilage on the sides of the knee cap. The incision may be either *lateral* (on the outer side of the joint), or *medial* (inner side), depending on the injury. Through the incision, the physician introduces an arthroscope, permitting him or her to see the extent of the damage.

2 With cutting instruments inserted in the arthroscope, the damaged cartilage is removed.

View from top

damaged cartilage

3 After closure, heavily padded dressing is applied.

Stages of recovery.

Limitations. Because your knee will remain sore and stiff for some time, you probably won't need to be warned not to run, jump or engage in strenuous exercise or competitive sports for several weeks. Your stitches will be removed after about 2 weeks. Then your doctor probably will have you begin an exercise program to regain strength.

Drugs. There will be some pain, but it usually can be controlled with oral medication.

Complications. There are usually no complications following this procedure.

Scar. You will have a small scar where the incision is made.

There are roughly 65,000 knee implants a year. The new joint alone (not counting installation) cost about $2500 in 1985. Knee and hip joint replacements are made out of the same material used to make fan blades in jet airplanes—a cobalt, molybdenum and chromium alloy that is heated to 2800 degress Fahrenheit before being poured into a mold.

Saturne

DESIGN: Pierre Praquin, France

PUBLISHER/CLIENT: CEA
Commissariat à L'Energie
Antomique/CNRS Centre
National de la Recherche
Scientifique

DATE OF 1ST PUBLICATION/USE:
1989

DESIGN RATIONALE: The peak
shows the mathematical
breakdown, the first level depicts
the conception of the researched
materials and the third level
shows these as well as the results.

CREDITS: Art director, Pierre
Praquin; photographer, Pierre
Jahan, Cen-Saclay; illustrator,
Pierre Praquin.

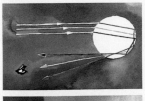

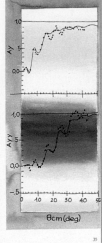

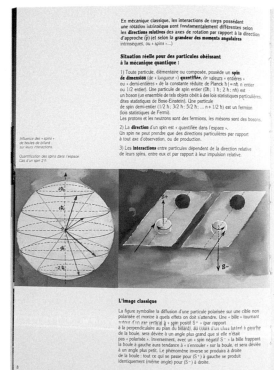

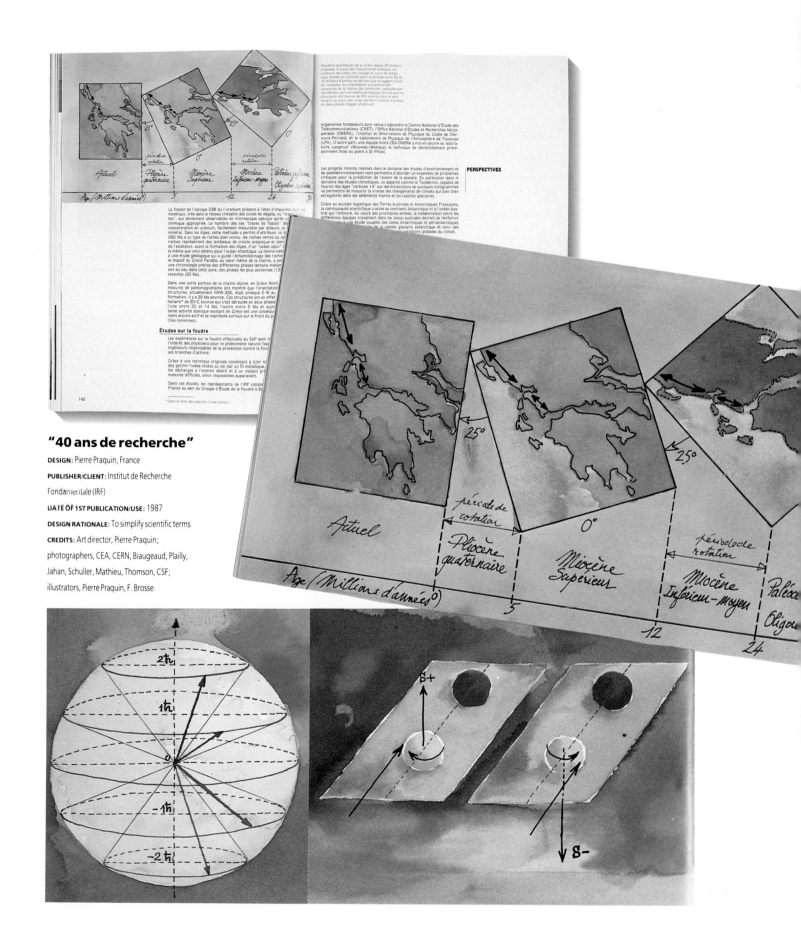

"40 ans de recherche"

DESIGN: Pierre Praquin, France

PUBLISHER/CLIENT: Institut de Recherche
Fondamentale (IRF)

DATE OF 1ST PUBLICATION/USE: 1987

DESIGN RATIONALE: To simplify scientific terms

CREDITS: Art director, Pierre Praquin;
photographers, CEA, CERN, Biaugeaud, Plailly,
Jahan, Schuller, Mathieu, Thomson, CSF;
illustrators, Pierre Praquin, F. Brosse.

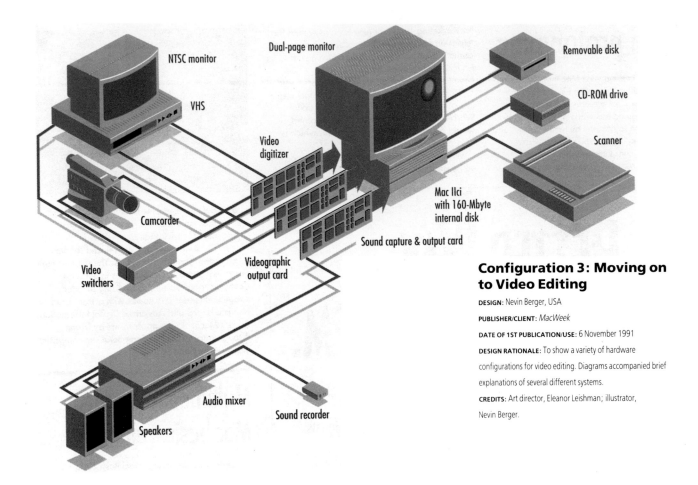

Configuration 3: Moving on to Video Editing

DESIGN: Nevin Berger, USA

PUBLISHER/CLIENT: *MacWeek*

DATE OF 1ST PUBLICATION/USE: 6 November 1991

DESIGN RATIONALE: To show a variety of hardware configurations for video editing. Diagrams accompanied brief explanations of several different systems.

CREDITS: Art director, Eleanor Leishman; illustrator, Nevin Berger.

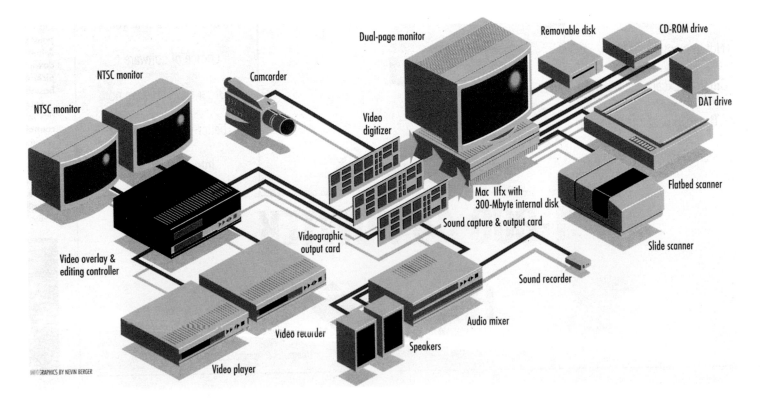

Document management in a mixed environment

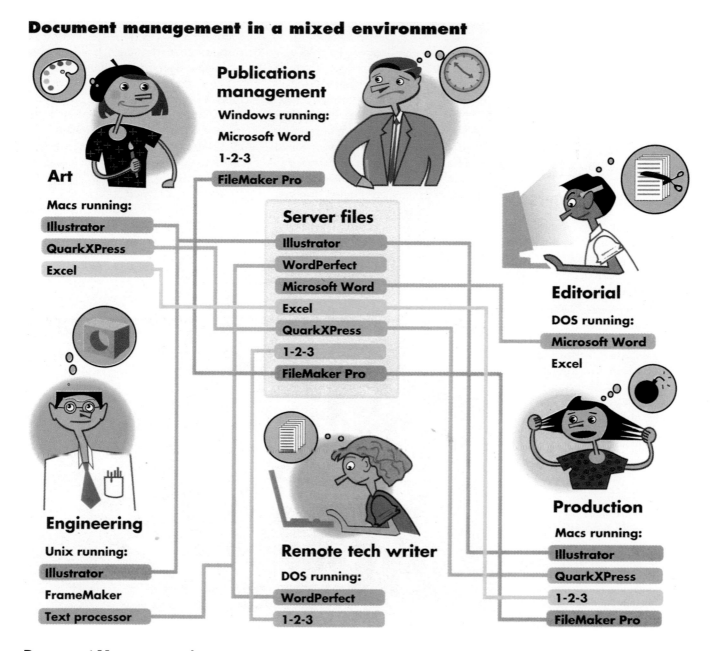

Document Management in a Mixed Environment

DESIGN: Nevin Berger, USA

PUBLISHER/CLIENT: *MacWeek*

DATE OF 1ST PUBLICATION/USE: 2 August 1993

DESIGN RATIONALE: A light-hearted approach shows the different paths documents take as they are used in a publication in a mixed platform environment. The graphic worked as an example of document flow, not as a literal diagram.

CREDITS: Art director, Eleanor Leishman; illustrator, Nevin Berger.

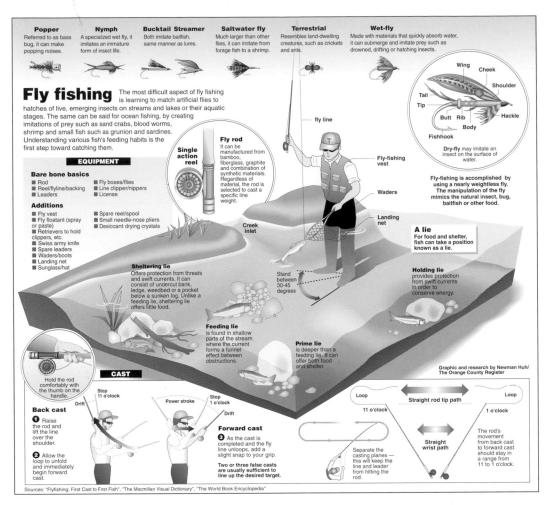

Popper
Referred to as bass bug, it can make popping noises.

Nymph
A specialized wet fly, it imitates an immature form of insect life.

Bucktail Streamer
Both imitate baitfish, same manner as lures.

Saltwater fly
Much larger than other flies, it can imitate from forage fish to a shrimp.

Terrestrial
Resembles land-dwelling creatures, such as crickets and ants.

Wet-fly
Made with materials that quickly absorb water, it can submerge and imitate prey such as drowned, drifting or hatching insects.

Fly fishing

The most difficult aspect of fly fishing is learning to match artificial flies to hatches of live, emerging insects on streams and lakes or their aquatic stages. The same can be said for ocean fishing, by creating imitations of prey such as sand crabs, blood worms, shrimp and small fish such as grunion and sardines. Understanding various fish's feeding habits is the first step toward catching them.

EQUIPMENT

Bare bone basics
- Rod
- Reel/flyline/backing
- Leaders
- Fly boxes/flies
- Line clipper/nippers
- License

Additions
- Fly vest
- Fly floatant (spray or paste)
- Retrievers to hold clippers, etc.
- Swiss army knife
- Spare leaders
- Waders/boots
- Landing net
- Sunglass/hat
- Spare reel/spool
- Small needle-nose pliers
- Desiccant drying crystals

Single action reel

Fly rod
It can be manufactured from bamboo, fiberglass, graphite and combination of synthetic materials. Regardless of material, the rod is selected to cast a specific line weight.

fly line

Wing **Cheek**
Tail **Shoulder**
Tip
Butt **Rib** **Hackle**
Fishhook **Body**

Dry-fly may imitate an insect on the surface of water.

Fly-fishing vest

Waders

Landing net

A lie
For food and shelter, fish can take a position known as a lie.

Fly-fishing is accomplished by using a nearly weightless fly. The manipulation of the fly mimics the natural insect, bug, baitfish or other food.

Creek inlet

Sheltering lie
Offers protection from threats and swift currents. It can consist of undercut bank, ledge, weedbed or a pocket below a sunken log. Unlike a feeding lie, sheltering lie offers little food.

Stand between 30-45 degrees

Holding lie
provides protection from swift currents in order to conserve energy.

Feeding lie
is found in shallow parts of the stream where the current forms a funnel effect between obstructions.

Prime lie
is deeper than a feeding lie. It can offer both food and shelter.

Graphic and research by Newman Huh/
The Orange County Register

CAST

Hold the rod comfortably with the thumb on the handle.

Back cast
❶ Raise the rod and lift the line over the shoulder.

❷ Allow the loop to unfold and immediately begin forward cast.

Stop 11 o'clock
Drift

Power stroke
Stop 1 o'clock
Drift

Forward cast
❸ As the cast is completed and the fly line unloops, add a slight snap to your grip.

Two or three false casts are usually sufficient to line up the desired target.

Loop
Straight rod tip path
Loop
11 o'clock
1 o'clock

Separate the casting planes — this will keep the line and leader from hitting the rod.

Straight wrist path

The rod's movement from back cast to forward cast should stay in a range from 11 to 1 o'clock.

Sources: "Flyfishing: First Cast to First Fish", "The Macmillan Visual Dictionary", "The World Book Encyclopedia"

Fly-fishing

DESIGN: Newman Huh, USA

PUBLISHER/CLIENT: The Orange County Register

DATE OF 1ST PUBLICATION/USE: 1992

DESIGN RATIONALE: To show techniques and equipment for fly-fishing and where the best areas are in a stream.

	PROPOSED HSCT	CONCORDE
Passenger capacity	200 to 300	100
Range	9,300 to 11,100 km	6,500 km
Speed	Mach 2.5 to 3	Mach 2
Revenue required (per passenger km)	$.06	$.54
Size of fleet	1,000 to 2,000	16
Fuselage length	95 meters	71 meters
Total gross weight	333,400 kg	186,000 kg

Proposed Boeing High Speed Civil Transport

Concorde

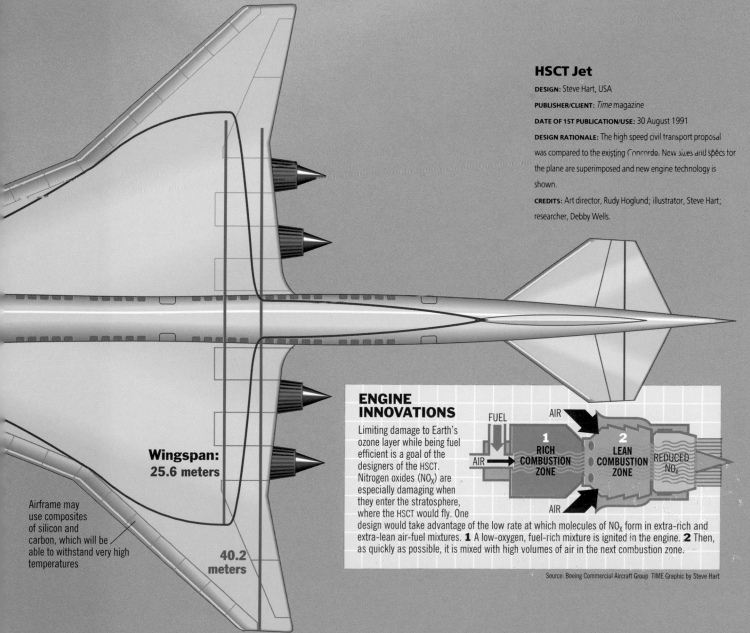

HSCT Jet

DESIGN: Steve Hart, USA

PUBLISHER/CLIENT: *Time* magazine

DATE OF 1ST PUBLICATION/USE: 30 August 1991

DESIGN RATIONALE: The high speed civil transport proposal was compared to the existing Concorde. New sizes and specs for the plane are superimposed and new engine technology is shown.

CREDITS: Art director, Rudy Hoglund; illustrator, Steve Hart; researcher, Debby Wells.

Wingspan:
25.6 meters

Airframe may use composites of silicon and carbon, which will be able to withstand very high temperatures

40.2 meters

ENGINE INNOVATIONS

Limiting damage to Earth's ozone layer while being fuel efficient is a goal of the designers of the HSCT. Nitrogen oxides (NO_X) are especially damaging when they enter the stratosphere, where the HSCT would fly. One design would take advantage of the low rate at which molecules of NO_X form in extra-rich and extra-lean air-fuel mixtures. **1** A low-oxygen, fuel-rich mixture is ignited in the engine. **2** Then, as quickly as possible, it is mixed with high volumes of air in the next combustion zone.

FUEL   AIR

AIR

1 RICH COMBUSTION ZONE

2 LEAN COMBUSTION ZONE

REDUCED NO_X

AIR

Source: Boeing Commercial Aircraft Group TIME Graphic by Steve Hart

What Are Quarks?

DESIGN: Joe Lertola, USA

PUBLISHER/CLIENT: *Time* magazine

DATE OF 1ST PUBLICATION/USE:

11 January 1993

DESIGN RATIONALE: To show how quarks fit into

larger articles.

Moon Chart

DESIGN: Steve Hart, USA

PUBLISHER/CLIENT: *Time* magazine

DATE OF 1ST PUBLICATION/USE: 8 March 1993

DESIGN RATIONALE: A quick-read diagram of a new finding

described in the text.

CREDITS: Art director, Rudy Hoglund; illustrator, Steve Hart.

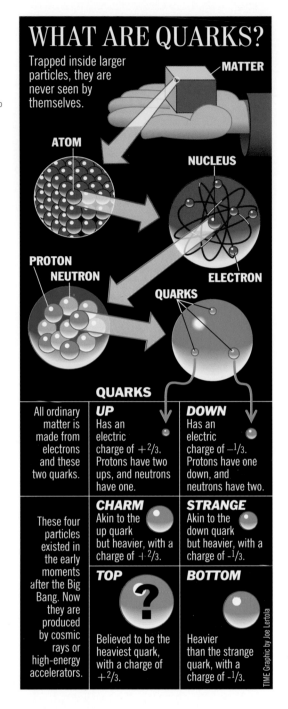

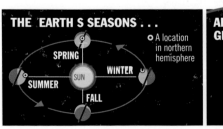

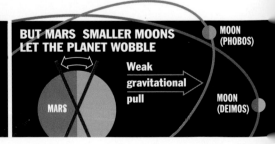

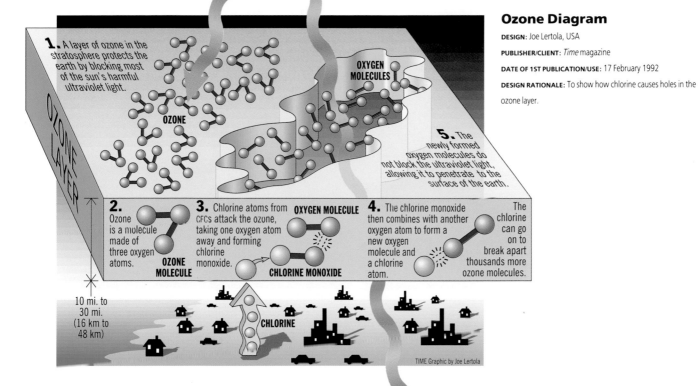

1. A layer of ozone in the stratosphere protects the earth by blocking most of the sun's harmful ultraviolet light.

OZONE

OXYGEN MOLECULES

OZONE LAYER

5. The newly formed oxygen molecules do not block the ultraviolet light, allowing it to penetrate to the surface of the earth.

2. Ozone is a molecule made of three oxygen atoms.

OZONE MOLECULE

3. Chlorine atoms from CFCs attack the ozone, taking one oxygen atom away and forming chlorine monoxide.

OXYGEN MOLECULE

CHLORINE MONOXIDE

4. The chlorine monoxide then combines with another oxygen atom to form a new oxygen molecule and a chlorine atom.

The chlorine can go on to break apart thousands more ozone molecules.

10 mi. to 30 mi. (16 km to 48 km)

CHLORINE

TIME Graphic by Joe Lertola

Ozone Diagram

DESIGN: Joe Lertola, USA

PUBLISHER/CLIENT: *Time* magazine

DATE OF 1ST PUBLICATION/USE: 17 February 1992

DESIGN RATIONALE: To show how chlorine causes holes in the ozone layer.

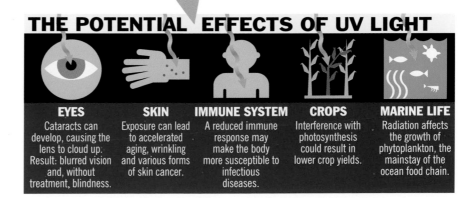

THE POTENTIAL EFFECTS OF UV LIGHT

EYES
Cataracts can develop, causing the lens to cloud up. Result: blurred vision and, without treatment, blindness.

SKIN
Exposure can lead to accelerated aging, wrinkling and various forms of skin cancer.

IMMUNE SYSTEM
A reduced immune response may make the body more susceptible to infectious diseases.

CROPS
Interference with photosynthesis could result in lower crop yields.

MARINE LIFE
Radiation affects the growth of phytoplankton, the mainstay of the ocean food chain.

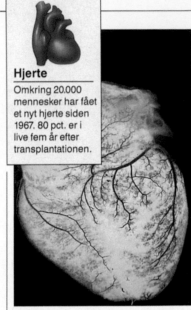

Hjerte

Omkring 20.000 mennesker har fået et nyt hjerte siden 1967. 80 pct. er i live fem år efter transplantationen.

Forkalkede årer ødelægger hjertet

Kranspulsårerne på hjertets overside er hjertemusklens blodforsyning. Hvis de forkalker, kan musklen ødelægges, så det bliver nødvendigt at transplantere.

▶ side 13

alder nye nyrer. I Danmark er der sket transplantationer til børn helt ned i toårsalderen, oplyser overlæge Sven Arvis Birkeland, Odense Sygehus. I nogle lande transplanteres også til spædbørn.

Som ved hjertetransplantationen er selve operationen ikke noget større problem. Tre rør skal forbindes: En pulsåre, en vene og urinlederen. Problemet ligger i patientens efterfølgende forsøg på afstødning. Nyren er, af endnu ukendte årsager, det organ, legemet har sværest ved at acceptere.

Leveren er svær at transplantere, men afstødes ikke så let

I modsætning til nyrer og hjerte er leveren vanskelig at transplantere. Alligevel fandt de første levertransplantationer sted så tidligt som i 1963 både i Europa og USA.

I dag er der udført omkring 15.000 levertransplantationer i verden, heraf 400 i Norden. Vanskelighederne ved denne operation skyldes dels, at der er mange kar, som skal forbindes, dels at det er svært for patienten at undvære leveren, mens operationen står på.

De faktorer, der får blod til at størkne, dannes i leveren, og mens der ingen lever er, kommer der let blødninger. Det er også vanskeligt at få blod nok til hjertet, mens leveren mangler, men det er nu løst

side 16 ▶

De otte trin i en hjertetransplantation

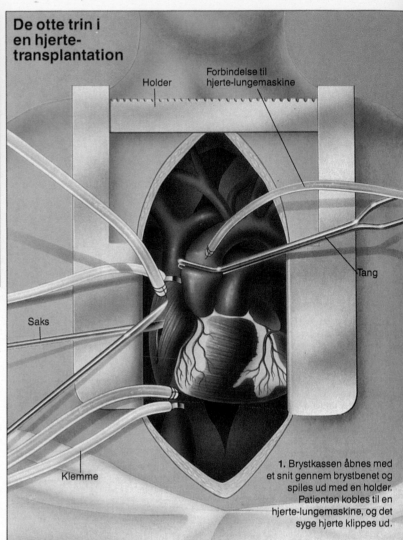

Holder

Forbindelse til hjerte-lungemaskine

Tang

Saks

Klemme

1. Brystkassen åbnes med et snit gennem brystbenet og spiles ud med en holder. Patienten kobles til en hjerte-lungemaskine, og det syge hjerte klippes ud.

SÅDAN FÅR MAN ET NYT HJERTE

Kirurgerne starter med at åbne brystkassen med et snit gennem brystbenet. Næste trin er at åbne hjertesækken, der er en sæk af bindevæv, så hjertet blottes. Nu kobles patienten til en hjerte-lungemaskine, som overtager hjertets og lungernes funktion. Herefter fjernes det syge hjerte. Af praktiske grunde lades den øverste del med for

kamrenes bagvægge tilbage. Herved undgås en tidskrævende tilkobling af vener til det nye hjerte.

Nu forbindes donorhjertet til lungepulsåren og den store legemspulsåre. De nerver, som kontrollerer hjertet, skæres over under indgrebet, men hjertet kan fungere godt uden dem. Til gengæld fastgøres elektroder til hjertet, så man senere nemt kan tilslutte en pacemaker.

Blodforsyningen til hjertet genoprettes, ved at tangen på legemspulsåren fjernes. Hvis hjertet starter med at flimre, opnås normal hjerterytme med et elektriske stød. Til sidst afkobles hjerte-lungemaskinen, og brystkassen lukkes.

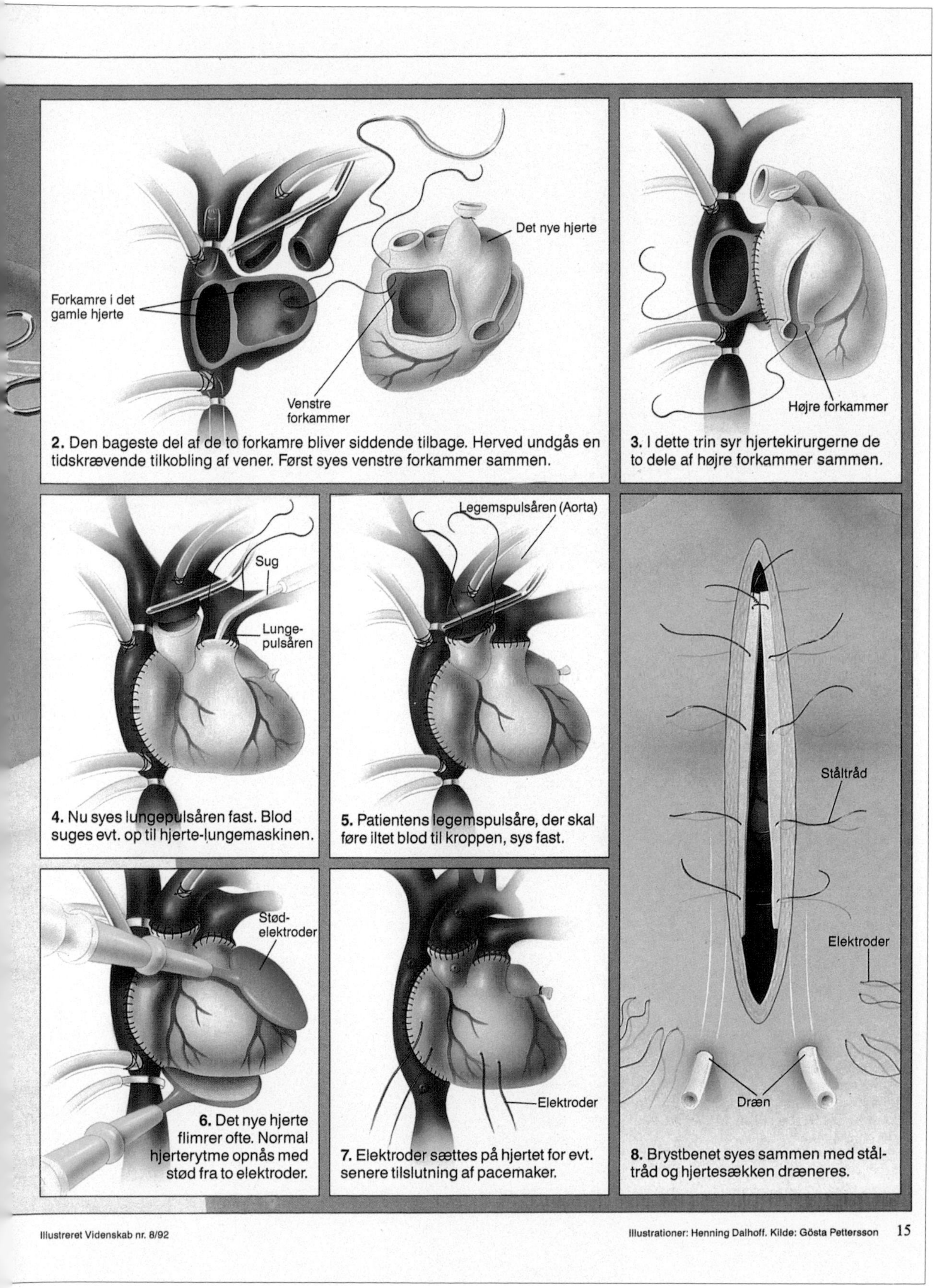

2. Den bageste del af de to forkamre bliver siddende tilbage. Herved undgås en tidskrævende tilkobling af vener. Først syes venstre forkammer sammen.

Forkamre i det gamle hjerte

Venstre forkammer

Det nye hjerte

3. I dette trin syr hjertekirurgerne de to dele af højre forkammer sammen.

Højre forkammer

4. Nu syes lungepulsåren fast. Blod suges evt. op til hjerte-lungemaskinen.

Sug

Lunge-pulsåren

5. Patientens legemspulsåre, der skal føre iltet blod til kroppen, sys fast.

Legemspulsåren (Aorta)

6. Det nye hjerte flimrer ofte. Normal hjerterytme opnås med stød fra to elektroder.

Stød-elektroder

7. Elektroder sættes på hjertet for evt. senere tilslutning af pacemaker.

Elektroder

8. Brystbenet syes sammen med stål-tråd og hjertesækken dræneres.

Ståltråd

Elektroder

Dræn

Illustrationer: Henning Dalhoff. Kilde: Gösta Pettersson 15

Heart Transplant

DESIGN: Hanne Poulson, Denmark

PUBLISHER/CLIENT: *Illustreret Videnskab*

DATE OF 1ST PUBLICATION/USE: 27 July 1992

DESIGN RATIONALE: The illustration shows a step-by-step heart transplant, from cutting loose the sick heart to closing the chest after surgery. It works as a "do-it-yourself" guide, taking you slowly and thoroughly through the process.

CREDITS: Art director, Hanne Poulsen; illustrator, Henning Dalhoff; writer, Marianne Hofstätter; researcher, Jens Henneberg, Henning Dalhoff, Gösta Pettersson.

Electro-Biology, Inc. Annual Report 1985

DESIGN: Donald W. Burg, USA

PUBLISHER/CLIENT:
Electro- Biology, Inc.

DATE OF 1ST PUBLICATION/USE:
1986

DESIGN RATIONALE: To show
how a range of EBI orthopaedic
products, both inside and outside
the patient's body, affects the
patient's mobility and lifestyle. It
showed the financial community,
shareholders and physicians, in
an entertaining and colourful
way, how and why EBI products
work.

CREDITS: Art director, Ellen
Shapiro, Shapiro Design Assoc.
Inc.; photographer, Michael
Melford; illustrators, Javier
Romero, Robert Demarest
(medical illustrations); researcher,
Mary Lynn Ament.

Bone Healing Products

Over the past eighteen months, EBI received numerous requests from orthopaedic surgeons for an electrical stimulation product that was **user friendly** and addressed the problem of patient non-compliance. In response, EBI developed and introduced the **Model 510**, a battery-powered new Bone Healing System that allows for complete patient ambulation during treatment. The Model 510 is **lightweight and portable**, simple for the patient to operate, and has a streamlined and attractive design. Equipped with both daily and cumulative treatment time monitors, the Model 510 makes it easier for the patient and doctor to monitor compliance. It delivers the same patented signal, proven to be effective in the treatment of **over 50,000 patients** with ununited fractures. By inducing pulsing electrical currents at the fracture site, the Model 510 promotes bone healing. These currents are generated by a low-energy electromagnetic field, produced when a **specific electrical signal** is transmitted from the battery-powered control unit to the treatment coil. The treatment coil delivers the therapeutic electromagnetic field to the fracture site. Total patient treatment time ranges from three to more than eight months, and averages six months. For maximum effect, the patient should receive ten hours of treatment per day. **EBI researchers and engineers** are currently developing additional coils to provide treatment for a wide variety of fracture sites. In addition, continued advances in microprocessor technology will allow for even smaller and lighter components, and even greater effectiveness due to enhanced patient compliance.

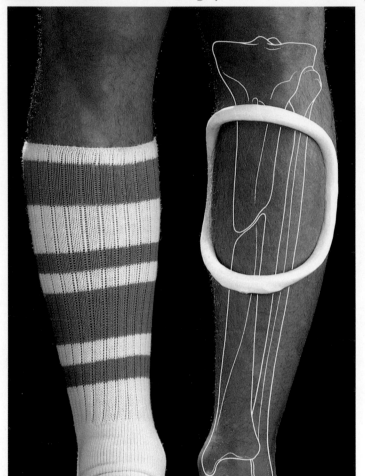

**Castable Coil–
Tibia placement**

4

New Strides in Patient Mobility

Using a treatment coil incorporated into the patient's cast, and a lightweight, battery-powered control unit, EBI's Model 510 Bone Healing System gives ununited fracture patients new mobility and flexibility.

Anthony J. Varrichio
Vice President
Development

"It took considerable technological and scientific discipline—plus old-fashioned teamwork—to bring EBI's new Castable Coil and portable bone healing system from the drawing board to market in less than one year. We built a product development team and established an environment conducive to innovation and creativity. We met our schedule and preempted the competition by beating them to the market with an approved portable product.

The project team included many disciplines—everything from Research Engineering up through and including Marketing. People were added in all areas who were capable of making significant contributions from their first day on the job. We developed a reliability program to assure that prototypes of the new product met clinical and regulatory requirements, as well as our own marketing and technical specifications.

Our successful development of the Castable Coil and Model 510 demonstrated that EBI has the human, technological, and financial resources to capitalize on its lead in electro-medicine. The Model 510 is a stepping stone to the future. We don't have to—and don't *intend* to—wait three to five years between significant product advances. For us, the future is now."

Aging in the Cell

PUBLISHER/CLIENT: *Chicago Tribune*

DATE OF 1ST PUBLICATION/USE: 8 December 1991

DESIGN RATIONALE: To illustrate the destructive and repair mechanism of tissues, cells and molecules of the body, and thereby the ageing process.

CREDITS: Art director, Steve Chengsos; illustrator, Stephen Ravenscraft; researcher, Terry Volpp.

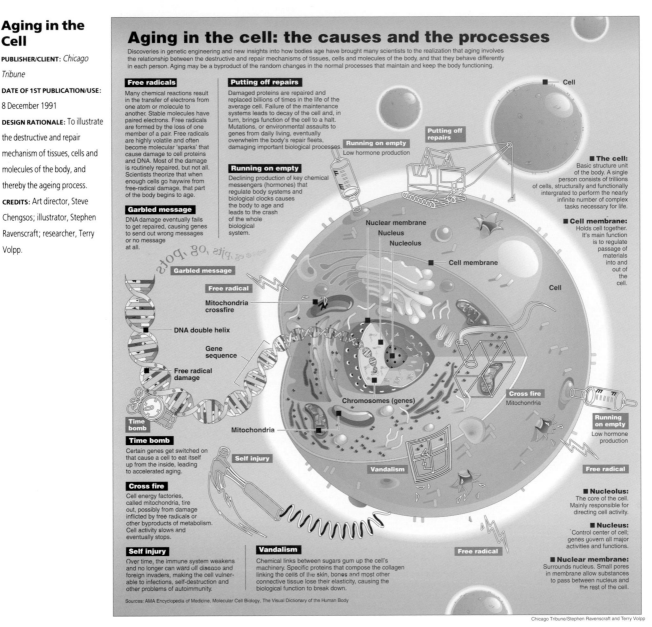

Aging in the cell: the causes and the processes

Discoveries in genetic engineering and new insights into how bodies age have brought many scientists to the realization that aging involves the relationship between the destructive and repair mechanisms of tissues, cells and molecules of the body, and that they behave differently in each person. Aging may be a byproduct of the random changes in the normal processes that maintain and keep the body functioning.

Free radicals
Many chemical reactions result in the transfer of electrons from one atom or molecule to another. Stable molecules have paired electrons. Free radicals are formed by the loss of one member of a pair. Free radicals are highly volatile and often become molecular 'sparks' that cause damage to cell proteins and DNA. Most of the damage is routinely repaired, but not all. Scientists theorize that when enough cells go haywire from free-radical damage, that part of the body begins to age.

Garbled message
DNA damage eventually fails to get repaired, causing genes to send out wrong messages or no message at all.

Time bomb
Certain genes get switched on that cause a cell to eat itself up from the inside, leading to accelerated aging.

Cross fire
Cell energy factories, called mitochondria, tire out, possibly from damage inflicted by free radicals or other byproducts of metabolism. Cell activity slows and eventually stops.

Self injury
Over time, the immune system weakens and no longer can ward off disease and foreign invaders, making the cell vulnerable to infections, self-destruction and other problems of autoimmunity.

Putting off repairs
Damaged proteins are repaired and replaced billions of times in the life of the average cell. Failure of the maintenance systems leads to decay of the cell and, in turn, brings function of the cell to a halt. Mutations, or environmental assaults to genes from daily living, eventually overwhelm the body's repair fleets, damaging important biological processes.

Running on empty
Declining production of key chemical messengers (hormones) that regulate body systems and biological clocks causes the body to age and leads to the crash of the whole biological system.

Vandalism
Chemical links between sugars gum up the cell's machinery. Specific proteins that compose the collagen linking the cells of the skin, bones and most other connective tissue lose their elasticity, causing biological function to break down.

Putting off repairs

Running on empty
Low hormone production

Running on empty

Garbled message

Free radical

Mitochondria crossfire

DNA double helix

Gene sequence

Free radical damage

Time bomb

Self injury

Vandalism

Nuclear membrane
Nucleus
Nucleolus

Cell membrane

Chromosomes (genes)

Mitochondria

Cross fire
Mitochondria

Running on empty
Low hormone production

Free radical

Cell

Cell

The cell: Basic structure unit of the body. A single person consists of trillions of cells, structurally and functionally intergrated to perform the nearly infinite number of complex tasks necessary for life.

Cell membrane: Holds cell together. It's main function is to regulate passage of materials into and out of the cell.

Nucleolus: The core of the cell. Mainly responsible for directing cell activity.

Nucleus: Control center of cell; genes govern all major activities and functions.

Nuclear membrane: Surrounds nucleus. Small pores in membrane allow substances to pass between nucleus and the rest of the cell.

Free radical

Sources: AMA Encyclopedia of Medicine, Molecular Cell Biology, The Visual Dictionary of the Human Body

Chicago Tribune/Stephen Ravenscraft and Terry Volpp

Important Functions of the Brain

DESIGN: Lew Calver, Meredith Hamilton, USA

PUBLISHER/CLIENT: *Newsweek*

DATE OF 1ST PUBLICATION/USE: 8 June 1992

DESIGN RATIONALE: The diagram shows important components in the brain. The accompanying story was about new research in the study of the brain. The graphics helped the reader visualize where important parts are located and also provided a quick glossary of terms.

CREDITS: Art director, Patricia Bradbury; illustrator, Lew Calver.

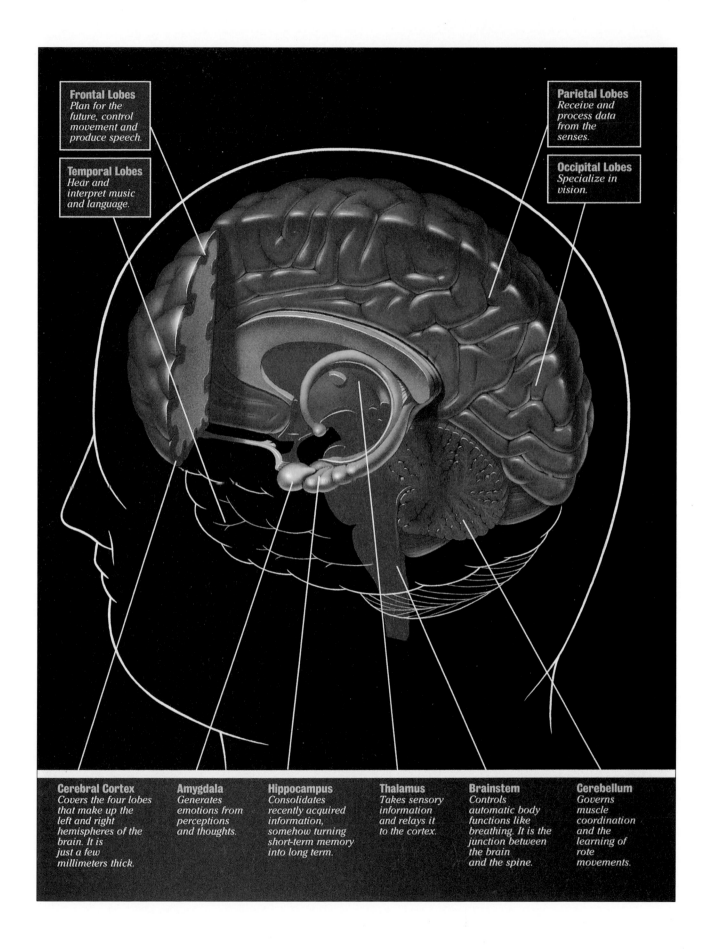

Frontal Lobes
Plan for the future, control movement and produce speech.

Temporal Lobes
Hear and interpret music and language.

Parietal Lobes
Receive and process data from the senses.

Occipital Lobes
Specialize in vision.

Cerebral Cortex
Covers the four lobes that make up the left and right hemispheres of the brain. It is just a few millimeters thick.

Amygdala
Generates emotions from perceptions and thoughts.

Hippocampus
Consolidates recently acquired information, somehow turning short-term memory into long term.

Thalamus
Takes sensory information and relays it to the cortex.

Brainstem
Controls automatic body functions like breathing. It is the junction between the brain and the spine.

Cerebellum
Governs muscle coordination and the learning of rote movements.

INSIDE THE NASSCO SHIPYARD

By KEN MARSHALL and JAMES W. CRAWLEY, photos by DAVE SICCARDI
The San Diego Union-Tribune

*F*ollowing three years of design and competitive bidding, San Diego's National Steel and Shipbuilding Co. was selected to build the container ship R.J. Pfeiffer, the first commercial ship to be constructed in a U.S. shipyard since 1985. The project meant hundreds of jobs and pumped millions into the local economy. Here is a look at how the R.J. Pfeiffer was built in NASSCO's shipyard.

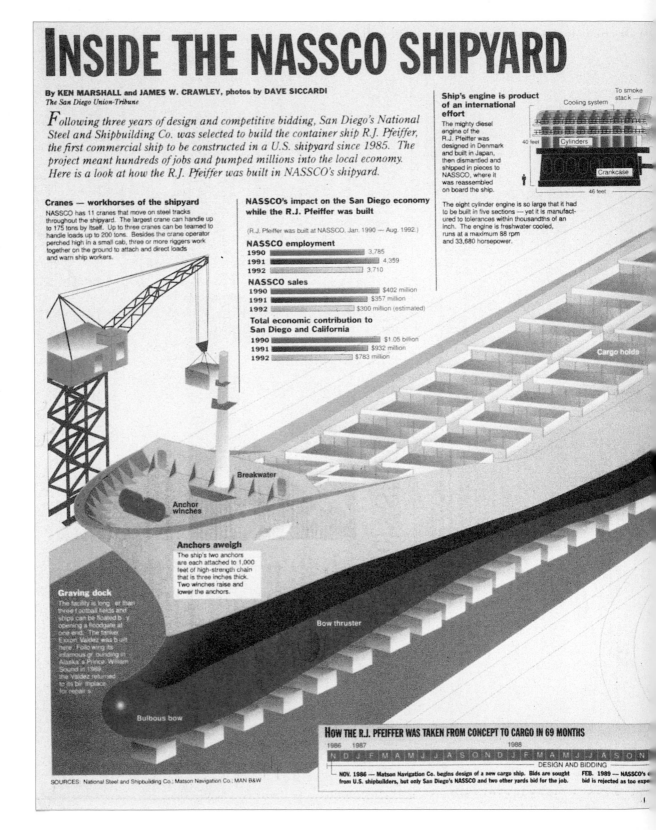

Cranes — workhorses of the shipyard

NASSCO has 11 cranes that move on steel tracks throughout the shipyard. The largest crane can handle up to 175 tons by itself. Up to three cranes can be teamed to handle loads up to 200 tons. Besides the crane operator perched high in a small cab, three or more riggers work together on the ground to attach and direct loads and warn ship workers.

NASSCO's impact on the San Diego economy while the R.J. Pfeiffer was built

(R.J. Pfeiffer was built at NASSCO. Jan. 1990 — Aug. 1992.)

NASSCO employment
- 1990 — 3,785
- 1991 — 4,359
- 1992 — 3,710

NASSCO sales
- 1990 — $402 million
- 1991 — $357 million
- 1992 — $300 million (estimated)

Total economic contribution to San Diego and California
- 1990 — $1.05 billion
- 1991 — $932 million
- 1992 — $783 million

Ship's engine is product of an international effort

The mighty diesel engine of the R.J. Pfeiffer was designed in Denmark and built in Japan, then dismantled and shipped in pieces to NASSCO, where it was reassembled on board the ship.

To smoke stack
Cooling system
40 feet
Cylinders
Crankcase
46 feet

The eight cylinder engine is so large that it had to be built in five sections — yet it is manufactured to tolerances within thousandths of an inch. The engine is freshwater cooled, runs at a maximum 88 rpm and 33,680 horsepower.

Cargo holds

Breakwater

Anchor winches

Anchors aweigh
The ship's two anchors are each attached to 1,000 feet of high-strength chain that is three inches thick. Two winches raise and lower the anchors.

Graving dock
The facility is long er than three football fields and ships can be floated by opening a floodgate at one end. The tanker Exxon Valdez was built here. Following its infamous grounding in Alaska's Prince William Sound in 1989, the Valdez returned to its birthplace for repairs.

Bow thruster

Bulbous bow

SOURCES: National Steel and Shipbuilding Co.; Matson Navigation Co.; MAN B&W

HOW THE R.J. PFEIFFER WAS TAKEN FROM CONCEPT TO CARGO IN 69 MONTHS

1986　1987　1988

N D J F M A M J J A S O N D J F M A M J J A S O N

DESIGN AND BIDDING

NOV. 1986 — Matson Navigation Co. begins design of a new cargo ship. Bids are sought from U.S. shipbuilders, but only San Diego's NASSCO and two other yards bid for the job.

FEB. 1989 — NASSCO's bid is rejected as too expe

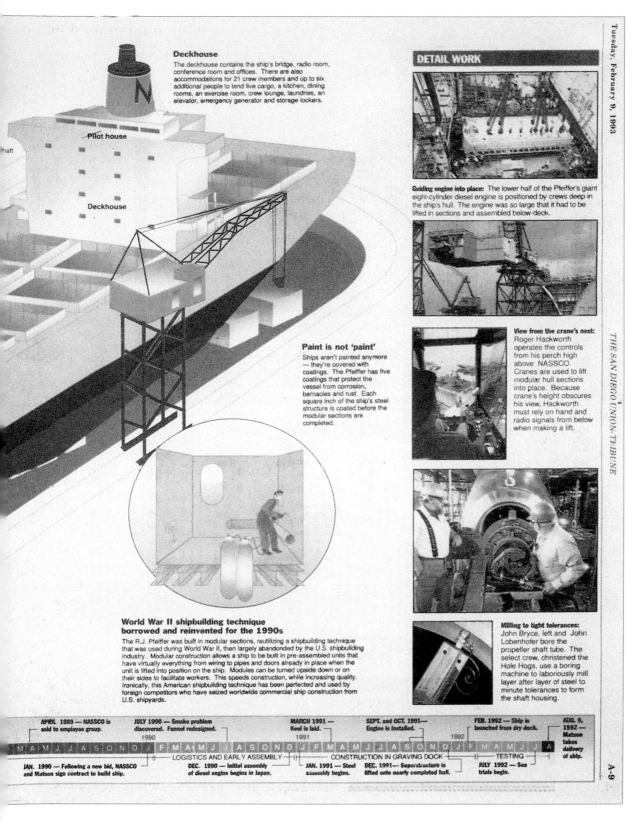

Deckhouse

The deckhouse contains the ship's bridge, radio room, conference room and offices. There are also accommodations for 21 crew members and up to six additional people to tend live cargo, a kitchen, dining rooms, an exercise room, crew lounge, laundries, an elevator, emergency generator and storage lockers.

Pilot house

Deckhouse

Paint is not 'paint'

Ships aren't painted anymore — they're covered with coatings. The Pfeiffer has five coatings that protect the vessel from corrosion, barnacles and rust. Each square inch of the ship's steel structure is coated before the modular sections are completed.

World War II shipbuilding technique borrowed and reinvented for the 1990s

The R.J. Pfeiffer was built in modular sections, reutilizing a shipbuilding technique that was used during World War II, then largely abandonded by the U.S. shipbuilding industry. Modular construction allows a ship to be built in pre-assembled units that have virtually everything from wiring to pipes and doors already in place when the unit is lifted into position on the ship. Modules can be turned upside down or on their sides to facilitate workers. This speeds construction, while increasing quality. Ironically, this American shipbuilding technique has been perfected and used by foreign competitors who have seized worldwide commercial ship construction from U.S. shipyards.

DETAIL WORK

Guiding engine into place: The lower half of the Pfeiffer's giant eight-cylinder diesel engine is positioned by crews deep in the ship's hull. The engine was so large that it had to be lifted in sections and assembled below-deck.

View from the crane's nest: Roger Hackworth operates the controls from his perch high above NASSCO. Cranes are used to lift modular hull sections into place. Because crane's height obscures his view, Hackworth must rely on hand and radio signals from below when making a lift.

Milling to tight tolerances: John Bryce, left and John Lobenhofer bore the propeller shaft tube. The select crew, christened the Hole Hogs, use a boring machine to laboriously mill layer after layer of steel to minute tolerances to form the shaft housing.

Tuesday, February 9, 1993

THE SAN DIEGO UNION-TRIBUNE

A-9

APRIL 1989 — NASSCO is sold to employee group.

JULY 1990 — Smoke problem discovered. Funnel redesigned.

MARCH 1991 — Keel is laid.

SEPT. and OCT. 1991— Engine is installed.

FEB. 1992 — Ship is launched from dry dock.

AUG. 9, 1992 — Matson takes delivery of ship.

JAN. 1990 — Following a new bid, NASSCO and Matson sign contract to build ship.

DEC. 1990 — Initial assembly of diesel engine begins in Japan.

JAN. 1991 — Steel assembly begins.

DEC. 1991 — Superstructure is lifted onto nearly completed hull.

JULY 1992 — Sea trials begin.

1990 | 1991 | 1992

M A M J J A S O N D J F M A M J J A S O N D J F M A M J J A S O N D J F M A M J J A

LOGISTICS AND EARLY ASSEMBLY — CONSTRUCTION IN GRAVING DOCK — TESTING

Inside the NASSCO Shipyard

DESIGN: Ken Marshall, USA

PUBLISHER/CLIENT: *San Diego Union-Tribune*

DATE OF 1ST PUBLICATION/USE: 9 February 1993

DESIGN RATIONALE: The graphic described the construction of the first commercial ship to be built in a US shipyard since 1985. The page detailed the methods used by the shipbuilders and examined the economic impact that the project had on the local economy.

CREDITS: Art director, Ken Marshall; photographer, Dave Siccardi; illustrator, Ken Marshall; writers and researchers, Ken Marshall, James W. Crawley.

A Sky Full of Clouds

DESIGN: Michael Kline, Acme Design Co., USA

PUBLISHER/CLIENT: *Kids Discover* magazine

DATE OF 1ST PUBLICATION/USE: April 1992

DESIGN RATIONALE: To show the relative heights of clouds compared to other flying objects like balloons, Concorde, etc.

CREDITS: Art directors, Will Hopkins, Mary K. Baumann, Hopkins Baumann, NYC; illustrator, Michael Kline, Acme Design Co.

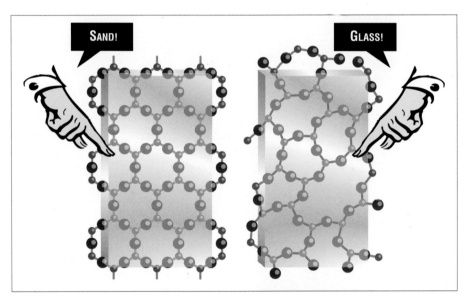

Sand/Glass Molecular Structure

DESIGN: John Baxter, Acme Design Co., USA

PUBLISHER/CLIENT: *Kids Discover* magazine

DATE OF 1ST PUBLICATION/USE: April 1993

DESIGN RATIONALE: The difference between the orderly structure of molecules in sand and the apparently random structure of glass molecules. The diagrams were scientifically presented, but the pointing hands added a humorous twist that would seize the attention of children.

CREDITS: Art directors, Will Hopkins, Mary K. Baumann, Hopkins Baumann, NYC; illustrator, John Baxter, Acme Design Co.

Layers within sumptuous layers

He was not especially tall—about five feet six inches—and in his early 30s, according to skeletal analysis. The Moche wrapped their fallen ruler in a lavish cocoon of tribute, including these elements:

Beneath the coffin's three-planked lid (1), feather ornaments, some in headdresses, appeared in groups (2) both above and below the body. Fabric banners with gilded copper platelets depicting a figure with turquoise-bead bracelets lay faceup above the body (3) and facedown below (4). Copper struts (5) made the lower banners rigid. Eleven chest coverings, called pectorals, of shell and copper beads (6), also appeared in layers. A gilded copper headdress (7) lay atop a textile headband to secure it (8).

An outer shirt covered with gilded copper platelets and cone-shaped tassels at the hem (9) and a simple inner white garment (10) clothed the body. The skull, face, ears, neck, and chest were festooned with gold, silver, and copper ornaments (11). Turquoise and gold-bead bracelets adorned the forearms (12). Gold and copper ingots lay on his hands; the right held a gold rattle (13); the left a copper knife (14). Seashells (15) lay at his feet, clad in ceremonial copper sandals (16).

Beneath the ruler a massive gold headdress ornament (17) overlay a wood support frame (18). Under it were crescent-shaped gold bells, two attached to backflaps of gold and copper (19). A small gold headdress ornament was found near a copper headdress chin strap (20). The significance of copper strips (21) remains a mystery. Three shrouds laid down with gilded copper platelets (22), enfolded the contents of the coffin, fastened together with copper strapping (23). At the very bottom lay shells, a miniature war club and shield (24), and copper-pointed atlatl darts (25).

PAINTING BY NED SEIDLER

Peruvian Tomb

PUBLISHER/CLIENT: *National Geographic* magazine

DATE OF 1ST PUBLICATION/USE: October 1988

DESIGN RATIONALE: A cutaway of a Moche tomb.

CREDITS: Art director, J. Robert Teringo; illustrator, Ned M. Seidler; researcher, Karen Gibbs.

JOURNEY OF AN IMAGE

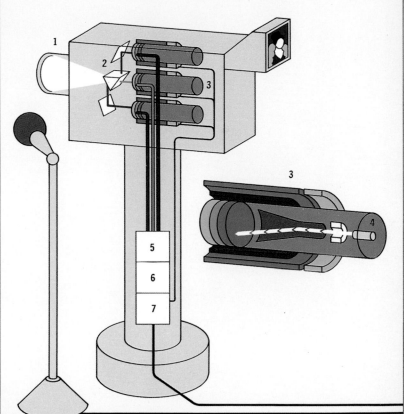

PACKAGING THE CARGO

The fabulous trek begins when the image—in this schematic, of an opera singer performing in a studio—passes through the lens of the camera (1), is reproduced in triplicate by a prism (2) and is directed by mirrors to each of three camera tubes (3). A beam emanating from an electron gun (4) at the back of each tube constantly scans the image, as it moves and changes, to determine the color of each element of the image and its varying degrees of brightness.

The tubes process their images in red, green and blue because all the shades we ultimately see on the screen will be mixed from these colors. Each tube then converts its colored copy of the image to an electronic signal. Next, a color encoder (5) merges the three signals into a master signal that contains the color balance for the entire picture. Our singer's dress, for example, would be reproduced with a strong red signal and relatively weak ones of green and blue. Her skin tones would be created by a combination of all three colors.

Information about brightness, too, is converted to electronic signals and combined into a master signal by what the industry calls a luminance unit (6). At the same time, a synchronization unit (7) ensures that the tubes are always gathering color and brightness in unison. (Without synchronization to coordinate reassembly of the image on your screen, utter chaos would ensue: Your television screen would become a battleground of information from conflicting images.)

Working simultaneously with the camera but independent of it, a microphone picks up the sound portion of the program. It is sent, parallel with the master signals for color and brightness, to a transmitter (8).

ILLUSTRATIONS BY JEAN WISENBAUGH

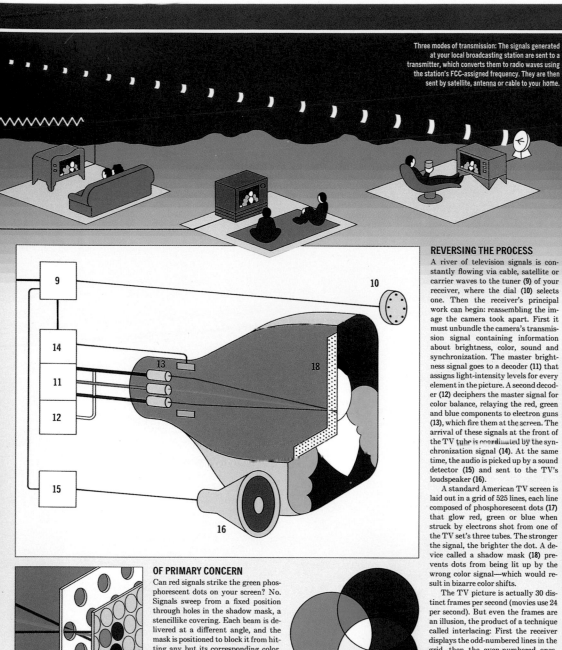

Three modes of transmission: The signals generated at your local broadcasting station are sent to a transmitter, which converts them to radio waves using the station's FCC-assigned frequency. They are then sent by satellite, antenna or cable to your home.

Journey of an Image

DESIGN: Jean Wisenbaugh, USA

PUBLISHER/CLIENT:

Life magazine

DATE OF 1ST PUBLICATION/USE:

March 1989

DESIGN RATIONALE: This diagram shows how television transmits an image. The reader is drawn into the diagram by the somewhat whimsical illustration showing the three major modes of transmission. The technical workings of camera and picture tube are then shown in detail. All aspects are tied together by the consistent use of the female television star image.

CREDITS: Art director, Dean Abatemarco; illustrator, Jean Wisenbaugh; writers, Joshua Simon, Joe Levine, Ann Bayer.

REVERSING THE PROCESS

A river of television signals is constantly flowing via cable, satellite or carrier waves to the tuner (9) of your receiver, where the dial (10) selects one. Then the receiver's principal work can begin: reassembling the image the camera took apart. First it must unbundle the camera's transmission signal containing information about brightness, color, sound and synchronization. The master brightness signal goes to a decoder (11) that assigns light-intensity levels for every element in the picture. A second decoder (12) deciphers the master signal for color balance, relaying the red, green and blue components to electron guns (13), which fire them at the screen. The arrival of these signals at the front of the TV tube is coordinated by the synchronization signal (14). At the same time, the audio is picked up by a sound detector (15) and sent to the TV's loudspeaker (16).

A standard American TV screen is laid out in a grid of 525 lines, each line composed of phosphorescent dots (17) that glow red, green or blue when struck by electrons shot from one of the TV set's three tubes. The stronger the signal, the brighter the dot. A device called a shadow mask (18) prevents dots from being lit up by the wrong color signal—which would result in bizarre color shifts.

The TV picture is actually 30 distinct frames per second (movies use 24 per second). But even the frames are an illusion, the product of a technique called interlacing: First the receiver displays the odd-numbered lines in the grid, then the even-numbered ones. The image of the first set of lines does not fade until after the second set of lines has been flashed. The sets alternate so quickly (60 times a second) it seems they are appearing together.

OF PRIMARY CONCERN

Can red signals strike the green phosphorescent dots on your screen? No. Signals sweep from a fixed position through holes in the shadow mask, a stencillike covering. Each beam is delivered at a different angle, and the mask is positioned to block it from hitting any but its corresponding color. Colored light, which mixes differently from solid pigments, has red, blue and green—rather than yellow—as primaries. Television yellow, for instance, is produced by combining red and green.

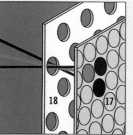

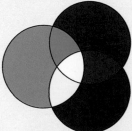

95

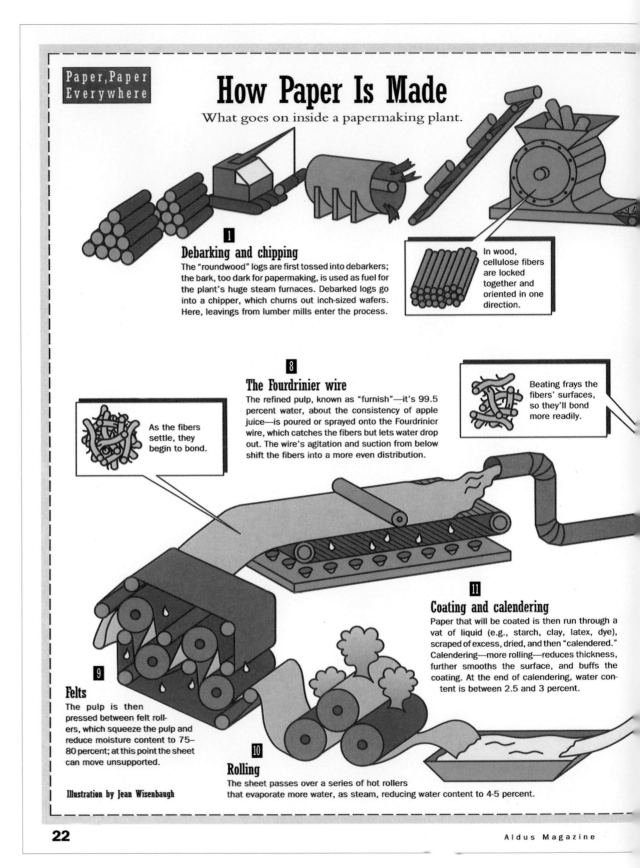

Paper, Paper Everywhere

How Paper Is Made
What goes on inside a papermaking plant.

1 Debarking and chipping
The "roundwood" logs are first tossed into debarkers; the bark, too dark for papermaking, is used as fuel for the plant's huge steam furnaces. Debarked logs go into a chipper, which churns out inch-sized wafers. Here, leavings from lumber mills enter the process.

In wood, cellulose fibers are locked together and oriented in one direction.

8 The Fourdrinier wire
The refined pulp, known as "furnish"—it's 99.5 percent water, about the consistency of apple juice—is poured or sprayed onto the Fourdrinier wire, which catches the fibers but lets water drop out. The wire's agitation and suction from below shift the fibers into a more even distribution.

Beating frays the fibers' surfaces, so they'll bond more readily.

As the fibers settle, they begin to bond.

11 Coating and calendering
Paper that will be coated is then run through a vat of liquid (e.g., starch, clay, latex, dye), scraped of excess, dried, and then "calendered." Calendering—more rolling—reduces thickness, further smooths the surface, and buffs the coating. At the end of calendering, water content is between 2.5 and 3 percent.

9 Felts
The pulp is then pressed between felt rollers, which squeeze the pulp and reduce moisture content to 75–80 percent; at this point the sheet can move unsupported.

10 Rolling
The sheet passes over a series of hot rollers that evaporate more water, as steam, reducing water content to 4-5 percent.

Illustration by Jean Wisenbaugh

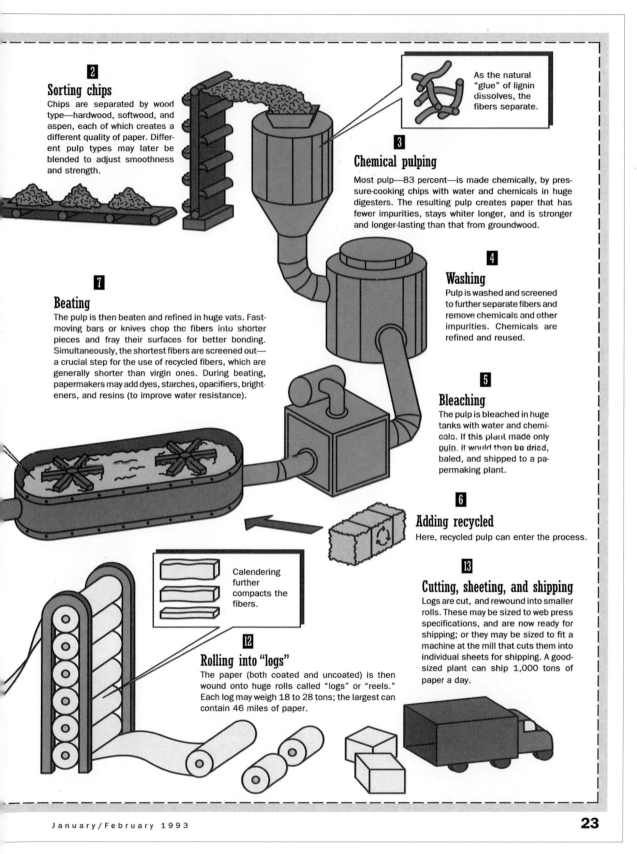

2

Sorting chips

Chips are separated by wood type—hardwood, softwood, and aspen, each of which creates a different quality of paper. Different pulp types may later be blended to adjust smoothness and strength.

As the natural "glue" of lignin dissolves, the fibers separate.

3

Chemical pulping

Most pulp—83 percent—is made chemically, by pressure-cooking chips with water and chemicals in huge digesters. The resulting pulp creates paper that has fewer impurities, stays whiter longer, and is stronger and longer-lasting than that from groundwood.

7

Beating

The pulp is then beaten and refined in huge vats. Fast-moving bars or knives chop the fibers into shorter pieces and fray their surfaces for better bonding. Simultaneously, the shortest fibers are screened out—a crucial step for the use of recycled fibers, which are generally shorter than virgin ones. During beating, papermakers may add dyes, starches, opacifiers, brighteners, and resins (to improve water resistance).

4

Washing

Pulp is washed and screened to further separate fibers and remove chemicals and other impurities. Chemicals are refined and reused.

5

Bleaching

The pulp is bleached in huge tanks with water and chemicals. If this plant made only pulp, it would then be dried, baled, and shipped to a papermaking plant.

6

Adding recycled

Here, recycled pulp can enter the process.

Calendering further compacts the fibers.

12

Rolling into "logs"

The paper (both coated and uncoated) is then wound onto huge rolls called "logs" or "reels." Each log may weigh 18 to 28 tons; the largest can contain 46 miles of paper.

13

Cutting, sheeting, and shipping

Logs are cut, and rewound into smaller rolls. These may be sized to web press specifications, and are now ready for shipping; or they may be sized to fit a machine at the mill that cuts them into individual sheets for shipping. A good-sized plant can ship 1,000 tons of paper a day.

23

How Paper is Made

DESIGN: Jean Wisenbaugh, USA

PUBLISHER/CLIENT:
Aldus magazine

DATE OF 1ST PUBLICATION/USE:
January 1993

DESIGN RATIONALE: The steps in making paper, from logs through to shipping, are illustrated. Simplified, colourful representations engage the reader while clearly showing the steps in papermaking. Detailed cutouts illustrate how the fibres change throughout the process.

CREDITS: Art director, Kristin Easterbrook; illustrator, Jean Wisenbaugh; writer/researcher, Paul Roberts.

Cholesterol

DESIGN: Alison Cocks, USA

PUBLISHER/CLIENT: *Dallas Morning News*

DATE OF 1ST PUBLICATION/USE: 8 February 1993

DESIGN RATIONALE: To illustrate the form of HDL or good cholesterol, sources of HDL constituents and cholesterol levels in men and women by age. The graphic addresses the concern that cholesterol is a determining factor in heart disease and discusses the role of "good" cholesterol as a necessary partner in the fatty build-up issue.

CREDITS: Art director, Ed Kohorst; illustrator, Alison Cocks; writer, Laura Beil.

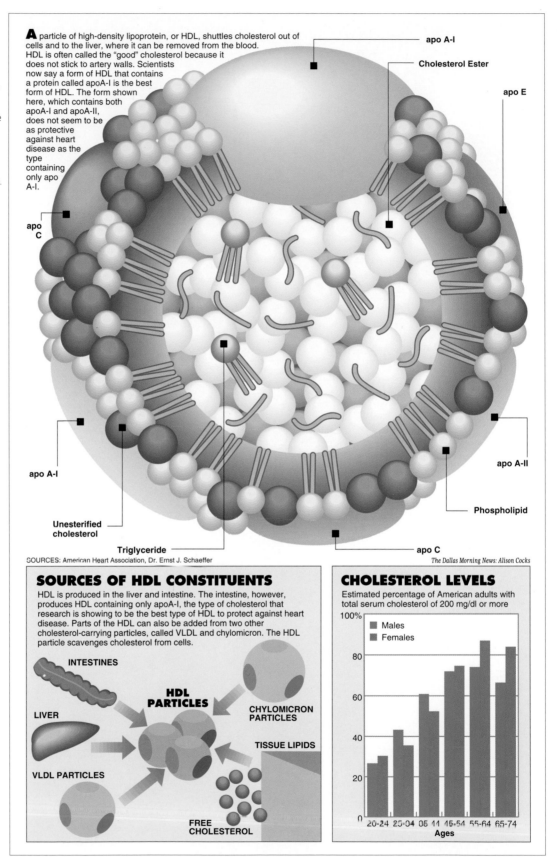

A particle of high-density lipoprotein, or HDL, shuttles cholesterol out of cells and to the liver, where it can be removed from the blood. HDL is often called the "good" cholesterol because it does not stick to artery walls. Scientists now say a form of HDL that contains a protein called apoA-I is the best form of HDL. The form shown here, which contains both apoA-I and apoA-II, does not seem to be as protective against heart disease as the type containing only apo A-I.

apo A-I

Cholesterol Ester

apo E

apo C

apo A-I

Unesterified cholesterol

Triglyceride

apo A-II

Phospholipid

apo C

SOURCES: American Heart Association, Dr. Ernst J. Schaeffer

The Dallas Morning News: Alison Cocks

SOURCES OF HDL CONSTITUENTS

HDL is produced in the liver and intestine. The intestine, however, produces HDL containing only apoA-I, the type of cholesterol that research is showing to be the best type of HDL to protect against heart disease. Parts of the HDL can also be added from two other cholesterol-carrying particles, called VLDL and chylomicron. The HDL particle scavenges cholesterol from cells.

INTESTINES

LIVER

HDL PARTICLES

CHYLOMICRON PARTICLES

TISSUE LIPIDS

VLDL PARTICLES

FREE CHOLESTEROL

CHOLESTEROL LEVELS

Estimated percentage of American adults with total serum cholesterol of 200 mg/dl or more

Males
Females

Ages: 20-24 25-04 06 11 15-54 55-64 65-74

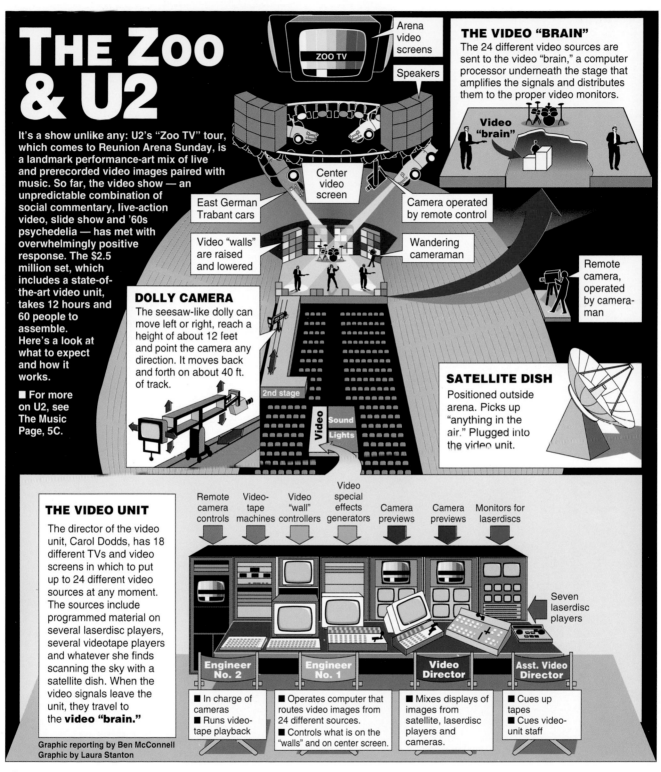

THE ZOO & U2

It's a show unlike any: U2's "Zoo TV" tour, which comes to Reunion Arena Sunday, is a landmark performance-art mix of live and prerecorded video images paired with music. So far, the video show — an unpredictable combination of social commentary, live-action video, slide show and '60s psychedelia — has met with overwhelmingly positive response. The $2.5 million set, which includes a state-of-the-art video unit, takes 12 hours and 60 people to assemble.
Here's a look at what to expect and how it works.

■ For more on U2, see The Music Page, 5C.

Arena video screens

Speakers

THE VIDEO "BRAIN"
The 24 different video sources are sent to the video "brain," a computer processor underneath the stage that amplifies the signals and distributes them to the proper video monitors.

Video "brain"

Center video screen

East German Trabant cars

Camera operated by remote control

Video "walls" are raised and lowered

Wandering cameraman

Remote camera, operated by camera-man

DOLLY CAMERA
The seesaw-like dolly can move left or right, reach a height of about 12 feet and point the camera any direction. It moves back and forth on about 40 ft. of track.

2nd stage

Video Sound Lights

SATELLITE DISH
Positioned outside arena. Picks up "anything in the air." Plugged into the video unit.

THE VIDEO UNIT
The director of the video unit, Carol Dodds, has 18 different TVs and video screens in which to put up to 24 different video sources at any moment. The sources include programmed material on several laserdisc players, several videotape players and whatever she finds scanning the sky with a satellite dish. When the video signals leave the unit, they travel to the **video "brain."**

Remote camera controls

Video-tape machines

Video "wall" controllers

Video special effects generators

Camera previews

Camera previews

Monitors for laserdiscs

Seven laserdisc players

Engineer No. 2
■ In charge of cameras
■ Runs video-tape playback

Engineer No. 1
■ Operates computer that routes video images from 24 different sources.
■ Controls what is on the "walls" and on center screen.

Video Director
■ Mixes displays of images from satellite, laserdisc players and cameras.

Asst. Video Director
■ Cues up tapes
■ Cues video-unit staff

Graphic reporting by Ben McConnell
Graphic by Laura Stanton

The Zoo & U2

DESIGN: Laura Stanton, Ben McConnel, USA

PUBLISHER/CLIENT: *The Dallas Morning News*

DATE OF 1ST PUBLICATION/USE: 2 April 1992

DESIGN RATIONALE: Illustrates the high-tech presentation which is the basis of the band U2's latest tour. On-site research and reports resulted in a first-time explanation of this production, and gave the Dallas fans an idea of what to expect.

CREDITS: Art director, Ed Kohorst; illustrator, Laura Stanton; writer/researcher, Ben McConnell.

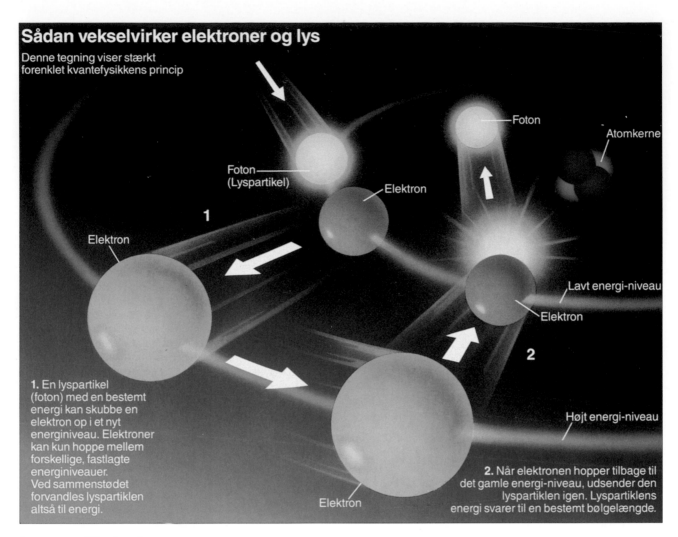

Sådan vekselvirker elektroner og lys

Denne tegning viser stærkt
forenklet kvantefysikkens princip

Foton

Atomkerne

Foton
(Lyspartikel)

Elektron

Elektron

Lavt energi-niveau

Elektron

1

2

Elektron

1. En lyspartikel
(foton) med en bestemt
energi kan skubbe en
elektron op i et nyt
energiniveau. Elektroner
kan kun hoppe mellem
forskellige, fastlagte
energiniveauer.
Ved sammenstødet
forvandles lyspartiklen
altså til energi.

Højt energi-niveau

Elektron

2. Når elektronen hopper tilbage til
det gamle energi-niveau, udsender den
lyspartiklen igen. Lyspartiklens
energi svarer til en bestemt bølgelængde.

Quantum Mechanics

DESIGN: Nanna Guldborg Andersen, Denmark

PUBLISHER/CLIENT: *Illustreret Videnskab*

DATE OF 1ST PUBLICATION/USE: 31 August 1992

DESIGN RATIONALE: The diagram shows the basics of quantum
mechanics: that electrons move in certain "lanes" and that they
only jump from one to the other, but do not exist between
"lanes". A photon (energy) enters top left, excites the electron
and makes it jump (1). The electron becomes unstable and falls
back to the lower energy level, re-emitting a photon (2).

CREDITS: Art director, Nana Guldborg Andersen; illustrator,
Klaus Westh; writers, Helle and Henrik Stub; researcher, Jens
Henneberg.

Loops and Whorls into Bits and Bytes: How One System Matches Prints

DESIGN: Anne Cronin, graphics editor, USA

PUBLISHER/CLIENT: *New York Times*

DATE OF 1ST PUBLICATION/USE: 10 January 1993

DESIGN RATIONALE: A diagram clarifying the method used in
computerized fingerprint identification, in which a print is
broken down into numbers, enabling users to search through
millions of prints on file for a match.

CREDITS: Art director, Nancy Kent; illustrator/writer/researcher,
Anne Cronin.

Loops and Whorls Into Bits and Bytes: How One System Matches Prints

Digitalized fingerprints have made regular searches of millions of print files possible. Here is how one version, the NEC Technologies Automated Fingerprint Identification System, works.

Old Way

Fingerprints used to be filed by Henry Classification, a method like the Dewey decimal system, that grouped prints by whorls, arches, etc., and counted print ridges. Fingerprints had to be checked manually against those it might resemble within its classification. In a large city, this could mean tens of thousands of prints. Without specifics, like a crime suspect's name, it was nearly impossible to make a match against a single crime-scene print.

New Way

The relationship of minutiae, or places at which fingerprint ridges end or split, are entered into a computer. This allows searches to be done electronically. The Los Angeles Police Department, for example, can now compare one print from a crime scene to every one of the almost 2 million sets of prints in their files in about an hour. If more information is available, (e.g. race, sex), this information can be used to narrow down the search and make it faster.

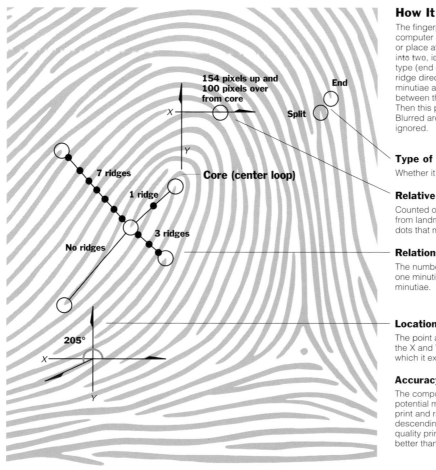

How It Works

The fingerprint is scanned into a computer and digitalized. Each minutia, or place at which ridge lines end or split into two, is noted and categorized by its type (end or split), by location, and ridge direction. Then four neighboring minutiae are also examined. The ridges between the minutiae are counted. Then this process is extended again. Blurred areas of the fingerprint are ignored.

Type of Minutia

Whether it is an end or a split.

Relative Position

Counted on a 512-pixel-per-inch scale from landmarks like the core. Pixels are the dots that make up computer images.

Relationship

The number of ridges between one minutia and the closest four minutiae.

Location and Angle

The point at which the minutia hits the X and Y axis and the angle at which it extends from that point.

Accuracy

The computer scores how closely a potential match comes to the search print and ranks the top contenders in descending order. With one good-quality print, the system is accurate better than 97 percent of the time.

Source: NEC Technologies, Inc.

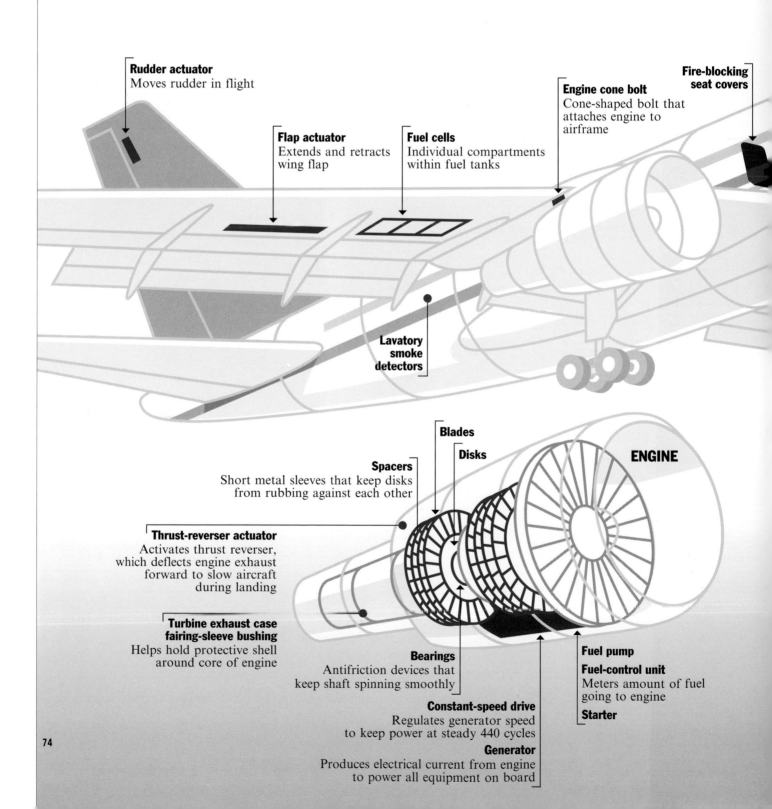

Rudder actuator
Moves rudder in flight

Flap actuator
Extends and retracts
wing flap

Fuel cells
Individual compartments
within fuel tanks

Engine cone bolt
Cone-shaped bolt that
attaches engine to
airframe

**Fire-blocking
seat covers**

**Lavatory
smoke
detectors**

Blades

Disks

ENGINE

Spacers
Short metal sleeves that keep disks
from rubbing against each other

Thrust-reverser actuator
Activates thrust reverser,
which deflects engine exhaust
forward to slow aircraft
during landing

**Turbine exhaust case
fairing-sleeve bushing**
Helps hold protective shell
around core of engine

Bearings
Antifriction devices that
keep shaft spinning smoothly

Fuel pump

Fuel-control unit
Meters amount of fuel
going to engine

Starter

Constant-speed drive
Regulates generator speed
to keep power at steady 440 cycles

Generator
Produces electrical current from engine
to power all equipment on board

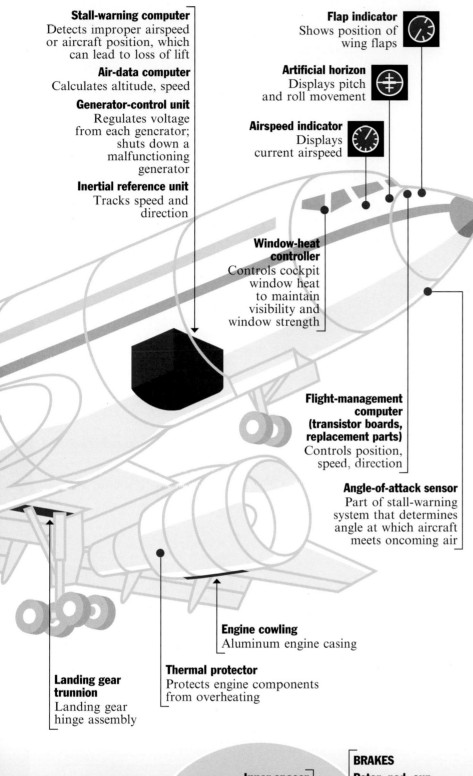

Stall-warning computer
Detects improper airspeed
or aircraft position, which
can lead to loss of lift

Air-data computer
Calculates altitude, speed

Generator-control unit
Regulates voltage
from each generator;
shuts down a
malfunctioning
generator

Inertial reference unit
Tracks speed and
direction

Flap indicator
Shows position of
wing flaps

Artificial horizon
Displays pitch
and roll movement

Airspeed indicator
Displays
current airspeed

**Window-heat
controller**
Controls cockpit
window heat
to maintain
visibility and
window strength

**Flight-management
computer (transistor boards,
replacement parts)**
Controls position,
speed, direction

Angle-of-attack sensor
Part of stall-warning
system that determines
angle at which aircraft
meets oncoming air

Engine cowling
Aluminum engine casing

**Landing gear
trunnion**
Landing gear
hinge assembly

Thermal protector
Protects engine components
from overheating

**WHEEL
ASSEMBLY**

Inner bearing

Inner spacer

BRAKES
Rotor, pad, cup

Brake key
Keeps entire
brake assembly
properly aligned

Outer bearing

Outer spacer

Counterfeit Aircraft Parts

DESIGN: John Grimwade, UK

PUBLISHER/CLIENT: *Condé Nast Traveler*

DATE OF 1ST PUBLICATION/USE: January 1993

DESIGN RATIONALE: To illustrate aircraft parts that have been
found to be counterfeit. The graphic gives an idea of the extent
of the problem, but is deliberately serious and calm in
presentation.

CREDITS: Art directors, Diana Laguardia, Mike Powers;
illustrator, John Grimwade; researcher, Lester Reingold.

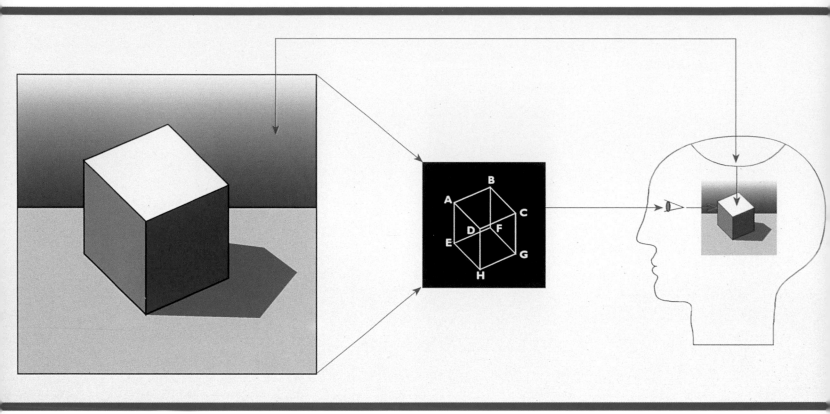

The Process of
Communication

DESIGN: Ronnie Peters, USA

PUBLISHER/CLIENT: *Information Technology Quarterly*, a
publication of Harvard University

DATE OF 1ST PUBLICATION/USE: Winter 1992

DESIGN RATIONALE: The illustration addresses the issue of the
relationship between reality and the perception of reality. It
shows how the human mind "reads" and reconstructs images of
seen objects.

CREDITS: Art director, Kris Lenk.

Illustration/Description of a
Car Accident

DESIGN: Ronnie Peters, USA

PUBLISHER/CLIENT: Ki-Won Wang

DATE OF 1ST PUBLICATION/USE: 1991

DESIGN RATIONALE: The diagrams (included in an insurance
claim) illustrate in a sequential form a collision between a truck
and a car.

CREDITS: Art director, Ronnie Peters; text, Paul Kahn.

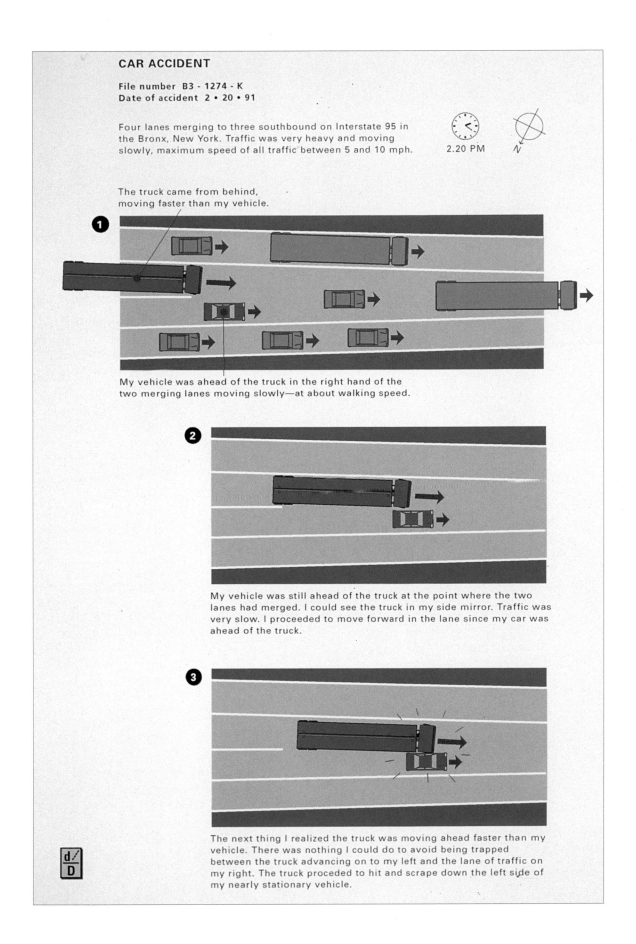

CAR ACCIDENT

File number B3 - 1274 - K
Date of accident 2 • 20 • 91

Four lanes merging to three southbound on Interstate 95 in the Bronx, New York. Traffic was very heavy and moving slowly, maximum speed of all traffic between 5 and 10 mph.

2.20 PM

The truck came from behind, moving faster than my vehicle.

My vehicle was ahead of the truck in the right hand of the two merging lanes moving slowly—at about walking speed.

My vehicle was still ahead of the truck at the point where the two lanes had merged. I could see the truck in my side mirror. Traffic was very slow. I proceeded to move forward in the lane since my car was ahead of the truck.

The next thing I realized the truck was moving ahead faster than my vehicle. There was nothing I could do to avoid being trapped between the truck advancing on to my left and the lane of traffic on my right. The truck proceded to hit and scrape down the left side of my nearly stationary vehicle.

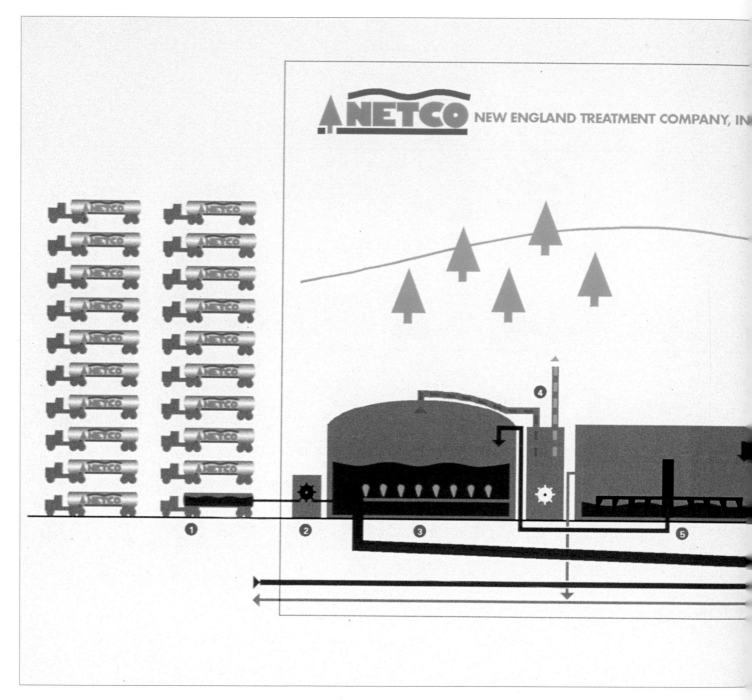

Process of Sludge Treatment

DESIGN: Ronnie Peters, USA

PUBLISHER/CLIENT: NETCO (New England Treatment
Company, Inc.)

DATE OF 1ST PUBLICATION/USE: 1991

DESIGN RATIONALE: The diagram from a NETCO brochure
describes an environmentally safe process of sludge treatment.
The illustration emphasizes an important aspect of the process
by which 20 trucks of wet sludge are reduced to a single truck
of dry ash.

CREDITS: Art director, Kris Lenk.

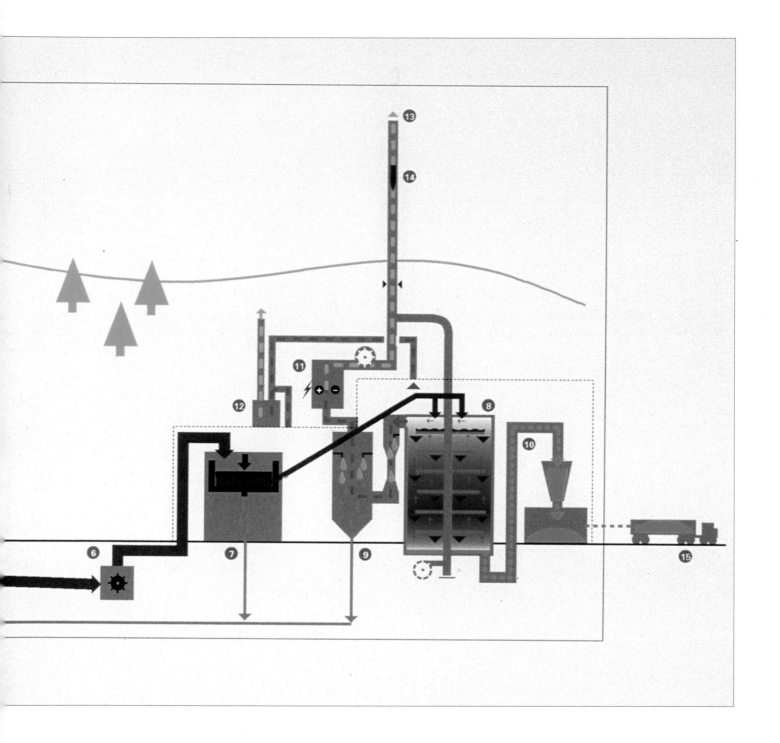

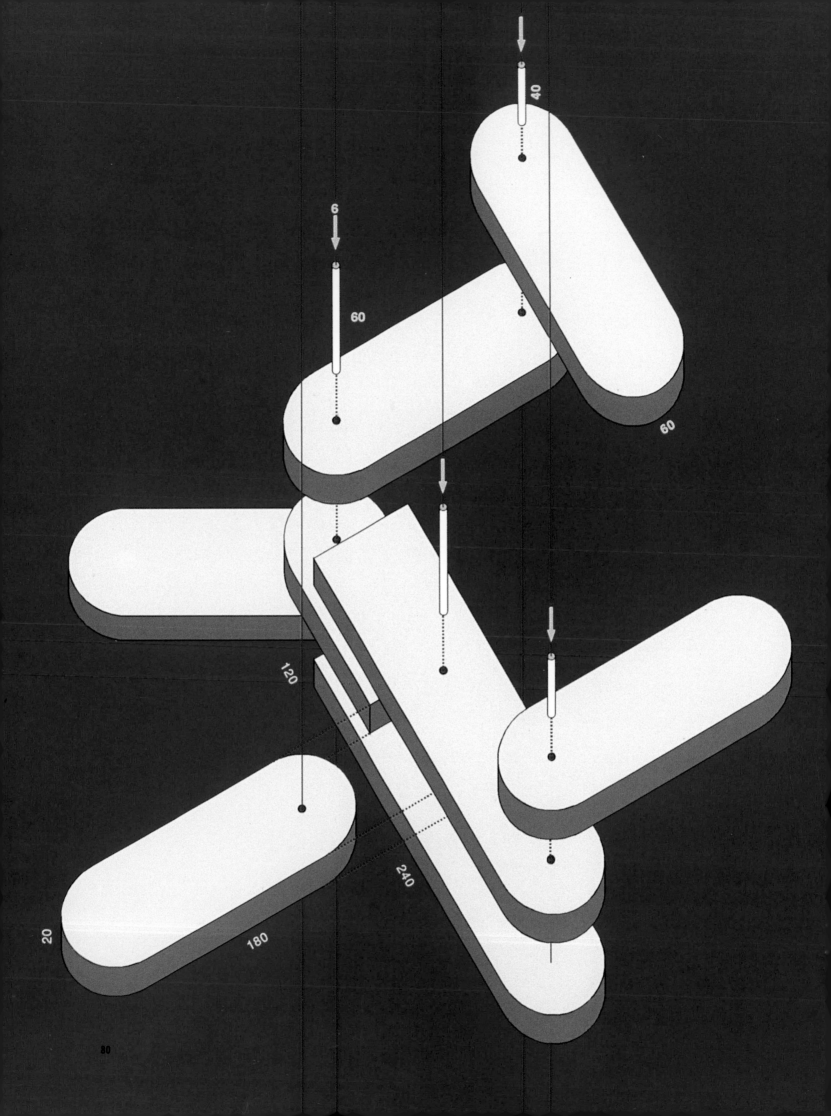

HOW POINTING DEVICES WORK

Mechanical Mouse

In an Apple mouse, a rubber ball touches two capstans, which are connected to slotted wheels sandwiched between two light-source-and-photosensor pairs (**A** and **B**). When the ball rolls, the capstans turn the wheels, whose slots interrupt the light. Each interruption is interpreted by the Mac as one increment of movement. The sensors are offset slightly so that, as the wheels turn, they produce a pair of signals with a pause between. The direction a wheel turns is indicated by which sensor, **A** or **B**, produces the first signal in each pair. Trackballs work similarly, except only the ball (not the entire housing) moves.

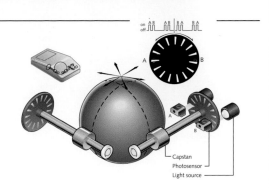

Capstan
Photosensor
Light source

Optical Mouse

In an optical mouse, light from two light sources (**A** and **B**) reflects off a pad covered with a fine grid of dots. The image of the grid is projected onto two separate photosensors. One senses vertical movement (**C**) and the other horizontal movement (**D**). As the reflection of the grid passes over the sensors, circuitry within the mouse counts the dots to determine the distance the mouse has moved in either direction.

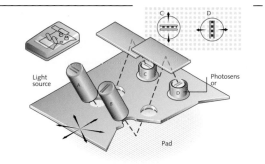

Light source
Photosensor
Pad

Tablet with Stylus

In a graphics tablet, a drawing stylus or cursor exchanges minute radio signals with the tablet through a grid of wires that crisscross the drawing area. The tablet determines the location of the stylus and transmits the location information to the Macintosh. The stylus doesn't need to touch the tablet surface itself; this means you can trace a drawing, even through several pages of a book.

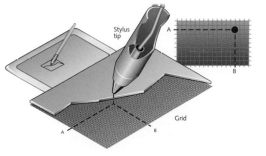

Stylus tip
Grid

How Pointing Devices Work

DESIGN: Arne Hurty, USA

PUBLISHER/CLIENT: *MacWorld* magazine

DATE OF 1ST PUBLICATION/USE: 1992

DESIGN RATIONALE: Three typical pointing devices – a detail of the main function of each pointing device shows how they differ.

CREDITS: Art director, Dennis McLeod; illustrator, Arne Hurty; writer, Jim Heid.

Instructional Diagram

DESIGN: Ronnie Peters, USA

PUBLISHER/CLIENT: Dynamic Diagrams, Inc.

DATE OF 1ST PUBLICATION/USE: 1990

DESIGN RATIONALE: The diagram illustrates the elements of a type toy and provides assembly instructions. By manipulating the various parts of the toy, one is able to create the entire Latin alphabet.

CREDITS: Art director, Ronnie Peters.

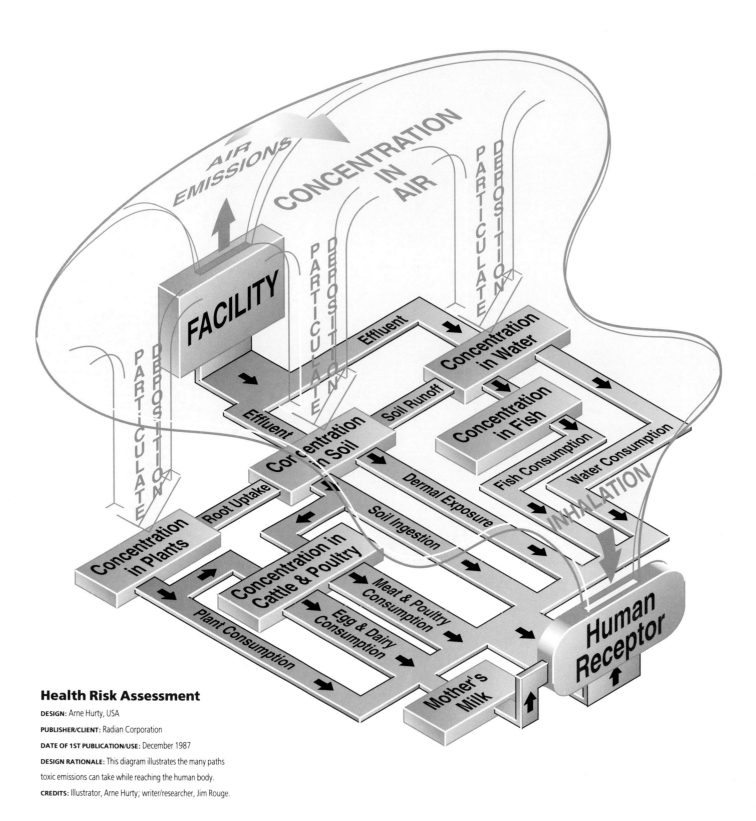

Health Risk Assessment

DESIGN: Arne Hurty, USA

PUBLISHER/CLIENT: Radian Corporation

DATE OF 1ST PUBLICATION/USE: December 1987

DESIGN RATIONALE: This diagram illustrates the many paths
toxic emissions can take while reaching the human body.

CREDITS: Illustrator, Arne Hurty; writer/researcher, Jim Rouge.

INSIDE THE MACINTOSH LC

The Macintosh LC was designed to be manufactured quickly and inexpensively. Five basic components—the logic board, the power supply, a fan-and-speaker unit, a 40MB hard drive, and a SuperDrive floppy drive—can be snapped into the plastic case by robots. The Macintosh LC uses only four cables to connect components. These cables can also be inserted by robots.

Adding a Board

A board such as Apple's IIe board connects to a new-style processor-direct slot on the Macintosh LC's logic board. An add-in board runs parallel to the logic board.

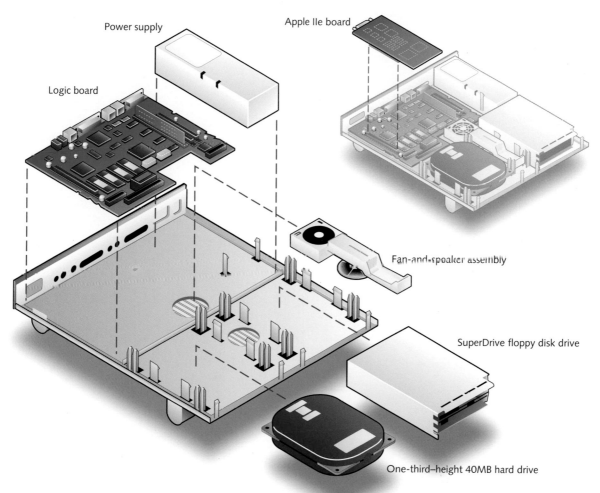

Power supply

Apple IIe board

Logic board

Fan-and-speaker assembly

SuperDrive floppy disk drive

One-third–height 40MB hard drive

Inside the Macintosh LC

DESIGN: Arne Hurty, USA

PUBLISHER/CLIENT: *MacWorld* magazine

DATE OF 1ST PUBLICATION/USE: December 1990

DESIGN RATIONALE: The diagram illustrates the inside of a Mac LC and shows the dramatic change in the internal configuration of a computer box.

CREDITS: Art director, Dennis McLeod; illustrator, Arne Hurty.

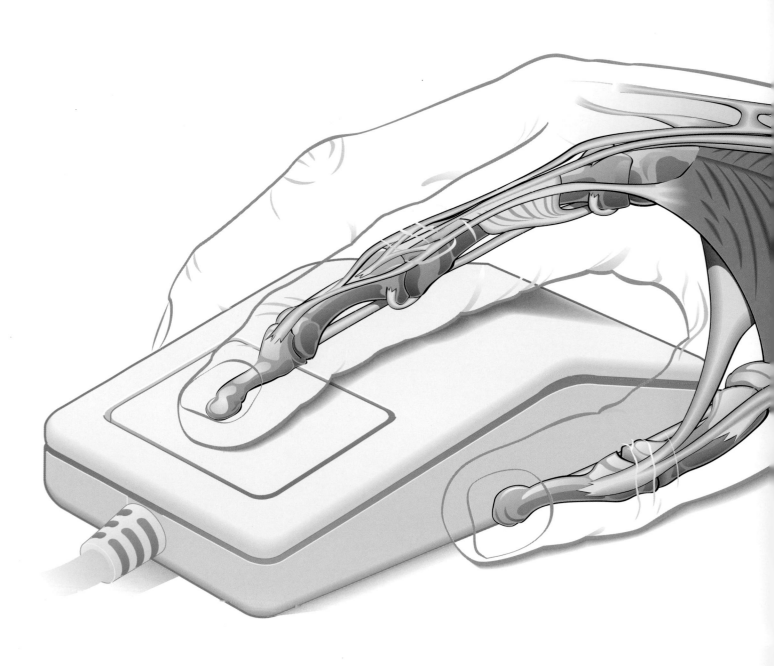

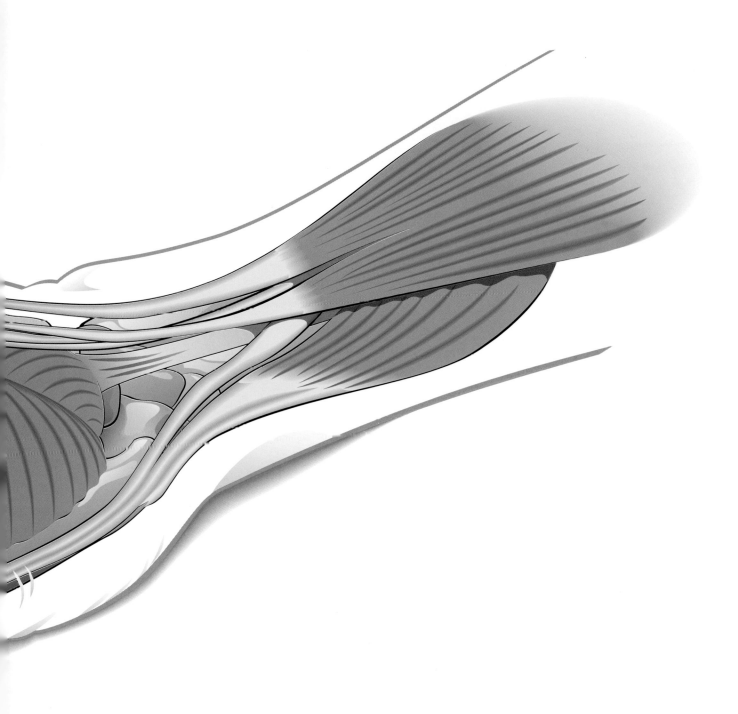

Using a Mouse

DESIGN: Arne Hurty, USA

PUBLISHER/CLIENT: *MacWorld* magazine

DATE OF 1ST PUBLICATION/USE: June 1992

DESIGN RATIONALE: The ligaments, bones and muscles of the hand as it holds a mouse. The illustration draws attention to the effect the mouse has on the hand during use.

CREDITS: Art director, Dennis McLeod; illustrator, Arne Hurty.

Charts

Charts are an area of diagrammatic graphics that have aroused an acrimonious debate between academia and the popular press in recent years. This is because the subject matter of charts (as opposed to most diagrams and all maps) is numbers. The numbers are made visible by the chart — and that's where the danger lies. It is the *other* things that are made visible at the same time as the numbers that cause the controversy. American statistics professors have rushed to the defence of numbers in the face of what they see to be a trivialization by graphic artists. These artists are sneered at for their lack of training in the proper science of statistics, and their work is ridiculed in articles and books that are read by the same group of academics who have written them. Sometimes the books find a larger audience, and the debate becomes more public.

Commerce exists for the express reason of making money, while academia does not. In the safe isolation of a school the theories of everything are studied and questioned, so it is not surprising that bad examples are found. They serve as just that — examples of the "wrong" way to do it. Academia is looking for reasons to find fault as well as to applaud.

Any debate has two sides. The academics would like all charts to conform to a strict code of rules whereas chartmakers in the non-academic world contend that the result of a rigorous application of this kind of thinking is that all charts become dull and uninteresting. The academics counter that if you think a chart is uninteresting you have the wrong numbers. There is no need to interest readers by attracting them with a picture or by

dramatizing the facts. Good statistics are intrinsically interesting. If the figures are right, the readers will read.

The readers of our daily and weekly press need to get the facts fast. Maybe they *are* in a simplified form, maybe they *do* have a little picture with them to aid understanding of the subject matter; these are justifiable means to the end of getting information off the printed page and into the readers' minds. And there are more reasons for a popular approach to chartmaking: let us say that the information to be displayed is important but of a highly technical nature, probably beyond the knowledge of most readers. Should they miss out because the rules demand a certain method of presentation? No, we should try to demystify such difficult information – that is what graphics are all about. The role of the graphic designer, and in particular the chartmaker, should be more than merely to inform – it should be to teach, to draw conclusions, to help the viewer understand.

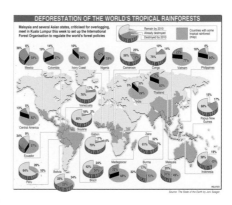

The examples on the following pages are from the rest of the world. They entertain unashamedly, while informing superbly. William Playfair, the inventor of charting, was also the first to say that a chart is a visualization of numbers, and that it would never have the same degree of accuracy as a simple listing of those same numbers. Graphic artists can go further than merely making the information available: they can illuminate it.

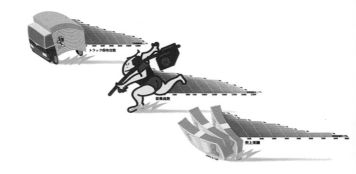

THE FAMILY TREE SUPERHEROES

When Joseph Campbell said the hero has a thousand faces, he might have been talking about the comic-book superhero. Superman, the original superhero, was the prototype in an art form that eventually drew on everything from Greek, Egyptian, and Norse mythology to science fiction and pulp detective serials. The Man of Steel, and successors like Captain Marvel and Captain America, embodied the mythical ideal, while Batman—"the Dark Knight"—drew on Zorro and the Shadow (whose gloomier shadings also turn up in Spiderman and the Punisher). Later figures, like the Hulk and the irradiated Fantastic Four, tapped into sci-fi Atomic Age anxiety.

Since the golden age of comics (1938-46), superheroes have endured an unending series of revisions by hundreds of artists, writers, and editors. Batman, for instance, developed from the stygian vigilante of the thirties into the campy Caped Crusader of the sixties, only to end up a neurotic avenger in the eighties. The Hulk's secret identity borrows from Superman, and his poor posture anticipates Swamp Thing. The success of the Justice League inspired X-Men, a band of solemn teenage mutants who, in turn, inspired spin-offs like the equally solemn but more traditional Teen Titans, the brash New Mutants, and, in 1983, a quartet of sarcastic pizza-eating turtles. And as the genre matured, the superhero grew from an invincible fantasy figure to a more complex character—compare Superman with the worried Spiderman or the existential Silver Surfer. Still, through the years the superhero has remained true to his or (rarely) her mission: to maintain moral certitude, to defend good against evil, and to conquer every conceivable kind of danger.

A Few of the Creators
Superman: Joe Shuster and Jerry Siegel (later revised by John Byrne)
Batman: Bob Kane (revised by Frank Miller)
Captain Marvel: C. C. Beck
Green Lantern: Bill Finger (revised by Neal Adams and Dennis O'Neil)
Wonder Woman: Dr. William Moulton Marston
Flash, Justice Society of America: Gardner Fox
Justice League of America: Julius Schwartz
Captain America: Jack Kirby (with Joe Simon)
Fantastic Four, Hulk, Silver Surfer, X-Men: Stan Lee and Jack Kirby
Spiderman: Stan Lee (with Jack Kirby and Steve Ditko)
Watchmen: Alan Moore and Dave Gibbons

The Owners
Three publishing companies own the rights to all the superheroes shown here: **D.C. Comics** (Superman, Batman, Wonder Woman, Captain Marvel, Flash, Green Lantern, Justice Society, Justice League, Swamp Thing, Teen Titans, Watchmen); **Marvel** (The Human Torch, Sub-Mariner, Daredevil, Captain America, Plastic Man, Fantastic Four, The Hulk, Spiderman, Silver Surfer, X-Men, The Avengers, New Mutants, The Punisher); and **Mirage Studios** (Teenage Mutant Ninja Turtles).

THE HUMAN TORCH (1939)

FLASH (1940)

GREEN LANTERN (1940)

PLASTIC MAN (1941)

X-MEN (1963) (ANGEL, CYCLOPS, BEAST, ICEMAN, AND MARVEL GIRL)

THE HULK (1962)

NEW MUTANTS (1983) (KARMA, WOLFBANE, MIRAGE, AND SUNSPOT)

TEENAGE MUTANT NINJA TURTLES (1983)

SWAMP THING (1971)

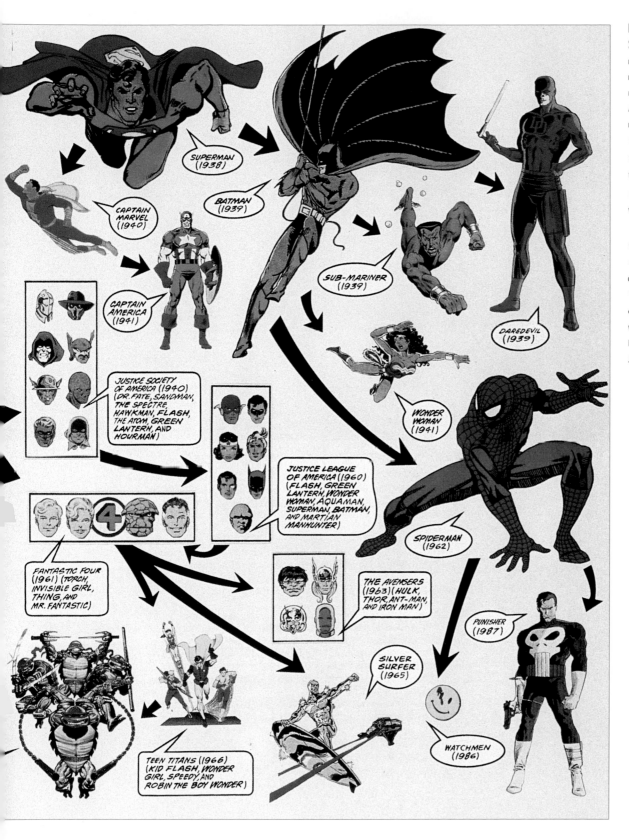

Family Tree of Superheroes

DESIGN: Alexandra Ginns, USA

PUBLISHER/CLIENT: Wigwag

DATE OF 1ST PUBLICATION/USE: August 1990

DESIGN RATIONALE: The idea behind the timeline was to show the history of a particular place through the evolution of a particular thing. This family tree was designed to show how the various participants in a field that we now think of as diverse and crowded all derived from a common point of origin – that is, to reveal the hidden connections.

CREDITS: Art director, Paul Davis; writers and researchers, Tom Hackett, Matthew Davis, Devon Johnson.

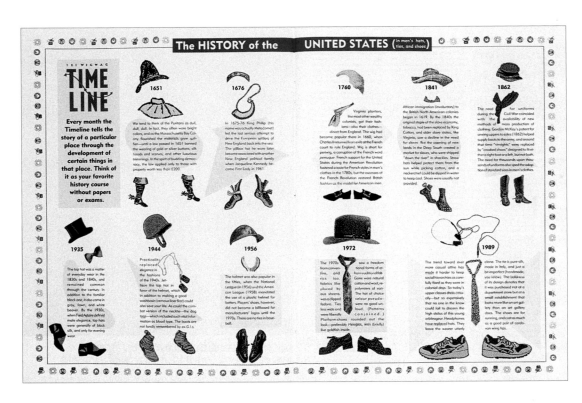

History of the United States (in men's hats, ties, and shoes)

DESIGN: Paul L. Davis, USA

PUBLISHER/CLIENT: Wigwag

DATE OF 1ST PUBLICATION/USE: October 1989

DESIGN RATIONALE: The idea behind the timeline was to show the history of a particular place through the evolution of a particular thing. This family tree was designed to show how the various participants in a field that we now think of as diverse and crowded all derived from a common point of origin – that is, to reveal the hidden connections.

CREDITS: Art director and illustrator, Paul Davis; writer, Evan Cornog.

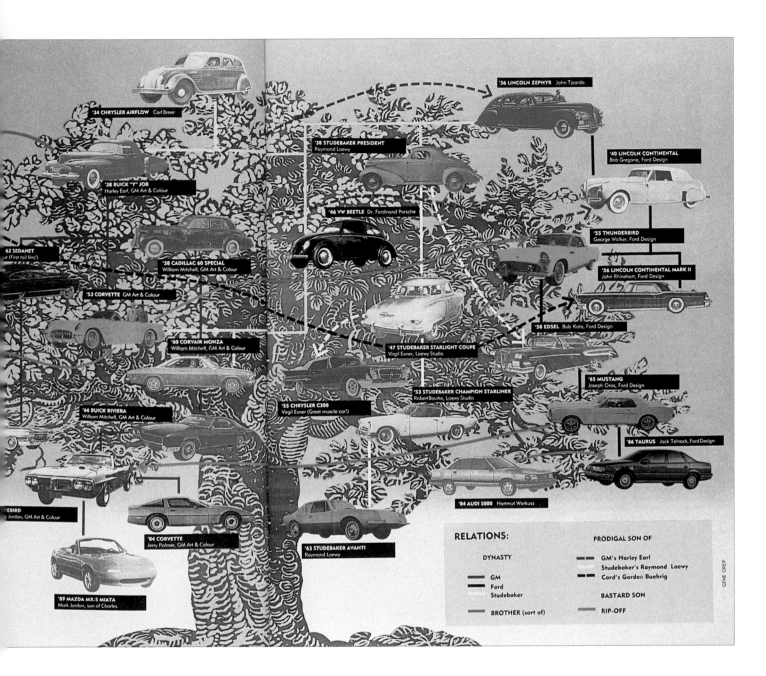

Within the illustration:

'34 CHRYSLER AIRFLOW Carl Breer

'36 LINCOLN ZEPHYR John Tjaarda

'38 STUDEBAKER PRESIDENT Raymond Loewy

'40 LINCOLN CONTINENTAL Bob Gregorie, Ford Design

'38 BUICK "Y" JOB Harley Earl, GM Art & Colour

'46 VW BEETLE Dr. Ferdinand Porsche

'55 THUNDERBIRD George Walker, Ford Design

'62 SEDANET (First tail fins')

'38 CADILLAC 60 SPECIAL William Mitchell, GM Art & Colour

'56 LINCOLN CONTINENTAL MARK II John Rhinehart, Ford Design

'53 CORVETTE GM Art & Colour

'58 EDSEL Bob Koto, Ford Design

'60 CORVAIR MONZA William Mitchell, GM Art & Colour

'47 STUDEBAKER STARLIGHT COUPE Virgil Exner, Loewy Studio

'65 MUSTANG Joseph Oros, Ford Design

'53 STUDEBAKER CHAMPION STARLINER Robert Bourke, Loewy Studio

'66 BUICK RIVIERA William Mitchell, GM Art & Colour

'55 CHRYSLER C300 Virgil Exner (Great muscle car!)

'86 TAURUS Jack Telnack, Ford Design

EBIRD Jordan, GM Art & Colour

'84 AUDI 5000 Hartmut Warkuss

'84 CORVETTE Jerry Palmer, GM Art & Colour

'63 STUDEBAKER AVANTI Raymond Loewy

'89 MAZDA MX-5 MIATA Mark Jordan, son of Charles

RELATIONS:

DYNASTY

— GM
— Ford
— Studebaker

— BROTHER (sort of)

PRODIGAL SON OF

— GM's Harley Earl
— Studebaker's Raymond Loewy
— Cord's Gordon Buehrig

BASTARD SON

— RIP-OFF

GENE GREIF

Family Tree of Cars

DESIGN: Risa, USA

PUBLISHER/CLIENT: Wigwag

DATE OF 1ST PUBLICATION/USE: November 1989

DESIGN RATIONALE: The idea behind the timeline was to show the history of a particular place through the evolution of a particular thing. This family tree was designed to show how the various participants in a field that we now think of as diverse and crowded all derived from a common point of origin – that is, to reveal the hidden connections.

CREDITS: Art director, Paul Davis; illustrator, Gene Greif; writer, Thomas Hackett.

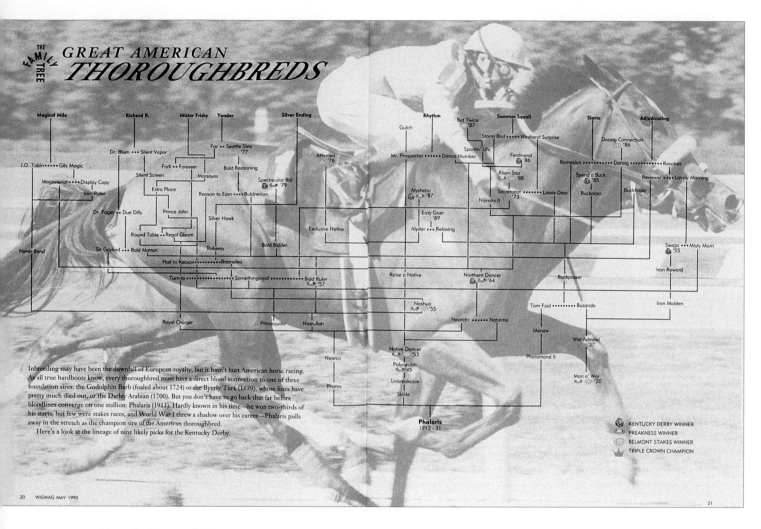

GREAT AMERICAN THOROUGHBREDS

Inbreeding may have been the downfall of European royalty, but it hasn't hurt American horse racing. As all true hardboots know, every thoroughbred must have a direct blood connection to one of three foundation sires: the Godolphin Barb (foaled about 1724) or the Byerly Turk (1679), whose lines have pretty much died out, or the Darley Arabian (1700). But you don't have to go back that far before bloodlines converge on one stallion: Phalaris (1913). Hardly known in his time—he won two-thirds of his starts, but few were stakes races, and World War I threw a shadow over his career—Phalaris pulls away in the stretch as the champion sire of the American thoroughbred.

Here's a look at the lineage of nine likely picks for the Kentucky Derby.

KENTUCKY DERBY WINNER
PREAKNESS WINNER
BELMONT STAKES WINNER
TRIPLE CROWN CHAMPION

Family Tree of Great American Thoroughbreds

DESIGN: Alexandra Ginns, USA

PUBLISHER/CLIENT: Wigwag

DATE OF 1ST PUBLICATION/USE: May 1990

DESIGN RATIONALE: The idea behind the timeline was to show the history of a particular place through the evolution of a particular thing. This family tree was designed to show how the various participants in a field that we now think of as diverse and crowded all derived from a common point of origin – that is, to reveal the hidden connections.

CREDITS: Art director, Paul Davis; writer, Thomas Hackett.

Family Tree of Paul Brown's NFL

DESIGN: Alexandra Ginns, USA

PUBLISHER/CLIENT: Wigwag

DATE OF 1ST PUBLICATION/USE: December 1990

DESIGN RATIONALE: The idea behind the timeline was to show the history of a particular place through the evolution of a particular thing. This family tree was designed to show how the various participants in a field that we now think of as diverse and crowded all derived from a common point of origin – that is, to reveal the hidden connections.

CREDITS: Art director, Paul Davis; writer, Lawrence Kaplen.

PAUL BROWN'S NFL

THE FAMILY TREE

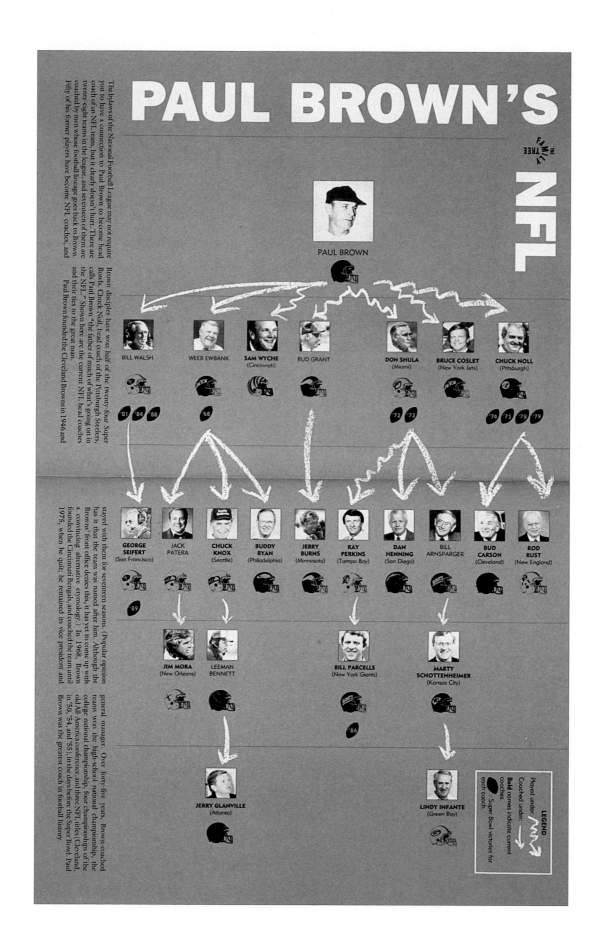

The bylaws of the National Football League may not require you to have a connection to Paul Brown to become head coach of an NFL team, but it clearly doesn't hurt. There are twenty-eight teams in the league, and seventeen of them are coached by men whose football lineage goes back to Brown. Fifty of his former players have become NFL coaches, and

Brown disciples have won half of the twenty-four Super Bowls. Chuck Noll, head coach of the Pittsburgh Steelers, calls Paul Brown "the father of much of what's going on in the NFL." Shown here are the current NFL head coaches and their ties to the great man.

Paul Brown founded the Cleveland Browns in 1946 and

stayed with them for seventeen seasons. (Popular opinion has it that the team was named after him. Although the Browns' front office denies this, it has yet to come up with a convincing alternative etymology.) In 1968, Brown founded the Cincinnati Bengals, and coached the team until 1975, when he quit; he remained its vice president and

general manager. Over forty-five years, Brown coached teams won the high-school national championship, the college national championship, four championships of the old All-America conference, and three NFL titles (Cleveland, in '50, '54, and '55), in the days before the Super Bowl. Paul Brown was the greatest coach in football history.

PAUL BROWN

BILL WALSH   WEEB EWBANK   **SAM WYCHE** (Cincinnati)   BUD GRANT   **DON SHULA** (Miami)   **BRUCE COSLET** (New York Jets)   **CHUCK NOLL** (Pittsburgh)

'81 '84 '88   '68   '72 '73   '74 '75 '78 '79

GEORGE SEIFERT (San Francisco)   JACK PATERA   **CHUCK KNOX** (Seattle)   **BUDDY RYAN** (Philadelphia)   **JERRY BURNS** (Minnesota)   **RAY PERKINS** (Tampa Bay)   **DAN HENNING** (San Diego)   BILL ARNSPARGER   **BUD CARSON** (Cleveland)   **ROD RUST** (New England)

'89

JIM MORA (New Orleans)   LEEMAN BENNETT   **BILL PARCELLS** (New York Giants)   **MARTY SCHOTTENHEIMER** (Kansas City)

'86

JERRY GLANVILLE (Atlanta)   **LINDY INFANTE** (Green Bay)

LEGEND

Played under/
Coached under
each coach.

Bold names indicate current coaches.

Super Bowl victories for each coach.

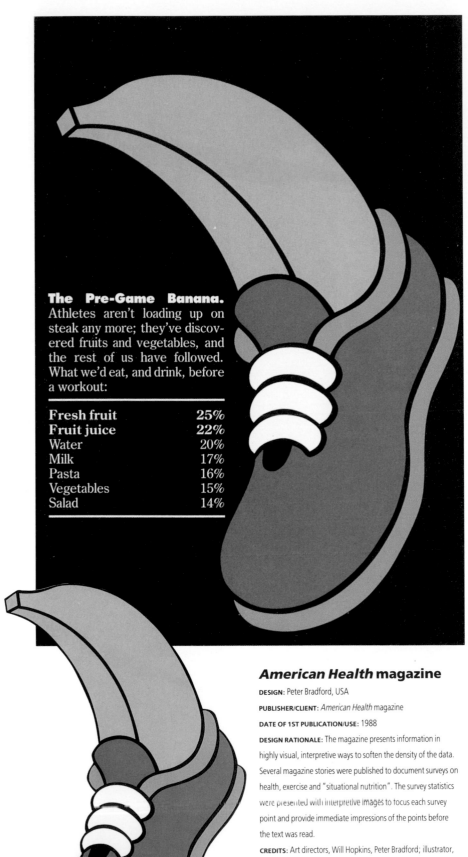

The Pre-Game Banana.

Athletes aren't loading up on steak any more; they've discovered fruits and vegetables, and the rest of us have followed. What we'd eat, and drink, before a workout:

Fresh fruit	**25%**
Fruit juice	**22%**
Water	20%
Milk	17%
Pasta	16%
Vegetables	15%
Salad	14%

The Romantic Crustacean.

When it comes to intimate dinners, lobster and wine set the mood. Here's our ultimate romantic meal:

Shellfish	**35%**
Salad	33%
Wine	**27%**
Vegetables	25%

American Health magazine

DESIGN: Peter Bradford, USA

PUBLISHER/CLIENT: *American Health* magazine

DATE OF 1ST PUBLICATION/USE: 1988

DESIGN RATIONALE: The magazine presents information in highly visual, interpretive ways to soften the density of the data. Several magazine stories were published to document surveys on health, exercise and "situational nutrition". The survey statistics were presented with interpretive images to focus each survey point and provide immediate impressions of the points before the text was read.

CREDITS: Art directors, Will Hopkins, Peter Bradford; illustrator, Peter Bradford.

Fordrea Community School

DESIGN: Peter Bradford, USA

PUBLISHER/CLIENT: Educational Facilities Laboratories

DATE OF 1ST PUBLICATION/USE: 1990

DESIGN RATIONALE: In a book promoting the sharing of facilities by schools and their communities, informal "sketch diagrams" of administrative processes and specific facilities were used to leaven the information. The diagrams emphasized the flexibility and options inherent in the text recommendations.

CREDITS: Art director, Peter Bradford; illustrators, Gary Fujiwara, Peter Bradford.

single organization to initiate cooperative community improvement instead of continuing to hire a community education director for each school. City officials established a new agency—the Sturgis Community-Schools Council—whose only mandate was to coordinate the community program.

The Community-Schools Council is neither a part of the school system nor the city government. The council is composed of the superintendent of schools, the city manager, a member of the city staff, a faculty member from a public school, a representative of a recreation day camp, a city commissioner and two citizens from the community. The council is a legal nonprofit organization empowered to administer programs, hire staff, purchase services and manage public facilities. It cannot own land, erect buildings or control an independent budget—but it can spend. State aid to education requires that all

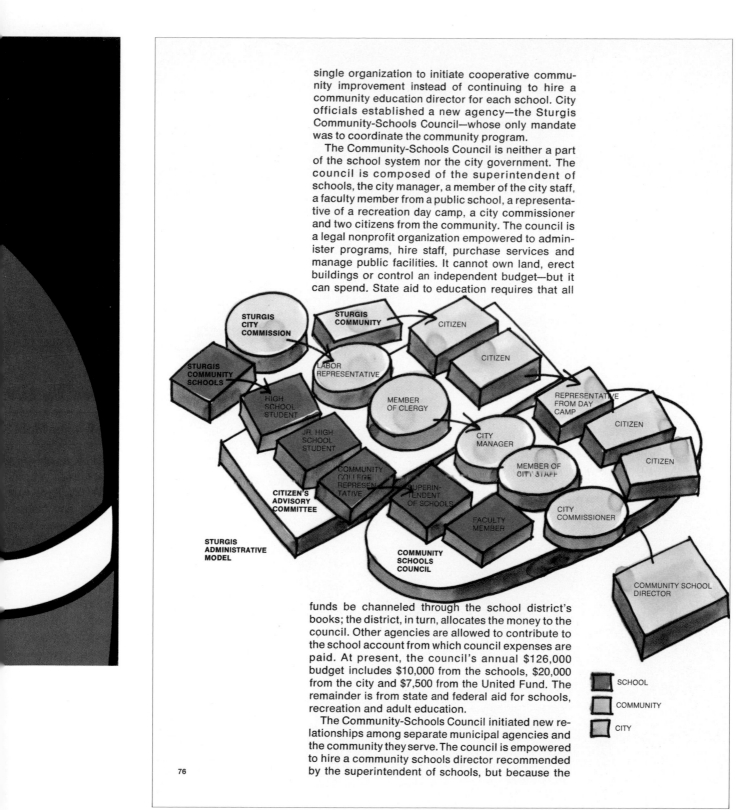

STURGIS
CITY
COMMISSION

STURGIS
COMMUNITY

CITIZEN

CITIZEN

STURGIS
COMMUNITY
SCHOOLS

LABOR
REPRESENTATIVE

REPRESENTATIVE
FROM DAY
CAMP

HIGH
SCHOOL
STUDENT

MEMBER
OF CLERGY

CITIZEN

JR. HIGH
SCHOOL
STUDENT

CITY
MANAGER

CITIZEN

COMMUNITY
COLLEGE
REPRESEN-
TATIVE

MEMBER OF
CITY STAFF

CITIZEN'S
ADVISORY
COMMITTEE

SUPERIN-
TENDENT
OF SCHOOLS

STURGIS
ADMINISTRATIVE
MODEL

FACULTY
MEMBER

CITY
COMMISSIONER

COMMUNITY
SCHOOLS
COUNCIL

COMMUNITY SCHOOL
DIRECTOR

funds be channeled through the school district's books; the district, in turn, allocates the money to the council. Other agencies are allowed to contribute to the school account from which council expenses are paid. At present, the council's annual $126,000 budget includes $10,000 from the schools, $20,000 from the city and $7,500 from the United Fund. The remainder is from state and federal aid for schools, recreation and adult education.

The Community-Schools Council initiated new relationships among separate municipal agencies and the community they serve. The council is empowered to hire a community schools director recommended by the superintendent of schools, but because the

SCHOOL

COMMUNITY

CITY

76

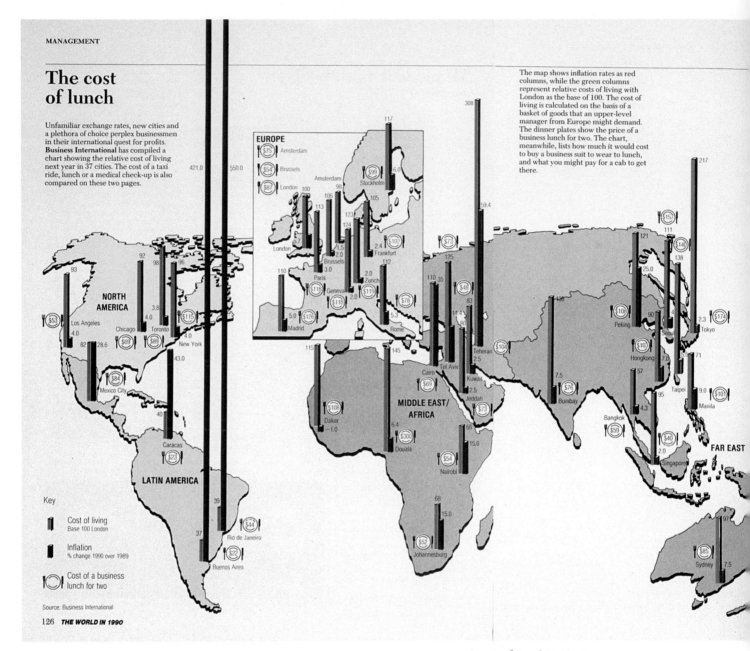

MANAGEMENT

The cost of lunch

Unfamiliar exchange rates, new cities and a plethora of choice perplex businessmen in their international quest for profits. **Business International** has compiled a chart showing the relative cost of living next year in 37 cities. The cost of a taxi ride, lunch or a medical check-up is also compared on these two pages.

The map shows inflation rates as red columns, while the green columns represent relative costs of living with London as the base of 100. The cost of living is calculated on the basis of a basket of goods that an upper-level manager from Europe might demand. The dinner plates show the price of a business lunch for two. The chart, meanwhile, lists how much it would cost to buy a business suit to wear to lunch, and what you might pay for a cab to get there.

EUROPE

$75 Amsterdam
$54 Brussels
$87 London

NORTH AMERICA

LATIN AMERICA

MIDDLE EAST/ AFRICA

FAR EAST

Key

Cost of living
Base 100 London

Inflation
% change 1990 over 1989

Cost of a business
lunch for two

Source: Business International

126 **THE WORLD IN 1990**

Cost of Eating Out

DESIGN: Michael Robinson, UK

PUBLISHER/CLIENT: World in 1990, *The Economist*

DATE OF 1ST PUBLICATION/USE: 1990

DESIGN RATIONALE: An illustration of the review of world business and political performance – in this case a comparison of the cost of going out to lunch throughout the world, plus the inflation cost to individuals in each country.

CREDITS: Art directors, Dennis Bailey, Mike Kenny; illustrator, Michael Robinson; editor, Dudley Fishburn.

Selected comparative costs

City	Cost of 10km taxi ride	Cost of business suit	Cost of medical checkup
EUROPE			
Amsterdam	$12.87	$545.61	$14.73
Brussels	$10.20	$882.33	$38.82
Frankfurt	$12.24	$453.96	$104.76
Geneva	$25.00	$508.40	$171.02
London	$10.19	$445.18	$124.64
Madrid	$5.27	$494.60	$46.66
Paris	$5.06	$447.38	$61.01
Rome	$10.83	$622.01	$58.17
Stockholm	$12.97	$644.85	$10.55
Zurich	$18.67	$763.32	$298.69
LATIN AMERICA			
Buenos Aires	$3.35	$350.00	$35.97
Caracas	$0.67	$318.81	$14.15
Mexico City	$20.89	$613.56	$56.58
Rio de Janeiro	$2.43	$457.00	$48.50
NORTH AMERICA			
Chicago	$10.50	$477.00	$60.00
Los Angeles	$19.56	$615.60	$84.98
New York	$8.35	$519.60	$60.00
Toronto	$12.80	$640.00	$40.86
FAR EAST			
Bangkok	$23.20	$222.71	$29.04
Peking	$5.79	n.a.	$18.46
Bombay	$2.63	$270.00	$8.02
Hongkong	$5.77	$556.64	$26.84
Manila	$3.12	$400.66	$17.50
Seoul	$4.12	$457.88	$7.39
Singapore	$3.22	$349.57	$28.81
Sydney	$7.91	$578.11	$18.74
Taipei	$5.65	$932.51	$91.00
Tokyo	$23.77	$1,079.69	$82.64
MIDDLE EAST/AFRICA			
Cairo	$7.50	$400.00	$34.70
Dakar	$6.29	$477.00	$35.95
Douala	$14.40	$699.19	$39.95
Johannesburg	$6.86	$605.64	$12.98
Kuwait	$7.92	$316.83	$29.52
Teheran	$2.09	$815.00	$22.25
Jeddah	$8.00	$432.00	$29.48
Nairobi	$9.63	$350.00	$13.23
Tel Aviv	$8.76	$558.35	$58.56

Pride and Productivity

DESIGN: Michael Robinson, UK

PUBLISHER/CLIENT: World in 1993, *The Economist*

DATE OF 1ST PUBLICATION/USE: 1992/93

DESIGN RATIONALE: A review of world business and political performance each year since 1989. This is part of a series of facts from the 1992 issues. In this case, a diagram compares Britain's pride and productivity with that of other European countries.

CREDITS: Art directors, Dennis Bailey, Mike Kenny; illustrator, Michael Robinson; editor, Dudley Fishburn.

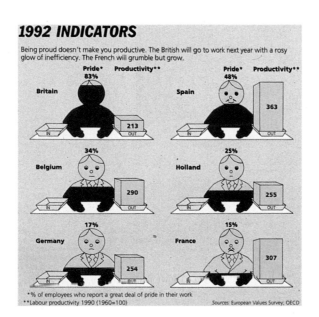

1992 INDICATORS

Being proud doesn't make you productive. The British will go to work next year with a rosy glow of inefficiency. The French will grumble but grow.

* % of employees who report a great deal of pride in their work
** Labour productivity 1990 (1960=100)

Sources: European Values Survey; OECD

Corporate Cutback

DESIGN: Michael Robinson, UK

PUBLISHER/CLIENT: *Management Today*

DATE OF 1ST PUBLICATION/USE: ?

DESIGN RATIONALE: A diagram showing how large BP had grown, having acquired many subsidiary companies, and what was left after Mr Horton's rationalization of the company.

CREDITS: Art director, Roland Schenk; illustrator, Michael Robinson.

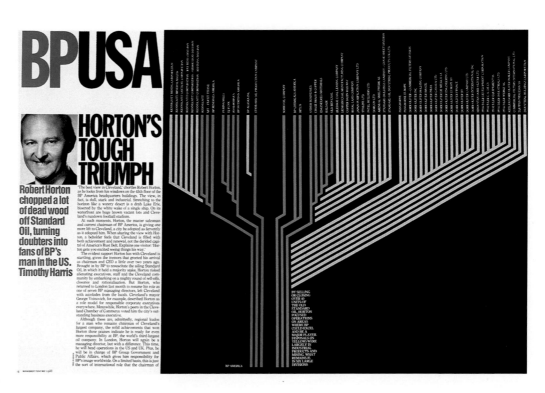

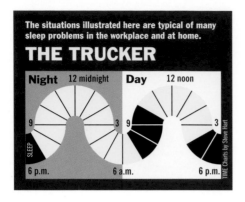

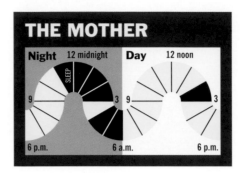

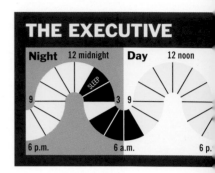

Wind & Fire

DESIGN: Sankei Design, Japan

PUBLISHER/CLIENT: *Sankei Shinbun* newspaper

DATE OF 1ST PUBLICATION/USE: 14 January –
19 December 1992

DESIGN RATIONALE: Various fields of data concerning history,
world development, etc. to illustrate articles written by
Taichi Sakaiya.

CREDITS: Art directors, Katsuhiko Nakazawa, Masataka
Tagawa; photographer, *Sankei Shinbun*; illustrator, Sankei
Design; writer, Taichi Sakaiya.

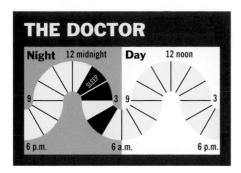

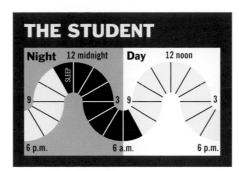

Sleep

DESIGN: Steve Hart, USA

PUBLISHER/CLIENT: *Time* magazine

DATE OF 1ST PUBLICATION/USE: 17 December 1990

DESIGN RATIONALE: Samples of different careers were compared showing a variety of sleep schedules. A new 24-hour "clock" was used.

CREDITS: Art director, Rudy Hoglund; illustrator, Steve Hart; researcher, Debby Wells.

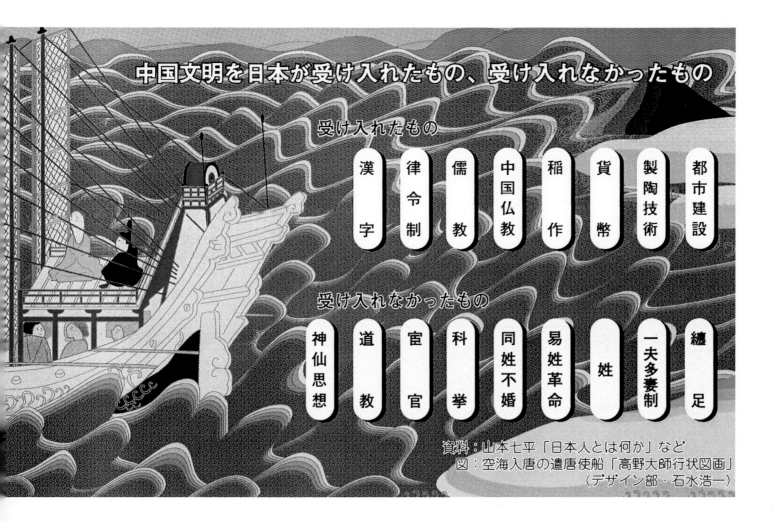

CHEMICAL PRECURSORS

ORIGIN OF LIFE

STROMATOLITES

FOUR BILLION YEARS AGO

AEROBIC RESPIRATION O₂

THREE BILLION

OZONE LAYER

EUKARYOTES

TWO BILLION

MULTICELLULAR LIFE

ONE BILLION

DIVERSIFICATION OF ANIMALS

MASS EXTINCTION   650 MILLION YEARS AGO

560

EARLY VERTEBRATES

500

420

VERTEBRATES INVADE THE LAND

360

COAL SWAMP FORESTS

300

230

DINOSAURS

MASS EXTINCTION

180

120

FLOWERING PLANTS   MAMMALS

65

MASS EXTINCTION

EMERGENCE OF MAN

TODAY

MAN-INDUCED EXTINCTIONS?

60 MILLION YEARS FROM NOW

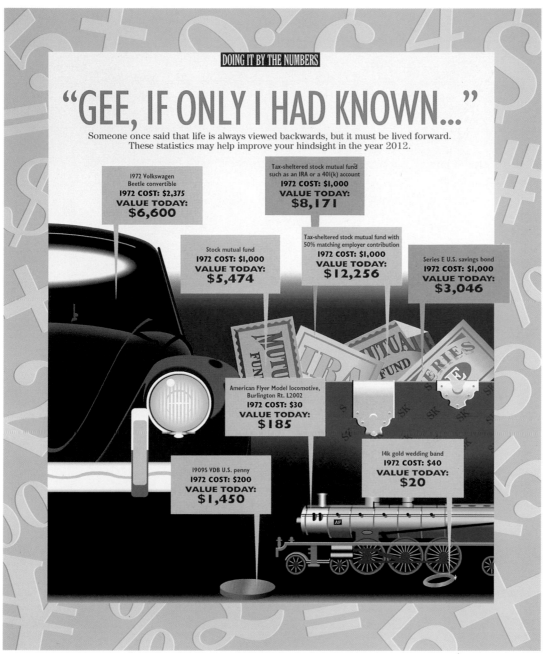

DOING IT BY THE NUMBERS

"GEE, IF ONLY I HAD KNOWN..."

Someone once said that life is always viewed backwards, but it must be lived forward.
These statistics may help improve your hindsight in the year 2012.

1972 Volkswagen
Beetle convertible
1972 COST: $2,375
VALUE TODAY:
$6,600

Tax-sheltered stock mutual fund
such as an IRA or a 401(k) account
1972 COST: $1,000
VALUE TODAY:
$8,171

Stock mutual fund
1972 COST: $1,000
VALUE TODAY:
$5,474

Tax-sheltered stock mutual fund with
50% matching employer contribution
1972 COST: $1,000
VALUE TODAY:
$12,256

Series E U.S. savings bond
1972 COST: $1,000
VALUE TODAY:
$3,046

American Flyer Model locomotive,
Burlington Rt. L2002
1972 COST: $30
VALUE TODAY:
$185

1909S VDB U.S. penny
1972 COST: $200
VALUE TODAY:
$1,450

14k gold wedding band
1972 COST: $40
VALUE TODAY:
$20

Gee, If Only I Had Known

DESIGN: Eliot Bergman, USA

PUBLISHER/CLIENT: *Stages* magazine, Fidelity Investments

DATE OF 1ST PUBLICATION/USE: 1992

DESIGN RATIONALE: The illustration compares Fidelity Investments products with common investments. The piece depicts a typical garage – a metaphor for things stored and forgotten – to dramatize the increase in value of mutual funds, IRAs and bonds.

CREDITS: Art director, Susan Yousem.

History of Earth

PUBLISHER/CLIENT: *National Geographic* magazine

DATE OF 1ST PUBLICATION/USE: August 1985

DESIGN RATIONALE: Summary of the geological and biological evolution of the planet Earth.

CREDITS: Art director, Allen T. Carroll; illustrator, Ned M. Seidler.

The Crooner Connection

In a summer of celebrity bios, if Marilyn Monroe is queen, Sinatra (no, not Elvis) must be king. On the 30th anniversary of her death, Marilyn has inspired five books. Frank just keeps popping up in *other* people's stories. But then, everybody seems to have known everybody else.

Noel Coward
By Clive Fisher. St. Martin's Press. $24.95.
Playwright, lyricist, actor—and no slouch as a celebrity hound. He made it his business to know *everyone.*

Dangerous Friends: At Large With Huston and Hemingway in the Fifties
By Peter Viertel. Doubleday. $24.50.
Screenwriter Viertel had a flirtation with Ava Gardner—Sinatra's second wife.

Papa called his pal 'the Kraut'

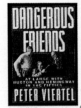

Huston directed Connery in 'The Man Who Would Be King' . . .

. . . and MM in 'The Asphalt Jungle'

Blue Angel: The Life of Marlene Dietrich
By Donald Spoto. Doubleday. $24.
Spoto says she had an affair with Sinatra. Which may explain why she played Vegas. But why did her pal Coward?

MM posed in Dietrich drag for Life magazine

Costarred in MM's last, unfinished movie

The Murder of Marilyn Monroe
By Leonore Canevari, Jeanette van Wyhe, Christian Dimas and Rachel Dimas. Carroll & Graf. $8.95.
Four psychics claim MM was murdered, based on "interviews" with her ghost and other phantoms.

MM appeared for 90 seconds in Groucho's 'Love Happy'

Marilyn: The Last Take
By Peter Harry Brown and Patte B. Barham. Dutton. $23.
Was Marilyn murdered? After looking into the traumas of her final weeks, these authors seem to think so.

Marilyn's Men: The Private Life of Marilyn Monroe
By Jane Ellen Wayne. St. Martin's Press. $18.95.
Speculation about almost every man MM ever married, worked with or met.

Why Norma Jean Killed Marilyn Monroe
By Lucy Freeman and Eddie Jaffe. Global Rights Ltd. of Chicago, Ill. $17.95.
Ghoulish probing of MM's childhood that led to what the authors call her "suicide on the installment plan."

Monroe: Her Life in Pictures
By James Spada with George Zeno. Doubleday. $22.50.
Oh, to be young, gifted and zaftig! Will this be reissued every decade? We hope so—it's full of great pix.

You See, I Haven't Forgotten
By Yves Montand. Knopf. $25.
During the filming of "Let's Make Love," Yves and MM did.

'Happy Birthday, Mr. President'

Capote called MM 'a beautiful child'

The Crooner Connection

DESIGN: Meredith Hamilton, USA

PUBLISHER/CLIENT: *Newsweek*

DATE OF 1ST PUBLICATION/USE: 17 August 1992

DESIGN RATIONALE: A humorous round-up of celebrity biographies to show that Hollywood is a small world. The piece allowed *Newsweek* to feature a number of biographies in a season during which there had been a plethora of such books.

CREDITS: Art director, Patricia Bradbury.

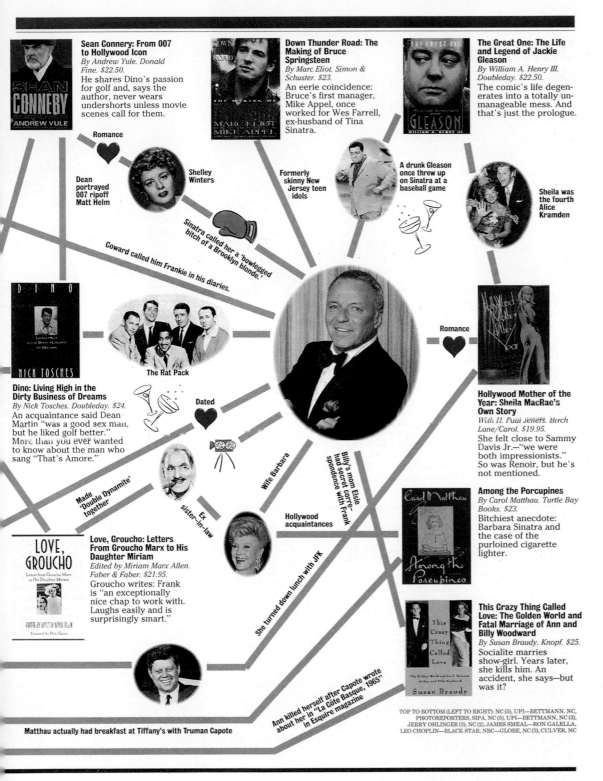

Sean Connery: From 007 to Hollywood Icon
By Andrew Yule. Donald Fine. $22.50.
He shares Dino's passion for golf and, says the author, never wears undershorts unless movie scenes call for them.

Down Thunder Road: The Making of Bruce Springsteen
By Marc Eliot. Simon & Schuster. $23.
An eerie coincidence: Bruce's first manager, Mike Appel, once worked for Wes Farrell, ex-husband of Tina Sinatra.

The Great One: The Life and Legend of Jackie Gleason
By William A. Henry III. Doubleday. $22.50.
The comic's life degenerates into a totally unmanageable mess. And that's just the prologue.

Romance

Dean portrayed 007 ripoff Matt Helm

Shelley Winters

Formerly skinny New Jersey teen idols

A drunk Gleason once threw up on Sinatra at a baseball game

Sheila was the fourth Alice Kramden

Sinatra called her a 'bowlegged bitch of a Brooklyn blonde.'

Coward called him Frankie in his diaries.

The Rat Pack

Romance

Dino: Living High in the Dirty Business of Dreams
By Nick Tosches. Doubleday. $24.
An acquaintance said Dean Martin "was a good sex man, but he liked golf better." More than you ever wanted to know about the man who sang "That's Amore."

Dated

Hollywood Mother of the Year: Sheila MacRae's Own Story
With H. Paul Jeffers. Birch Lane/Carol. $19.95.
She felt close to Sammy Davis Jr.—"we were both impressionists." So was Renoir, but he's not mentioned.

Made 'Double Dynamite' together

Ex sister-in-law

Wife Barbara

Billy's mom Elsie had secret correspondence with Frank

Hollywood acquaintances

Among the Porcupines
By Carol Matthau. Turtle Bay Books. $23.
Bitchiest anecdote: Barbara Sinatra and the case of the purloined cigarette lighter.

Love, Groucho: Letters From Groucho Marx to His Daughter Miriam
Edited by Miriam Marx Allen. Faber & Faber. $21.95.
Groucho writes: Frank is "an exceptionally nice chap to work with. Laughs easily and is surprisingly smart."

She turned down lunch with JFK

This Crazy Thing Called Love: The Golden World and Fatal Marriage of Ann and Billy Woodward
By Susan Braudy. Knopf. $25.
Socialite marries show-girl. Years later, she kills him. An accident, she says—but was it?

Ann killed herself after Capote wrote about her in "La Côte Basque, 1965" in Esquire magazine

Matthau actually had breakfast at Tiffany's with Truman Capote

Inflow and Outflow
Secondary Education

DESIGN: Liza Snook, NL

PUBLISHER/CLIENT: Ministry of Education and Science

DATE OF 1ST PUBLICATION/USE: June 1991

DESIGN RATIONALE: Major and minor currents of pupils, within and between school-types that are part of the Dutch system of secondary education. When data are filled in, the diagrams make one general view possible.

Duration of Registration

DESIGN: Liza Snook, NL

PUBLISHER/CLIENT: Ministry of Education and Science

DATE OF 1ST PUBLICATION/USE: May/June 1991

DESIGN RATIONALE: In this diagram students can read for how many years they are allowed to be registered in higher professional education and/or at universities.

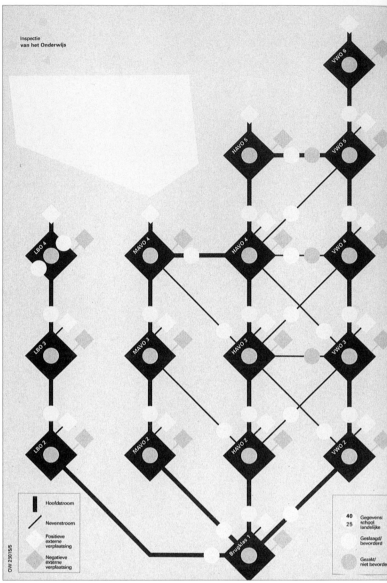

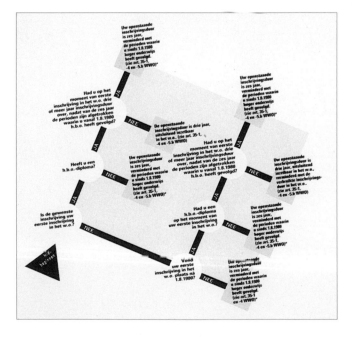

Het Groenere Boekje
(The Green Book)

DESIGN: Rene Hofman, NL, Nick Feeney, UK

PUBLISHER/CLIENT: PTT Telecom

DATE OF 1ST PUBLICATION/USE: March 1992

DESIGN RATIONALE: The diagram gives procedures that are part of a TQM (Total Quality Management) campaign. The goal of the procedures is optimal service to clients.

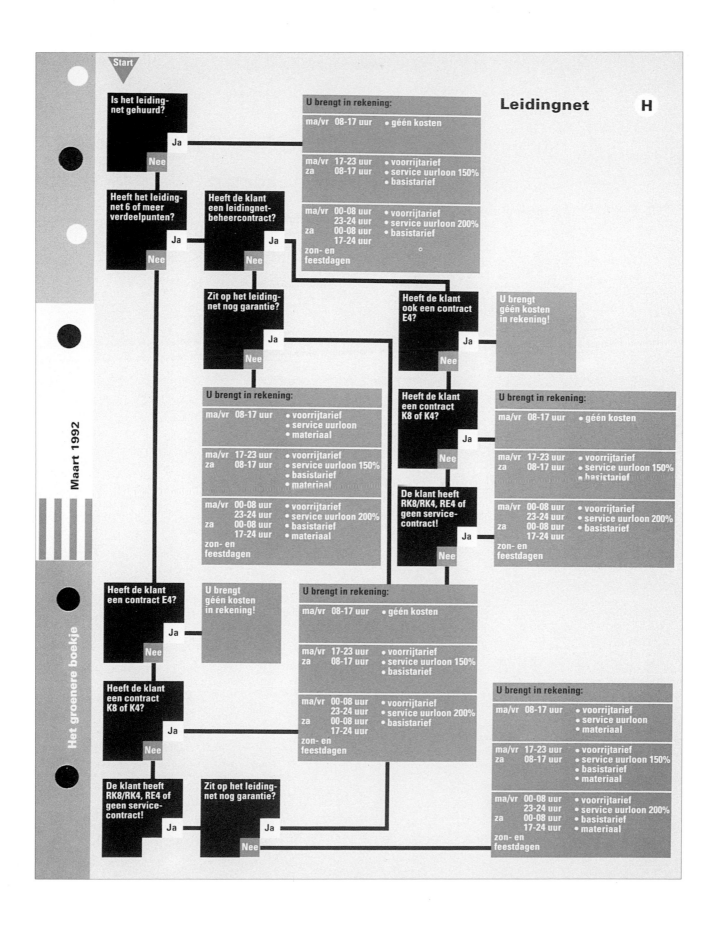

Start

Is het leiding-net gehuurd?
Ja
Nee

U brengt in rekening:

| ma/vr | 08-17 uur | • géén kosten |

ma/vr	17-23 uur	• voorrijtarief
za	08-17 uur	• service uurloon 150%
		• basistarief

ma/vr	00-08 uur	• voorrijtarief
	23-24 uur	• service uurloon 200%
za	00-08 uur	• basistarief
	17-24 uur	
zon- en		
feestdagen		

Heeft het leiding-net 6 of meer verdeelpunten?
Ja
Nee

Heeft de klant een leidingnet-beheercontract?
Ja
Nee

Zit op het leiding-net nog garantie?
Ja
Nee

Heeft de klant ook een contract E4?
Ja
Nee

U brengt géén kosten in rekening!

U brengt in rekening:

ma/vr	08-17 uur	• voorrijtarief
		• service uurloon
		• materiaal

ma/vr	17-23 uur	• voorrijtarief
za	08-17 uur	• service uurloon 150%
		• basistarief
		• materiaal

ma/vr	00-08 uur	• voorrijtarief
	23-24 uur	• service uurloon 200%
za	00-08 uur	• basistarief
	17-24 uur	• materiaal
zon- en		
feestdagen		

Heeft de klant een contract K8 of K4?
Ja
Nee

De klant heeft RK8/RK4, RE4 of geen service-contract!
Ja
Nee

U brengt in rekening:

| ma/vr | 08-17 uur | • géén kosten |

ma/vr	17-23 uur	• voorrijtarief
za	08-17 uur	• service uurloon 150%
		• basistarief

ma/vr	00-08 uur	• voorrijtarief
	23-24 uur	• service uurloon 200%
za	00-08 uur	• basistarief
	17-24 uur	
zon- en		
feestdagen		

Heeft de klant een contract E4?
Ja
Nee

U brengt géén kosten in rekening!

U brengt in rekening:

| ma/vr | 08-17 uur | • géén kosten |

ma/vr	17-23 uur	• voorrijtarief
za	08-17 uur	• service uurloon 150%
		• basistarief

ma/vr	00-08 uur	• voorrijtarief
	23-24 uur	• service uurloon 200%
za	00-08 uur	• basistarief
	17-24 uur	
zon- en		
feestdagen		

Heeft de klant een contract K8 of K4?
Ja
Nee

De klant heeft RK8/RK4, RE4 of geen service-contract!
Ja

Zit op het leiding-net nog garantie?
Ja
Nee

U brengt in rekening:

ma/vr	08-17 uur	• voorrijtarief
		• service uurloon
		• materiaal

ma/vr	17-23 uur	• voorrijtarief
za	08-17 uur	• service uurloon 150%
		• basistarief
		• materiaal

ma/vr	00-08 uur	• voorrijtarief
	23-24 uur	• service uurloon 200%
za	00-08 uur	• basistarief
	17-24 uur	• materiaal
zon- en		
feestdagen		

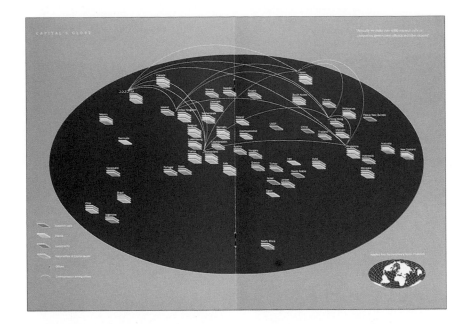

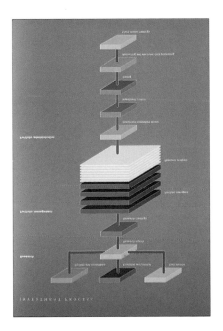

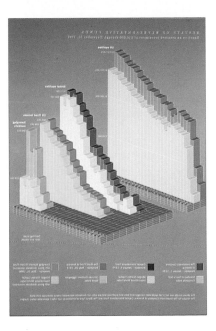

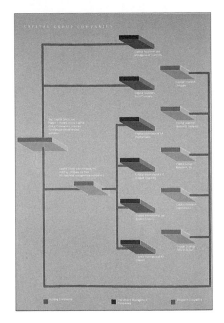

The Capital Group Brochure

DESIGN: Mervyn Kurlansky, South Africa

PUBLISHER/CLIENT: The Capital Group

DATE OF 1ST PUBLICATION/USE: 1992

DESIGN RATIONALE: The Capital Group is a privately owned global investment management organization which manages assets for institutional accounts and publicly owned mutual funds and unit trusts. The group's brochure was designed to explain its philosophy, practices and track record, using succinct copy and simple graphic charts.

CREDITS: Art director, Mervyn Kurlansky; designers, Richard Fisher-Smith, Mandy Nolan.

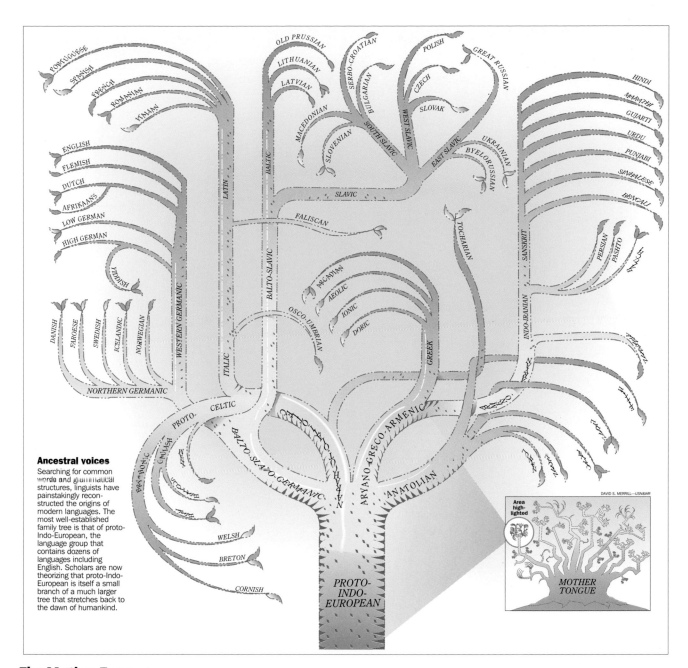

Ancestral voices

Searching for common words and grammatical structures, linguists have painstakingly reconstructed the origins of modern languages. The most well-established family tree is that of proto-Indo-European, the language group that contains dozens of languages including English. Scholars are now theorizing that proto-Indo-European is itself a small branch of a much larger tree that stretches back to the dawn of humankind.

The Mother Tongue

DESIGN: Dave Merrill, USA

PUBLISHER/CLIENT: *US News & World Report*

DATE OF 1ST PUBLICATION/USE: 5 November 1990

DESIGN RATIONALE: The diagram is an updated version of the human languages tree often found in encyclopedias. It reveals the writer's contention that this traditional tree is but a small branch of a much larger tree. New language names and branches update the information.

CREDITS: Art director, Rob Covey; illustrator, Dave Merrill; writer/researcher, William Allhman.

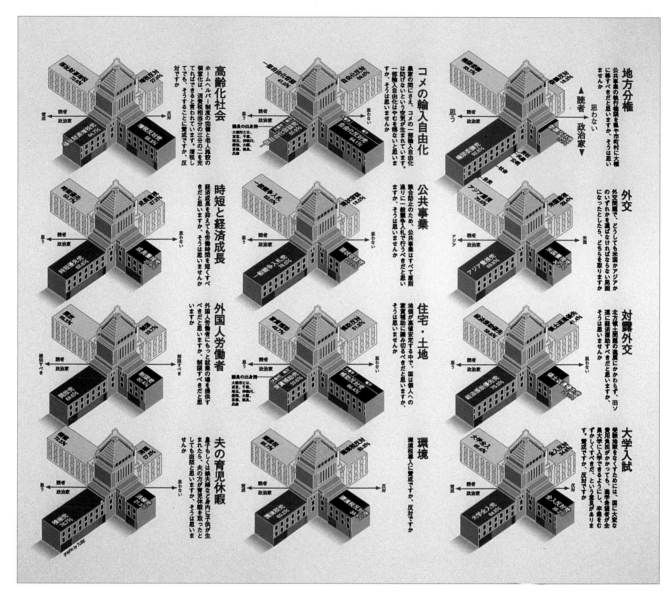

Japanese Government

DESIGN: Hiroyuki Kimura, Yuko Minoura, Japan

PUBLISHER/CLIENT: Asahi Shimbun, *AERA* magazine

DATE OF 1ST PUBLICATION/USE: 22 December 1992

DESIGN RATIONALE: Charts founded on an opinion poll regarding the Japanese government. The noughts represent "Yes" and the crosses represent "No"

CREDITS: Art director, Hiroyuki Kimura.

Sumitomo Bank

DESIGN: Hiroyuki Kimura, Sachiko Hagiwara, Japan

PUBLISHER/CLIENT: Asahi Shimbun, *AERA* magazine

DATE OF 1ST PUBLICATION/USE: 3 March 1992

DESIGN RATIONALE: Where are the branch managers of the Heiwa Sogo bank now, after the bank was absorbed by the Sumitomo Bank five years ago?

CREDITS: Art director, Hiroyuki Kimura.

Japanese Government

DESIGN: Hiroyuki Kimura, Yuko Minoura, Sachiko Hagiwara, Japan

PUBLISHER/CLIENT: Asahi Shimbun, *AERA* magazine

DATE OF 1ST PUBLICATION/USE: 22 December 1992

DESIGN RATIONALE: A chart founded on an opinion poll regarding the Japanese government. Noughts represent "Yes" and crosses represent "No"

CREDITS: Art director, Hiroyuki Kimura.

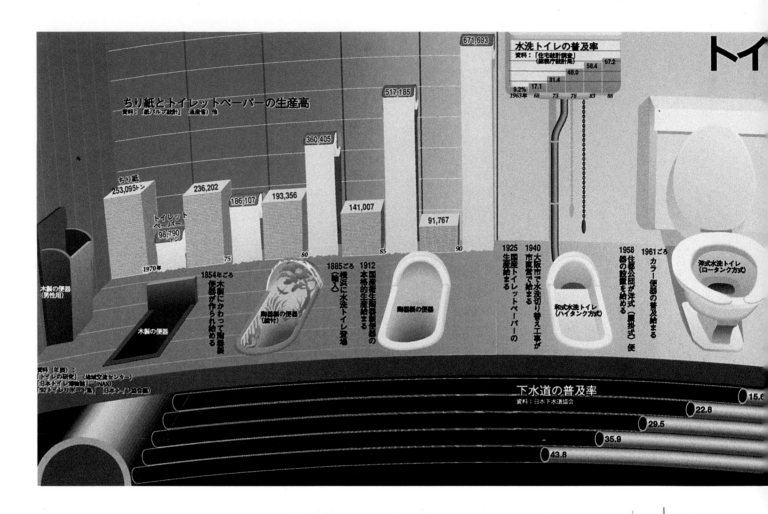

Comparison of Building Heights

DESIGN: Misako Tsunemi, Miroshita Ltd, Japan

PUBLISHER/CLIENT: *Sankei Shinbun* in *Scope* series

DATE OF 1ST PUBLICATION/USE: 21 August 1992

DESIGN RATIONALE: To illustrate two types of building in Japan and the USA so that readers can easily understand the difference between them.

CREDITS: Art director, Nobuo Morishita; illustrator, Misako Tsunemi; writer, Tetsuya Nakamoto; researcher, *Sankei Shibun,* Tokusyo-Han.

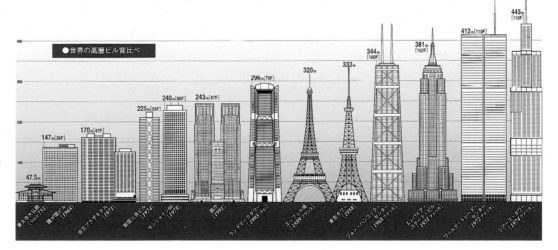

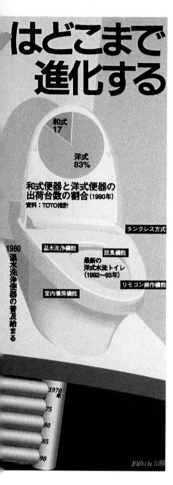

The Lavatory

DESIGN: Hiroyuki Kimura, Sachiko Hagiwara, Japan

PUBLISHER/CLIENT: Asahi Shimbun, *AERA* magazine

DATE OF 1ST PUBLICATION/USE: 26 January 1993

DESIGN RATIONALE: To illustrate the history of the lavatory, especially the chamber pot.

CREDITS: Art director, Hiroyuki Kimura.

Self-promotional Diagram

DESIGN: Tilly Northedge, UK

PUBLISHER/CLIENT: Self-promotion

DATE OF 1ST PUBLICATION/USE: 1990

DESIGN RATIONALE: A self-set brief of a self-portrait, demonstrating how the artist works for clients and considers their needs and also those of the end-users.

CREDITS: Art director/illustrator, Tilly Northedge.

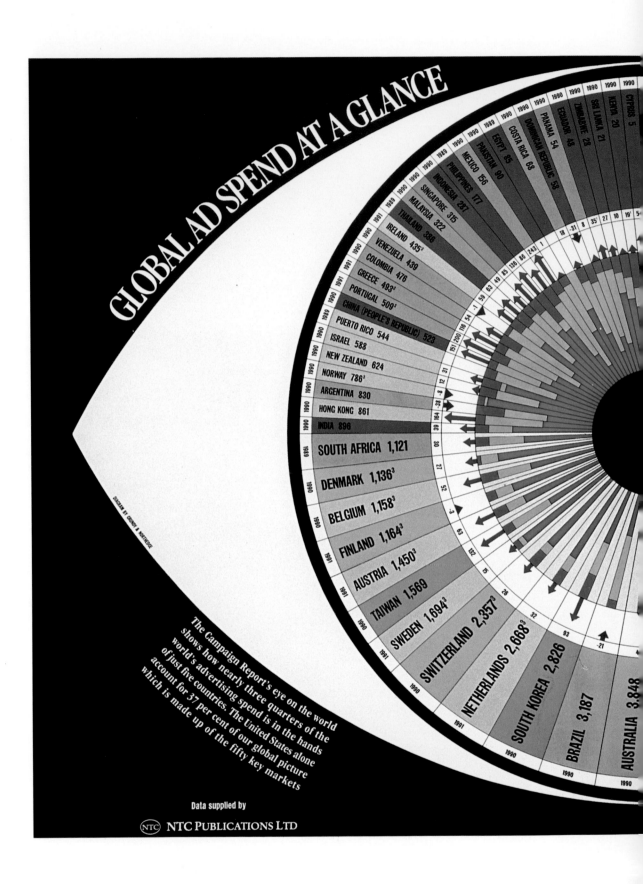

GLOBAL AD SPEND AT A GLANCE

The Campaign Report's eye on the world shows how nearly three quarters of the world's advertising spend is in the hands of just five countries. The United States alone account for 37 per cent of our global picture which is made up of the fifty key markets

Data supplied by

NTC PUBLICATIONS LTD

CYPRUS 5
KENYA 20
SRI LANKA 21
ZIMBABWE 28
ECUADOR 48
PANAMA 54
DOMINICAN REPUBLIC 58
COSTA RICA 68
EGYPT 85
PAKISTAN 90
MEXICO 156
PHILIPPINES 177
INDONESIA 287
SINGAPORE 315
MALAYSIA 322
THAILAND 388
IRELAND 435²
VENEZUELA 439
COLOMBIA 476
GREECE 493²
PORTUGAL 509²
CHINA (PEOPLE'S REPUBLIC) 523
PUERTO RICO 544
ISRAEL 588
NEW ZEALAND 624
NORWAY 786²
ARGENTINA 830
HONG KONG 861
INDIA 896
SOUTH AFRICA 1,121
DENMARK 1,136³
BELGIUM 1,158³
FINLAND 1,164³
AUSTRIA 1,450³
TAIWAN 1,569
SWEDEN 1,694³
SWITZERLAND 2,357³
NETHERLANDS 2,668³
SOUTH KOREA 2,826
BRAZIL 3,187
AUSTRALIA 3,848

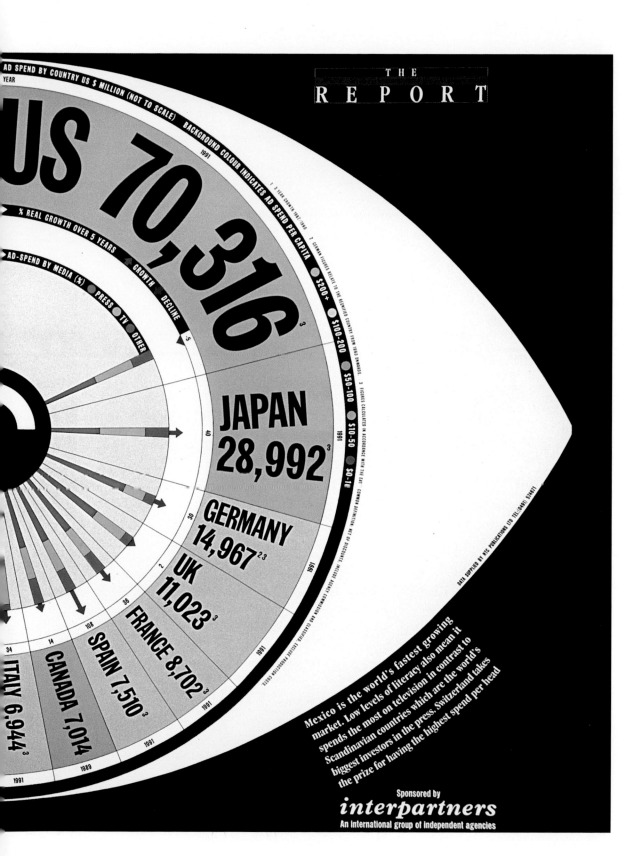

AD SPEND BY COUNTRY US $ MILLION (NOT TO SCALE)

YEAR

BACKGROUND COLOUR INDICATES AD SPEND PER CAPITA

% REAL GROWTH OVER 5 YEARS

AD-SPEND BY MEDIA (%)   GROWTH   DECLINE

PRESS   TV   OTHER

US 70,316 [3]

JAPAN 28,992 [3]

GERMANY 14,967 [2,3]

UK 11,023 [3]

FRANCE 8,702 [3]

SPAIN 7,510 [3]

CANADA 7,014

ITALY 6,944 [3]

$200 +
$100-200
$50-100
$10-50
$0-10

Mexico is the world's fastest growing market. Low levels of literacy also mean it spends the most on television in contrast to Scandinavian countries which are the world's biggest investors in the press. Switzerland takes the prize for having the highest spend per head

Sponsored by
interpartners
An international group of independent agencies

Ad-Spend At a Glance

DESIGN: Tilly Northedge, UK

PUBLISHER/CLIENT: *Campaign* magazine

DATE OF 1ST PUBLICATION/USE: September 1992

DESIGN RATIONALE: To show advertising budgets around the world and how those budgets are apportioned among the different media. The graphic was featured in the centre spread of the magazine in order to demonstrate the statistics in an arresting manner.

CREDITS: Art director/ illustrator, Tilly Northedge; writer/researcher, Tracey Taylor.

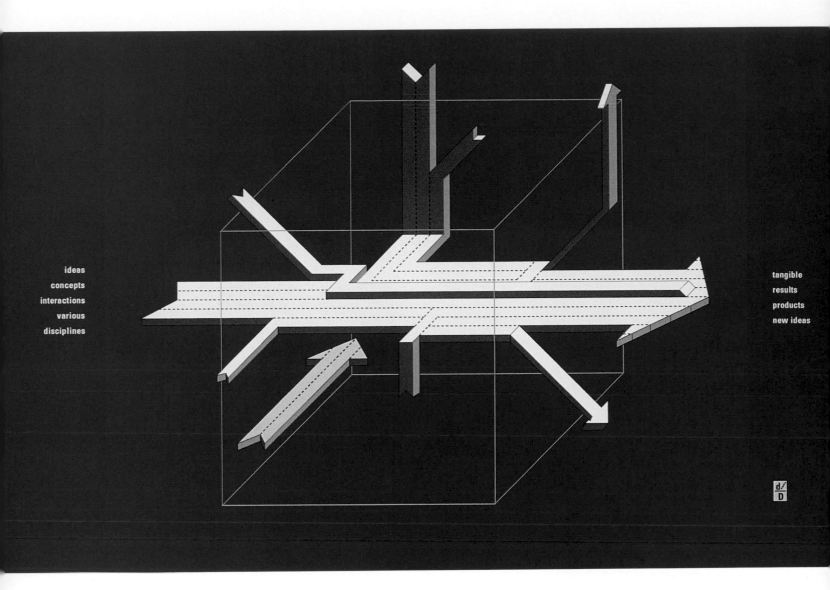

ideas
concepts
interactions
various
disciplines

tangible
results
products
new ideas

Converging Trends

DESIGN: Ronnie Peters, USA

PUBLISHER/CLIENT: Design for the brochure of Sigchi's (Special Interest Group for Computer – Human Interaction) 1992 Conference

DATE OF 1ST PUBLICATION/USE: 1991

DESIGN RATIONALE: The diagram illustrates the convergence of various resources (ideas, concepts, interactions between disciplines) that is necessary for the creation of new products.

CREDITS: Art director, Kris Lenk.

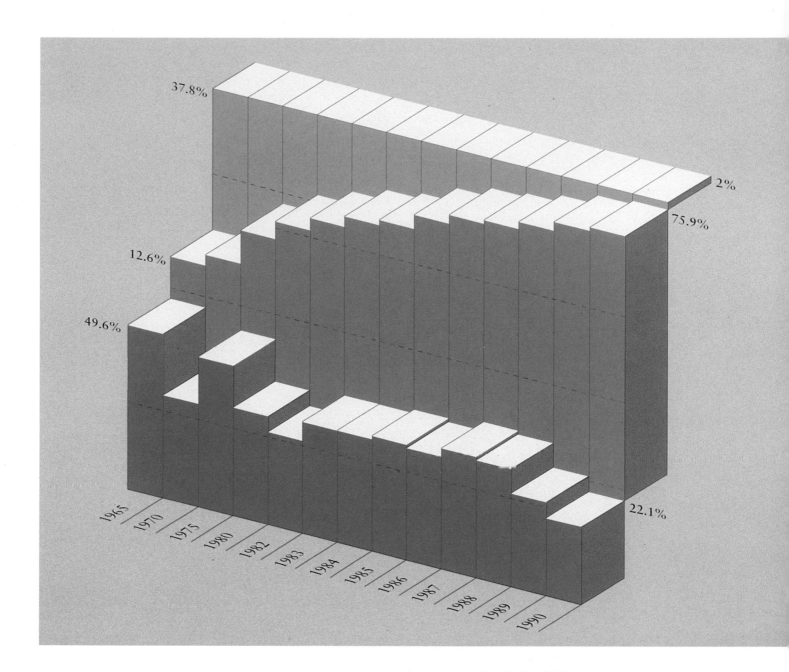

Statistical Diagram

DESIGN: Ronnie Peters, USA

PUBLISHER/CLIENT: Yale University Hospital

DATE OF 1ST PUBLICATION/USE: 1993

DESIGN RATIONALE: The diagram analyses the number of federal grant proposals for medical research submitted between 1965 and 1990. It indicates the number of projects approved, accepted and financed, the number of projects accepted but not financed and the percentage of rejected proposals.

CREDITS: Art director, Kris Lenk.

Tenses of the English Language

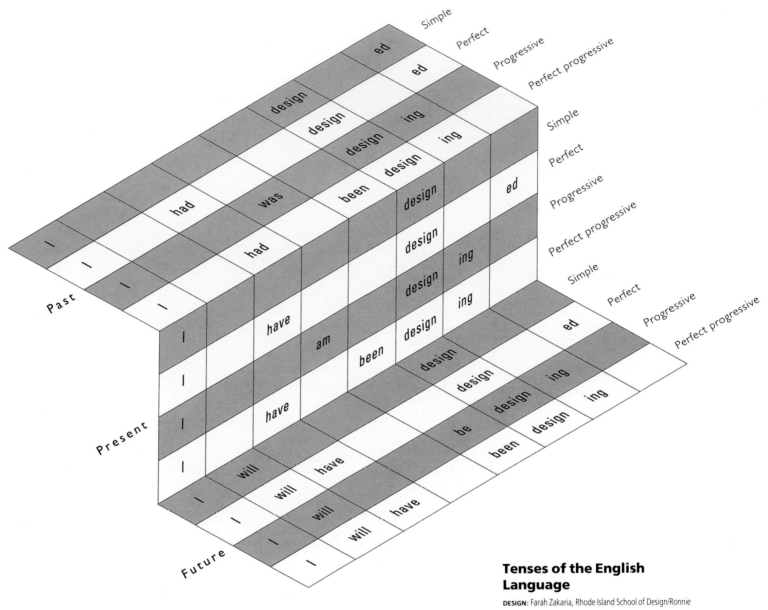

Tenses of the English Language

DESIGN: Farah Zakaria, Rhode Island School of Design/Ronnie Peters, USA

PUBLISHER/CLIENT: Dynamic Diagrams, Inc.

DATE OF 1ST PUBLICATION/USE: 1991

DESIGN RATIONALE: The diagram presents in a single grid the 12 forms of a regular verb in English. Repeating patterns are grouped into clear visual hierarchy.

CREDITS: Art director, Kris Lenk; text, Paul Kahn.

DEFORESTATION OF THE WORLD'S TROPICAL RAINFORESTS

Malaysia and several Asian states, criticised for overlogging, meet in Kuala Lumpur this week to set up the International Forest Organisation to regulate the world's forest policies

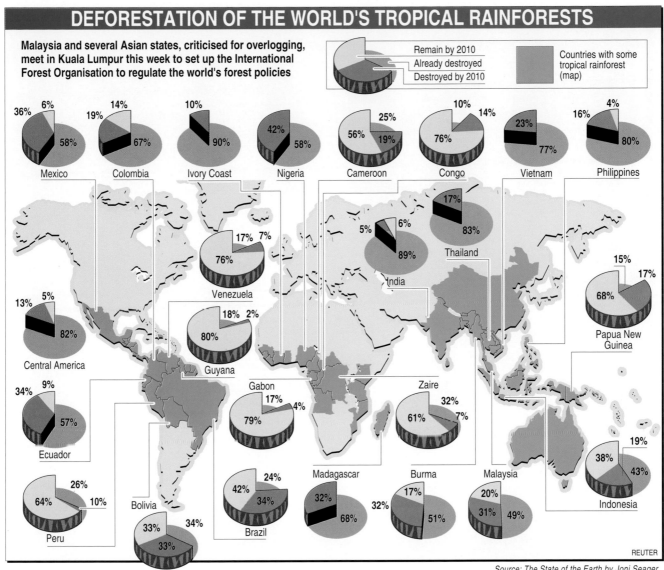

Remain by 2010
Already destroyed
Destroyed by 2010

Countries with some tropical rainforest (map)

Mexico — 36% / 6% / 58%
Colombia — 19% / 14% / 67%
Ivory Coast — 10% / 90%
Nigeria — 42% / 58%
Cameroon — 56% / 25% / 19%
Congo — 76% / 10% / 14%
Vietnam — 23% / 77% / 4%
Philippines — 16% / 4% / 80%
Venezuela — 76% / 17% / 7%
Thailand — 83% / 17%
India — 89% / 5% / 6%
Central America — 13% / 5% / 82%
Guyana — 80% / 18% / 2%
Papua New Guinea — 68% / 15% / 17%
Ecuador — 34% / 9% / 57%
Gabon — 79% / 17% / 4%
Zaire — 61% / 32% / 7%
Peru — 64% / 26% / 10%
Bolivia — 33% / 33% / 34%
Brazil — 42% / 24% / 34%
Madagascar — 32% / 68%
Burma — 32% / 17% / 51%
Malaysia — 31% / 20% / 49%
Indonesia — 38% / 19% / 43%

REUTER

Source: The State of the Earth by Joni Seager

Deforestation of the World's Tropical Rainforests

DESIGN: Chan Chee Kin, Singapore

PUBLISHER/CLIENT: Reuter News Graphics Service

DATE OF 1ST PUBLICATION/USE: 15 February 1993

DESIGN RATIONALE: Map of the world locating tropical rainforests with pie charts for each country showing how much forest has been destroyed, will be destroyed by 2010 (at present logging levels) and how much will remain.

CREDITS: Researcher, Sandra Maler.

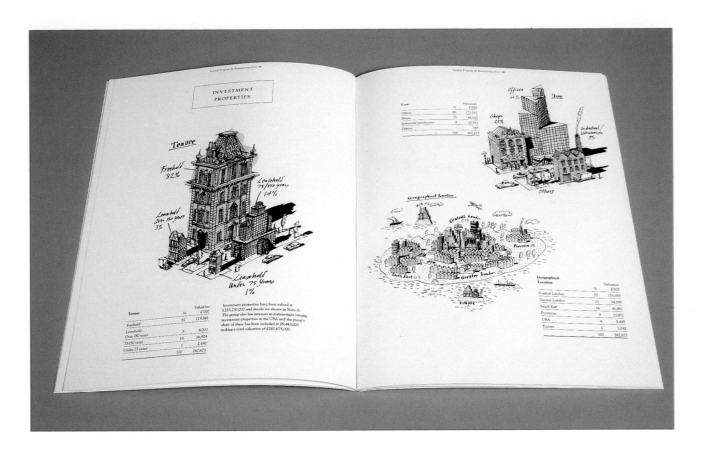

Lynton Annual Report 1988

DESIGN: Michael Peters Ltd, Jonathan Davis, UK

PUBLISHER/CLIENT: Lynton plc

DATE OF 1ST PUBLICATION/USE: June 1989

DESIGN RATIONALE: Three investment pie charts showing different types of tenure and user. The third chart represents geographical location across Lynton's property portfolio. The pie charts use the illustrative theme of the report to make an appealing feature of this information. Some of the buildings illustrated have architectural features of real buildings in Lynton's portfolio.

CREDITS: Art director, Jonathan Davis; illustrator, Benoit Jacques.

Oil Share Prices (Oil L709)

DESIGN: Branislav Radovic, UK

PUBLISHER/CLIENT: *Financial Times*

DATE OF 1ST PUBLICATION/USE: 24 July 1991

DESIGN RATIONALE: A graphic illustrating four share prices.

CREDITS: Art director/photographer/illustrator/writer/researcher, David Case.

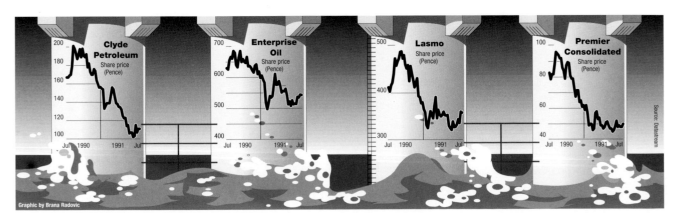

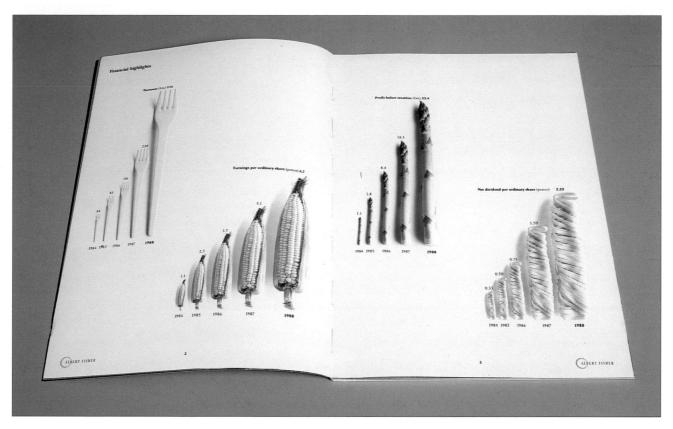

Albert Fisher Group plc
Annual Report 1988

DESIGN: Michael Peters Ltd, Stuart Redfern, UK

PUBLISHER/CLIENT: The Albert Fisher Group plc

DATE OF 1ST PUBLICATION/USE: April 1989

DESIGN RATIONALE: A double-page spread for financial highlights, including graphs for turnover and profit figures. The client is a major food sourcer and service organization; it was decided to use the company's "tools of the trade" to animate the financial graphs, normally a dull part of an annual report.

CREDITS: Art director, Stuart Redfern.

How 11.1 Million Voters
Changed Their Minds

DESIGN: Phil Green, UK

PUBLISHER/CLIENT: *Sunday Times*/Mori

DATE OF 1ST PUBLICATION/USE: 12 April 1992

DESIGN RATIONALE: A flow diagram to show the movement of voters in the British election between three main parties and 'don't knows'. Arrow width shows the relative size of movement. The original movement arrows between parties were on vertical and horizontal axes, which looked complicated and did not clearly show the flow.

CREDITS: Illustration, Phil Green; researcher, Mori.

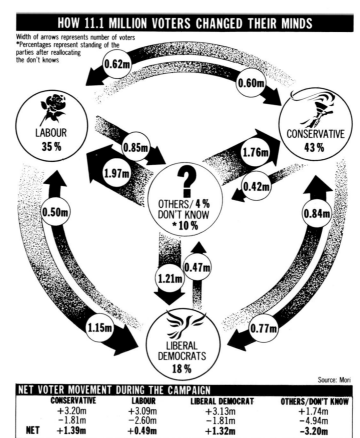

HOW 11.1 MILLION VOTERS CHANGED THEIR MINDS

Width of arrows represents number of voters
*Percentages represent standing of the parties after reallocating the don't knows

Source: Mori

NET VOTER MOVEMENT DURING THE CAMPAIGN			
CONSERVATIVE	**LABOUR**	**LIBERAL DEMOCRAT**	**OTHERS/DON'T KNOW**
+3.20m	+3.09m	+3.13m	+1.74m
−1.81m	−2.60m	−1.81m	−4.94m
NET +1.39m	+0.49m	+1.32m	−3.20m

American Depository Receipts

DESIGN: Williams and Phoa, UK

PUBLISHER/CLIENT: Warburg Securities

DATE OF 1ST PUBLICATION/USE: 1989

DESIGN RATIONALE: As in the S. G. Warburg corporate brochure, the theme based on security patterns is continued through the diagrams and illustrations. The constant (but evolving) theme projects a consistent image that is fresh in its detailing and application.

CREDIT: Art director, Phoa Kia Boon.

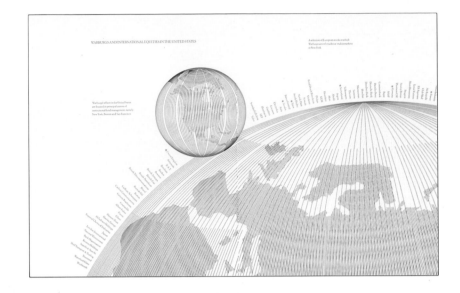

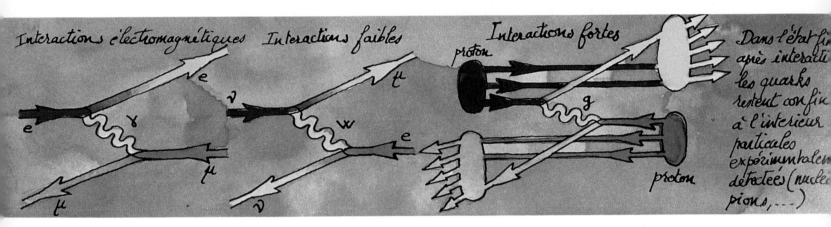

Institut de Recherche Fondamentale (IRF) "40 ans de recherche"

DESIGN: Pierre Praquin, France

PUBLISHER/CLIENT: Institut de Recherche Fondamentale

DATE OF 1ST PUBLICATION/USE: 1987

DESIGN RATIONALE: Using acrylic and ink, the map uses calligraphy, diagrams and illustrations to simplify scientific terms.

CREDITS: Art director, Pierre Praquin; photographers, CEA, CERN, Biaugeaud, Plailly, Jahan, Schuller, Mathieu, Thomson, CSF; illustrators, Pierre Praquin, F. Brosse.

Social Stratification in the United States

DESIGN: Dennis Livingston, USA

DATE OF 1ST PUBLICATION/USE: 1983

DESIGN RATIONALE: Demographic characteristics of the population of the United States including income, wealth, race, occupation (as single or couple) and single family with dependants. It functions as poster and chart. From a distance the patterns of income by occupation are easily seen. On closer examination, wealth patterns and other information can be discerned.

CREDITS: Art director/illustrator, Kathryn Shagas; researcher, Stephen Rose.

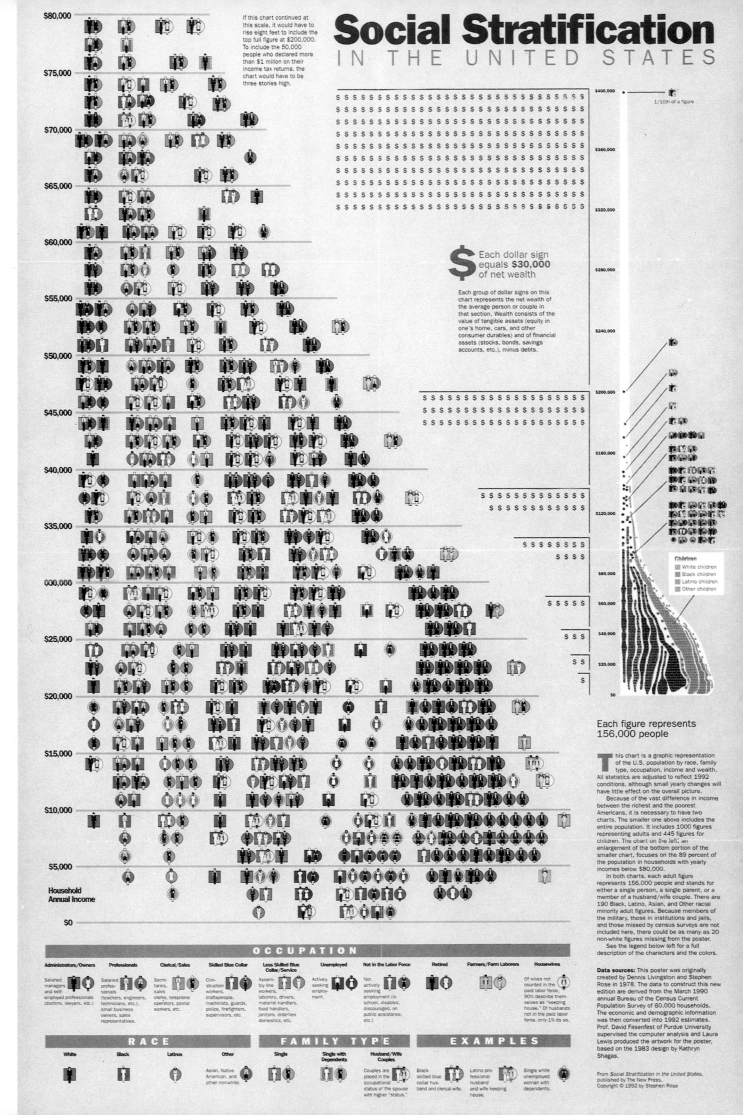

Social Stratification
IN THE UNITED STATES

If this chart continued at this scale, it would have to rise eight feet to include the top full figure at $200,000. To include the 50,000 people who declared more than $1 million on their income tax returns, the chart would have to be three stories high.

$ Each dollar sign equals **$30,000** of net wealth

Each group of dollar signs on this chart represents the net wealth of the average person or couple in that section. Wealth consists of the value of tangible assets (equity in one's home, cars, and other consumer durables) and of financial assets (stocks, bonds, savings accounts, etc.), minus debts.

1/10th of a figure

Children
- White children
- Black children
- Latino children
- Other children

Each figure represents 156,000 people

This chart is a graphic representation of the U.S. population by race, family type, occupation, income and wealth. All statistics are adjusted to reflect 1992 conditions, although small yearly changes will have little effect on the overall picture.

Because of the vast difference in income between the richest and the poorest Americans, it is necessary to have two charts. The smaller one above includes the entire population. It includes 1000 figures representing adults and 445 figures for children. The chart on the left, an enlargement of the bottom portion of the smaller chart, focuses on the 89 percent of the population in households with yearly incomes below $80,000.

In both charts, each adult figure represents 156,000 people and stands for either a single person, a single parent, or a member of a husband/wife couple. There are 190 Black, Latino, Asian, and Other racial minority adult figures. Because members of the military, those in institutions and jails, and those missed by census surveys are not included here, there could be as many as 20 non-white figures missing from the poster.

See the legend below left for a full description of the characters and the colors.

Data sources: This poster was originally created by Dennis Livingston and Stephen Rose in 1978. The data to construct this new edition are derived from the March 1990 annual Bureau of the Census Current Population Survey of 60,000 households. The economic and demographic information was then converted into 1992 estimates. Prof. David Fasenfest of Purdue University supervised the computer analysis and Laura Lewis produced the artwork for the poster, based on the 1983 design by Kathryn Shagas.

From *Social Stratification in the United States*, published by The New Press. Copyright © 1992 by Stephen Rose.

Household Annual Income

$80,000 / $75,000 / $70,000 / $65,000 / $60,000 / $55,000 / $50,000 / $45,000 / $40,000 / $35,000 / $30,000 / $25,000 / $20,000 / $15,000 / $10,000 / $5,000 / $0

$400,000 / $360,000 / $320,000 / $280,000 / $240,000 / $200,000 / $160,000 / $120,000 / $80,000 / $60,000 / $40,000 / $20,000 / $0

OCCUPATION

Administrators/Owners	Professionals	Clerical/Sales	Skilled Blue Collar	Less Skilled Blue Collar/Service	Unemployed	Not in the Labor Force	Retired	Farmers/Farm Laborers	Housewives
Salaried managers and self-employed professionals (doctors, lawyers, etc.).	Salaried professionals (teachers, engineers, technicians, etc.), small business owners, sales representatives.	Secretaries, sales clerks, telephone operators, postal workers, etc.	Construction workers, craftspeople, machinists, guards, police, firefighters, supervisors, etc.	Assembly line workers, laborers, drivers, material handlers, food handlers, janitors, orderlies, domestics, etc.	Actively seeking employment.	Not actively seeking employment (in school, disabled, discouraged, on public assistance, etc.)			Of wives not counted in the paid labor force, 90% describe themselves as "keeping house." Of husbands not in the paid labor force, only 1% do so.

RACE

White	Black	Latinos	Other
			Asian, Native American, and other non-white.

FAMILY TYPE

Single	Single with Dependents	Husband/Wife Couples
		Couples are placed in the occupational status of the spouse with higher "status."

EXAMPLES

Black skilled blue collar husband and clerical wife.

Latino professional husband and wife keeping house.

Single white unemployed woman with dependents.

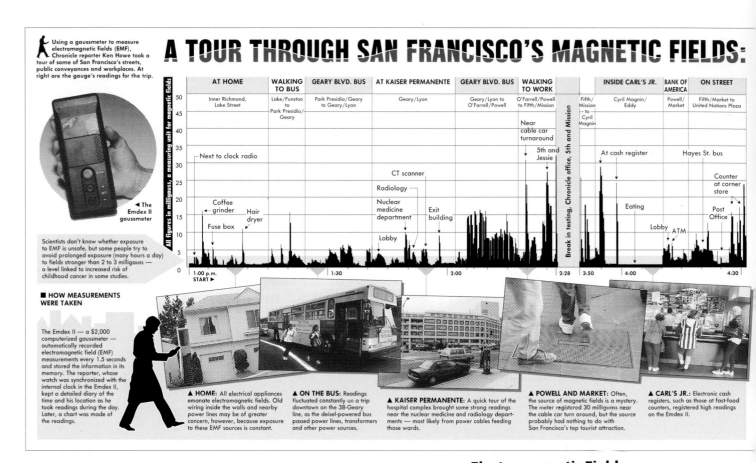

Using a gaussmeter to measure electromagnetic fields (EMF), Chronicle reporter Ken Howe took a tour of some of San Francisco's streets, public conveyances and workplaces. At right are the gauge's readings for the trip.

A TOUR THROUGH SAN FRANCISCO'S MAGNETIC FIELDS:

◄ The Emdex II gaussmeter

Scientists don't know whether exposure to EMF is unsafe, but some people try to avoid prolonged exposure (many hours a day) to fields stronger than 2 to 3 milligauss — a level linked to increased risk of childhood cancer in some studies.

■ HOW MEASUREMENTS WERE TAKEN

The Emdex II — a $2,000 computerized gaussmeter — automatically recorded electromagnetic field (EMF) measurements every 1.5 seconds and stored the information in its memory. The reporter, whose watch was synchronized with the internal clock in the Emdex II, kept a detailed diary of the time and his location as he took readings during the day. Later, a chart was made of the readings.

▲ HOME: All electrical appliances emanate electromagnetic fields. Old wiring inside the walls and nearby power lines may be of greater concern, however, because exposure to these EMF sources is constant.

▲ ON THE BUS: Readings fluctuated constantly on a trip downtown on the 38-Geary line, as the diesel-powered bus passed power lines, transformers and other power sources.

▲ KAISER PERMANENTE: A quick tour of the hospital complex brought some strong readings near the nuclear medicine and radiology departments — most likely from power cables feeding those wards.

▲ POWELL AND MARKET: Often, the source of magnetic fields is a mystery. The meter registered 30 milligauss near the cable car turn around, but the source probably had nothing to do with San Francisco's top tourist attraction.

▲ CARL'S JR.: Electronic cash registers, such as those at fast-food counters, registered high readings on the Emdex II.

Electromagnetic Fields Walking Tour

DESIGN: Kristine Strawser, USA

PUBLISHER/CLIENT: *San Francisco Chronicle*

DATE OF 1ST PUBLICATION/USE: 8 March 1993

DESIGN RATIONALE: Charting the results, measured with a gaussmeter, of magnetic fields in different places and areas of San Francisco.

CREDITS: Graphics editor, Steve Outing; writers, Ken Howe, Steve Outing; researcher, Ken Howe.

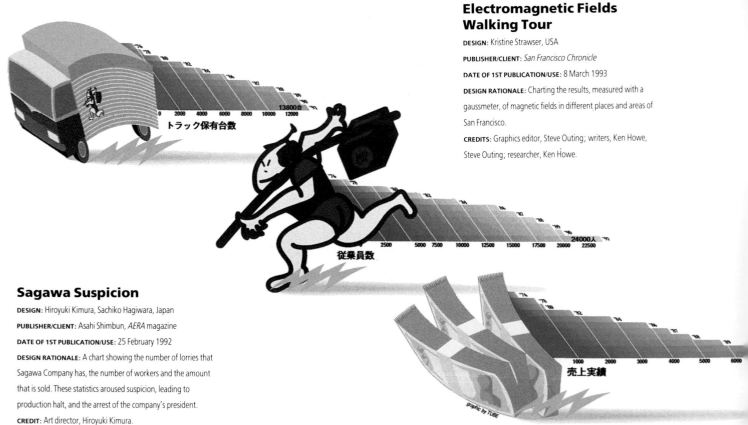

Sagawa Suspicion

DESIGN: Hiroyuki Kimura, Sachiko Hagiwara, Japan

PUBLISHER/CLIENT: Asahi Shimbun, *AERA* magazine

DATE OF 1ST PUBLICATION/USE: 25 February 1992

DESIGN RATIONALE: A chart showing the number of lorries that Sagawa Company has, the number of workers and the amount that is sold. These statistics aroused suspicion, leading to production halt, and the arrest of the company's president.

CREDIT: Art director, Hiroyuki Kimura.

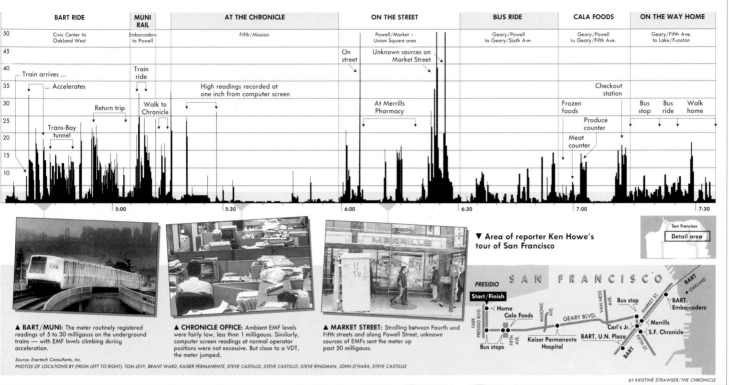

THEY ARE EVERYWHERE, AS OUR STROLL THROUGH THE CITY SHOWS —
BUT SHOULD WE BE CONCERNED ABOUT EXPOSURE TO ELECTROMAGNETIC FIELDS? SCIENCE DOESN'T HAVE A FINAL ANSWER

| BART RIDE | MUNI RAIL | AT THE CHRONICLE | ON THE STREET | BUS RIDE | CALA FOODS | ON THE WAY HOME |

Civic Center to Oakland West / Embarcadero to Powell / Fifth/Mission / Powell/Market – Union Square area / Geary/Powell to Geary/Sixth Ave. / Geary/Powell to Geary/Fifth Ave. / Geary/Fifth Ave. to Lake/Funston

▲ **BART/MUNI:** The meter routinely registered readings of 5 to 30 milligauss on the underground trains — with EMF levels climbing during acceleration.

Source: Enertech Consultants, Inc.

▲ **CHRONICLE OFFICE:** Ambient EMF levels were fairly low, less than 1 milligauss. Similarly, computer screen readings at normal operator positions were not excessive. But close to a VDT, the meter jumped.

▲ **MARKET STREET:** Strolling between Fourth and Fifth streets and along Powell Street, unknown sources of EMFs sent the meter up past 50 milligauss.

▼ Area of reporter Ken Howe's tour of San Francisco

San Francisco — Detail area

SAN FRANCISCO

PRESIDIO — Start/Finish

PHOTOS OF LOCATIONS BY (FROM LEFT TO RIGHT): TOM LEVY, BRANT WARD, KAISER PERMANENTE, STEVE CASTILLO, STEVE CASTILLO, STEVE RINGMAN, JOHN O'HARA, STEVE CASTILLO

BY KRISTINE STRAWSER/THE CHRONICLE

現代哲学の宇宙

Philosophy

DESIGN: Hiroyuki Kimura, Sachiko Hagiwara, Japan

PUBLISHER/CLIENT: Asahi Shimbun, *AERA* magazine

DATE OF 1ST PUBLICATION/USE: 18 August 1992

DESIGN RATIONALE: To illustrate modern philosophies using the cosmos as a correlative.

CREDIT: Art director, Hiroyuki Kimura.

1,000 Years At a Glance

DESIGN: Nigel Holmes, UK

PUBLISHER/CLIENT: *Time* magazine

DATE OF 1ST PUBLICATION/USE: October 1992

DESIGN RATIONALE: To show key world events occurring in the last millennium.

CREDITS: Art director/illustrator/writer, Nigel Holmes; researchers, Debby Wells, Rata Kamlani.

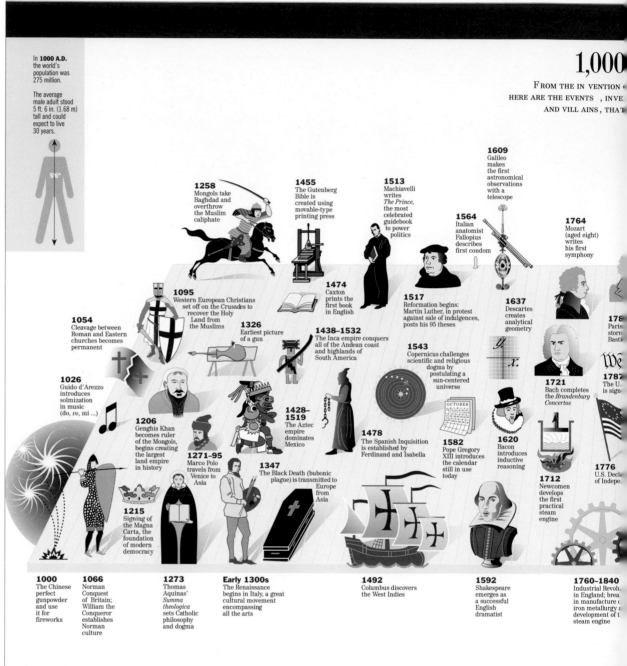

In **1000 A.D.** the world's population was 275 million.

The average male adult stood 5 ft. 6 in. (1.68 m) tall and could expect to live 30 years.

5'6"

1,000

FROM THE INVENTION
HERE ARE THE EVENTS, INVE
AND VILLAINS, THAT

1609 Galileo makes the first astronomical observations with a telescope

1258 Mongols take Baghdad and overthrow the Muslim caliphate

1455 The Gutenberg Bible is created using movable-type printing press

1513 Machiavelli writes *The Prince,* the most celebrated guidebook to power politics

1564 Italian anatomist Fallopius describes first condom

1764 Mozart (aged eight) writes his first symphony

1095 Western European Christians set off on the Crusades to recover the Holy Land from the Muslims

1474 Caxton prints the first book in English

1517 Reformation begins: Martin Luther, in protest against sale of indulgences, posts his 95 theses

1637 Descartes creates analytical geometry

178 Paris storm Basti

1054 Cleavage between Roman and Eastern churches becomes permanent

1326 Earliest picture of a gun

1438–1532 The Inca empire conquers all of the Andean coast and highlands of South America

1543 Copernicus challenges scientific and religious dogma by postulating a sun-centered universe

1787 The U. is sign

1026 Guido d'Arezzo introduces solmization in music (do, re, mi ...)

1206 Genghis Khan becomes ruler of the Mongols, begins creating the largest land empire in history

1428–1519 The Aztec empire dominates Mexico

1478 The Spanish Inquisition is established by Ferdinand and Isabella

1582 Pope Gregory XIII introduces the calendar still in use today

1620 Bacon introduces inductive reasoning

1721 Bach completes the *Brandenburg Concertos*

1776 U.S. Decla of Indepe.

1271–95 Marco Polo travels from Venice to Asia

1347 The Black Death (bubonic plague) is transmitted to Europe from Asia

1712 Newcomen develops the first practical steam engine

1215 Signing of the Magna Carta, the foundation of modern democracy

1000 The Chinese perfect gunpowder and use it for fireworks

1066 Norman Conquest of Britain; William the Conqueror establishes Norman culture

1273 Thomas Aquinas' *Summa theologica* sets Catholic philosophy and dogma

Early 1300s The Renaissance begins in Italy, a great cultural movement encompassing all the arts

1492 Columbus discovers the West Indies

1592 Shakespeare emerges as a successful English dramatist

1760–1840 Industrial Revolu in England; brea in manufacture iron metallurgy development of t steam engine

TIME

ears at a Glance

NP OWDER T O THE S ECOND R USSIAN REV OLUTION,
S AND P OLITICAL MO VEMENTS , THE CONFLICTS , HEROE S
ED OUR W ORLD DURING THE P AST MILLENNIUM

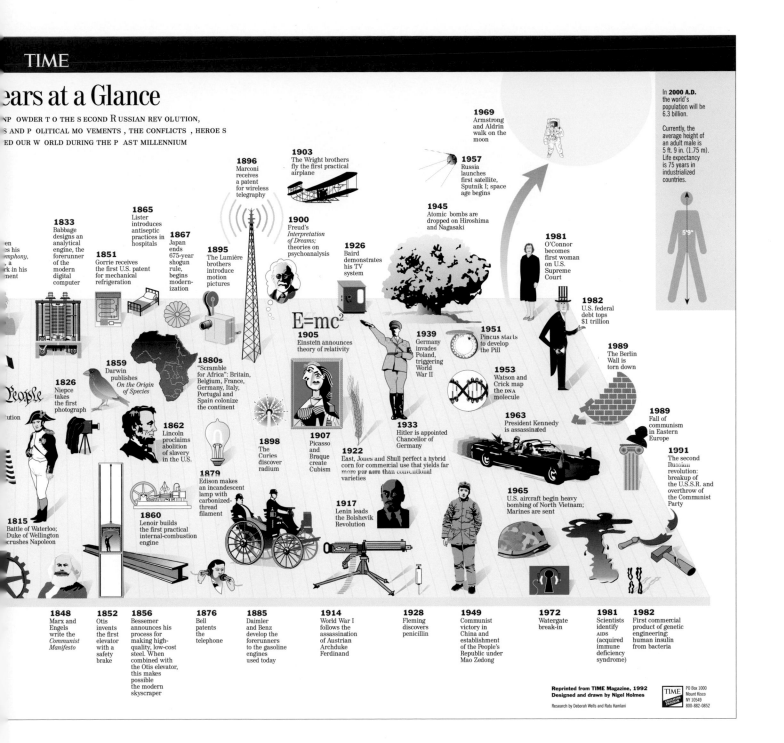

In **2000 A.D.**
the world's
population will be
6.3 billion.

Currently, the
average height of
an adult male is
5 ft. 9 in. (1.75 m).
Life expectancy
is 75 years in
industrialized
countries.

5'9"

1969
Armstrong
and Aldrin
walk on the
moon

1957
Russia
launches
first satellite,
Sputnik I; space
age begins

1896
Marconi
receives
a patent
for wireless
telegraphy

1903
The Wright brothers
fly the first practical
airplane

1945
Atomic bombs are
dropped on Hiroshima
and Nagasaki

1833
Babbage
designs an
analytical
engine, the
forerunner
of the
modern
digital
computer

1865
Lister
introduces
antiseptic
practices in
hospitals

1867
Japan
ends
675-year
shogun
rule,
begins
modern-
ization

1900
Freud's
*Interpretation
of Dreams;*
theories on
psychoanalysis

1926
Baird
demonstrates
his TV
system

1981
O'Connor
becomes
first woman
on U.S.
Supreme
Court

1851
Gorrie receives
the first U.S. patent
for mechanical
refrigeration

1895
The Lumière
brothers
introduce
motion
pictures

1982
U.S. federal
debt tops
$1 trillion

$E=mc^2$

1905
Einstein announces
theory of relativity

1939
Germany
invades
Poland,
triggering
World
War II

1951
Pincus starts
to develop
the Pill

1989
The Berlin
Wall is
torn down

1859
Darwin
publishes
*On the Origin
of Species*

1880s
"Scramble
for Africa": Britain,
Belgium, France,
Germany, Italy,
Portugal and
Spain colonize
the continent

1953
Watson and
Crick map
the DNA
molecule

1826
Niepce
takes
the first
photograph

1862
Lincoln
proclaims
abolition
of slavery
in the U.S.

1898
The
Curies
discover
radium

1907
Picasso
and
Braque
create
Cubism

1933
Hitler is appointed
Chancellor of
Germany

1963
President Kennedy
is assassinated

1989
Fall of
communism
in Eastern
Europe

1922
East, Jones and Shull perfect a hybrid
corn for commercial use that yields far
more per acre than conventional
varieties

1991
The second
Russian
revolution:
breakup of
the U.S.S.R. and
overthrow of
the Communist
Party

1879
Edison makes
an incandescent
lamp with
carbonized-
thread
filament

1815
Battle of Waterloo;
Duke of Wellington
crushes Napoleon

1860
Lenoir builds
the first practical
internal-combustion
engine

1917
Lenin leads
the Bolshevik
Revolution

1965
U.S. aircraft begin heavy
bombing of North Vietnam;
Marines are sent

People

1848
Marx and
Engels
write the
*Communist
Manifesto*

1852
Otis
invents
the first
elevator
with a
safety
brake

1856
Bessemer
announces his
process for
making high-
quality, low-cost
steel. When
combined with
the Otis elevator,
this makes
possible
the modern
skyscraper

1876
Bell
patents
the
telephone

1885
Daimler
and Benz
develop the
forerunners
to the gasoline
engines
used today

1914
World War I
follows the
assassination
of Austrian
Archduke
Ferdinand

1928
Fleming
discovers
penicillin

1949
Communist
victory in
China and
establishment
of the People's
Republic under
Mao Zedong

1972
Watergate
break-in

1981
Scientists
identify
AIDS
(acquired
immune
deficiency
syndrome)

1982
First commercial
product of genetic
engineering:
human insulin
from bacteria

Reprinted from TIME Magazine, 1992
Designed and drawn by Nigel Holmes

Research by Deborah Wells and Ratu Kamlani

TIME | PO Box 1000
Mount Kisco
NY 10549
800-882-0852

The Body Shop

DESIGN: Robert Lockwood, USA

PUBLISHER/CLIENT: Associated Press

DATE OF 1ST PUBLICATION/USE: February 1992

DESIGN RATIONALE: An informative graphic package done as a full newspaper broadsheet page explaining recent developments in replacement body parts, using text, icons, illustrations and a timeline. The work is one of a series of graphic reports delivered by the Associated Press. This page put the topic of replacement body parts in the context of history and recent discoveries. It explained the availability, cost, durability and risk involved in common operations. It was prepared and delivered ready for camera to AP's members' Macintosh computers using QuarkXPress 3.1.

CREDITS: Art director, John Monahan, Associated Press; illustrator, Steve McCracken; writer, Daniel Q. Haney, Associated Press.

Special report Newspaper's nameplate

The Body Shop

Ear implants
Cochlear implants help the deaf to hear. Developed in the early 1970s, they are widely used for profoundly deaf adults. Routine use in children was approved in 1990. The device cannot restore normal hearing but allows users to understand some words without lipreading and makes lipreading much easier. Users hear noise that's different from normal speech, but with training can interpret the noise. About 1,000 implanted annually.
AVAILABILITY: Device from one company on the market. Another may be approved this year. Implants done at major medical centers.
COST: $14,000 to $15,000 for the device. With surgery and training, total is $25,000 to $35,000.
DURABILITY: Failure rate low, probably under 5 percent. Should last indefinitely.
RISK: Slight chance of paralysis of facial nerves and infection.

Lenses
Surgeons remove clouded eye lenses and replace them with permanent implants. Since the first operation in 1945, it has become standard treatment for cataracts. Vision is often good, though glasses may be necessary. New cutting and polishing techniques have vastly improved lens quality. About 1.5 million operations done yearly.
AVAILABILITY: Operation performed at virtually all hospitals and surgical outpatient centers.
COST: $90 to $200 for each lens. Total procedure, $4,500 to $6,000.
DURABILITY: Lenses should last a lifetime.
RISK: Lens becomes dislocated in less than 1 percent of cases. Inflammation rare.

Hips
Doctors replace damaged or arthritic hip joints with synthetic ones. Operation dramatically relieves pain. New ball and sockets are made from polyethylene, titanium, ceramics, chrome and cobalt. Cement usually used to anchor the new joint in place. Patients walk a few days after the surgery. About 150,000 done annually.
AVAILABILITY: Operation routine at most large and medium hospitals.
COST: $800 to $3,000 for new joint. Total cost, $25,000 to $30,000.
DURABILITY: About 1 percent to 2 percent fail annually. Loosening is biggest problem. Polyethylene socket lining may wear out and need replacement.
RISK: Dislocation possible during initial healing. Breakdown of cement and polyethylene can cause bone-damaging inflammation.

Heart valves
Damaged heart valves are too narrow or fail to shut completely. Replacing them can save lives and relieve severe symptoms, such as constant fatigue. Mechanical valves are made from metal and plastic; recycled valves come from pigs or corpses. First operation done in 1960. About 50,000 performed yearly.
AVAILABILITY: Major hospitals with heart surgery programs.
COST: $4,000 to $4,800 per valve, $25,000 to $30,000 in all.
DURABILITY: Bjork-Shiley Convexo-Concave valve recalled because it might break. Other mechanical valves highly reliable.
RISK: Valve failure can cause death. Mechanical valves increase risk of clots. Blood-

Breast implants
Breast implants are used to enlarge breasts or for repair after cancer surgery. Operation has been done since 1960s. Implants filled with silicone gel most common, but use suspended because of safety questions. Implants filled with salt water still available and considered safe. About 125,000 women got breast implants last year, 8 percent of them receiving saline implants.
AVAILABILITY: Salt-water implants widely used. Operation done in large and medium hospitals and out-patient surgical centers.
COST: Salt-water implants cost about $500 a pair. Total cost, $4,500 to $7,500.
DURABILITY: Accidents, puncture wounds and ordinary wear can break implant, letting water drain out. Happens in 1 percent to 3 percent of recipients.
RISK: Infection, bleeding and scarring possible. Sometimes breast grows hard around implant.

Knees
Most common joint replacement operation. Relieves pain, usually resulting from arthritis. Doctors replace the damaged ends of the bones that meet at the knee, as well as underside of the kneecap. Like other joint replacements, operation should be performed by surgeons who do at least 25 to 50 annually. About 160,000 done yearly.
AVAILABILITY: Operation routine at most large and medium hospitals.
COST: $2,300 to $2,500 for new knee. Total cost, $28,000 to $30,000.
DURABILITY: Loosening most common problem. One percent or less fail each year.
RISK: Slight risk of infection or blood clots. Disintegration of cement and polyethylene can cause inflammation, eroding bone.

Illustrations by Steve McCracken

Timeline

FIRST USE OF EXTERNAL ARTIFICIAL KIDNEY — FIRST SUCCESSFUL KNEE REPLACEMENT — FIRST TOTAL HIP REPLACEMENT — FIRST COCHLEAR EAR TRANSPLANT — BARNEY CLARK RECEIVES JARVIK-7 ARTIFICIAL HEART

| 1945 | 1950 | 1955 | 1960 | 1965 | 1970 | 1975 | 1980 | 1985 | 1990 |

FIRST LENS REPLACEMENT FOR CATARACTS — FIRST HEART VALVE REPLACEMENT — FIRST HUMAN TEST OF EXTERNAL ARTIFICIAL PANCREAS

A buyer's guide to new parts

To ease pain, replace what wears out, science designs new body parts

By DANIEL Q. HANEY
Associated Press Writer

Once, we made do with our original equipment. Eyes dimmed. Knees stiffened. Hearts gave out. And that was that.

But times change, and now when nature's own parts go bad, a fusion of technology and surgery is ready with replacements.

30 YEARS OF PROGRESS
Of course, humans are not quite like '57 Chevys: Just pop in a new carburetor and the old baby purrs again. But over 30 years, manufacturers have dramatically improved the quality and durability of an assortment of parts for worn out humans. And surgeons have grown adept at installing them.

MORE CHOICES AVAILABLE
Artificial teeth, screwed to the jaw with titanium screws, are common. So are artificial heart valves, artificial ears, new hips. More are on the

way: Synthetic livers and pancreases are in the labs. Work continues on the artificial heart.

"I can't think of a place in the body where there isn't a substitute being considered," said Robert Baier, president-elect of the Society for Biomaterials.

DRAMATIC PAIN RELIEF
Among the most impressive are new hips and knees. The originals are vulnerable to the wear of aging and the damage of arthritis. Without help, each step can be a pain. But now surgeons routinely put in new ones, more than 100,000 a year.

"It's called the most miraculous advance in the treatment of arthritis in the last 30 years. You can count on dramatic pain relief after hip or knee replacement in 95 percent of patients," said Dr. Clement Sledge of Brigham and Women's Hospital in Boston.

IMPROVEMENTS ON THE WAY
Good as they are, they could be better. New hips can come loose as the

"It's called the most miraculous advance in the treatment of arthritis in the last 30 years. You can count on dramatic pain relief after hip or knee replacement in 95 percent of patients."
Dr. Clement Sledge

cement that holds them in place eventually gives way. On the horizon: hormone coatings that spur bone to grow around the new joint, holding it in place.

THE EYES HAVE IT
Even more common are new eye lenses. When cataracts cloud sight, surgeons take out the murky lens and put in a plastic one.

Thanks to exacting manufacturing techniques, the replacements are durable, stable and well tolerated. But not perfect. Wearers may still need glasses. In the works are multifocal lenses so users see well both near and afar.

MORE STUDIES NEEDED
Of course, caution is wise, for new parts can go disastrously awry. Six years ago, the Bjork-Shiley Convexo-Concave valve, implanted in 86,000 people, was recalled. It has been blamed for about 300 deaths. In January, use of silicone breast implants was stopped because of fear they could leak, causing harm.

Rio Summit

DESIGN: Robert Lockwood, USA

PUBLISHER/CLIENT: Associated Press

DATE OF 1ST PUBLICATION/USE: May 1992

DESIGN RATIONALE: An information graphic package done as a full newspaper broadsheet page explaining the 1992 Rio Summit using text, maps, a timeline, icons and charts. This page put news stories of the Rio Summit in the context of history, key issues and major problems. It was prepared and delivered ready for camera to AP's members' Macintosh computers using QuarkXPress software.

CREDITS: Art director, John Monahan, Associated Press; illustrator, Michael Leary, Robert Lockwood, Inc.; writer, Paul Raeburn, Associated Press.

Special report Newspaper's nameplate

The largest summit in history

*More than sixty heads of state will converge on **Rio de Janeiro** to discuss the most important global issue of the 21st century:* **The Environment**

Dateline ENVIRONMENT

1970
UNITED STATES. *First **Earth Day** celebrated. **U.S. Environmental Protection Agency** established. U.S. phases out DDT. Oregon passes first **bottle-recycling bill.** STOCKHOLM, SWEDEN. First U.N. conference on the environment.*

1973
UNITED NATIONS *Convention on **International Trade in Endangered Species** adopted. U.S. passes **Endangered Species Act.** Arab oil embargo.*

1976
MASSACHU-SETTS. **Argo Merchant oil spill** off Mass. coast.

1978
FRANCE **Amoco Cadiz** oil spill off French coast.

EARTH SUMMIT

By PAUL RAEBURN The Associated Press

IT WILL BE THE LARGEST SUMMIT MEETING IN HISTORY. SIXTY heads of state and delegates from 160 nations will converge in Rio de Janeiro in June for a landmark conference to set the world's agenda for the next century.

The United Nations Conference on Environment and Development, otherwise known as the Earth Summit, marks a historic shift in international relations. East-West tensions have relaxed, and the threat of nuclear war has receded. But a new issue has arisen: the growing disparity between rich and poor.

Most of the world's wealth is in the industrialized countries of the Northern Hemisphere. Poverty, hunger and overpopulation shackle the poor countries of the South. East-West tensions have given way to North-South debate.

Much of the tension revolves around the twin issues of development and the environment. In December 1989, the United Nations began planning the Earth Summit to address these problems. The summit comes 20 years after the Stockholm Conference on the Human Environment, which established the United Nations Environment Program. Since then, the U.N. Environment Program has coordinated the negotiation of treaties to control hazardous waste exports, ocean dumping and trade in endangered species.

It also helped nations agree on a convention to reduce damage to the ozone layer, an agreement that is serving as a model for the agreement to be negotiated at the Earth Summit.

Foremost among the Earth Summit treaties is an agreement to try to limit the greenhouse gases that can lead to global warming. Delegates have completed work on a convention that asks nations to assess and report on their greenhouse gas emissions with the aim of reducing them to 1990 levels by the year 2000.

Delegates will also address difficult issues on the preservation of species diversity, the transfer of environmentally benign technology to developing countries and on the protection of the world's remaining forests.

Many environmentalists, diplomats and world leaders say the time to act is now. In a few decades, there will be few forests left to protect, and the oceans and atmosphere could be damaged beyond recovery.

"Breakdown at Rio will have a tremendous negative impact," says Maurice Strong, the secretary general of the Earth Summit. "The consequences will be very severe. And when will we be able to pick up the pieces again?"

1985
UNITED STATES AND GREAT BRITAIN *Live Aid concert raises $83 million for **African famine victims.***

1986
U.S.S.R. *Chernobyl nuclear power plant accident **kills 31, injures 300.*** UNITED STATES *Dioxin found in Times Beach, Mo., leading to town's **evacuation.***

1987
UNITED STATES *Long Island **garbage barge** roams the East Coast in search of a place to dump waste.* CANADA *Montreal Protocol to **limit ozone-depleting chemicals** is signed.*

A WORLD IN DISTRESS

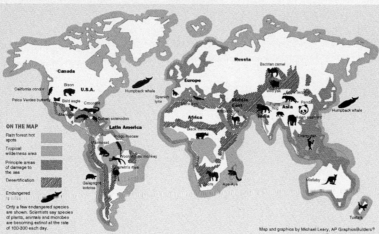

ON THE MAP

Rain forest hot spots

Tropical wilderness area

Principle areas of damage to the sea

Desertification

Endangered

Only a few endangered species are shown. Scientists say species of plants, animals and microbes are becoming extinct at the rate of 100-300 each day.

Map and graphics by Michael Leary, AP GraphicsBuilders®

1988
UNITED STATES *U.S. suffers worst drought since Dust-Bowl days, heightening fears of greenhouse effect.*

UNITED STATES *Love Canal, in upstate New York, evacuated after discovery of chemical waste dump.*

1979
UNITED STATES *Three Mile Island nuclear power plant accident. Burmah Agate oil spill, Galveston Bay, Texas.*

1984
INDIA *Deadly gas leaks from Union Carbide plant in Bhopal, India, killing 3,400.*

NEGOTIATORS AT THE EARTH SUMMIT WILL ADDRESS SEVEN CRITICAL ISSUES THAT COULD MARK A HISTORIC TURNING POINT IN INTERNATIONAL RELATIONS: **GLOBAL WARMING,** **TECHNOLOGY TRANSFER,** OCEAN POLLUTION, FOREST PROTECTION, POPULATION CONTROL, THE PRESERVATION OF SPECIES AND THE ENCOURAGEMENT OF **SUSTAINABLE DEVELOPMENT.**

GLOBAL WARMING

Before the industrial age, the atmosphere contained 575 billion metric tons of carbon in the form of carbon dioxide. Now it contains 750 billion metric tons, and the number continues to climb. Carbon dioxide traps the sun's heat, and researchers worry that this excessive build-up of the gas could radically alter Earth's climate, melting polar ice caps, flooding coastal cities and shifting the U.S. grain belt northward into Canada. Negotiators are expected to sign a treaty encouraging — but not requiring — reductions in carbon dioxide emissions.

Per Capita CO² emissions

United States	5.3
Canada	4.6
Trin. and Tobago	4.0
Brazil	3.0
Mexico	1.0
Colombia	0.5
El Salvador	0.1
Haiti	0.031

Source: Carbon Dioxide Information Analysis Center

TECHNOLOGY TRANSFER

So-called "clean" technologies for producing energy and cutting pollution are being developed in industrialized countries, but developing countries can't afford them. Negotiators will be asked to find a way to pay for the transfer of these technologies to countries that aren't able to pay for them.

OCEAN POLLUTION

Much of the damage to the oceans comes from hundreds of miles inland. Winds carry pollutants from smokestacks to the oceans. Industrial wastes dumped into rivers flow into the sea. Fertilizers, pesticides and salt are washed into the sea by rain and irrigation. The coastal regions where this pollution ends up are home to 85 percent of the world's fish. Negotiators will try to devise better ways to manage marine ecosystems.

FOREST PROTECTION

Forests absorb carbon dioxide from the atmosphere. They protect watersheds and shelter millions of plant and animal species. Yet to farmers and ranchers they are obstacles that must be burned or cleared. Negotiations for a treaty to protect forests broke down. Negotiators hope at least to produce a statement of principles on environmentally benign forest management.

POPULATION CONTROL

The population of industrialized countries has nearly stabilized. But in developing countries, population is skyrocketing. Up to 97 percent of population growth between now and 2050 will occur in developing countries. By that time, today's population of 5.48 billion will have reached 10 billion. Negotiators will try to draft measures to stabilize population.

World Population Growth
Each figure represents 1 billion people

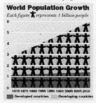

1970 1975 1980 1985 1990 1995 2000 2005 2010
Developed countries   Developing countries

PRESERVATION OF SPECIES

Scientists estimate that there are 5 million to 50 million species on Earth. They are becoming extinct at the rate of 100-300 per day, by some estimates. Negotiators have been struggling to produce a treaty to conserve biological diversity. Whether such a treaty will be concluded at the Earth Summit is uncertain.

SUSTAINABLE DEVELOPMENT

Business leaders and environmentalists are increasingly realizing that they must be allies, not adversaries. "Sustainable development" refers to economic growth that doesn't plunder the environment. Earth Summit negotiators will search for standards and strategies to promote development that meets the needs of the present without compromising the future.

1989
ALASKA. *Exxon Valdez oil **spill**, Prince William Sound, Alaska.*

1990
UNITED STATES *Clean Air Act amended.*

1991
ANTARCTICA *Nations agree to prohibit mineral exploration in Antarctica and protect native species.*

The Heart: A User's Guide No. 4

DESIGN: Robert Lockwood, USA

PUBLISHER/CLIENT: Associated Press

DATE OF 1ST PUBLICATION/USE: November 1991

DESIGN RATIONALE: An information graphic package done as a full newspaper broadsheet page explaining medical problems of the heart and solutions, using text, icons, illustrations and tables. This page was done as an explanatory graphic showing recent developments in medication, diet, exercise and tests. It was prepared and delivered ready for camera to AP's members' Macintosh computers using QuarkXPress 3.1.

CREDITS: Art director, John Monahan, Associated Press; illustrator, David Suter; writer, Daniel Q. Haney, Associated Press.

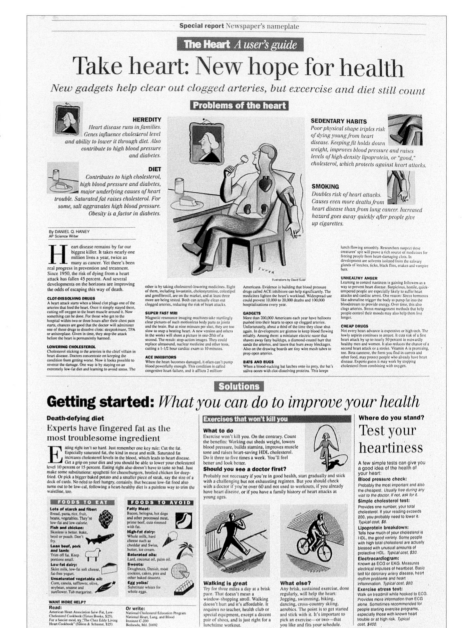

Community Hospitals Annual Report 1992

DESIGN: Michael Peters Ltd, Jackie Vicary, Tim Handsford, UK

PUBLISHER/CLIENT: Community Hospitals Group plc

DATE OF 1ST PUBLICATION/USE: December 1992

DESIGN RATIONALE: The company's financial highlights are depicted in a strong, colourful way, using graphic elements that linked into the front cover and inside spreads.

CREDITS: Art director, Tim Handsford.

	1992	1991	
	£,000	£,000	%
Turnover	42,068	35,063	+20
Operating Profit	6,837	5,698	+20
Profit Before Tax	6,752	5,814	+16.1
Profit After Tax	5,182	4,221	+22.8
Earnings Per Share	16.0p	15.6p	+2.6
Dividend Per Share	6.5p	6.0p	+8.3

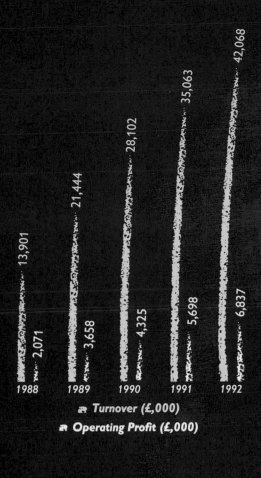

13,901   21,444   28,102   35,063   42,068

2,071   3,658   4,325   5,698   6,837

1988   1989   1990   1991   1992

▧ **Turnover (£,000)**
▧ **Operating Profit (£,000)**

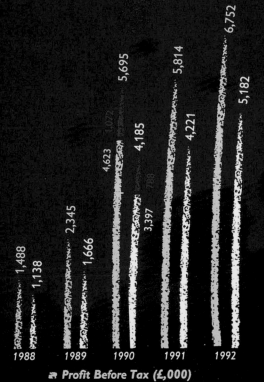

1,488   2,345   4,623   5,695   5,814   6,752

1,138   1,666   4,185   3,397   4,221   5,182

1988   1989   1990   1991   1992

▧ **Profit Before Tax (£,000)**
▧ **Profit After Tax (£,000)**

▧ *Exceptional Item*

8.3   11.1   13.4   16.5   15.6   16.0

3.0   4.5   5.2   6.0   6.5

1988   1989   1990   1991   1992

▧ **Earnings per Share (pence)**
▧ **Dividend per Share (pence)**

▧ *Exceptional Item*

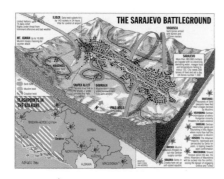

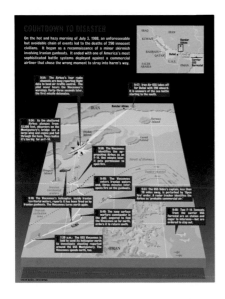

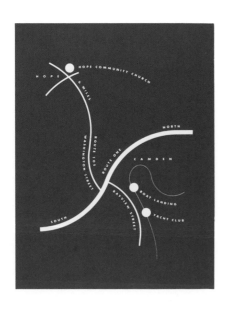

Maps

News maps, like their counterparts news diagrams, generally appear in daily newspapers and weekly magazines to help locate places and remind readers of the geography of a war region, an area of flooding or a part of a town where an event has occurred. Such maps are usually produced under the same rushed conditions as news diagrams. However, there is a significant difference between making maps — of any kind — and making charts and diagrams. The work of a mapmaker starts with a set of coastlines, boundaries and city locations that cannot be moved around for reasons of design clarity. A map does come with a set of rules, which, if broken, render it useless.

Besides, in a news map, the artist's job is to illustrate geography for the reader, and it would be nonsense not to use the conventions and shapes already known. Creativity in such maps comes from choosing the angle from which to view the scene, not in designing it from scratch. Will that view be as if from a satellite looking down at an angle, or will it be more like a page from an atlas — a plan view?

Orientation maps help you to find your way around. Strangely, this function might lead the designer to break all the rules outlined above and tailor the map to the specific requirements of the user, to the exclusion of much other detail. In the 17th century the roads on maps for coachmen were drawn as a straight line, just like the road stretching out in front of the coach and horses. It was the compass arrow that moved to show changes of direction, while the road kept relentlessly on up the narrow pages of a concertina-folded pack that was unfolded as the journey proceeded. On either side of the road were shown landmarks and intersections that would be passed along the way, but nothing out of the coachman's view was included. The map therefore served for that particular journey alone and could, of course, be used in both directions. Today's best orientation maps address the user in this efficient way. As a tourist what do you need to know? As a new arrival at an airport, how do you find your connecting flight? What attractions will you try first in a holiday theme park?

Statistical and pictorial maps combine quantities and pictures on a geographic base. Population maps, for example, show by colour the numbers of people living in given areas. Maps of wildlife in Africa make the animals visible as well as their geographical distribution.

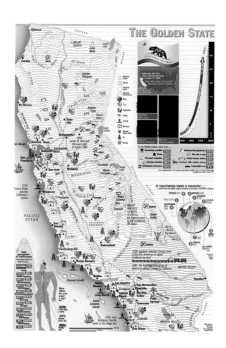

This is a branch of diagrammatic graphics that can become very busy with illustration and decoration if they are not carefully controlled: the best examples balance the two equally important forms of information into an aesthetically pleasing whole. In the case of abstract statistics applied to maps, a less pictorial approach is often the best way to do the job. If cricitisms of overdone charts in general have any validity, they probably have most when it comes to maps with charts. Getting across exactly the right amount of geographical information while not allowing it to clash with the statistics that must also be shown is not easy.

Here, all the examples skilfully combine elements of pictorial interest with strictly accurate maps.

① **Sunday, Feb 16:** Israelis launch unmanned drones carrying cameras to track Sheikh Abbas Moussawi, Hezbollah leader.

② **Sunday, Feb 16:** Five helicopter gunships attack Moussawi motorcade returning from memorial service in Jibshit. Moussawi, his wife and son are killed after a direct hit on their Mercedes.

⑦ **Friday, Feb 21:** More than 8,000 refugees flee villages for the safety of Tyre.

⑥ **Thursday, Feb 20:** Helicopter gunships strafe Kafra and Yater with missiles in search for Katyusha launchers.

③ **Wednesday, Feb 19:** Hezbollah militia fires 20 Katyusha rockets into villages in upper Galilee in revenge for Moussawi killings. Israelis begin artillery barrage.

④ **Thursday, Feb 20:** Israeli army advances into southern Lebanon with 36 Merkava and M-60 tanks.

⑤ **Thursday, Feb 20:** UN roadblock swept aside by Israeli bulldozers as troops attack Kafra and Yater. 2 Israeli soldiers killed; 3 wounded. Army kills 17. Two civilians die and 19 are injured

Tyre · Kafra · Yater · Srobbine · Rashaf · Beit

MEDITERRANEAN SEA · LEBANON · Beirut · **SHEIKH KILLED HERE** · Toufahta · Nabatiyeh · Jibshit · SYRIA · Tyre · Area of map · Israeli security zone · Haifa · ISRAEL · 0 20 miles

Assassination of Moussawi

DESIGN: Chris Sargent, UK

PUBLISHER/CLIENT: *Sunday Times*

DATE OF 1ST PUBLICATION: 23 February 1992

DESIGN RATIONALE: The graphic shows the well-planned sequence of events that led to the assassination of Moussawi.

CREDITS: Illustrator and researcher, Chris Sargent.

Countdown to Disaster

DESIGN: Dixon Rohr

PUBLISHER/CLIENT: *Newsweek*

DATE OF 1ST PUBLICATION/USE: 13 July 1992

DESIGN RATIONALE: A blow-by-blow account of the events that resulted in a US ship mistakenly shooting down an Iranian Airbus filled with civilian passengers. The map was part of a series of graphics that illustrated several fatal errors made by the US ship.

CREDITS: Art director, Patricia Bradbury; designer, Doris Downes-Jewett; writer, John Barry.

COUNTDOWN TO DISASTER

On the hot and hazy morning of July 3, 1988, an unforeseeable but avoidable chain of events led to the deaths of 290 innocent civilians. It began as a reconnaissance of a minor skirmish involving Iranian gunboats. It ended with one of America's most sophisticated battle systems deployed against a commercial airliner that chose the wrong moment to stray into harm's way.

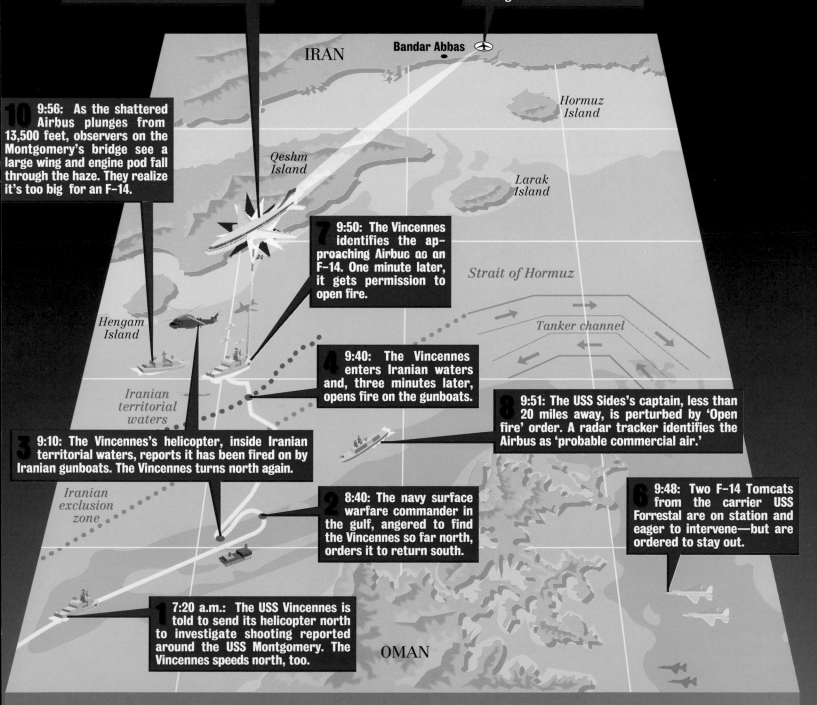

9 **9:54:** The Airbus's four radio channels are busy reporting flight data to local air-traffic control. The pilot never hears the Vincennes's warnings. Forty-three seconds later, the first missile detonates.

5 **9:47: Iran Air 655 takes off** for Dubai with 290 aboard. It is unaware of the sea battle starting to the south.

10 **9:56:** As the shattered Airbus plunges from 13,500 feet, observers on the Montgomery's bridge see a large wing and engine pod fall through the haze. They realize it's too big for an F-14.

7 **9:50:** The Vincennes identifies the approaching Airbus as an F-14. One minute later, it gets permission to open fire.

4 **9:40:** The Vincennes enters Iranian waters and, three minutes later, opens fire on the gunboats.

8 **9:51: The USS Sides's captain, less than** 20 miles away, is perturbed by 'Open fire' order. A radar tracker identifies the Airbus as 'probable commercial air.'

3 **9:10: The Vincennes's helicopter, inside Iranian** territorial waters, reports it has been fired on by Iranian gunboats. The Vincennes turns north again.

2 **8:40: The navy surface** warfare commander in the gulf, angered to find the Vincennes so far north, orders it to return south.

6 **9:48: Two F-14 Tomcats** from the carrier USS Forrestal are on station and eager to intervene—but are ordered to stay out.

1 **7:20 a.m.: The USS Vincennes is** told to send its helicopter north to investigate shooting reported around the USS Montgomery. The Vincennes speeds north, too.

DIXON ROHR—NEWSWEEK

Manhattan circa 1776

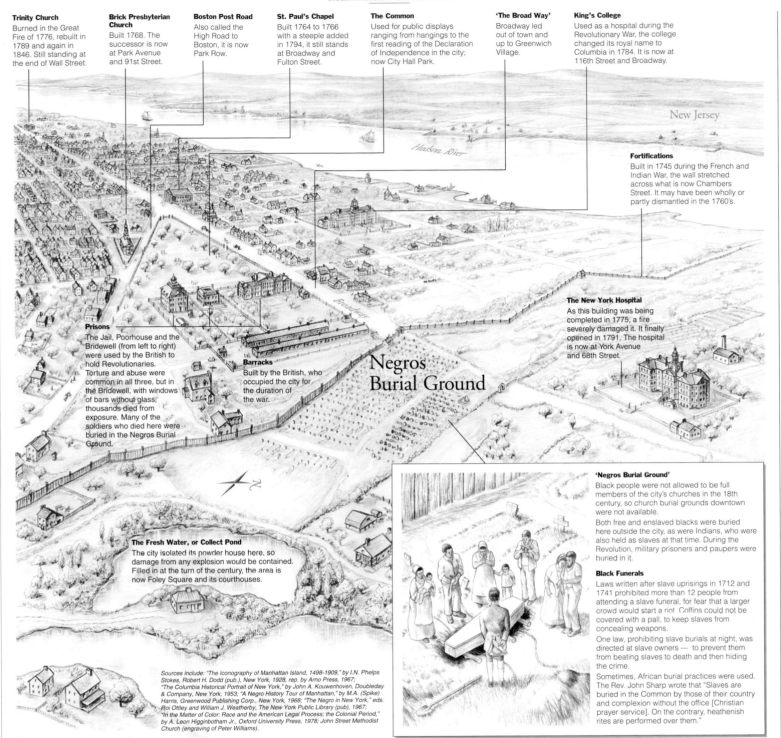

Trinity Church
Burned in the Great Fire of 1776, rebuilt in 1789 and again in 1846. Still standing at the end of Wall Street.

Brick Presbyterian Church
Built 1768. The successor is now at Park Avenue and 91st Street.

Boston Post Road
Also called the High Road to Boston, it is now Park Row.

St. Paul's Chapel
Built 1764 to 1766 with a steeple added in 1794, it still stands at Broadway and Fulton Street.

The Common
Used for public displays ranging from hangings to the first reading of the Declaration of Independence in the city; now City Hall Park.

'The Broad Way'
Broadway led out of town and up to Greenwich Village.

King's College
Used as a hospital during the Revolutionary War, the college changed its royal name to Columbia in 1784. It is now at 116th Street and Broadway.

New Jersey

Hudson River

Fortifications
Built in 1745 during the French and Indian War, the wall stretched across what is now Chambers Street. It may have been wholly or partly dismantled in the 1760's.

The New York Hospital
As this building was being completed in 1775, a fire severely damaged it. It finally opened in 1791. The hospital is now at York Avenue and 68th Street.

Prisons
The Jail, Poorhouse and the Bridewell (from left to right) were used by the British to hold Revolutionaries. Torture and abuse were common in all three, but in the Bridewell, with windows of bars without glass, thousands died from exposure. Many of the soldiers who died here were buried in the Negros Burial Ground.

Barracks
Built by the British, who occupied the city for the duration of the war.

Negros Burial Ground

The Fresh Water, or Collect Pond
The city isolated its powder house here, so damage from any explosion would be contained. Filled in at the turn of the century, the area is now Foley Square and its courthouses.

Sources include: "The Iconography of Manhattan Island, 1498-1909," by I.N. Phelps Stokes, Robert H. Dodd (pub.), New York, 1928, rep. by Arno Press, 1967; "The Columbia Historical Portrait of New York," by John A. Kouwenhoven, Doubleday & Company, New York, 1953; "A Negro History Tour of Manhattan," by M.A. (Spike) Harris, Greenwood Publishing Corp., New York, 1968; "The Negro in New York," eds. Roi Ottley and William J. Weatherby, The New York Public Library (pub), 1967; "In the Matter of Color: Race and the American Legal Process; the Colonial Period," by A. Leon Higginbotham Jr., Oxford University Press, 1978; John Street Methodist Church (engraving of Peter Williams).

Anne Cronin/The New York Times; illustrations by Hank Iken (city view) and Al Granberg (funeral)

'Negros Burial Ground'
Black people were not allowed to be full members of the city's churches in the 18th century, so church burial grounds downtown were not available.

Both free and enslaved blacks were buried here outside the city, as were Indians, who were also held as slaves at that time. During the Revolution, military prisoners and paupers were buried in it.

Black Funerals
Laws written after slave uprisings in 1712 and 1741 prohibited more than 12 people from attending a slave funeral, for fear that a larger crowd would start a riot. Coffins could not be covered with a pall, to keep slaves from concealing weapons.

One law, prohibiting slave burials at night, was directed at slave owners — to prevent them from beating slaves to death and then hiding the crime.

Sometimes, African burial practices were used. The Rev. John Sharp wrote that "Slaves are buried in the Common by those of their country and complexion without the office [Christian prayer service]. On the contrary, heathenish rites are performed over them."

The Struggle for Freedom and a Proper Burial

By ANNE CRONIN

PATRICK M'ROBERT, an Englishman touring New York City in 1774, wrote: "It rather hurts an Europian eye to see so many negro slaves upon the streets tho' they are said to deminish yearly here." M'Robert estimated the city population between 26,000 and 30,000 and thought that non-whites were about a fifth of it. Most slaves were black, some were captured Indians.

One hundred and fifty years after the Dutch brought the first slaves to New Amsterdam, abolitionists in New York City were arguing that people striving for their freedom from Great Britain should not be holding other people as slaves.

Slave uprisings in the city in 1712 and 1741 brought curfews, prohibitions on meeting and burial restrictions. As war began in 1775, racial tensions were still high.

The British, making this tension a tactic, promised freedom to any slave who served in their army. After slaves began to flee to the Redcoats in great numbers, the Revolutionaries adopted the same policy. On March 20, 1781, the New York General Assembly authorized the enlistment of slaves: "And such slave, so entered as aforesaid, who shall serve for a term of three years, or until regularly discharged, shall immediately after such service or discharge be, and is hereby declared to be a free man of this state."

One historian of that time, William Smith, wrote that blacks in Washington's army "mix, march, mess & sleep with the Whites." Smith also took note that the black soldiers complained of a "want of Pay" and many were "in Rags without Shoes & Stockings." By the war's end

Peter Williams

in 1783, 5,000 black men had served as Revolutionary soldiers.

By the time the new Federal Government conducted its first census in 1790, New York City's population was about 10 percent non-white — 7 percent slaves and 3 percent free.

One of the slaves who rose above the indignities of the time was Peter Williams. His Loyalist owner fled to Britain after the war. The Trustees of John Street Methodist Church bought Williams for $40 in 1783. He worked as the sexton, and purchased his freedom in 1785, then became a prosperous tobacconist and undertaker.

At that time, blacks were not not allowed to be full members of New York's churches. They were relegated to balconies or back pews, and had to bury their dead out of town instead of in sanctified church yards.

Frustrated, Williams and other black members of the John Street Church founded the city's first black congregation, Mother African Methodist Episcopal Zion Church, in 1796. (The congregation is now

located at 137th Street near Lenox Avenue.) Because Williams had donated the land and much of the money to build the first church, he laid the cornerstone on July 30, 1800, at Church and Leonard Streets, a year after New York State passed a law to abolish slavery.

In 1794, black New Yorkers petitioned the City Common Council for a better cemetery and proposed a plot on Chrystie Street. After the city determined that it was "in a proper Place," the Council chipped in £100 of the £450 price tag, and set up a "trust for a burying Ground for the black People."

As this new burying ground and other black churches with cemeteries began to be built, those bodies at the Negros Burial Ground who could still be identified were disinterred and moved to safer ground. But an unknown number of graves remained.

By the end of the 1700's, the city's growing population was forcing expansion uptown. The Collect Pond was filled in, the burial ground was built over and the city's street grid continued northward directly over the dead.

The Negros' Burial Ground

DESIGN: Anne Cronin, USA

PUBLISHER/CLIENT: *New York Times*

DATE OF 1ST PUBLICATION/USE: 28 February 1993

DESIGN RATIONALE: To show Manhattan at the time that blacks had to be buried "out of town". It was the first time any publication showed a diagram of the site at the time it was being used. Now this section of the city is a canyon of tall office buildings.

CREDITS: Art director, John Cayea; illustrators, Hank Iken, Al Granberg; writers, David W. Dunlap, Anne Cronin; researcher, Anne Cronin.

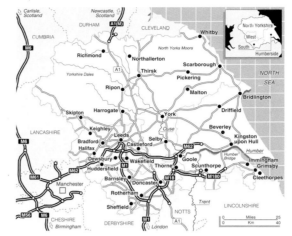

Map of Yorkshire and Humberside

DESIGN: Bob Hutchison, UK

PUBLISHER/CLIENT: *Financial Times*

DATE OF 1ST PUBLICATION/USE: July 1992

DESIGN RATIONALE: A map showing the concentration of the motorway network in the south of the Yorkshire and Humberside area. This map was achieved by showing all the main roads in Yorkshire and Humberside with emphasis on the motorway network and its link-up with the surrounding counties.

CREDITS: Art director, David Case; illustrator/researcher, Bob Hutchison.

Map of India

DESIGN: Bob Hutchison, UK

PUBLISHER/CLIENT: *Financial Times*

DATE OF 1ST PUBLICATION/USE: June 1992

DESIGN RATIONALE: A map was commissioned to provide geographical background for a number of wide-ranging articles forming the editorial content of a pull-out supplement on India. The above was achieved by showing main cities and towns, all the states, surrounding countries and a locator globe.

CREDITS: Art director, David Case; illustrator/researcher, Bob Hutchison.

A NEW ROOST

SPRUCE GOOSE
A LONG JOURNEY

It seemed like an ingenious idea during early WWII: Keep US soldiers and materiel out of the reach of marauding German submarines by flying men and supplies to Europe. But in 1942, no airplane could do the job and the metal needed to build one was in short supply.

Aviator Howard Hughes and shipbuilder Henry Kaiser were convinced they could build the mammoth transport craft from wood, and the government gave them a contract for three flying boats.

As Allied anti-submarine efforts became more successful, the government's interest in the plane waned. By 1947, with Kaiser and the original money gone, Hughes sunk $7 million of his own into the single plane, now called the H-4 Hughes Flying Boat.

**Spruce Goose creator
Howard Hughes
(1905-1976)**

Under government pressure to scrap the project, Hughes was accused of illegally profiting from his government contract. One senator called the plane "a flying lumberyard." Newspapers took up the jibe, calling it the Spruce Goose.

But Hughes pressed on. On Nov. 2, 1947, the plane was finally ready for testing.

Hughes piloted taxi tests in Long Beach Harbor. On the third test, Hughes unexpectedly took the plane aloft. It lifted about 70 feet off the water as thousands of spectators watched from shore. The 1.6-mile flight was the only one the plane would ever make although it would remain flight-ready in a humidity-controlled hangar until 1976.

Its future was in doubt for a time, but in 1980 the boat was turned over to the Aero Club of Southern California, a non-profit group that cared for the Spruce Goose until this year. The boat became a tourist attraction housed next to the Queen Mary in Long Beach.

By 1992, attraction manager Walt Disney Co. was losing money and did not renew its lease and the Aero Club was forced to look for a buyer for the plane.

Evergreen International Aviation, a company with an already impressive collection of vintage aircraft, bought the plane for an undisclosed sum and will move it next month to Oregon, where it is building a climate-controlled museum to house it.

▼ **Howard Hughes takes a last look into the cockpit of the H-4 Flying Boat prior to its first and only flight over the waters of Long Beach on Nov. 2, 1947.**

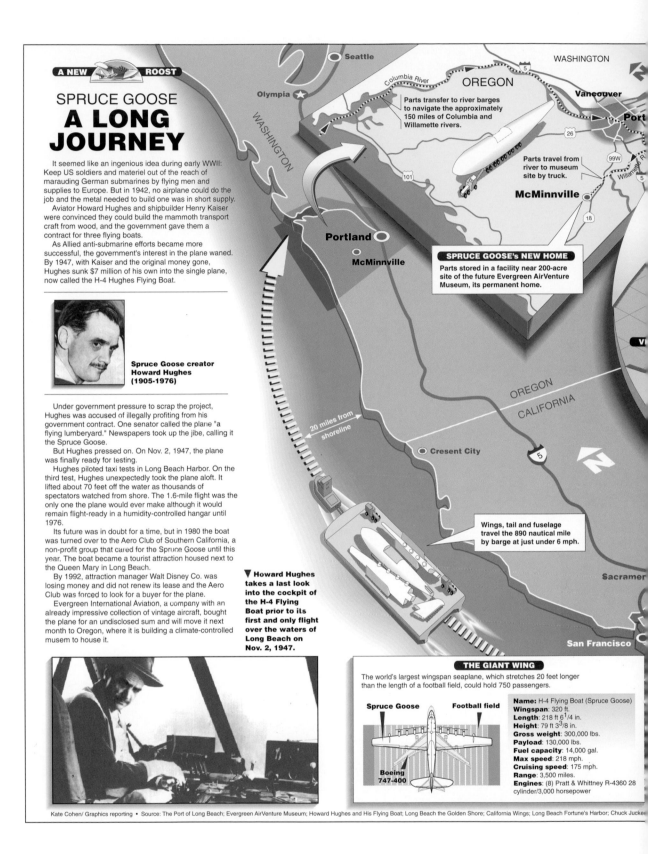

Parts transfer to river barges to navigate the approximately 150 miles of Columbia and Willamette rivers.

Parts travel from river to museum site by truck.

SPRUCE GOOSE's NEW HOME
Parts stored in a facility near 200-acre site of the future Evergreen AirVenture Museum, its permanent home.

20 miles from shoreline

Wings, tail and fuselage travel the 890 nautical mile by barge at just under 6 mph.

WASHINGTON
OREGON
Columbia River
Seattle
Olympia
Vancouver
Port
McMinnville
Portland
McMinnville
Cresent City
OREGON
CALIFORNIA
Sacramer
San Francisco

THE GIANT WING

The world's largest wingspan seaplane, which stretches 20 feet longer than the length of a football field, could hold 750 passengers.

Spruce Goose   Football field

Boeing
747-400

Name: H-4 Flying Boat (Spruce Goose)
Wingspan: 320 ft.
Length: 218 ft 6 1/4 in.
Height: 79 ft 3 3/8 in.
Gross weight: 300,000 lbs.
Payload: 130,000 lbs.
Fuel capacity: 14,000 gal.
Max speed: 218 mph.
Cruising speed: 175 mph.
Range: 3,500 miles.
Engines: (8) Pratt & Whittney R-4360 28 cylinder/3,000 horsepower

Kate Cohen/ Graphics reporting • Source: The Port of Long Beach; Evergreen AirVenture Museum; Howard Hughes and His Flying Boat; Long Beach the Golden Shore; California Wings; Long Beach Fortune's Harbor; Chuck Jucker

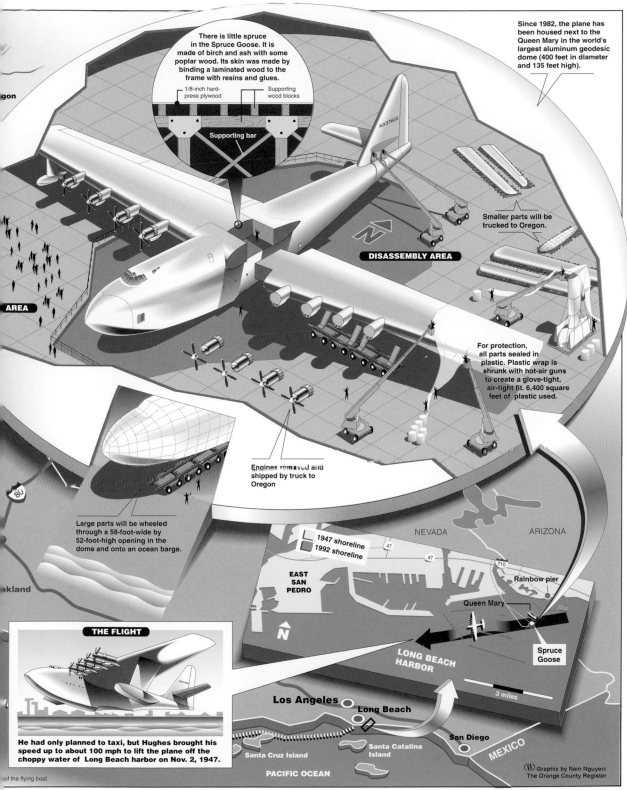

Spruce Goose – A Long Journey

DESIGN: Nam Nguyeh, USA

PUBLISHER/CLIENT: The Orange County Register

DATE OF 1ST PUBLICATION/USE: 1992

DESIGN RATIONALE: To show how a Spruce Goose is dismantled and moved to a new site.

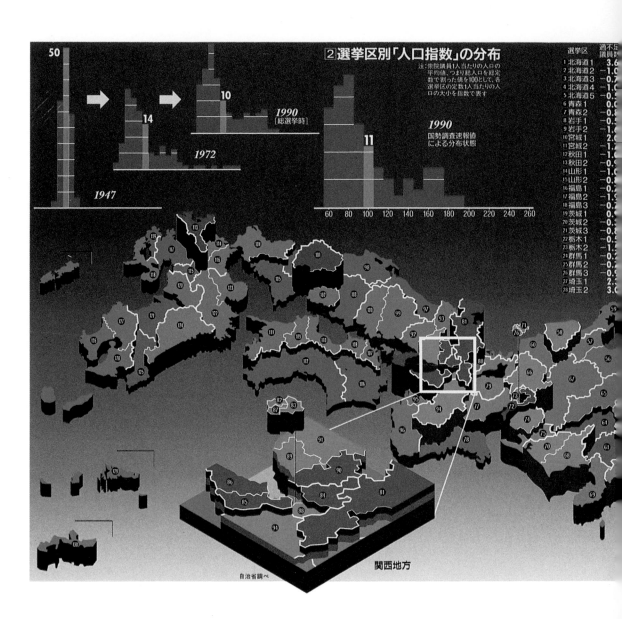

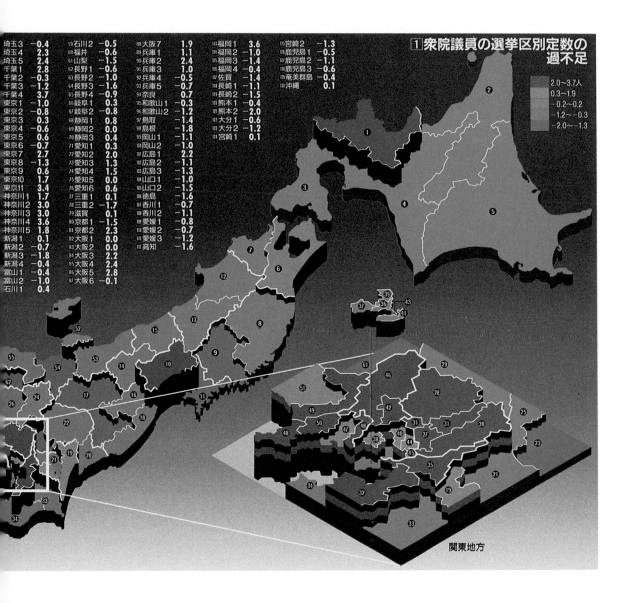

Inequality in the value of "one vote" throughout Japan

DESIGN: Nobuo Morishita and Nuboko Edotsune, Japan

PUBLISHER/CLIENT: Asahi Shimbun, *AERA* magazine

DATE OF 1ST PUBLICATION/USE: 4 June 1991

DESIGN RATIONALE: A graphic to show the allotted number of representative seats for each constituency.

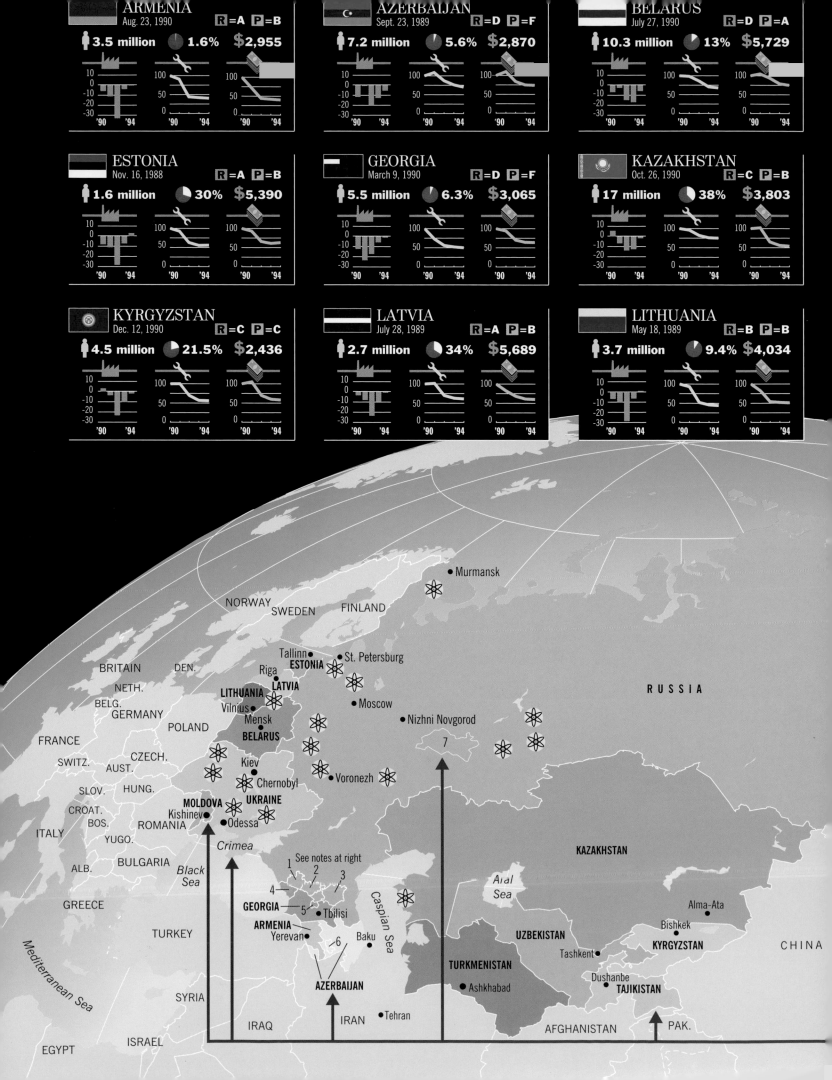

ARMENIA
Aug. 23, 1990   **R**=A **P**=B

3.5 million   1.6% $2,955

AZERBAIJAN
Sept. 23, 1989   **R**=D **P**=F

7.2 million   5.6% $2,870

BELARUS
July 27, 1990   **R**=D **P**=A

10.3 million   13% $5,729

ESTONIA
Nov. 16, 1988   **R**=A **P**=B

1.6 million   30% $5,390

GEORGIA
March 9, 1990   **R**=D **P**=F

5.5 million   6.3% $3,065

KAZAKHSTAN
Oct. 26, 1990   **R**=C **P**=B

17 million   38% $3,803

KYRGYZSTAN
Dec. 12, 1990   **R**=C **P**=C

4.5 million   21.5% $2,436

LATVIA
July 28, 1989   **R**=A **P**=B

2.7 million   34% $5,689

LITHUANIA
May 18, 1989   **R**=B **P**=B

3.7 million   9.4% $4,034

Murmansk

NORWAY   SWEDEN   FINLAND

Tallinn   St. Petersburg

BRITAIN   DEN.

Riga   ESTONIA

NETH.

LITHUANIA   LATVIA

BELG.   Moscow

GERMANY   Vilnius

RUSSIA

FRANCE   POLAND   Mensk   Nizhni Novgorod

BELARUS

SWITZ.   CZECH.

AUST.   Kiev

SLOV.   HUNG.   Chernobyl

ITALY   CROAT.   Voronezh

BOS.   MOLDOVA   UKRAINE

YUGO.   ROMANIA   Kishinev

ALB.   BULGARIA   Odessa

Black   Crimea

Sea

GREECE   See notes at right

KAZAKHSTAN

1

2

3

4

Aral

Sea

GEORGIA   5

TURKEY   Tbilisi

Alma-Ata

ARMENIA   Caspian   Bishkek

Yerevan   Baku   Sea

UZBEKISTAN   KYRGYZSTAN

6   Tashkent   CHINA

SYRIA   AZERBAIJAN   TURKMENISTAN

Dushanbe

IRAN   Tehran   Ashkhabad   TAJIKISTAN

IRAQ

AFGHANISTAN   PAK.

ISRAEL

EGYPT

Mediterranean Sea

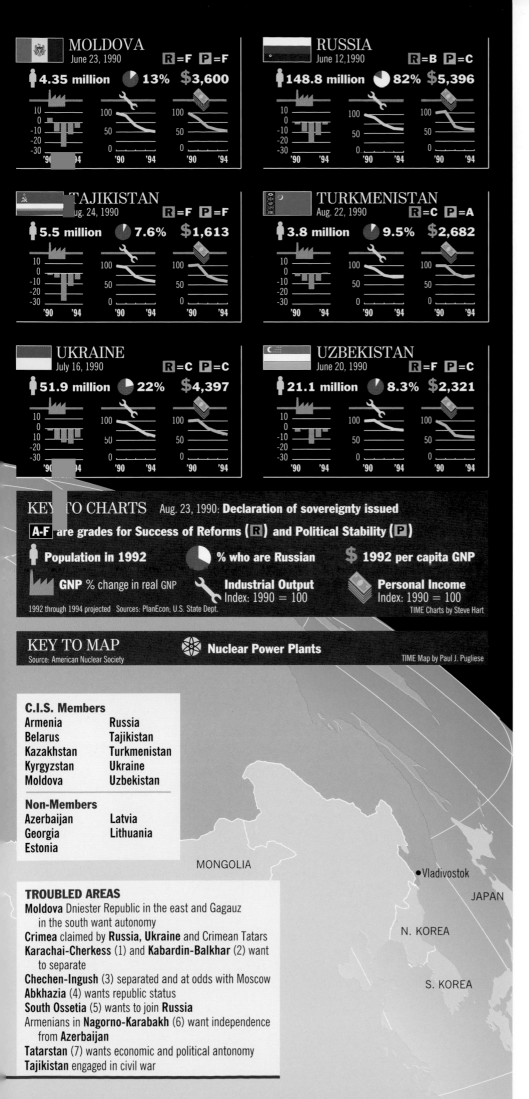

MOLDOVA
June 23, 1990 R=F P=F
4.35 million 13% $3,600

RUSSIA
June 12, 1990 R=B P=C
148.8 million 82% $5,396

TAJIKISTAN
Aug. 24, 1990 R=F P=F
5.5 million 7.6% $1,613

TURKMENISTAN
Aug. 22, 1990 R=C P=A
3.8 million 9.5% $2,682

UKRAINE
July 16, 1990 R=C P=C
51.9 million 22% $4,397

UZBEKISTAN
June 20, 1990 R=F P=C
21.1 million 8.3% $2,321

KEY TO CHARTS Aug. 23, 1990: **Declaration of sovereignty issued**

A-F are grades for Success of Reforms (**R**) and Political Stability (**P**)

Population in 1992   % who are Russian $ 1992 per capita GNP

GNP % change in real GNP   **Industrial Output** Index: 1990 = 100   **Personal Income** Index: 1990 = 100

1992 through 1994 projected   Sources: PlanEcon; U.S. State Dept.   TIME Charts by Steve Hart

KEY TO MAP
Source: American Nuclear Society   ✸ **Nuclear Power Plants**   TIME Map by Paul J. Pugliese

C.I.S. Members
Armenia	Russia
Belarus	Tajikistan
Kazakhstan	Turkmenistan
Kyrgyzstan	Ukraine
Moldova	Uzbekistan

Non-Members
Azerbaijan	Latvia
Georgia	Lithuania
Estonia	

MONGOLIA
•Vladivostok
JAPAN
N. KOREA
S. KOREA

TROUBLED AREAS
Moldova Dniester Republic in the east and Gagauz in the south want autonomy
Crimea claimed by **Russia, Ukraine** and Crimean Tatars
Karachai-Cherkess (1) and **Kabardin-Balkhar** (2) want to separate
Chechen-Ingush (3) separated and at odds with Moscow
Abkhazia (4) wants republic status
South Ossetia (5) wants to join **Russia**
Armenians in **Nagorno-Karabakh** (6) want independence from **Azerbaijan**
Tatarstan (7) wants economic and political antonomy
Tajikistan engaged in civil war

Former Soviet Union Republics

DESIGN: Steve Hart, USA

PUBLISHER/CLIENT: *Time* magazine

DATE OF 1ST PUBLICATION/USE: 7 December 1992

DESIGN RATIONALE: The economics of each republic are charted, and the map locates nuclear plants and trouble areas. The key to the charts uses icons for quick identification of the information in 15 charts.

CREDITS: Art director, Rudy Hoglund; illustrator, Steve Hart; cartographer, Paul Pugliese; researcher, Debby Wells.

Under the Gun

DESIGN: Anne Cronin, USA

PUBLISHER/CLIENT: *New York Times*

DATE OF 1ST PUBLICATION/USE: 9 August 1992

DESIGN RATIONALE: To show Sarajevo's location in the mountains of Bosnia so that readers could understand how a handful of Serbs could fire at will on the city without fear of retaliation. Flat maps could not show the impossibility of launching a counterattack up the side of a mountain.

CREDITS: Art director, John Cayea; illustrator, Al Granberg; researcher/graphics editor Anne Cronin.

The Sarajevo Battleground

DESIGN: Gary Cook, Ian Moores, UK

PUBLISHER/CLIENT: *Sunday Times*

DATE OF 1ST PUBLICATION/USE: 3 January 1993

DESIGN RATIONALE: A view of Sarajevo surrounded by Serbian forces plus a map of Balkan flashpoints. The intention was to show flashpoints in the Balkans, particularly the forces and arms build-up around Sarajevo.

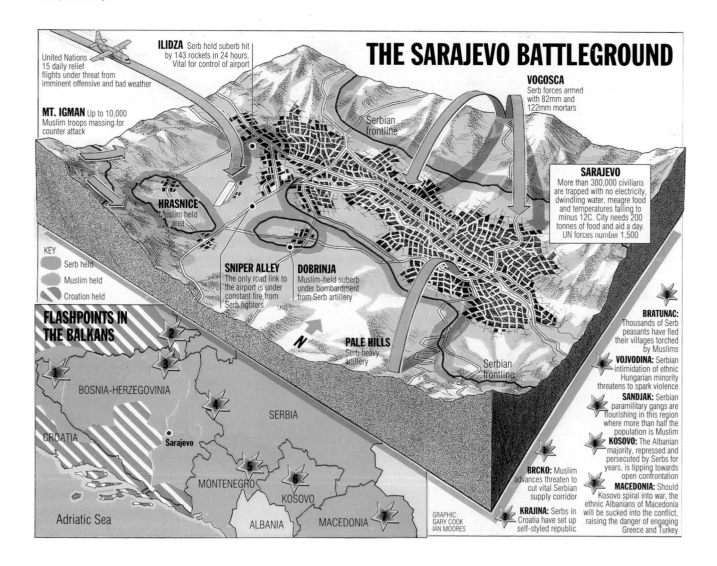

THE SARAJEVO BATTLEGROUND

ILIDZA Serb held suburb hit by 143 rockets in 24 hours. Vital for control of airport

United Nations 15 daily relief flights under threat from imminent offensive and bad weather

MT. IGMAN Up to 10,000 Muslim troops massing for counter attack

VOGOSCA Serb forces armed with 82mm and 122mm mortars

Serbian frontline

SARAJEVO More than 380,000 civilians are trapped with no electricity, dwindling water, meagre food and temperatures falling to minus 12C. City needs 200 tonnes of food and aid a day. UN forces number 1,500

HRASNICE Muslim held area

KEY
Serb held
Muslim held
Croation held

SNIPER ALLEY The only road link to the airport is under constant fire from Serb fighters

DOBRINJA Muslim-held suberb under bombardment from Serb artillery

FLASHPOINTS IN THE BALKANS

BOSNIA-HERZEGOVINIA

CROATIA

Sarajevo

SERBIA

MONTENEGRO

KOSOVO

Adriatic Sea

ALBANIA

MACEDONIA

PALE HILLS Serb heavy artillery

Serbian frontline

N

GRAPHIC: GARY COOK IAN MOORES

BRATUNAC: Thousands of Serb peasants have fled their villages torched by Muslims

VOJVODINA: Serbian intimidation of ethnic Hungarian minority threatens to spark violence

SANDJAK: Serbian paramilitary gangs are flourishing in this region where more than half the population is Muslim

KOSOVO: The Albanian majority, repressed and persecuted by Serbs for years, is tipping towards open confrontation

MACEDONIA: Should Kosovo spiral into war, the ethnic Albanians of Macedonia will be sucked into the conflict, raising the danger of engaging Greece and Turkey

BRCKO: Muslim advances threaten to cut vital Serbian supply corridor

KRAJINA: Serbs in Croatia have set up self-styled republic

Under The Gun

Bjelasnica, former Olympic ski slope

Jahorina, former Olympic ski slope

Serb guns

Bosnian-held

Serb tank, artillery and mortar forces in the mountains include 150 to 200 heavy guns.

From Split and Dubrovnik

Serb guns Trebevic Mountain

Former bobsled run

Butmir Airport

U.N. forces

Serb adquarters Pale

Bosnian attack was repelled here Wednesday

Ilidza

Dobrinja

Serb snipers

Bosnian-held

Bosna River

m Belgrade

Miljacka River,

Ruins of Olympic Hall

Serb snipers

Serb snipers

Sarajevo

Former Olympic Village

"Sniper Alley"

Kosevo Hospital

Cemetery

Ruins of Olympic Stadium

Bosnian-held

From Zagreb

Serb guns

Grandmother mourning her 2-year-old granddaughter was wounded here Tuesday

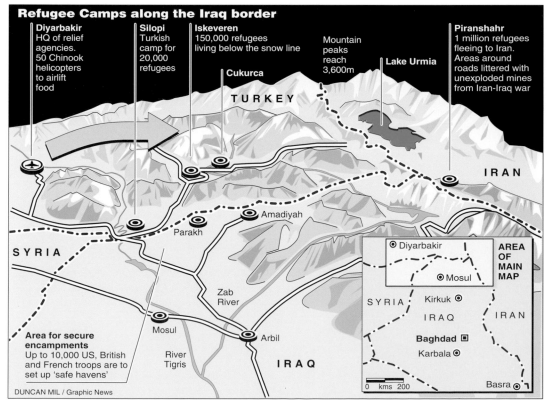

Refugee Camps along the Iraq border

Diyarbakir HQ of relief agencies. 50 Chinook helicopters to airlift food

Silopi Turkish camp for 20,000 refugees

Iskeveren 150,000 refugees living below the snow line

Cukurca

Mountain peaks reach 3,600m

Lake Urmia

Piranshahr 1 million refugees fleeing to Iran. Areas around roads littered with unexploded mines from Iran-Iraq war

TURKEY

IRAN

Amadiyah

Parakh

SYRIA

Zab River

Mosul

Arbil

Area for secure encampments Up to 10,000 US, British and French troops are to set up 'safe havens'

River Tigris

IRAQ

DUNCAN MIL / Graphic News

Inset map — AREA OF MAIN MAP

⊙ Diyarbakir

⊙ Mosul

SYRIA

Kirkuk ⊙

IRAQ

IRAN

Baghdad ▣

Karbala ⊙

Basra ⊙

0 kms 200

Refugee Camps along the Iraq border

DESIGN: Duncan Mil, UK

PUBLISHER/CLIENT: Graphic News

DATE OF 1ST PUBLICATION/USE: 17 April 1991

DESIGN RATIONALE: To illustrate Kurdish refugee camps along the Iraqi border.

CREDITS: Art director, Duncan Mil; illustrators, Duncan Mil, Russell Lewis; writer/researcher, Julie Hacking.

Rebuilding the Oakland Hills

DESIGN: Steve Kearsley, USA

PUBLISHER/CLIENT: *San Francisco Chronicle*

DATE OF 1ST PUBLICATION/USE: 13 October 1992

DESIGN RATIONALE: One year after a devastating urban wildfire that destroyed 2,500 homes in an affluent neighbourhood of Oakland, California, very few homeowners had successfully navigated through the process of negotiating settlements with their insurance companies, selecting architects and builders. The majority had not even begun the rebuilding process.

CREDITS: Map artist, Bruce Krefting; researcher, Alyx Meltzer.

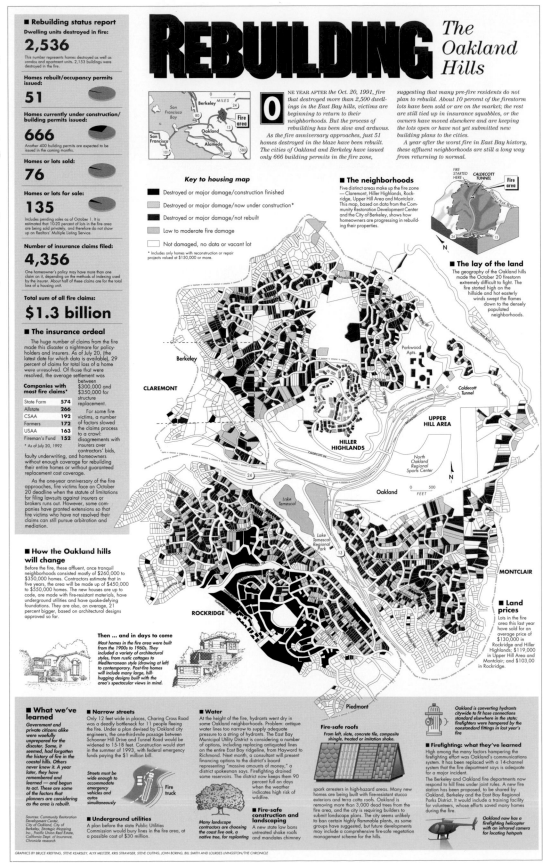

■ Rebuilding status report

Dwelling units destroyed in fire:

2,536

This number represents homes destroyed as well as condos and apartment units. 2,153 buildings were destroyed in the fire.

Homes rebuilt/occupancy permits issued:

51

Homes currently under construction/ building permits issued:

666

Another 400 building permits are expected to be issued in the coming months.

Homes or lots sold:

76

Homes or lots for sale:

135

Includes pending sales as of October 1. It is estimated that 10-20 percent of lots in the fire area are being sold privately, and therefore do not show up on Realtors' Multiple Listing Service.

Number of insurance claims filed:

4,356

One homeowner's policy may have more than one claim on it, depending on the methods of indexing used by the insurer. About half of these claims are for the total loss of a housing unit.

Total sum of all fire claims:

$1.3 billion

■ The insurance ordeal

The huge number of claims from the fire made this disaster a nightmare for policy-holders and insurers. As of July 20, (the latest date for which data is available), 29 percent of claims for total loss of a home were unresolved. Of those that were resolved, the average settlement was between $300,000 and $350,000 for structure replacement.

Companies with most fire claims*	
State Farm	574
Allstate	266
CSAA	192
Farmers	172
USAA	163
Fireman's Fund	152

* As of July 20, 1992

For some fire victims, a number of factors slowed the claims process to a crawl: disagreements with insurers over contractors' bids, faulty underwriting, and homeowners without enough coverage for rebuilding their entire homes or without guaranteed replacement cost coverage.

As the one-year anniversary of the fire approaches, fire victims face an October 20 deadline when the statute of limitations for filing lawsuits against insurers or brokers runs out. However, some companies have granted extensions so that fire victims who have not resolved their claims can still pursue arbitration and mediation.

■ How the Oakland hills will change

Before the fire, these affluent, once tranquil neighborhoods consisted mostly of $260,000 to $350,000 homes. Contractors estimate that in five years, the area will be made up of $450,000 to $550,000 homes. The new houses are up to code, and made with fire-resistant materials, have underground utilities and have quake-defying foundations. They are also, on average, 21 percent bigger, based on architectural designs approved so far.

Then ... and in days to come

Most homes in the fire area were built from the 1900s to 1960s. They included a variety of architectural styles, from rustic cottages to Mediterranean style (drawing at left) to contemporary. Post-fire homes will include many large, hill-hugging designs built with the area's spectacular views in mind.

REBUILDING *The Oakland Hills*

O NE YEAR AFTER *the Oct. 20, 1991, fire that destroyed more than 2,500 dwellings in the East Bay hills, victims are beginning to return to their neighborhoods. But the process of rebuilding has been slow and arduous.*

As the fire anniversary approaches, just 51 homes destroyed in the blaze have been rebuilt. The cities of Oakland and Berkeley have issued only 666 building permits in the fire zone,

suggesting that many pre-fire residents do not plan to rebuild. About 10 percent of the firestorm lots have been sold or are on the market; the rest are still tied up in insurance squabbles, or the owners have moved elsewhere and are keeping the lots open or have not yet submitted new building plans to the cities.

A year after the worst fire in East Bay history, these affluent neighborhoods are still a long way from returning to normal.

Key to housing map

- ■ Destroyed or major damage/construction finished
- ■ Destroyed or major damage/now under construction*
- ■ Destroyed or major damage/not rebuilt
- □ Low to moderate fire damage
- □ Not damaged, no data or vacant lot

* Includes only homes with reconstruction or repair projects valued at $150,000 or more.

■ The neighborhoods

Five distinct areas make up the fire zone — Claremont, Hiller Highlands, Rockridge, Upper Hill Area and Montclair. This map, based on data from the Community Restoration Development Center and the City of Berkeley, shows how homeowners are progressing in rebuilding their properties.

■ The lay of the land

The geography of the Oakland hills made the October 20 firestorm extremely difficult to fight. The fire started high on the hillside and hot easterly winds swept the flames down to the densely populated neighborhoods.

■ Land prices

Lots in the fire area this last year have sold for an average price of $130,000 in Rockridge and Hiller Highlands; $119,000 in Upper Hill Area and Montclair; and $103,00 in Rockridge.

■ What we've learned

Government and private citizens alike were woefully unprepared for the disaster. Some, it seemed, had forgotten the history of fire in the coastal hills. Others never knew it. A year later, they have remembered and learned — and begun to act. These are some of the factors that planners are considering as the area is rebuilt.

Sources: Community Restoration Development Center, City of Oakland, City of Berkeley, Strategic Mapping Inc., Pacific Union Real Estate, California Dept. of Insurance, Chronicle research

■ Narrow streets

Only 12 feet wide in places, Charing Cross Road was a deadly bottleneck for 11 people fleeing the fire. Under a plan devised by Oakland city engineers, the one-third-mile passage between Schooner Hill Drive and Tunnel Road would be widened to 15-18 feet. Construction would start in the summer of 1993, with federal emergency funds paying the $1 million bill.

Streets must be wide enough to accommodate emergency vehicles and autos simultaneously

■ Underground utilities

A plan before the state Public Utilities Commission would bury lines in the fire area, at a possible cost of $30 million.

■ Water

At the height of the fire, hydrants went dry in some Oakland neighborhoods. Problem: antique water lines too narrow to supply adequate pressure to a string of hydrants. The East Bay Municipal Utility District is considering a number of options, including replacing antiquated lines on the entire East Bay ridgeline, from Hayward to Richmond. Next month, a consultant will present financing options to the district's board representing "massive amounts of money," a district spokesman says. Firefighting drained some reservoirs. The district now keeps them 90 percent full on days when the weather indicates high risk of wildfire.

Many landscape contractors are choosing the coast live oak, a native tree, for replanting

■ Fire-safe construction and landscaping

A new state law bans untreated shake roofs and mandates chimney spark arresters in high-hazard areas. Many new homes are being built with fire-resistant stucco exteriors and terra cotta roofs. Oakland is removing 3,000 dead trees from the fire area, and the city is requiring builders to submit landscape plans. The city seems unlikely to ban certain highly flammable plants, as some groups have suggested, but future developments may include a comprehensive fire-safe vegetation management scheme for the hills.

Fire-safe roofs

From left, slate, concrete tile, composite shingle, treated or imitation shake.

Oakland is converting hydrants citywide to fit hose connections standard elsewhere in the state; firefighters were hampered by the nonstandard fittings in last year's fire

■ Firefighting: what they've learned

High among the many factors hampering the firefighting effort was Oakland's communications system. It has been replaced with a 14-channel system that the fire department says is adequate for a major incident.

The Berkeley and Oakland fire departments now respond to hill fires under joint rules. A new fire station has been proposed, to be shared by Oakland, Berkeley and the East Bay Regional Parks District. It would include a training facility for volunteers, whose efforts saved many homes during the fire.

Oakland now has a firefighting helicopter with an infrared camera for locating hotspots

GRAPHICS BY BRUCE KREFTING, STEVE KEARSLEY, ALYX MELTZER, KRIS STRAWSER, STEVE OUTING, JOHN BORING, BILL SMITH AND LOURDES LIVINGSTON/THE CHRONICLE

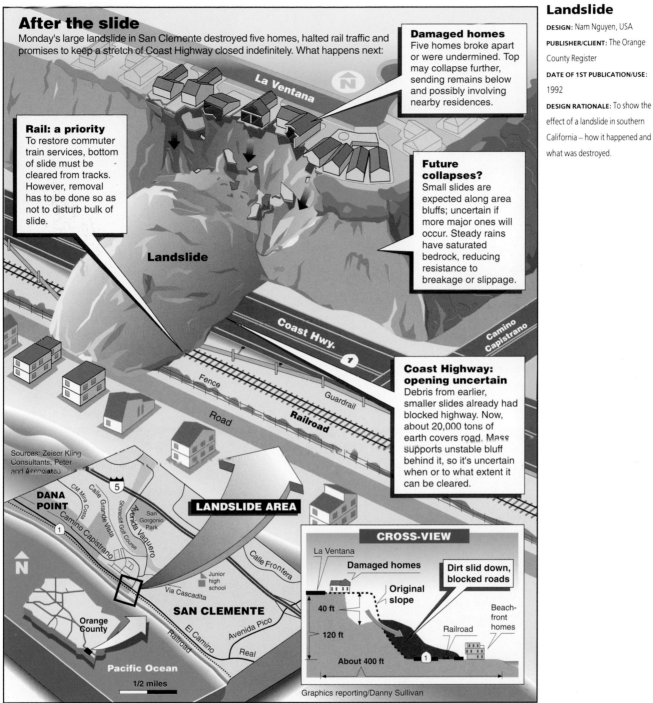

After the slide

Monday's large landslide in San Clemente destroyed five homes, halted rail traffic and promises to keep a stretch of Coast Highway closed indefinitely. What happens next:

Damaged homes
Five homes broke apart or were undermined. Top may collapse further, sending remains below and possibly involving nearby residences.

Rail: a priority
To restore commuter train services, bottom of slide must be cleared from tracks. However, removal has to be done so as not to disturb bulk of slide.

Future collapses?
Small slides are expected along area bluffs; uncertain if more major ones will occur. Steady rains have saturated bedrock, reducing resistance to breakage or slippage.

Coast Highway: opening uncertain
Debris from earlier, smaller slides already had blocked highway. Now, about 20,000 tons of earth covers road. Mass supports unstable bluff behind it, so it's uncertain when or to what extent it can be cleared.

La Ventana

Landslide

Coast Hwy.

Camino Capistrano

Fence
Guardrail
Road
Railroad

Sources: Zeiser Kling Consultants; Peter and Associates

DANA POINT
CM Mira Costa
Calle Grande Vista
Shorecliff Golf Course
Avenida Vaquero
San Gorgonio Park
LANDSLIDE AREA
Calle Frontera
Junior high school
Via Cascadita
SAN CLEMENTE
El Camino Real
Avenida Pico
Orange County
Railroad
Pacific Ocean

N

1/2 miles

CROSS-VIEW
La Ventana
Damaged homes
Dirt slid down, blocked roads
Original slope
40 ft
120 ft
Beach-front homes
Railroad
About 400 ft

Graphics reporting/Danny Sullivan

Nam Nguyen/The Orange County Register

Landslide

DESIGN: Nam Nguyen, USA

PUBLISHER/CLIENT: The Orange County Register

DATE OF 1ST PUBLICATION/USE: 1992

DESIGN RATIONALE: To show the effect of a landslide in southern California – how it happened and what was destroyed.

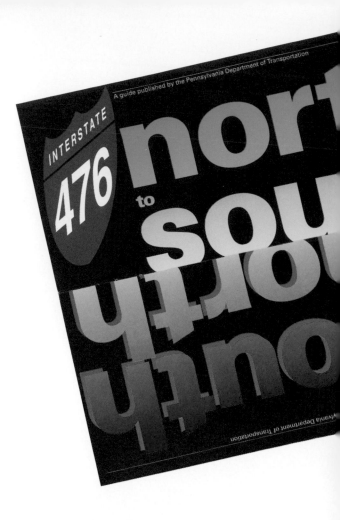

Interstate 676 Guide

DESIGN: Katz Wheeler Design, Joel Katz, USA

PUBLISHER/CLIENT: Pennsylvania Department of Transportation

DATE OF 1ST PUBLICATION/USE: 1990

DESIGN RATIONALE: A short but complex downtown interstate.
Spreading the geography makes it possible for the user to follow
and understand the on-ramps and off-ramps in the direction he
or she is travelling.

CREDIT: Art director, Joel Katz (of Paradigm: Design).

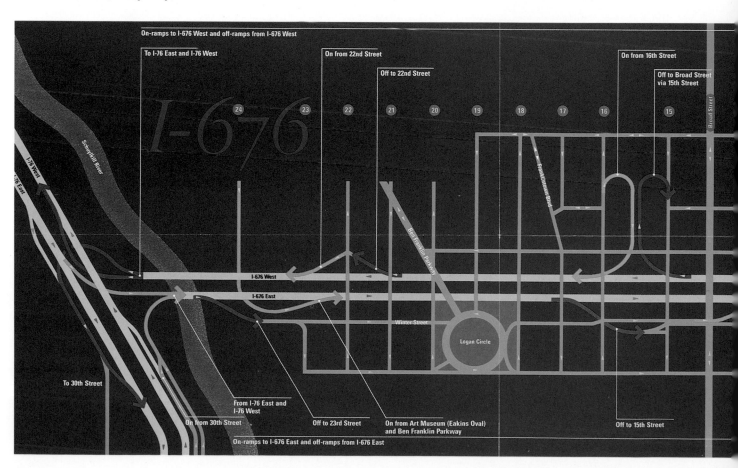

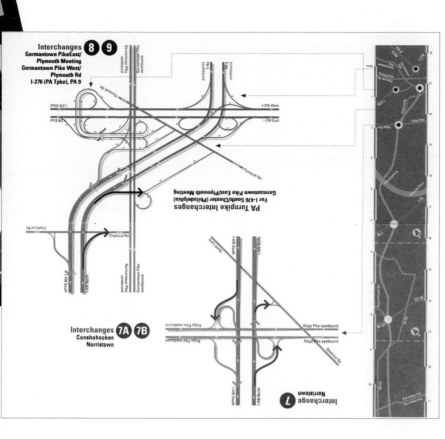

Interstate 476 Guide

DESIGN: Katz Wheeler Design, Joel Katz, USA

PUBLISHER/CLIENT: Pennsylvania Department of Transportation

DATE OF 1ST PUBLICATION/USE: 1991

DESIGN RATIONALE: A new north–south interstate with all its interchanges, opened after 30 years of planning, construction and legal challenges. The graphics fulfilled the brief by utilizing a format that permits all diagrams to be viewed both from the north and from the south. The driver can use "heads up" mapping so that right on the map represents a right turn in his or her car.

CREDIT: Art director, Joel Katz (of Paradigm: Design).

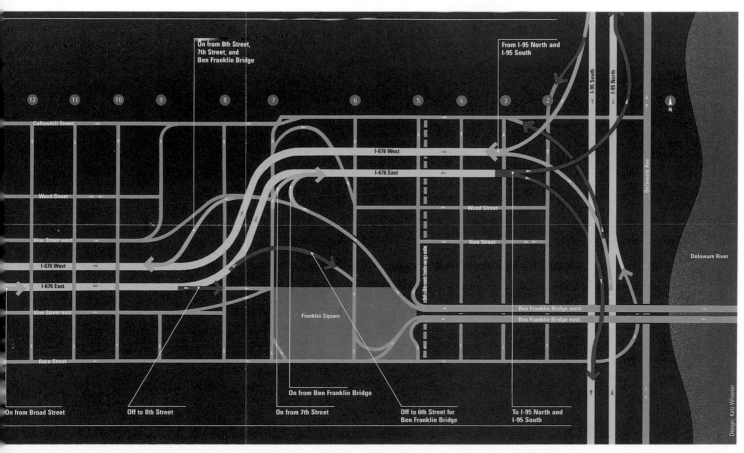

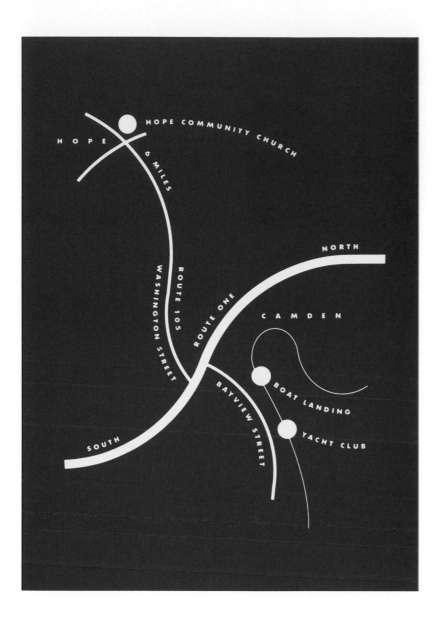

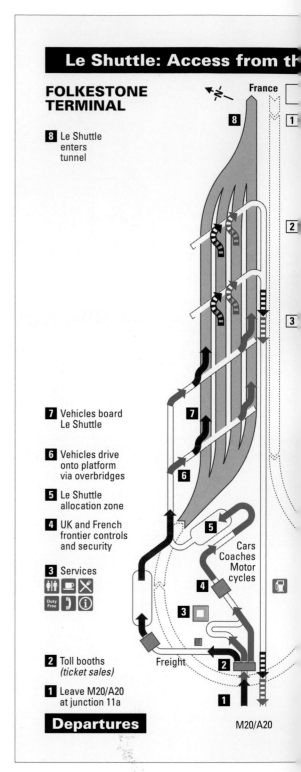

Camden Map

DESIGN: Peter Bradford, USA

PUBLISHER/CLIENT: Snyder and May

DATE OF 1ST PUBLICATION/USE: 1990

DESIGN RATIONALE: A simple, playful, freestanding map was designed to provide directions to a church wedding and reception in Camden, Maine. The occasion was the marriage of two political scientists. The map was given an Alexander Calder flavour to reflect the background of the couple – the groom was an architect and builder, and the bride managed the Isamu Noguchi Museum and was the granddaughter of Buckminster Fuller

CREDITS: Art director, Peter Bradford; illustrator, Lorraine Christiani.

Le Shuttle Terminal Maps

DESIGN: Trevor Bounford, UK

PUBLISHER/CLIENT: Eurotunnel

DATE OF 1ST PUBLICATION/USE: December 1992

DESIGN RATIONALE: A map to show routes followed by passenger vehicles on departure and arrival via the two terminals. The object was to show how simple the process is as a step-by-step procedure while indicating the geographical layout of the terminals for passenger orientation. The diagram was designed to accommodate translated labels in French, Dutch and German. Departure and arrival routes had to be differentiated and the diagram was also designed to reproduce in black and white.

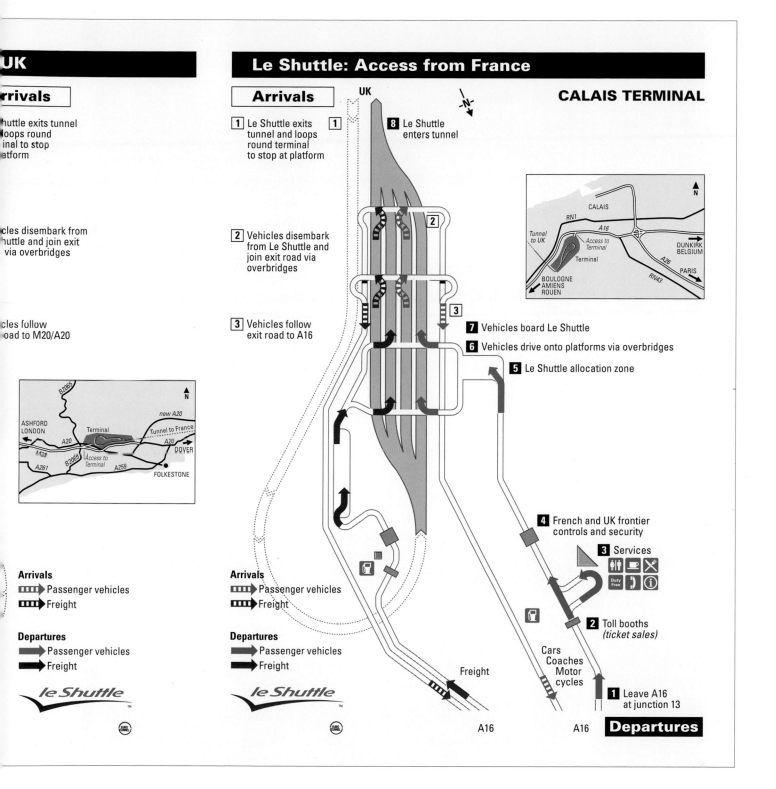

UK

rivals

huttle exits tunnel
oops round
inal to stop
atform

cles disembark from
huttle and join exit
via overbridges

cles follow
oad to M20/A20

Arrivals
▧▶ Passenger vehicles
▧▶ Freight

Departures
➤ Passenger vehicles
➤ Freight

le Shuttle™

EURO TUNNEL

Le Shuttle: Access from France

Arrivals

UK

CALAIS TERMINAL

N

1 Le Shuttle exits tunnel and loops round terminal to stop at platform [1]

8 Le Shuttle enters tunnel

2 Vehicles disembark from Le Shuttle and join exit road via overbridges [2]

3 Vehicles follow exit road to A16 [3]

7 Vehicles board Le Shuttle

6 Vehicles drive onto platforms via overbridges

5 Le Shuttle allocation zone

4 French and UK frontier controls and security

3 Services

Duty Free

2 Toll booths *(ticket sales)*

Cars
Coaches
Motor
cycles

1 Leave A16 at junction 13

Freight

A16

A16

Departures

CALAIS
RN1
A16
Tunnel to UK
Access to Terminal
Terminal
DUNKIRK BELGIUM
A26
PARIS
RN43
BOULOGNE
AMIENS
ROUEN
N

Arrivals
▧▶ Passenger vehicles
▧▶ Freight

Departures
➤ Passenger vehicles
➤ Freight

le Shuttle™

EURO TUNNEL

B2065
new A20
ASHFORD
LONDON
Terminal
Tunnel to France
A20
A20
DOVER
M20
B2068
A261
Access to Terminal
A259
FOLKESTONE
N

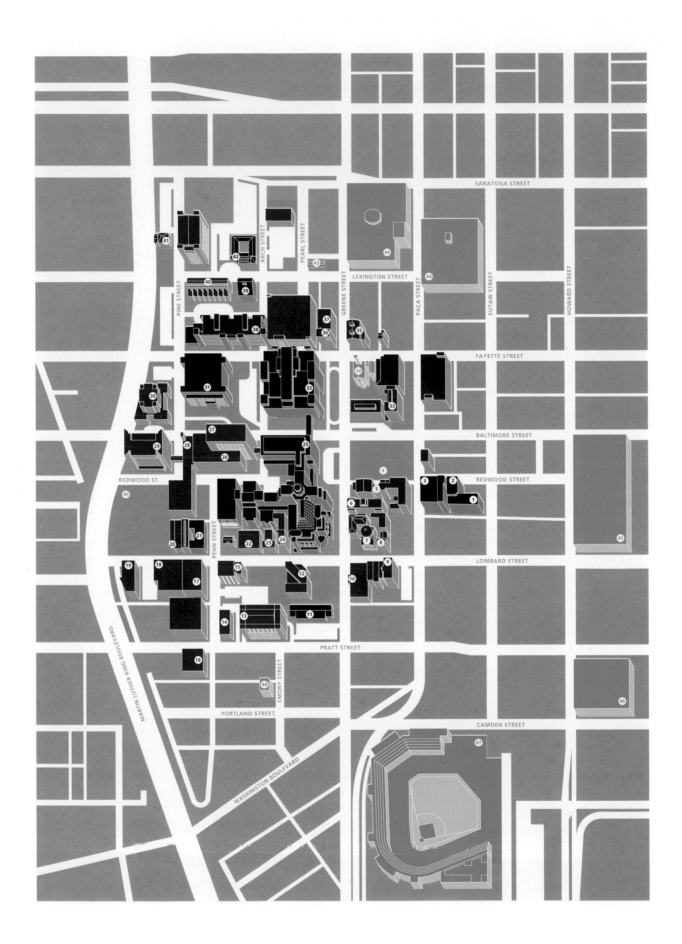

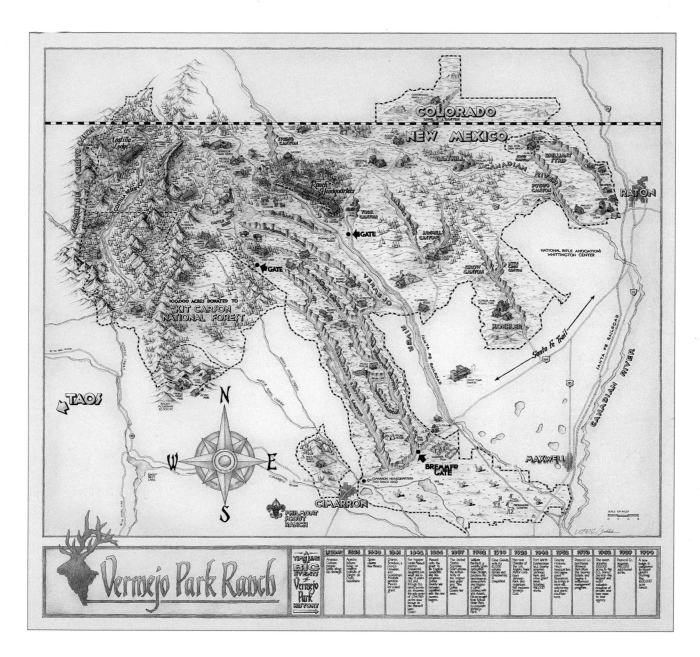

Baltimore Map

DESIGN: Julie Marable, 212 Associates

PUBLISHER/CLIENT: University of Maryland

DATE OF 1ST PUBLICATION/USE: 1993

DESIGN RATIONALE: This is a map of downtown Baltimore, highlighting the buildings of the University of Maryland. As this work was intended for use on a large enamelled sign, the structures have been rendered simply yet distinctly. Colour was used to distinguish the functions of the various buildings.

CREDITS: Art director, David Gibson, 212 Associates; illustrators, Guilbert Gates, Jared Schneidman Design.

Vermejo Park Ranch

DESIGN: Albert Lorenz, USA

PUBLISHER/CLIENT: Pennzoil Company

DATE OF 1ST PUBLICATION/USE: 1988

DESIGN RATIONALE: An accurate map showing a hunting and hiking nature reserve. The brief was to be accurate but slightly playful.

CREDITS: Art director, Dave Webster; illustrator, Albert Lorenz.

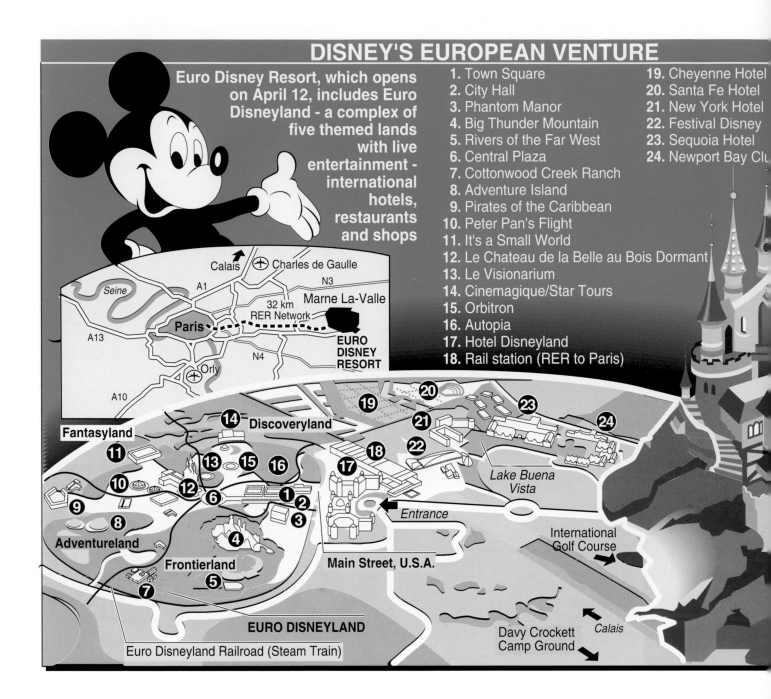

DISNEY'S EUROPEAN VENTURE

Euro Disney Resort, which opens on April 12, includes Euro Disneyland - a complex of five themed lands with live entertainment - international hotels, restaurants and shops

1. Town Square
2. City Hall
3. Phantom Manor
4. Big Thunder Mountain
5. Rivers of the Far West
6. Central Plaza
7. Cottonwood Creek Ranch
8. Adventure Island
9. Pirates of the Caribbean
10. Peter Pan's Flight
11. It's a Small World
12. Le Chateau de la Belle au Bois Dormant
13. Le Visionarium
14. Cinemagique/Star Tours
15. Orbitron
16. Autopia
17. Hotel Disneyland
18. Rail station (RER to Paris)

19. Cheyenne Hotel
20. Santa Fe Hotel
21. New York Hotel
22. Festival Disney
23. Sequoia Hotel
24. Newport Bay Clu

Calais
Charles de Gaulle
Seine
A1
N3
Marne La-Valle
32 km
RER Network
Paris
A13
EURO DISNEY RESORT
N4
Orly
A10

Fantasyland
Discoveryland
Lake Buena Vista
Entrance
International Golf Course
Adventureland
Main Street, U.S.A.
Frontierland
EURO DISNEYLAND
Euro Disneyland Railroad (Steam Train)
Davy Crockett Camp Ground
Calais

Euro Disney Resort

DESIGN: Viki Ramsay, Australia

PUBLISHER/CLIENT: Reuter News Graphics Service

DATE OF 1ST PUBLICATION/USE: 24 March 1992

DESIGN RATIONALE: Illustrations and map locating Euro-Disney and its facilities ahead of its grand opening on 12 April 1993.

CREDITS: Art director/researcher, Corrie Parsonson.

Resort value: **$U.S. 3.9 billion**
Resort area: **1,943 hectares**
Euro Disneyland: **57 hectares**
Expected number of visits
in first year: **11 million**
Staff and 'cast
members': **14,000**

⑫
Le Chateau
de la Belle au
bois Dormant

REUTER/
RAMSAY

New York City UNFOLDS®

DESIGN: Stephen VanDam, Switzerland

PUBLISHER/CLIENT: VanDam Inc., USA

DATE OF 1ST PUBLICATION/USE: 1985

DESIGN RATIONALE: VanDam's NYC UNFOLDS® presents the
essence of Manhattan in a compact, easy-to-follow and instantly
accessible format: three sectional maps to Downtown,
Midtown and Uptown unfold to 18 times their original size,
then refold themselves when the cover is closed.

CREDITS: Art director/writer, Stephen VanDam; researcher,
Nicholas Dalton.

Council Estate Signage

DESIGN: Peter Grundy, Tilly Northedge, UK

PUBLISHER/CLIENT: Hammersmith & Fulham Council

DATE OF 1ST PUBLICATION/USE: March 1993

DESIGN RATIONALE: The first map designed for the council estates of Hammersmith and Fulham. There are 30 estates in all. The brief was for an outdoor sign showing the layout of each council estate for residents and visitors alike. The sign had to be functional but friendly. The colours were set by the client in accordance with its corporate scheme.

CREDITS: Art directors and illustrators, Peter Grundy, Tilly Northedge.

Self-promotion Brochure for the Neue Bank AG

DESIGN: Fritz Gottschalk, Andreas Gossweiler, Switzerland

PUBLISHER/CLIENT: Neue Bank AG

DATE OF 1ST PUBLICATION/USE: 1992

DESIGN RATIONALE: Access map to Vaduz (base of the Neue Bank).

CREDIT: Art director, Fritz Gottschalk.

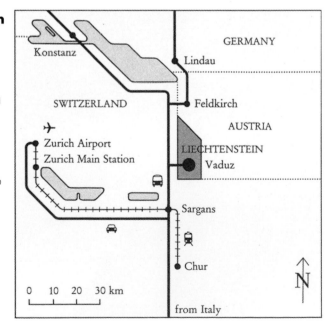

Jerusalem

DESIGN: John Grimwade, UK

PUBLISHER/CLIENT: *Condé Nast Traveler*

DATE OF 1ST PUBLICATION/USE: March 1993

DESIGN RATIONALE: A walking tour of the Old City, Jerusalem. Tightly linked to facing text, with landmarks drawn to help the reader stay on course.

CREDITS: Art director, Diana Laguardia, Christin Gangi; illustrator, John Grimwade.

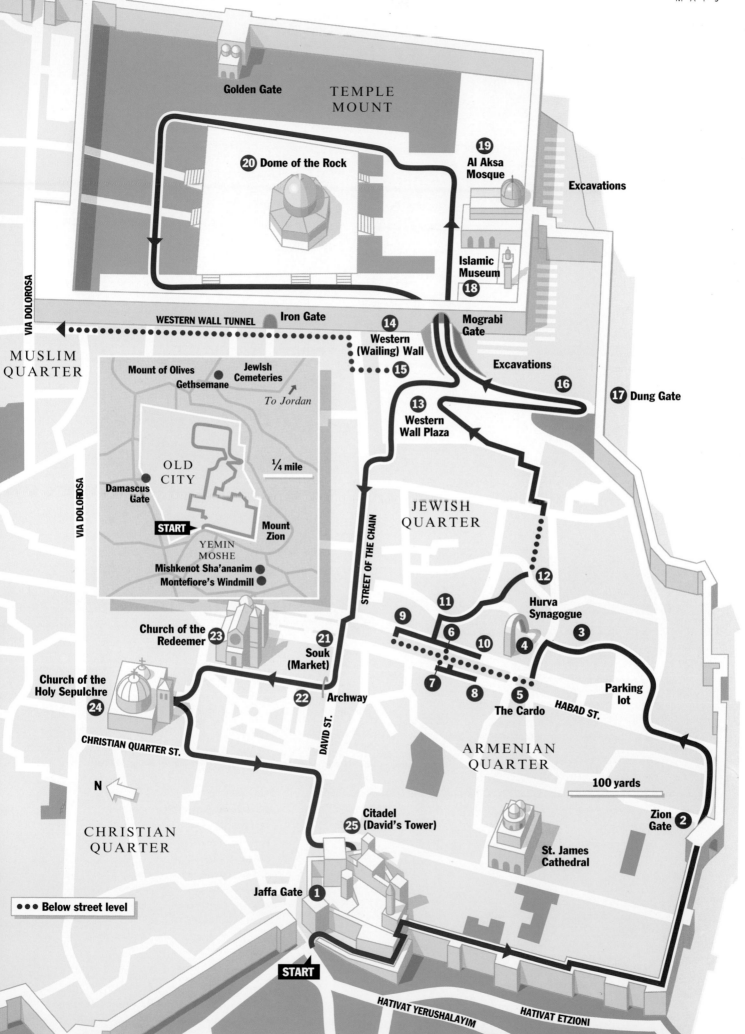

Golden Gate

TEMPLE MOUNT

20 Dome of the Rock

19 Al Aksa Mosque

Excavations

Islamic Museum

18

VIA DOLOROSA

MUSLIM QUARTER

WESTERN WALL TUNNEL   Iron Gate   Mograbi Gate

14 Western (Wailing) Wall

15

Excavations

16

17 Dung Gate

Mount of Olives   Jewish Cemeteries
Gethsemane

To Jordan

13 Western Wall Plaza

OLD CITY

¼ mile

VIA DOLOROSA

Damascus Gate

JEWISH QUARTER

START

Mount Zion

YEMIN MOSHE

Mishkenot Sha'ananim
Montefiore's Windmill

12

STREET OF THE CHAIN

11

Hurva Synagogue

9

6   **10**   **4**   **3**

Church of the Redeemer **23**

21 Souk (Market)

7   **8**   **5**   The Cardo

22 Archway

Parking lot

HABAD ST.

Church of the Holy Sepulchre **24**

CHRISTIAN QUARTER ST.

DAVID ST.

ARMENIAN QUARTER

N

100 yards

CHRISTIAN QUARTER

Citadel (David's Tower) 25

St. James Cathedral

Zion Gate **2**

Jaffa Gate **1**

••• **Below street level**

START

HATIVAT YERUSHALAYIM   HATIVAT ETZIONI

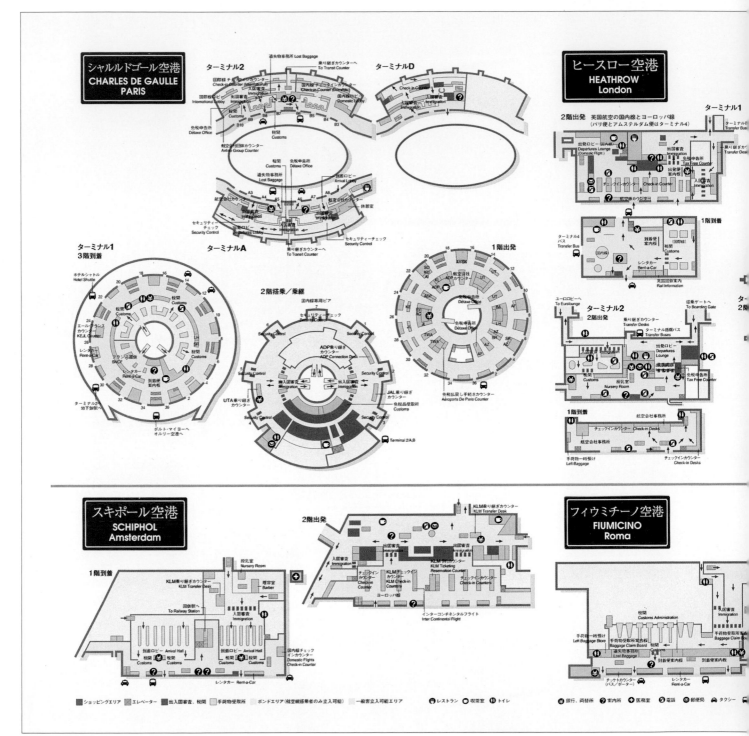

Guide Map to European Airports

DESIGN: Misako Tsunemi, Morishita Ltd, Japan

PUBLISHER/CLIENT: Pia Co. Ltd

DATE OF 1ST PUBLICATION/USE: September 1992

DESIGN RATIONALE: A guide to European airports.

CREDITS: Art director, Nobuo Morishita; illustrator, Misako Tsunemi; writer/researcher, Pia Co. Ltd.

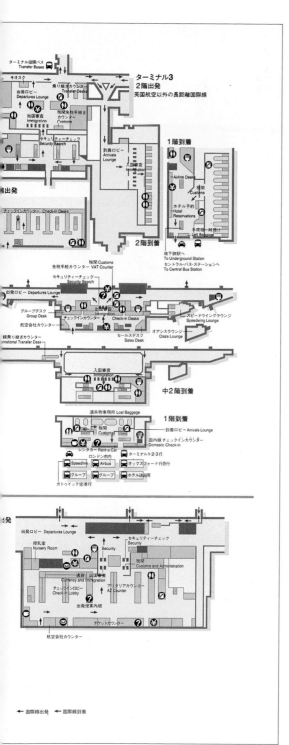

Motorola IVHS User Interface Design Project

DESIGN: Aaron Marcus and Associates, USA

PUBLISHER/CLIENT: Automative and Industrial Electronics Group, Motorola Corporation

DATE OF 1ST PUBLICATION/USE: March 1992

DESIGN RATIONALE: The 12.24 cm-diagonal LCD touch-sensitive screens of a prototype user interface design for Motorola's intelligent vehicle/highway system in-car navigation device depict maps of traffic/weather conditions, road classes, sites of interest, system status, controls and displays of route guidance information in equivalent symbol, map and text formats.

CREDIT: Principal designer, Aaron Marcus.

Figures copyright 1992 by Motorola and used with permission.

Sturgis Administration Model

DESIGN: Peter Bradford, USA

PUBLISHER/CLIENT: Educational Facilities Laboratories

DATE OF 1ST PUBLICATION/USE: 1990

DESIGN RATIONALE: In a book promoting the sharing of facilities by schools and their communities, informal "sketch diagrams" of administrative processes and specific facilities were used to leaven the information. The diagrams emphasized the flexibility and options inherent in the text recommendations.

CREDITS: Art director, Peter Bradford; illustrators, Gary Fujiwara, Peter Bradford.

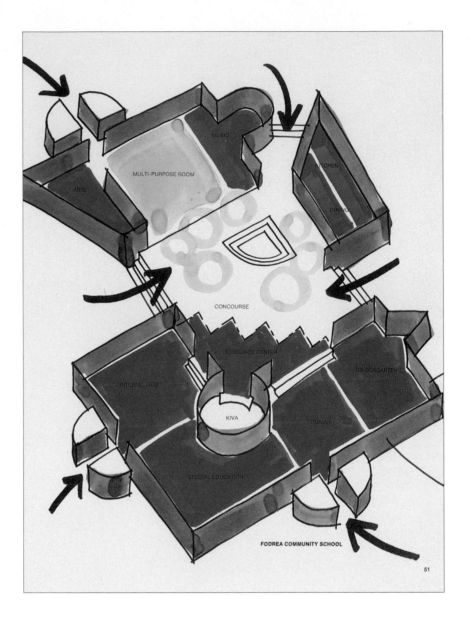

The Golden State

DESIGN: Nigel Holmes, Joe Lertola, Paul Pugliese, USA

PUBLISHER/CLIENT: *Time* magazine

DATE OF 1ST PUBLICATION/USE: 18 November 1991

DESIGN RATIONALE: To produce an illustrated map of California.

CREDIT: Debby Wells.

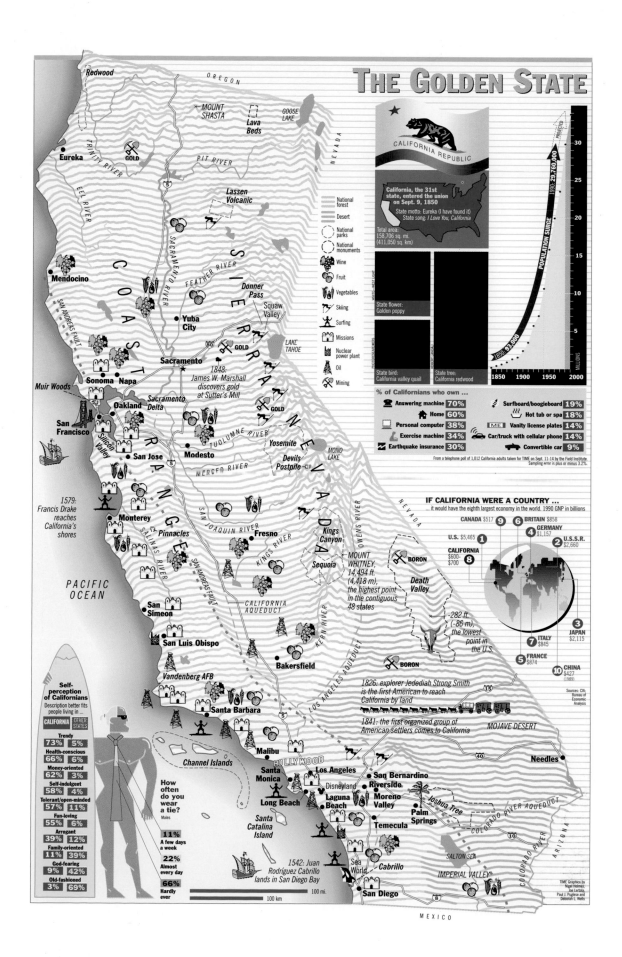

Cardiff in Europe

DESIGN: Peter Grundy, UK

PUBLISHER/CLIENT: Cardiff Bay Brochure, Forward Publishing

DATE OF 1ST PUBLICATION/USE: April 1992

DESIGN RATIONALE: The use of a modern map to show the location of Cardiff in the British Isles and its connection to other major cities in the UK and Europe.

CREDITS: Art director, William Scott, Forward Publishing; illustrator, Peter Grundy.

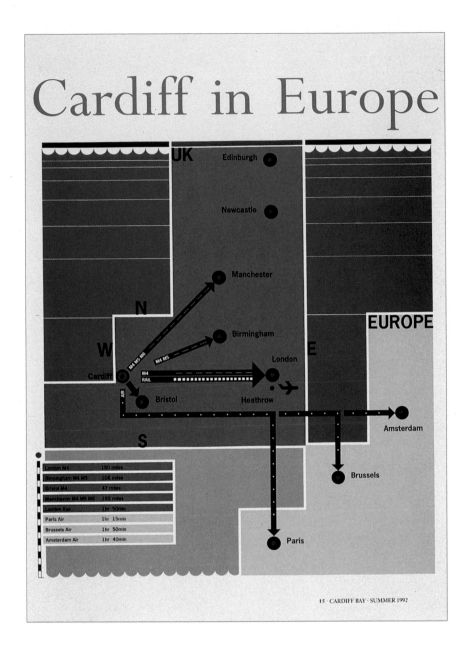

London M4	160 miles
Birmingham M4 M5	108 miles
Bristol M4	47 miles
Manchester M4 M5 M6	192 miles
London Rail	1hr 50min
Paris Air	1hr 15min
Brussels Air	1hr 50min
Amsterdam Air	1hr 40min

15 · CARDIFF BAY · SUMMER 1992

North America in the Age of Dinosaurs

PUBLISHER/CLIENT: *National Geographic* magazine

DATE OF 1ST PUBLICATION/USE: January 1993

DESIGN RATIONALE: To show the types of dinosaur which ranged across North America during the Mesozoic era, with a physical map of North America as it was during that era (showing fossil distributions).

CREDITS: Art director, Bob Pratt; illustrators, John A. Bonner, John Sibbick; researcher, Debbie Gibbons.

NORTH AMERICA
IN THE AGE OF DINOSAURS

Produced by the Cartographic Division
National Geographic Society
GILBERT M. GROSVENOR, PRESIDENT AND CHAIRMAN
NATIONAL GEOGRAPHIC MAGAZINE
WILLIAM GRAVES, EDITOR
JOHN F. SHUPE, CHIEF CARTOGRAPHER
WASHINGTON, D. C., JANUARY 1993

A fabulous array of dinosaurs ranged across North America during the Mesozoic era. Descendants of ancient reptiles, dinosaurs had evolved as continents shifted, climates changed, and plants blossomed into modern forms. Diverse in size, shape, and behavior, dinosaurs faced no animal challenge. Yet none survived an end-of-era cataclysm. Perhaps they perished after a gigantic asteroid flung enormous amounts of pulverized rock into the atmosphere. The global cooling and darkness that likely followed are prime suspects in the snuffing out of flying reptiles, scores of marine creatures, and the lost lords of earth.

THE CONTINENTS SHAPE UP

At the dawn of the dinosaur age, some 15 million years after the Mesozoic era began, continental plates were crowded together into the supercontinent Pangaea. After early dinosaurs established themselves throughout this landmass, the continents drifted apart. By 74 million years ago, the time of this map, North America was taking its present shape. Seas, at full flood, separated the North American continent into sections and split Asia from Europe.

74 Million Years Ago

DINOSAUR FOSSIL DISTRIBUTION

Late Cretaceous ●
Early Cretaceous ○
Late and middle Jurassic ◆
Early Jurassic □
Triassic △

Dot in the symbol identifies site that includes footprints; wave indicates marine-reptile fossils.

The Tanks: ANKYLOSAURS

Intimidating ankylosaurs wore bony-plated armor primarily for defense—they were peaceful plant-eaters. The heaviest browsers belonged to two families: Ankylosauridae, with heavy clubs at the end of their tails, and Nodosauridae, without. *Edmontonia*, one of the last of North America's Nodosauridae, probably hunkered down and waited for a predator to retreat. *Euoplocephalus*, the most common of North America's Ankylosauridae, could have clobbered an attacker's legs with its tail club. Bony eyelids gave extra protection. At two and a half tons, it weighed almost half as much as an African elephant.

Giants Among Giants: SAUROPODS

Enormous in its own time, the 30-ton *Alamosaurus* was a dwarf compared with earlier sauropods, which may have reached a hundred tons. A herbivore, *Alamosaurus* probably browsed through forests and moved to new feeding grounds in herds, the adults protecting the young. Its sheer mass must have deterred most predators, but it could also lash out with its long tail or slash out with the large curved claw on each elephantine foot. Some scientists suggest that *Alamosaurus* may have reared up and crushed attackers with its massive legs.

Duckbills and Boneheads: HADROSAURS AND PACHYCEPHALOSAURS

Hoots, honks, and bellows of the bipedal hadrosaurs may have rung across lowland plains and meandering rivers like the sounds of a noisy zoo. The hollow crests of *Parasaurolophus*, *Lambeosaurus*, and *Corythosaurus* probably resonated their calls. Though otherwise similar to these animals, *Saurolophus* had a solid crest, and *Edmontosaurus* none at all.

Crests and calls could have been mating displays. After mating, females likely nested in colonies and tended their broods after hatching.

Hadrosaurs cropped twigs, pine needles, leaves, and seeds with a wide toothless beak, which has given them the nickname "duckbills." Banks of as many as 2,000 rasping teeth chewed thoroughly.

Another group of herding herbivores, pachycephalosaurs such as *Stygimoloch* and *Pachycephalosaurus*, roamed upland areas. Males may have butted their thick-boned, domed heads to establish dominance and win mates. Fossilized impressions of some dinosaurs' skin reveal texture, but their coloring is always fanciful.

The Rhino Dinos: CERATOPSIANS

The plant-eating ceratopsians bristled with an armory of horns and neck shields. Some, like *Pachyrhinosaurus* and *Styracosaurus*, weighed several tons and would have been formidable foes to any predator. Males' shields may also have intimidated rivals or helped attract mates.

Undisturbed, these hoof-toed quadrupeds browsed quietly in herds on open plains, snipping bunches of tough plants with their pointed, bony beaks, then chewing with scissor-like teeth.

Unlike *Anchiceratops* and *Triceratops*, the 200-pound *Leptoceratops* (left) had no horns and almost no shield. Though it lived at the same time as its shielded relatives, its small size, partly bipedal gait, and clawed toes set it apart.

Along with hadrosaurs, the ceratopsians appear to have been the most numerous of the continent's dinosaurs in the late Cretaceous.

Leptoceratops length 6 ft

Bird Mimics: ORNITHOMIMIDS AND TROODONTIDS

Amid the other dinosaurs—the massive, the fantastically crested and horned—lived smaller, streamlined creatures reminiscent of birds: dinosaurs' only living relatives. The long-necked, slightly built, leggy *Dromiceiomimus* belongs to the Ornithomimidae (bird-mimic) family. Its running speed—some 30 miles an hour, as fast as an ostrich—and keen eyesight enabled it to escape predators and perhaps to catch such quick prey as insects, small mammals, and lizards. It also probably used its toothless beak to browse on leaves, fruits, and seeds. Its light, flexible skull and neck bones allowed it to maneuver food into its mouth with great speed and precision.

Troodon, from a different family, developed similar body lines as well as a brain whose relative size matches those of some modern birds and mammals.

This speedy predator, with opposable digits on its hands, probably hunted a variety of small animals. Many of its saw-edged teeth have been found in hadrosaur nests, suggesting that it often fed on their young.

THE ENVIRONMENT

Great sun-warmed seas covered much of the earth during the late Cretaceous, a time of mild climates and ice-free polar regions. Densely forested with sequoia-like trees, Alaska felt winter's chill but saw little frost.

The Western Interior Seaway, almost a thousand miles wide at times, flooded one-third of North America. The modern Gulf Coast was underwater, a huge bay spread over the confluence of the Ohio and Mississippi Rivers, and an arm of the sea stretched across the Hudson Bay area to the North Atlantic.

On land, flowering plants and trees like magnolias, roses, oaks, and walnuts spread among the conifers, ferns, and palmlike cycads that had dominated most of the Mesozoic. Geologic pressures were thrusting up many of the world's high mountain ranges, including the Rockies.

LIFE IN THE INLAND SEA

Leviathans as strange as the dinosaurs on land included mosasaurs (marine lizards) such as the *Tylosaurus* and *Platecarpus*. These relatives of today's monitor lizards were top predators of the inland sea. Covered with diamond-shaped scales, they undulated their slim bodies and long, flat tails to move through the water like eels. Front fins probably enabled the animals to turn quickly, and back fins acted as stabilizers. Some *Tylosaurus* fossils preserve meals being digested: fish, flightless swimming birds, and even other mosasaurs.

Mosasaurs also ate giant squid and a now extinct class of spiral-shelled mollusks called ammonites—and left bite marks still visible on fossilized remains. Fish swallowed squid whole: One eight-foot specimen ate such a large squid that it must have choked to death with its tentacles hanging out of its mouth. One of the largest fish ever, *Xiphactinus* was longer than modern swordfish. It ate a variety of other fish, and its cousin *Gillicus* usually about half its size, was apparently a favorite.

Elasmosaurus, a plesiosaur (marine reptile) with no living relatives, also preyed on fish. Moving its catlike limbs up and down to swim, it may have approached schools from below, positioning its long neck so as to attack from beneath the belly and to the rear prey—their blind spot. Like the alligator of today it swallowed stones, perhaps for the same reasons—to grind up food in a gizzard and to provide ballast.

Largest of sea turtles, the rare *Archelon* most likely swam as its living relatives do, working its paddles like birds' wings.

Still missing from the fossil record are many of the smaller animals that must have supported these large marine predators.

Flesh-eaters: TYRANNOSAURS

Striding on trunklike legs, the seven-ton *Tyrannosaurus* towered among the trees. Though smaller, its relatives *Daspletosaurus* and *Albertosaurus* looked no less savage. All had massive heads, lethal serrated teeth, arms capable of lifting hundreds of pounds, sharp claws on birdlike feet and on two-fingered hands.

Were these—the biggest of all carnivores—terrifying predators lumbering carrion feeders, or something of both? Some experts believe that *Tyrannosaurus* ambushed prey, slamming its open jaws into unprotected flesh. Others think that the hands could have held prey like a meat hook while the jaws did their deadly work. Perhaps the feet dealt crippling kicks. In shared hunting grounds *Daspletosaurus* might have stalked the horned ceratopsians, while the slighter *Albertosaurus* took off after bipedal hadrosaurs.

Carcasses of animals felled by accident or nature may have supplemented the tyrannosaurs' hunting—or made up their entire diet if they were not agile enough to bring down prey themselves.

Labeled species (map illustrations)

Pteranodon wingspan 20 ft
Anchiceratops 20 ft
Triceratops 30 ft
Pachyrhinosaurus 18 ft
Styracosaurus 18 ft
Troodon 8 ft
Dromiceiomimus 12 ft
Quetzalcoatlus wingspan 35 ft
Euoplocephalus 20 ft
Edmontonia 23 ft
Alamosaurus 69 ft
Elasmosaurus 32 ft
Platecarpus 20 ft
Tylosaurus 29 ft
Xiphactinus 16 ft
Archelon 15 ft
Ammonite 2 ft
Pachycephalosaurus 26 ft
Stygimoloch
Parasaurolophus 33 ft
Corythosaurus 33 ft
Edmontosaurus 40 ft
Tyrannosaurus 45 ft
Albertosaurus juveniles, adult length 26 ft
Daspletosaurus 28 ft

Map labels

GREENLAND
NORTH AMERICA
WESTERN INTERIOR SEAWAY
HUDSON SEAWAY
LABRADOR SEAWAY
NORTHWEST TERRITORIES
ALBERTA
SASKATCHEWAN
MANITOBA
QUEBEC
ONTARIO
NORTH DAKOTA
SOUTH DAKOTA
NEBRASKA
WISCONSIN
MICH.
IOWA
WYOMING
COLO.
KANSAS
KENTUCKY
NEW MEXICO
OKLAHOMA
TEXAS
LA.
MISS.
ALA.
GA.
FLA.
MEXICO
BELIZE
GUATEMALA
EL SALVADOR

Transverse Mercator Projection
SCALE 1:19,112,000 OR 1 INCH = 302 MILES

DOUGHNUT LONDON

Three decades that saw a city explode

A rapid shift in population has made old definitions of London redundant. The defunct Greater London Council was a belated attempt in the 1960s to catch up with the fact that the city had spilled far beyond the boundaries of what is now called inner London. But even then, the focus of the capital was already shifting further and further towards its edges, into the nebulously defined metropolitan area and beyond.

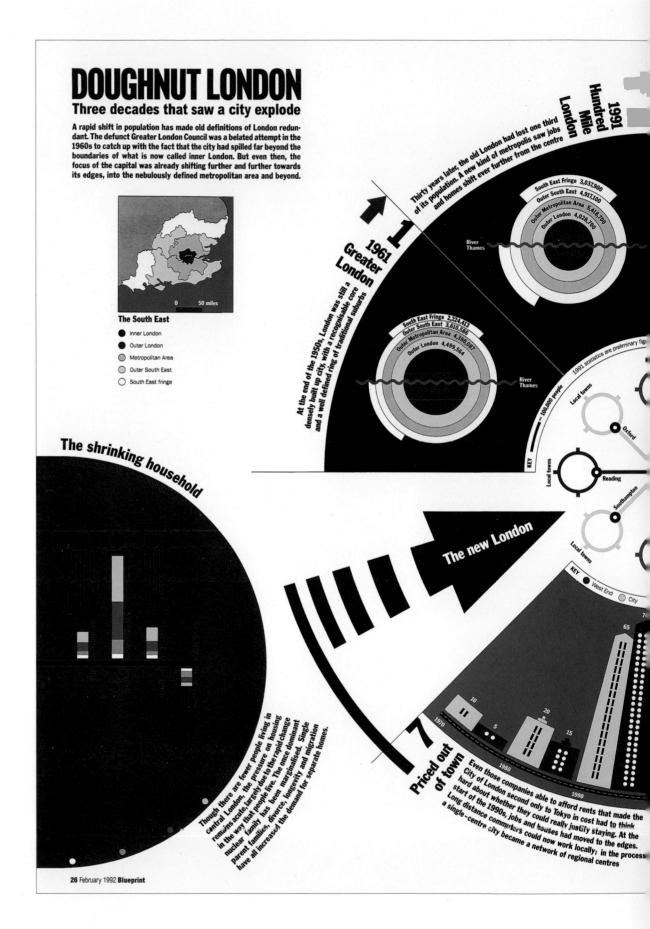

The South East

- Inner London
- Outer London
- Metropolitan Area
- Outer South East
- South East fringe

0   50 miles

1991 Hundred Mile London

1961 Greater London

Thirty years later, the old London had lost one third of its population. A new kind of metropolis saw jobs and homes shift ever further from the centre

At the end of the 1950s, London was still a densely built up city with a recognisable core and a well defined ring of traditional suburbs

South East Fringe 3,037,900
Outer South East 4,917,100
Outer Metropolitan Area 5,418,700
Outer London 4,026,700

South East Fringe 2,224,413
Outer South East 3,610,586
Outer Metropolitan Area 4,390,087
Outer London 4,499,564

River Thames

River Thames

KEY = 100,000 people

1991 statistics are preliminary figu

The shrinking household

Though there are fewer people living in central London, the pressure on housing remains acute, largely due to the rapid change in the way that people live. The once dominant nuclear families has been marginalised. Single parent families, divorce, longevity and migration have all increased the demand for separate homes.

The new London

Local towns

Local towns

Oxford

Reading

Southampton

Local towns

KEY ● West End ○ City

Priced out of town

Even those companies able to afford rents that made the City of London second only to Tokyo in cost had to think hard about whether they could really justify staying. At the start of the 1990s, jobs and houses had moved to the edges. Long distance commuters could now work locally; in the process a single-centre city became a network of regional centres

1970

1980

1990

10

5

20

15

65

7

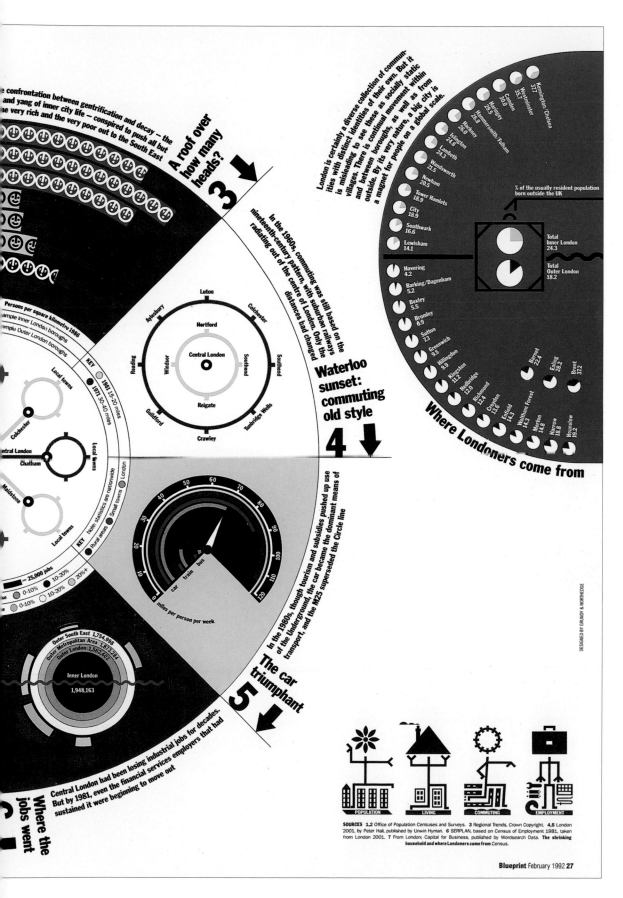

Doughnut London

DESIGN: Peter Grundy, Tilly Northedge, UK

PUBLISHER/CLIENT: *Blueprint* magazine

DATE OF 1ST PUBLICATION/USE: February 1992

DESIGN RATIONALE: Statistics on employment, housing, commuting, etc. were used to present a view of how London has evolved over the last 30 years from a large, single centre to a smaller one with a large ring of outlying conurbations.

CREDITS: Art directors and illustrators, Peter Grundy, Tilly Northedge; writer, Deyan Sudjic; researcher, Liz Farrelly.

Tesco plc Annual Report 1989

DESIGN: Michael Peters Ltd, Peter Chodel, UK

PUBLISHER/CLIENT: Tesco plc

DATE OF 1ST PUBLICATION/USE: July 1989

DESIGN RATIONALE: Photographic map of the UK using fresh produce and groceries. The map was intended to enliven the page/spread which listed all Tesco stores and to be an innovative way of showing what Tesco does.

CREDITS: Art director, Peter Chodel; photographer, Tessa Traeger.

PARADIGM:LONDON

PARADIGM:ROMA

Urban Icons (London, Rome, Philadelphia)

DESIGN: Katz Wheeler Design, Joel Katz, USA

PUBLISHER/CLIENT: Katz Wheeler Design

DATE OF 1ST PUBLICATION/USE: 1990

DESIGN RATIONALE: A series of symbolic, iconic diagrams of world cities within circles: London, Philadelphia, Rome. This practice of "fictional iconography" uses city maps as the starting point for an exploration of functional and hierarchical (rather than geographic) relationships in cities.

CREDIT: Art director, Joel Katz (of Paradigm: Design).

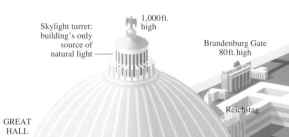

PHILADELPHIA PARADIGM

Hitler's Berlin, 1963

DESIGN: John Grimwade, UK

PUBLISHER/CLIENT: Random House

DATE OF 1ST PUBLICATION/USE: 1992

DESIGN RATIONALE: Hitler's grand scheme for Berlin, based on models and drawings, used as endpapers for *Fatherland* by Robert Harris to create a sense of place for this fiction work based on the premise that in 1963 there was a Berlin run by Hitler.

Skylight turret: building's only source of natural light

1,000 ft. high

Brandenburg Gate 80 ft. high

Grand Avenue 400 ft. wide, 3 miles long

Arch of Triumph 400 ft. high

Railway Station

GREAT HALL

Room inside hall for more than 150,000 people to stand

Reichstag

Grand Plaza

POTSDAMER STRASSE

TIERGARTEN

Hitler's Palace

RIVER SPREE

165

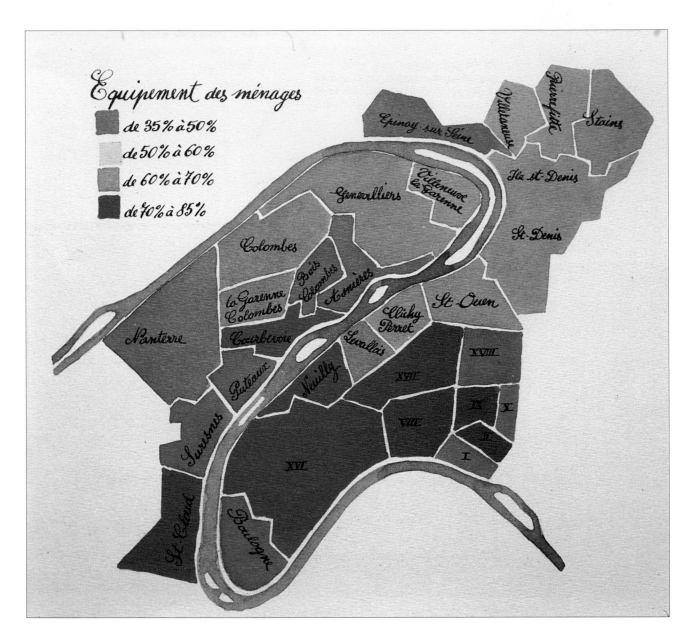

**Brochure
Telecommunication – Dot
Nanterre France**

DESIGN: Pierre Praquin, France

PUBLISHER/CLIENT: Ministère des Telecommunication Dot
Nanterre France

DATE OF 1ST PUBLICATION/USE: 1986

DESIGN RATIONALE: Completely illustrated and annotated using
watercolour and ink.

CREDITS: Art director and illustrator, Pierre Praquin.

**1990 New York City
Marathon**

DESIGN: Jean Wisenbaugh, USA

PUBLISHER/CLIENT: *New York* magazine

DATE OF 1ST PUBLICATION/USE: October 1990

DESIGN RATIONALE: A map of the course of the New York City
Marathon. Colourful depictions of points of interest along the
route combine with the actual course and mile markers to give
the reader a sense of the festive event and provide the spectator
with a guide for watching the race.

CREDITS: Art director, Richard Mantel; illustrator, Jean
Wisenbaugh.

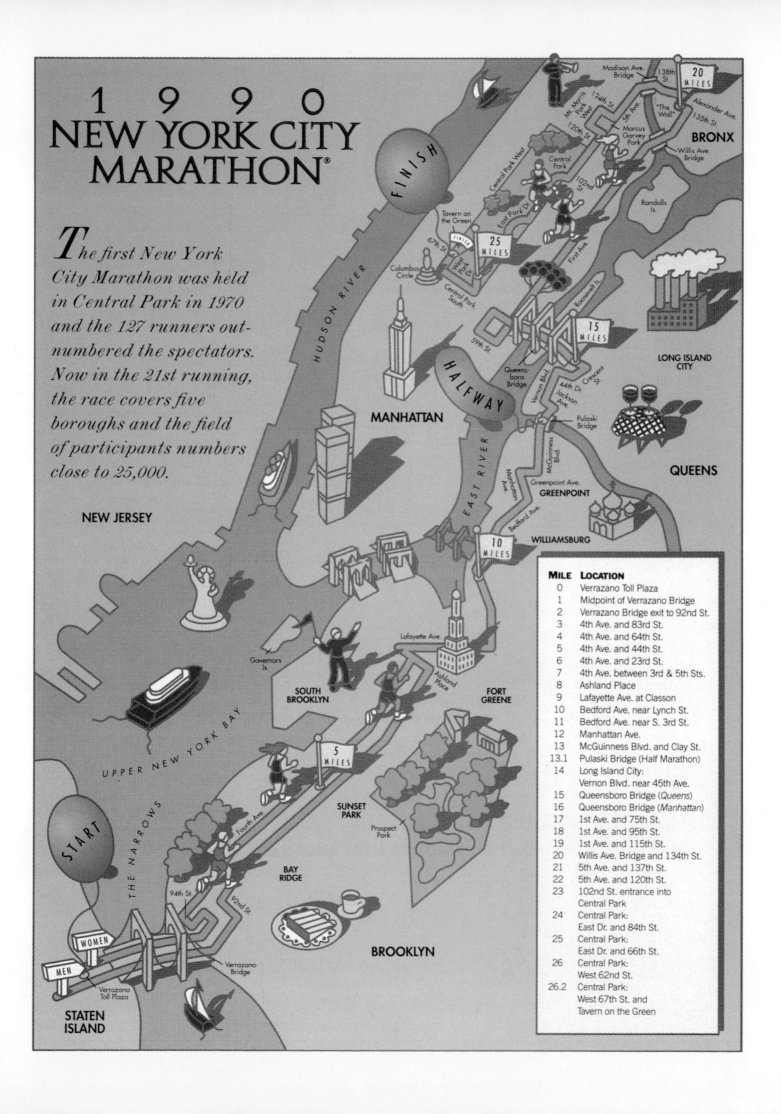

1990 NEW YORK CITY MARATHON®

The first New York City Marathon was held in Central Park in 1970 and the 127 runners outnumbered the spectators. Now in the 21st running, the race covers five boroughs and the field of participants numbers close to 25,000.

MILE	LOCATION
0	Verrazano Toll Plaza
1	Midpoint of Verrazano Bridge
2	Verrazano Bridge exit to 92nd St.
3	4th Ave. and 83rd St.
4	4th Ave. and 64th St.
5	4th Ave. and 44th St.
6	4th Ave. and 23rd St.
7	4th Ave. between 3rd & 5th Sts.
8	Ashland Place
9	Lafayette Ave. at Classon
10	Bedford Ave. near Lynch St.
11	Bedford Ave. near S. 3rd St.
12	Manhattan Ave.
13	McGuinness Blvd. and Clay St.
13.1	Pulaski Bridge (Half Marathon)
14	Long Island City: Vernon Blvd. near 45th Ave.
15	Queensboro Bridge (*Queens*)
16	Queensboro Bridge (*Manhattan*)
17	1st Ave. and 75th St.
18	1st Ave. and 95th St.
19	1st Ave. and 115th St.
20	Willis Ave. Bridge and 134th St.
21	5th Ave. and 137th St.
22	5th Ave. and 120th St.
23	102nd St. entrance into Central Park
24	Central Park: East Dr. and 84th St.
25	Central Park: East Dr. and 66th St.
26	Central Park: West 62nd St.
26.2	Central Park: West 67th St. and Tavern on the Green

Greater Yellowstone

Looking from the north across Yellowstone National Park toward Grand Teton in the south, panoramist Heinrich Berann depicts scenic park features and the 28- by 46-mile caldera, or basin, created by a massive volcanic eruption 600,000 years ago.

For sale by the Superintendent of Documents U.S. Government Printing Office, Washington, DC 20402.   © GPO, 1991 — 281-953/20002.

Hot Springs, Old Faithful, Yellowstone Lake,
n—the far-reaching Greater Yellowstone area
s with places symbolizing the American West.

Today federal land agencies and other groups work together
to protect this magnificent natural habitat of the grizzly bear,
elk, bison, trumpeter swan, and other wildlife.

National Park / Wyoming, Montana, and Idaho
National Park / Wyoming

National Park Service
U.S. Department of the Interior

Greater Yellowstone

DESIGN: Vincent Gleason, USA

PUBLISHER/CLIENT: US National Park Service

DATE OF 1ST PUBLICATION/USE: 1991

DESIGN RATIONALE: Looking from the north across Yellowstone
National Park, Wyoming, Montana and Idaho, toward Grand
Teton in the south, this panorama depicts scenic park features
and the 28 by 48 mile (45 × 77km) caldera or basin created by a
massive volcanic eruption 600,000 years ago.

CREDITS: Art director, Vincent Gleason; illustrator,
Heinrich Berann.

Everglades

DESIGN: Megan Kealy, R. R. Donelly, Cartographic Services, USA

PUBLISHER/CLIENT: US National Park Service

DATE OF 1ST PUBLICATION/USE: 1992

DESIGN RATIONALE: The map depicts the variety of ecosystems and visitor facilities found in the Everglades Park, Florida.

CREDITS: Art director, Vincent Gleason; cartographer, Megan Kealy.

Exploring the Everglades

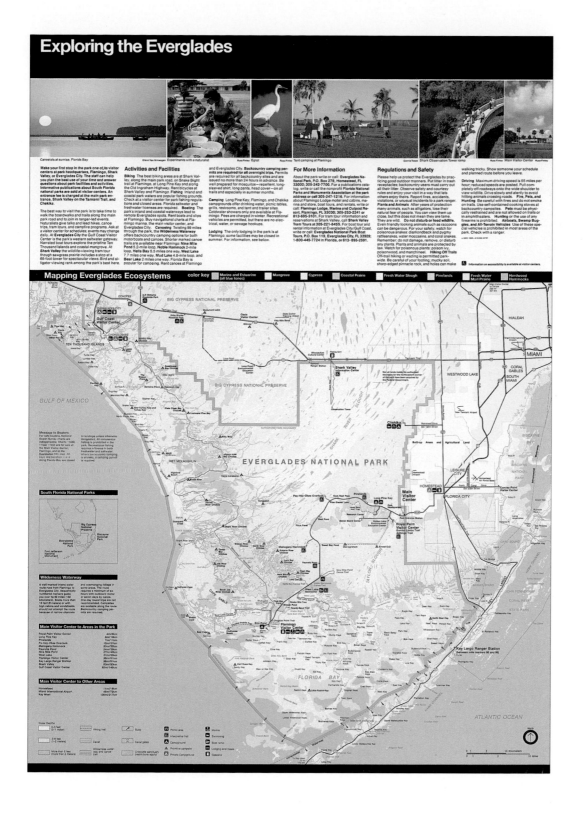

Canoeists at sunrise, Florida Bay · Experiments with a naturalist · Egret · Tent camping at Flamingo · Shark Observation Tower ramp · Main Visitor Center

Make your first stop in the park one of its visitor centers at park headquarters, Flamingo, Shark Valley, or Everglades City. The staff can help you plan the best use of your time and answer questions about park facilities and activities. Informative publications are sold at visitor centers. An entrance fee is charged at the main park entrance, Shark Valley on the Tamiami Trail, and Chekika.

The best way to visit the park is to take time to walk the boardwalks and trails along the main park road and to join in ranger-led events. Naturalists give talks and lead hikes, canoe trips, tram tours, and campfire programs. Ask a visitor center for schedules; events may change daily. At Everglades City the Gulf Coast Visitor Center is the park's western saltwater gateway. Narrated boat tours explore the pristine Ten Thousand Islands and coastal mangrove. At Shark Valley the wildlife-viewing tram tour through sawgrass prairie includes a stop at a 65-foot tower for spectacular views. Bird and alligator viewing rank among the park's best here.

Activities and Facilities

Biking The best biking areas are at Shark Valley, along the main park road, on Snake Bight trail at Flamingo, at Long Pine Key and along the Old Ingraham Highway. Rent bicycles at Shark Valley and Flamingo. **Fishing** Inland and coastal park waters are popular fishing grounds. Check at a visitor center for park fishing regulations and closed areas. Florida saltwater and freshwater licenses are required. **Boating** The park's inland and coastal waterways lead to remote Everglades spots. Rent boats and slips at Flamingo. Buy navigational charts at Flamingo marina, the main visitor center, and Everglades City. **Canoeing** Twisting 99 miles through the park, the **Wilderness Waterway** offers backcountry camping options for both motorboats and canoes. Shorter marked canoe trails are available near Flamingo: **Nine Mile Pond** 5.2-mile loop, **Noble Hammock** 2-mile loop, **Hells Bay** 5.5 miles one way, **West Lake** 7.7 miles one way, **Mud Lake** 4.8-mile loop, and **Bear Lake** 2 miles one way. Florida Bay is popular for canoeing. Rent canoes at Flamingo and Everglades City. Backcountry camping permits are required for all overnight trips. Permits are required for all backcountry sites and are issued no more than 24 hours in advance. Be well prepared for mosquitos—repellent, long-sleeved shirt, long pants, head cover—on all trails and especially in summer months.

Camping Long Pine Key, Flamingo, and Chekika campgrounds offer drinking water, picnic tables, grills, restrooms, and tent and trailer sites. Coldwater showers only are available at Flamingo. Fees are charged in winter. Recreational vehicles are permitted, but there are no electrical, water, or sewage hookups.

Lodging The only lodging in the park is at Flamingo; some facilities may be closed in summer. For information, see below.

For More Information

About the park write or call: Everglades National Park, P.O. Box 279, Homestead, FL 33030; 305-242-7700. For a publications catalog, write or call the nonprofit Florida National Parks and Monuments Association at the park address or call 305-247-1216. For information about Flamingo Lodge motel and cabins, marina and store, boat tours, and rentals, write or call: Flamingo Lodge, Marina and Outpost Resort, Flamingo, FL 33030; 305-253-2241 or 813-695-3101. For tram tour information and reservations at Shark Valley, call Shark Valley Tram Tours at 305-221-8455. For boat tour and rental information at Everglades City/Gulf Coast, write or call: Everglades National Park Boat Tours, P.O. Box 119, Everglades City, FL 33929; 1-800-445-7724 in Florida, or 813-695-2591.

Regulations and Safety

Please help us protect the Everglades by practicing good outdoor manners. Put litter in trash receptacles; backcountry users must carry out all their litter. Observe safety and courtesy rules and enjoy your visit in a way that lets others enjoy theirs. Report fires, accidents, violations, or unusual incidents to a park ranger. **Plants and Animals** After years of protection many animals, such as alligators, lose their natural fear of people. You can view them up close, but this does not mean they are tame. They are wild. **Do not disturb or feed wildlife.** Even friendly looking animals such as raccoons can be dangerous. For your safety, watch for poisonous snakes: diamondback and pygmy rattlesnakes, water moccasins, and coral snakes. Remember: do not damage, remove, or disturb any plants. Plants and animals are protected by law. Watch for poisonous plants: poison ivy, poisonwood, and manchineel. **Hiking Off Trails** Off-trail hiking or wading is permitted parkwide. Be careful of your footing; mucky soil, sharp-edged pinnacle rock, and holes can make

walking tricky. Show someone your schedule and planned route before you leave.

Driving Maximum driving speed is 55 miles per hour; reduced speeds are posted. Pull completely off roadways onto the wide shoulder to view wildlife. Drive slowly and alertly to avoid hitting animals crossing roads. **Fire, Pets, and Hunting** Use self-contained cooking stoves at backcountry campsites. Pets must be physically restrained and are not allowed on trails or in amphitheaters. Hunting or the use of any firearms is prohibited. **Airboats, Swamp Buggies, and All-Terrain Vehicles** Use of these special vehicles is prohibited in most areas of the park. Check with a ranger.

Information on accessibility is available at visitor centers.

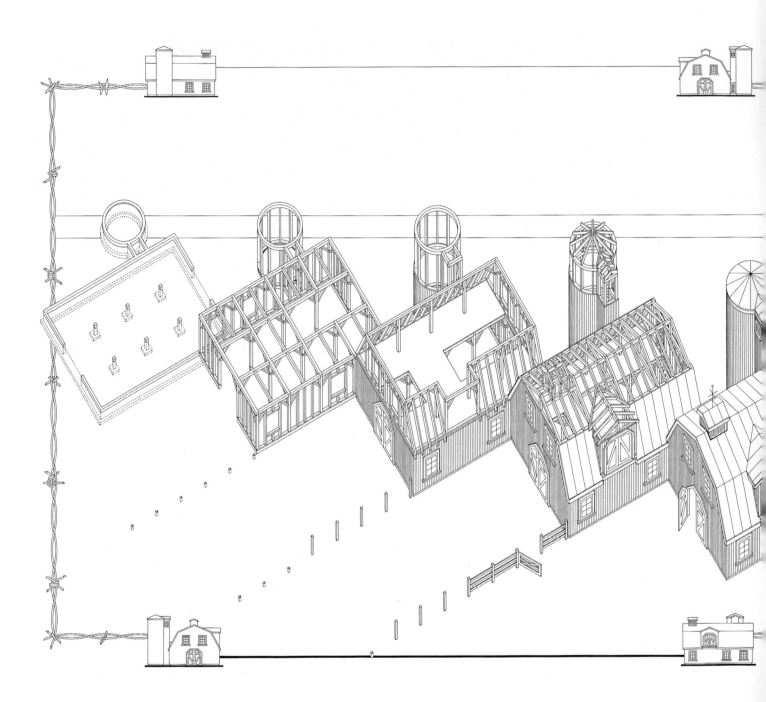

Barn Dance

DESIGN: Guy Peckham, USA

PUBLISHER/CLIENT: Self-promotion

DATE OF 1ST PUBLICATION/USE: 1986

DESIGN RATIONALE: The various stages in the construction of a barn. The construction process was separated into five phases with illustrative "snap shot" drawings collected together to describe how the barn might look at the end of each phase. Finished views of the barn were grouped with barbed wire to frame the ensemble.

CREDITS: Illustrator, Guy Peckham Architect

Seattle Poster

DESIGN: Guy Peckham, USA

PUBLISHER/CLIENT: Self-promotion

DATE OF 1ST PUBLICATION/USE: 1985

DESIGN RATIONALE: To illustrate downtown Seattle buildings which are distinctive for their size and shape. The buildings are shown as if in a "family portrait", with portions of the widest and tallest buildings partially hidden behind those in front. Colour was added to focus attention to the group.

CREDITS: Illustrator, Guy Peckham Architect

53rd Street Map

DESIGN: Steven Guarnaccia, USA

PUBLISHER/CLIENT: 53rd Street Association

DATE OF 1ST PUBLICATION/USE: 1986

DESIGN RATIONALE: To show the cultural institutions on 53rd Street between 2nd and 8th Avenues in New York City.

CREDITS: Art directors, Kaspar Shmid, Michael Gericke, Pentagram; illustrator, Steven Guarnaccia.

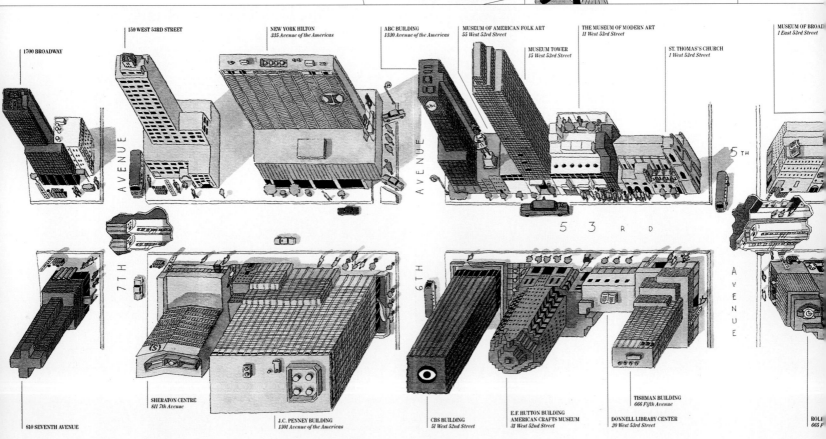

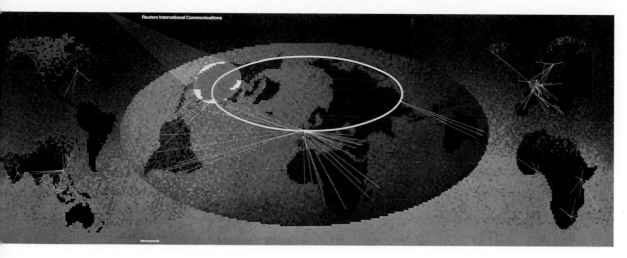

Reuters
Annual Report
1986 – Cover

DESIGN: Mervyn Kurlansky,
South Africa

PUBLISHER/CLIENT: Reuters
Holding plc

DATE OF 1ST PUBLICATION/USE:
1987

DESIGN RATIONALE: Reuters is
an international news agency
with a worldwide communication
network supplying press
information and a data service for
businesses and financial
institutions. The cover of the
1986 Annual Report was based
on the Reuters global network.

CREDITS: Art director, Mervyn
Kurlansky; illustrator, Dan Fern;
designer, Claire Johnson.

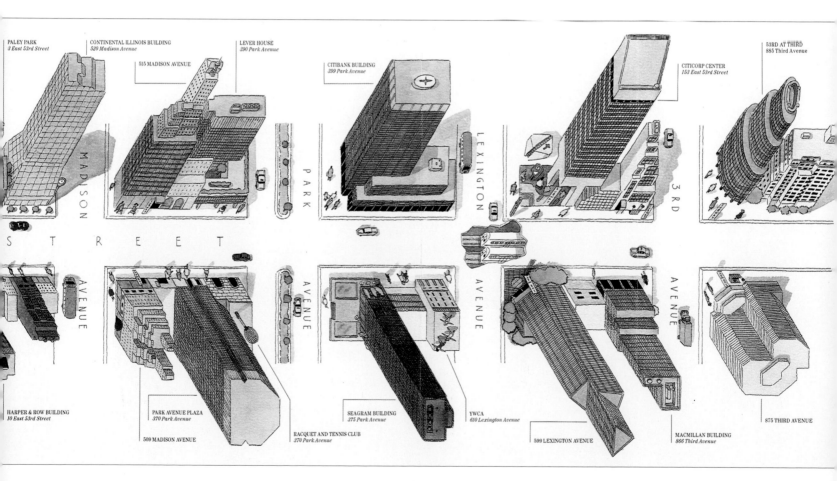

Alaska

DESIGN: Hiroyuki Kimura,
Sachiko Hagiwara, Japan

PUBLISHER/CLIENT: *Alaska-Kaze
no yona monogatari,*
Shogakukan Inc.

DATE OF 1ST PUBLICATION/USE:
1 July 1991

DESIGN RATIONALE: Map of
Alaska.

CREDITS: Art director, Hiroyuki
Kimura.

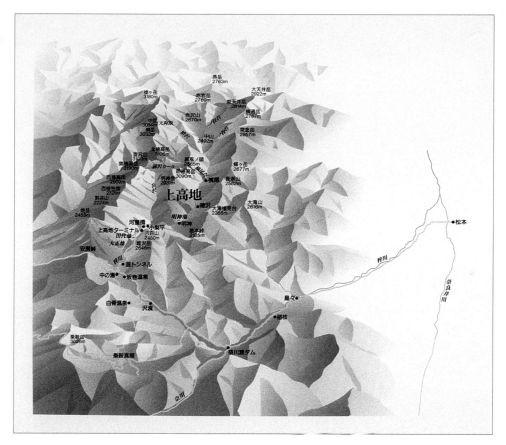

Kamikochi

DESIGN: Hiroyuki Kimura, Sachiko Hagiwara, Japan

PUBLISHER/CLIENT: A Rainy Day/Shogaku Kan, Inc.

DATE OF 1ST PUBLICATION/USE: 1 July 1991

DESIGN RATIONALE: A bird's eye view of Kamakochi.

CREDITS: Art director, Hiroyuki Kimura.

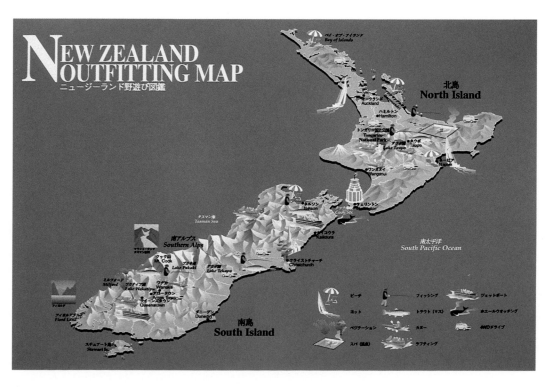

New Zealand Outfitting Map

DESIGN: Hiroyuki Kimura, Sachiko Hagiwara, Japan

PUBLISHER/CLIENT: The Best Selection/Yomiuri Shimbun-sha

DATE OF 1ST PUBLICATION/USE: 11 April 1992

DESIGN RATIONALE: A bird's eye view of New Zealand

CREDITS: Art director, Hiroyuki Kimura.

Dimensions: The Design of the Earth

DESIGN: James Cross, USA

PUBLISHER/CLIENT: Simpson Paper Company

DATE OF 1ST PUBLICATION/USE: 1991

DESIGN RATIONALE: A poster entitled "The Earth in True Dimensions" to accompany a book titled *Dimensions: The Design of the Earth*, which was a promotional piece designed for the Simpson Paper Company. The purpose of the poster was to show how immense our universe is and yet how fragile our human environment is.

CREDITS: Writer/researcher, James Cross.

RUNNING THE GA
Some predators follow the w
migration, awaiting an oppo
huge herds also pass throug
predator colonies. Su
that the wildebeest
with 20 million po

CHEETAHS

POACHERS
At least 40,000 to
50,000 wildebeest
fall annually to meat
poachers.

VULTURES
The Ruppell's vulture
is able to follow the
migration along its
entire route.

CROCODILES
Dominate the rivers.

WILD DOGS
Wander over a home
range of up to 750
square miles.

**MONITOR
LIZARDS**

TANZANIA

**SEVEN GREAT
MIGRATIONS**
For a foldout map of where
and when to see wildlife in
the Western Hemisphere,
turn to page 152.

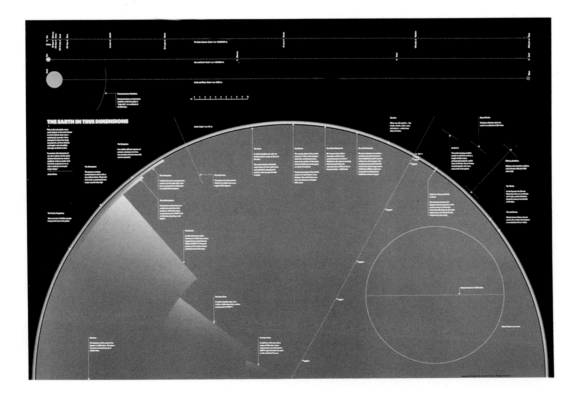

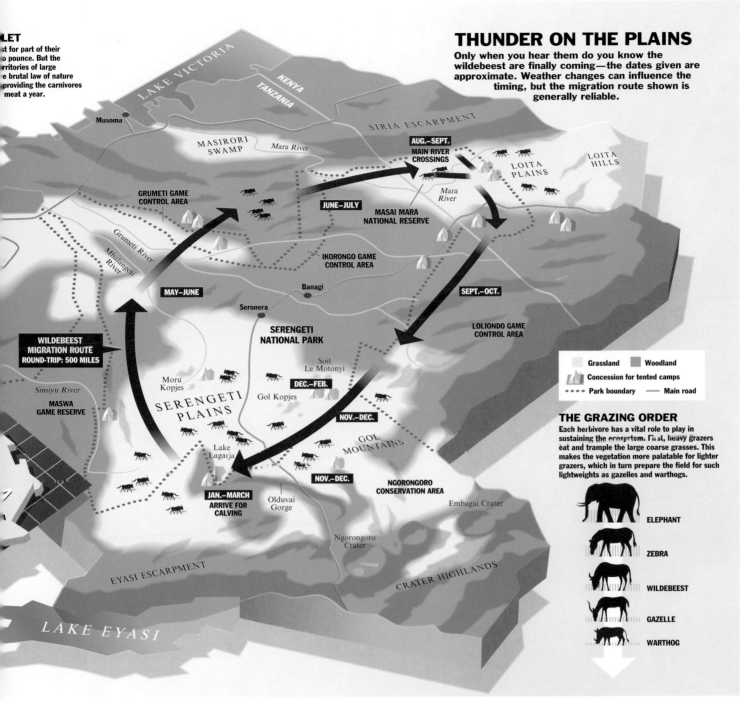

THUNDER ON THE PLAINS

Only when you hear them do you know the wildebeest are finally coming—the dates given are approximate. Weather changes can influence the timing, but the migration route shown is generally reliable.

LAKE VICTORIA

KENYA
TANZANIA

Musoma

SIRIA ESCARPMENT

MASIRORI SWAMP

Mara River

AUG.–SEPT.
MAIN RIVER CROSSINGS

LOITA PLAINS

LOITA HILLS

GRUMETI GAME CONTROL AREA

Mara River

JUNE–JULY

MASAI MARA NATIONAL RESERVE

Grumeti River

Mbalangeti River

IKORONGO GAME CONTROL AREA

MAY–JUNE

Banagi

SEPT.–OCT.

Seronera

LOLIONDO GAME CONTROL AREA

SERENGETI NATIONAL PARK

WILDEBEEST MIGRATION ROUTE ROUND-TRIP: 500 MILES

Simiyu River

MASWA GAME RESERVE

Moru Kopjes

Soit Le Motonyi

DEC.–FEB.

Gol Kopjes

SERENGETI PLAINS

NOV.–DEC.

GOL MOUNTAINS

NOV.–DEC.

Lake Lagarja

NGORONGORO CONSERVATION AREA

JAN.–MARCH
ARRIVE FOR CALVING

Olduvai Gorge

Embagai Crater

Ngorongoro Crater

EYASI ESCARPMENT

CRATER HIGHLANDS

LAKE EYASI

Legend

- ☐ Grassland   ■ Woodland
- ⛰ Concession for tented camps
- ···· Park boundary   — Main road

THE GRAZING ORDER

Each herbivore has a vital role to play in sustaining the ecosystem. First, heavy grazers eat and trample the large coarse grasses. This makes the vegetation more palatable for lighter grazers, which in turn prepare the field for such lightweights as gazelles and warthogs.

ELEPHANT

ZEBRA

WILDEBEEST

GAZELLE

WARTHOG

Serengeti

DESIGN: John Grimwade, UK

PUBLISHER/CLIENT: *Condé Nast Traveler*

DATE OF 1ST PUBLICATION/USE: June 1992

DESIGN RATIONALE: The migration route of wildebeest in Tanzania and Kenya. A virtually self-contained diagram, built to support a large feature story about wildebeest migration.

CREDITS: Art directors, Diana Laguardia, Christin Gangi; illustrator, John Grimwade.

LET

...t for part of their
...o pounce. But the
...rritories of large
...e brutal law of nature
...providing the carnivores
...meat a year.

Architecture

Architects often make the best information designers. Some, like Richard Saul Wurman, even switch from architecture to graphics. There is something about an architect's training that is immensely suitable to the art of explaining: indeed, Wurman's information design company is called The Understanding Business.

The responsibility of designing a building in which people are going to live or work instils in the architect a respect for numbers and facts, and the means by which architects must make their work visible – drawing – is, of course, the other half of any graphics job. There is a necessary precision to architecture, a fitting together of many parts into one cohesive whole, that is a nice parallel to information processing and designing.

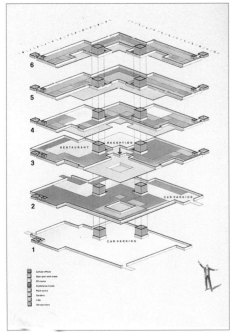

Sometimes the architect turns to illustration to make the point graphically clearer. Here you will see renderings of Rockefeller Center in New York City, cut away to show the intricacies of the underground passages, but done in a friendly, illustrative manner rather than the cooler cross-section and plan views that one might expect from an architect. The capacity to visualize an unbuilt project is a skill that comes in very useful when an existing building must be drawn, especially when an interior view is required.

The revelation of the cutaway is one of the stars of any information graphics portfolio, for it is truly an example of something that can be shown in no other way: it does not exist in reality, yet paradoxically it is entirely based on reality.

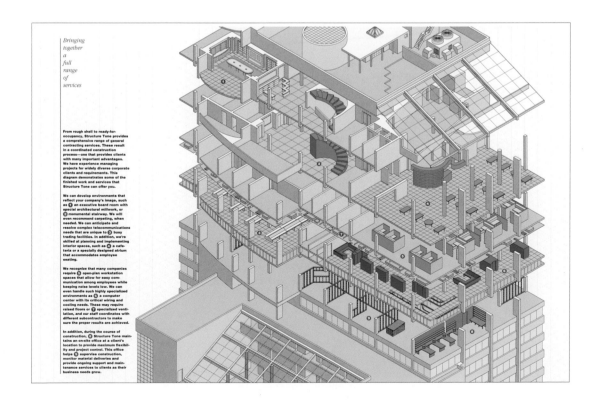

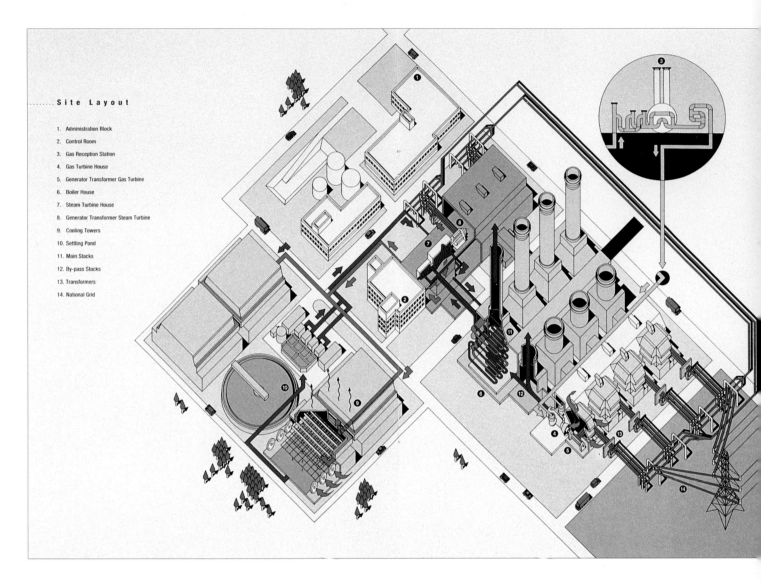

........Site Layout

1. Administration Block
2. Control Room
3. Gas Reception Station
4. Gas Turbine House
5. Generator Transformer Gas Turbine
6. Boiler House
7. Steam Turbine House
8. Generator Transformer Steam Turbine
9. Cooling Towers
10. Settling Pond
11. Main Stacks
12. By-pass Stacks
13. Transformers
14. National Grid

Killingholme Power Station – Site Layout

DESIGN: Tilly Northedge, UK

PUBLISHER/CLIENT: Powergen: Killingholme Brochure

DATE OF 1ST PUBLICATION/USE: April 1993

DESIGN RATIONALE: A diagrammatic site layout showing the components of the first purpose-built gas-fired power station in the UK. Colour is used informatively to group the components rather than realistically. The graphic provides a three-dimensional site layout for the centre spread of the brochure showing the main parts of the gas-fired power station.

CREDITS: Art director, John Perlmutter, Uffindell & West; illustrator, Tilly Northedge.

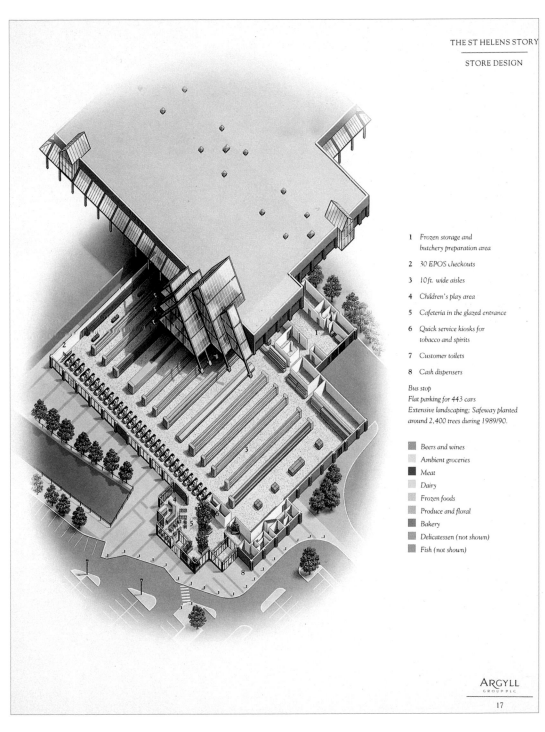

THE ST HELENS STORY

STORE DESIGN

1 Frozen storage and
  butchery preparation area

2 30 EPOS checkouts

3 10 ft. wide aisles

4 Children's play area

5 Cafeteria in the glazed entrance

6 Quick service kiosks for
  tobacco and spirits

7 Customer toilets

8 Cash dispensers

Bus stop
Flat parking for 443 cars
Extensive landscaping; Safeway planted
around 2,400 trees during 1989/90.

Beers and wines
Ambient groceries
Meat
Dairy
Frozen foods
Produce and floral
Bakery
Delicatessen (not shown)
Fish (not shown)

ARGYLL
GROUP PLC

17

Argyll Group plc Annual Report 1990

DESIGN: Michael Peters Ltd,
Jackie Vicary, UK

PUBLISHER/CLIENT:
Argyll Group plc

DATE OF 1ST PUBLICATION/USE:
July 1991

DESIGN RATIONALE: An exploded view of a Safeway store at St Helens, Lancashire, showing the internal store layout and facilities. The illustration was part of a special feature about the store, supported by a photographic essay and case studies about the people who work there and the customer services they provide.

CREDITS: Art director, Jackie Vicary; illustrator, David Draper.

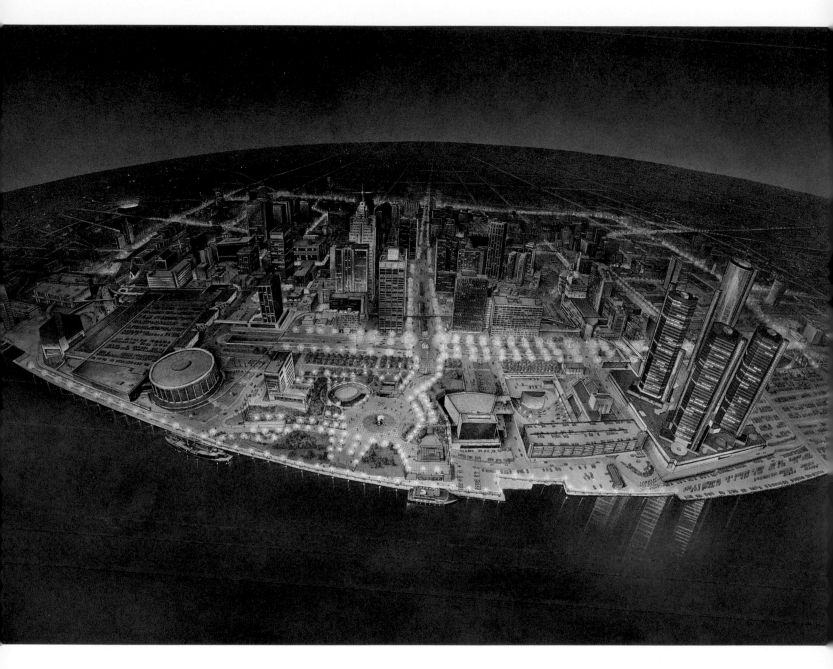

Detroit at Night

DESIGN: Albert Lorenz, USA

PUBLISHER/CLIENT: W. B. Doner & Co., commissioned by
City of Detroit

DATE OF 1ST PUBLICATION/USE: 1987

DESIGN RATIONALE: A view of Detroit at night to show the
lighting design of the city.

CREDITS: Art director, Dean Charlton.

Rockefeller Center

DESIGN: Albert Lorenz, USA

PUBLISHER/CLIENT: Soskin/ Thompson Assoc.

DATE OF 1ST PUBLICATION/USE: 1986

DESIGN RATIONALE: An exploded view of British and French buildings in Rockefeller Center in which an exaggerated perspective lifts the buildings and shows retail activity below.

CREDITS: Art director, Jan Leth.

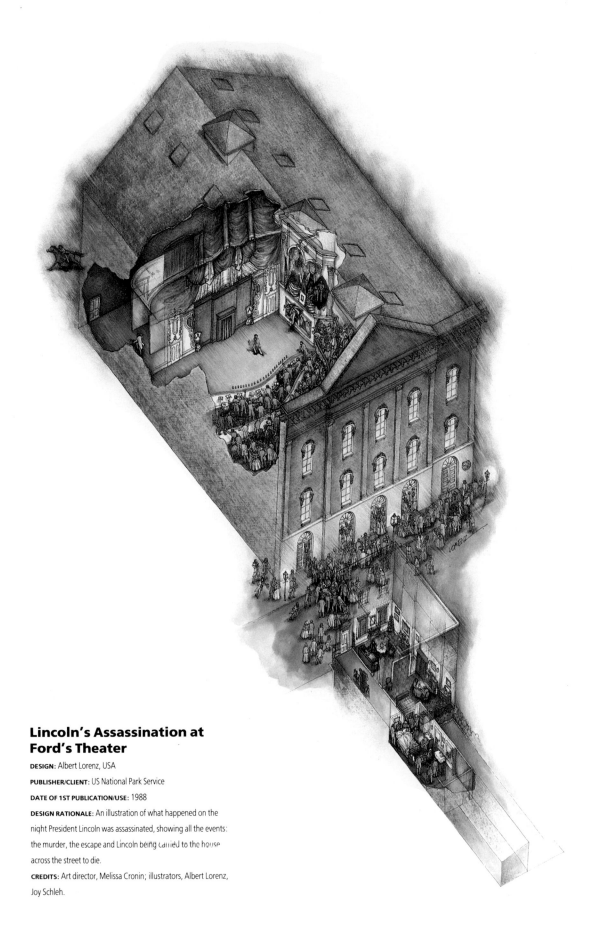

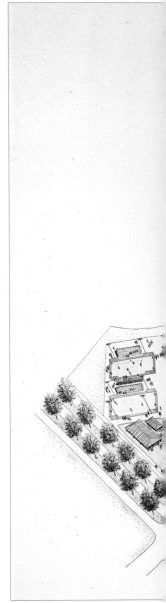

Lincoln's Assassination at Ford's Theater

DESIGN: Albert Lorenz, USA

PUBLISHER/CLIENT: US National Park Service

DATE OF 1ST PUBLICATION/USE: 1988

DESIGN RATIONALE: An illustration of what happened on the night President Lincoln was assassinated, showing all the events: the murder, the escape and Lincoln being carried to the house across the street to die.

CREDITS: Art director, Melissa Cronin; illustrators, Albert Lorenz, Joy Schleh.

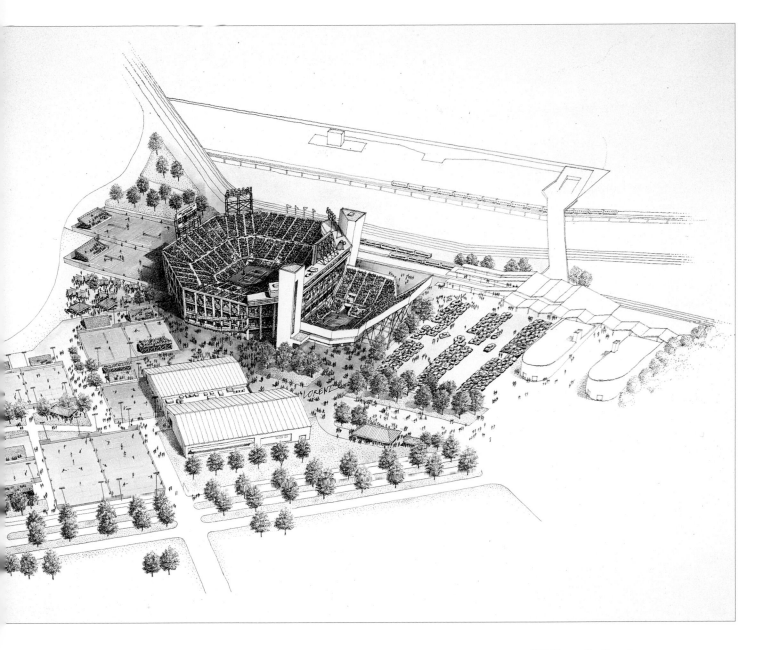

US Tennis Center

DESIGN: Albert Lorenz, USA

PUBLISHER/CLIENT: *Golf Digest/Tennis* magazine

DATE OF 1ST PUBLICATION/USE: 1986

DESIGN RATIONALE: An exploded perspective of the National Tennis Center in New York, home of the US Open. A pen and ink illustration that concentrates the viewer's eye on the Center.

CREDITS: Art director, Julie Francis; illustrator, Albert Lorenz.

Dream to Reality – The Bay Area Dream House

DESIGN: Kelly Frankeny, Chris Morris, USA

PUBLISHER/CLIENT: *San Francisco Examiner*

DATE OF 1ST PUBLICATION/USE: 16 March 1992

DESIGN RATIONALE: The roof, top floor and lower floor of a house that was designed after suggestions were submitted from all over the Bay Area. The cutaway shows the design of the house and how it was furnished, while not neglecting any aspect of the house.

CREDITS: Art director, Kelly Frankeny; illustrator, Chris Morris; writer, Bruce Koon.

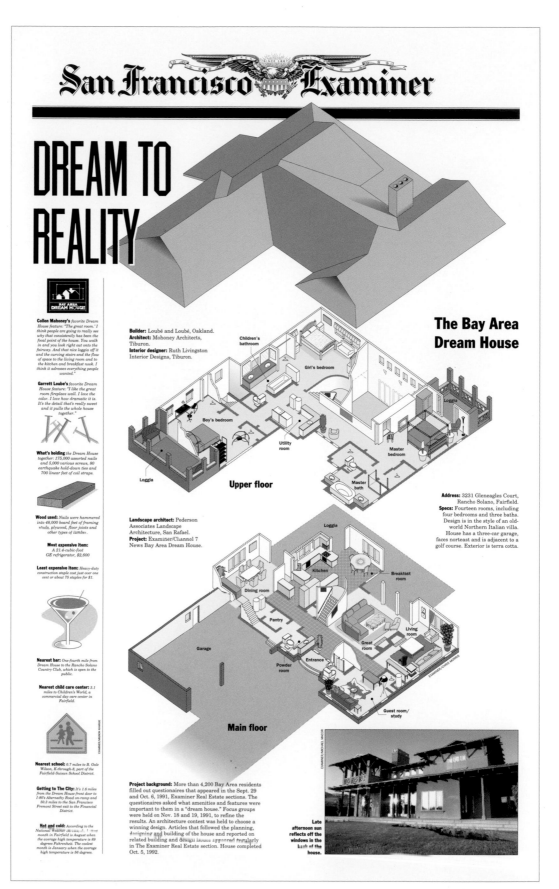

San Francisco Examiner

DREAM TO REALITY

BAY AREA DREAM HOUSE

Collen Mahoney's *favorite Dream House feature: "The great room. I think people are going to really see why that consistently has been the focal point of the house. You walk in and you look right out onto the fairway. And that nice loggia off it and the curving stairs and the flow of space to the living room and to the kitchen and breakfast nook. I think it adresses everything people wanted."*

Garrett Loube's *favorite Dream House feature: "I like the great room fireplace wall. I love the color. I love how dramatic it is. It's the detail that's really sweet and it pulls the whole house together."*

What's holding *the Dream House together: 175,000 assorted nails and 5,000 various screws, 80 earthquake hold-down ties and 700 linear feet of coil straps.*

Wood used: *Nails were hammered into 48,000 board feet of framing studs, plywood, floor joists and other types of lumber.*

Most expensive item: *A 21.4-cubic-foot GE refrigerator, $2,600*

Least expensive item: *Heavy-duty construction staple cost just over one cent or about 75 staples for $1.*

Nearest bar: *One-fourth mile from Dream House to the Rancho Solano Country Club, which is open to the public.*

Nearest child care center: *3.1 miles to Children's World, a commercial day care center in Fairfield.*

Nearest school: *0.7 miles to B. Gale Wilson, K-through-8, part of the Fairfield-Suisun School District.*

Getting to The City: *It's 1.6 miles from the Dream House front door to I-80's Abernathy Road on-ramp and 50.3 miles to the San Francisco Fremont Street exit to the Financial District.*

Hot and cold: *According to the National Weather Service, the most month in Fairfield is August when the average high temperature is 89 degrees Fahrenheit. The coolest month is January when the average high temperature is 56 degrees.*

The Bay Area Dream House

Builder: Loubé and Loubé, Oakland.
Architect: Mohoney Architects, Tiburon.
Interior designer: Ruth Livingston Interior Designs, Tiburon.

Children's bathroom
Girl's bedroom
Boy's bedroom
Loggia
Utility room
Master bedroom
Loggia
Master bath

Upper floor

Address: 3231 Gleneagles Court, Rancho Solano, Fairfield.
Specs: Fourteen rooms, including four bedrooms and three baths. Design is in the style of an old-world Northern Italian villa. House has a three-car garage, faces noreast and is adjacent to a golf course. Exterior is terra cotta.

Landscape architect: Pederson Associates Landscape Architecture, San Rafael.
Project: Examiner/Channel 7 News Bay Area Dream House.

Loggia
Kitchen
Breakfast room
Dining room
Pantry
Garage
Great room
Living room
Powder room
Entrance
Guest room/ study

Main floor

Project background: More than 4,200 Bay Area residents filled out questionaires that appeared in the Sept. 29 and Oct. 6, 1991, Examiner Real Estate sections. The questionaires asked what amenities and features were important to them in a "dream house." Focus groups were held on Nov. 18 and 19, 1991, to refine the results. An architecture contest was held to choose a winning design. Articles that followed the planning, designing and building of the house and reported on related building and design issues appeared regularly in The Examiner Real Estate section. House completed Oct. 5, 1992.

Late afternoon sun reflects off the windows in the back of the house.

SAN FRANCISCO EXAMINER

CITY HALL: A CLOSEUP

On this third anniversary of the Loma Prieta earthquake, plans are finally under way for San Francisco's City Hall to undergo $128.5 million worth of dismantling, evacuation and retrofitting. The hall, virtually the West's only structure comparable in scale and ornamentation design to European palaces, faces a virtual tip-to-turf refurbishing for seismic

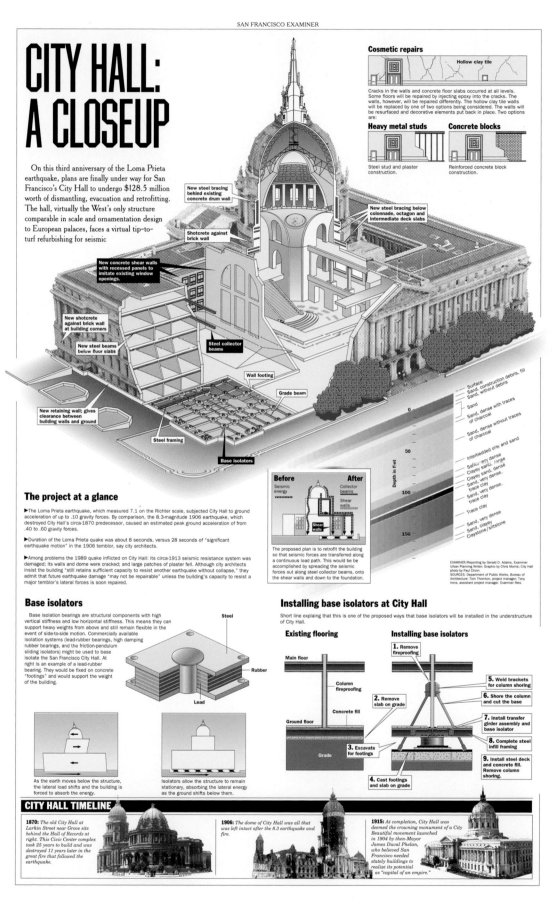

Cosmetic repairs

Hollow clay tile

Cracks in the walls and concrete floor slabs occurred at all levels. Some floors will be repaired by injecting epoxy into the cracks. The walls, however, will be repaired differently. The hollow clay tile walls will be replaced by one of two options being considered. The walls will be resurfaced and decorative elements put back in place. Two options are:

Heavy metal studs

Steel stud and plaster construction.

Concrete blocks

Reinforced concrete block construction.

New steel bracing behind existing concrete drum wall

New steel bracing below colonnade, octagon and intermediate deck slabs

Shotcrete against brick wall

New concrete shear walls with recessed panels to imitate existing window openings.

New shotcrete against brick wall at building corners

New steel beams below floor slabs

Steel collector beams

Wall footing

Grade beam

New retaining wall; gives clearance between building walls and ground

Steel framing

Base isolators

The project at a glance

▶The Loma Prieta earthquake, which measured 7.1 on the Richter scale, subjected City Hall to ground acceleration of up to .10 gravity forces. By comparison, the 8.3-magnitude 1906 earthquake, which destroyed City Hall's circa-1870 predecessor, caused an estimated peak ground acceleration of from .40 to .60 gravity forces.

▶Duration of the Loma Prieta quake was about 8 seconds, versus 28 seconds of "significant earthquake motion" in the 1906 temblor, say city architects.

▶Among problems the 1989 quake inflicted on City Hall: its circa-1913 seismic resistance system was damaged; its walls and dome cracked; and large patches of plaster fell. Although city architects insist the building "still retains sufficient capacity to resist another earthquake without collapse," they admit that future earthquake damage "may not be repairable" unless the building's capacity to resist a major temblor's lateral forces is soon repaired.

Before — **After**

Seismic energy — Collector beams / Shear walls / Shear walls

The proposed plan to retrofit the building so that seismic forces are transferred along a continuous load path. This would be accomplished by spreading the seismic forces out along steel collector beams, onto the shear walls and down to the foundation.

Surface / Sand, construction debris, fill / Sand, without debris
Sand
Sand, dense with traces of charcoal
Sand, dense without traces of charcoal
Interbedded clay and sand
Sand, very dense
Clayey sand, dense
Clayey sand, dense
Sand, very dense
trace clay
Sand, very dense
trace clay
Trace clay
Sand, very dense
Sand, clayey
Claystone/siltstone

Depth in Feet — 0, 50, 100, 150

EXAMINER/Reporting by Gerald D. Adams, Examiner Urban Planning Writer; Graphic by Chris Morris; City Hall photo by Paul Chinn.
SOURCES: Department of Public Works, Bureau of Architecture: Tom Thornton, project manager; Tony Irons, assistant project manager. Examiner files.

Base isolators

Base isolation bearings are structural components with high vertical stiffness and low horizontal stiffness. This means they can support heavy weights from above and still remain flexible in the event of side-to-side motion. Commercially available isolation systems (lead-rubber bearings, high damping rubber bearings, and the friction-pendulum sliding isolators) might be used to base isolate the San Francisco City Hall. At right is an example of a lead-rubber bearing. They would be fixed on concrete "footings" and would support the weight of the building.

Steel

Rubber

Lead

As the earth moves below the structure, the lateral load shifts and the building is forced to absorb the energy.

Isolators allow the structure to remain stationary, absorbing the lateral energy as the ground shifts below them.

Installing base isolators at City Hall

Short line explaing that this is one of the proposed ways that base isolators will be installed in the understructure of City Hall.

Existing flooring

Main floor
Column fireproofing
Concrete fill
Ground floor
Grade

Installing base isolators

1. Remove fireproofing
2. Remove slab on grade
3. Excavate for footings
4. Cast footings and slab on grade
5. Weld brackets for column shoring
6. Shore the column and cut the base
7. Install transfer girder assembly and base isolator
8. Complete steel infill framing
9. Install steel deck and concrete fill. Remove column shoring.

CITY HALL TIMELINE

1870: The old City Hall at Larkin Street near Grove sits behind the Hall of Records at right. This Civic Center complex took 25 years to build and was destroyed 11 years later in the great fire that followed the earthquake.

1906: The dome of City Hall was all that was left intact after the 8.3 earthquake and fire.

1915: At completion, City Hall was deemed the crowning monument of a City Beautiful movement launched in 1904 by then-Mayor James Duval Phelan, who believed San Francisco needed stately buildings to realize its potential as "capital of an empire."

City Hall: A Close Up

DESIGN: Chris Morris, Kelly Frankeny, USA

PUBLISHER/CLIENT: *San Francisco Examiner*

DATE OF 1ST PUBLICATION/USE: 17 October 1992

DESIGN RATIONALE: On the anniversary of the earthquake that damaged this building, the graphic illustrates the work that is underway to make it safe in the event of another earthquake and the work being done cosmetically. Employing cross-sections and exploded views, and superimposing the graphic on top of an aerial photo of City Hall, it gives much insight into the scope of the work necessary to fix a structure so large.

CREDITS: Art director, Kelly Frankeny; photographer, Paul Chinn; illustrator, Chris Morris; writer, Gerald Adams; researcher, Stewart Huntington.

Broadgate

DESIGN: Michael Robinson, UK

PUBLISHER/CLIENT: Broadgate

DATE OF 1ST PUBLICATION/USE: 1987

DESIGN RATIONALE: Part of a series of drawings for the Broadgate Development, London. In this case a whole building was cut through to show the shell and core to possible tenants. The series of drawings proved very effective, and the development was and still is one of the few successes of the property boom. Design and Art Direction awards were given for illustration, photograph and design (Davenport Associates, Peter Davenport).

CREDITS: Art director, Peter Davenport, Davenport Associates; illustrator, Michael Robinson.

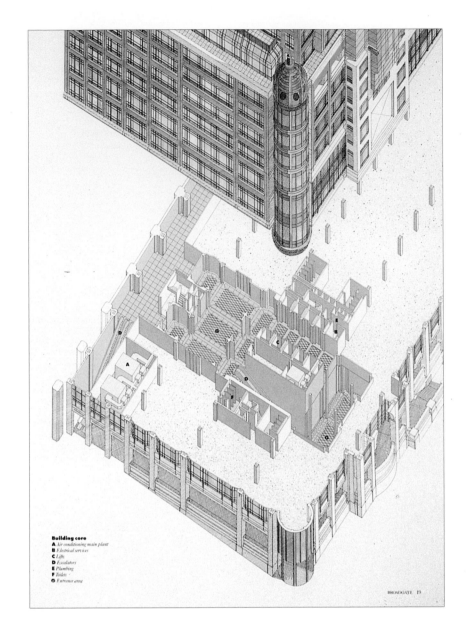

Building core
A *Air conditioning main plant*
B *Electrical services*
C *Lifts*
D *Escalators*
E *Plumbing*
F *Toilets*
G *Entrance area*

BROADGATE 19

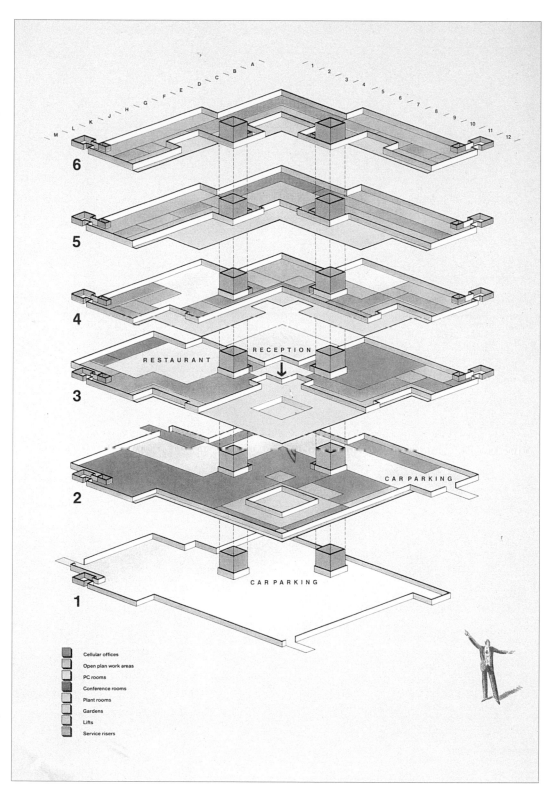

6

5

4

RESTAURANT   RECEPTION

3

CAR PARKING

2

CAR PARKING

1

■ Cellular offices
□ Open plan work areas
□ PC rooms
■ Conference rooms
□ Plant rooms
□ Gardens
□ Lifts
■ Service risers

IBM Building Plan

DESIGN: Michael Robinson, UK

PUBLISHER/CLIENT: IBM

DESIGN RATIONALE: A plan of a building IBM took over from Wiggins Teap as a new office, this diagram was to help explain where areas were in this rather complex building., Condensing the perspective helped to get the plan down to this small area.

CREDITS: Art director, Robert Carter (DEGW); illustrator, Michael Robinson.

Bringing
together
a
full
range
of
services

From rough shell to ready-for-occupancy, Structure Tone provides a comprehensive range of general contracting services. These result in a coordinated construction process—one that provides clients with many important advantages. We have experience managing projects for widely diverse corporate clients and requirements. This diagram demonstrates some of the finished work and services that Structure Tone can offer you.

We can develop environments that reflect your company's image, such as ❶ an executive board room with special architectural millwork, or ❷ monumental stairway. We will even recommend carpeting, when needed. We can anticipate and resolve complex telecommunications needs that are unique to ❸ busy trading facilities. In addition, we're skilled at planning and implementing interior spaces, such as ❹ a cafeteria or a specially designed atrium that accommodates employee seating.

We recognize that many companies require ❺ open-plan workstation spaces that allow for easy communication among employees while keeping noise levels low. We can even handle such highly specialized environments as ❻ a computer center with its critical wiring and cooling needs. These may require raised floors or ❼ specialized ventilation, and our staff coordinates with different subcontractors to make sure the proper results are achieved.

In addition, during the course of construction, ❽ Structure Tone maintains an on-site office at a client's location to provide maximum flexibility and project control. This office helps ❾ supervise construction, monitor material deliveries and provide ongoing support and maintenance services to clients as their business needs grow.

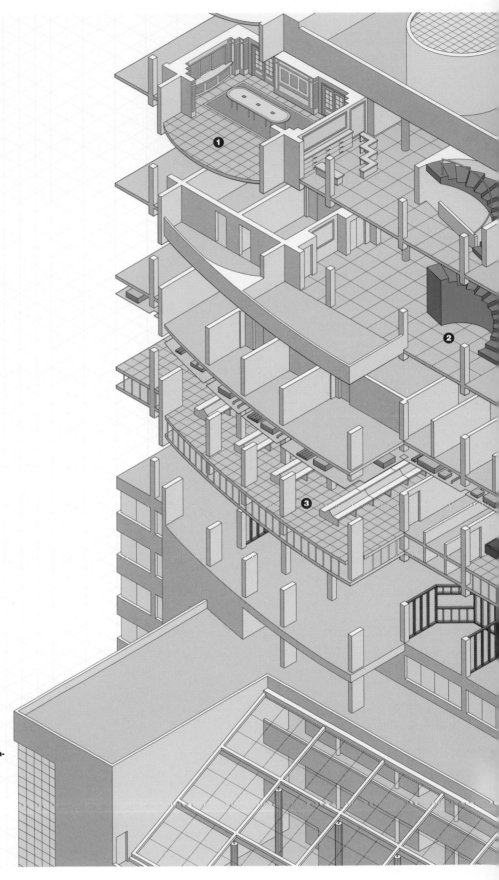

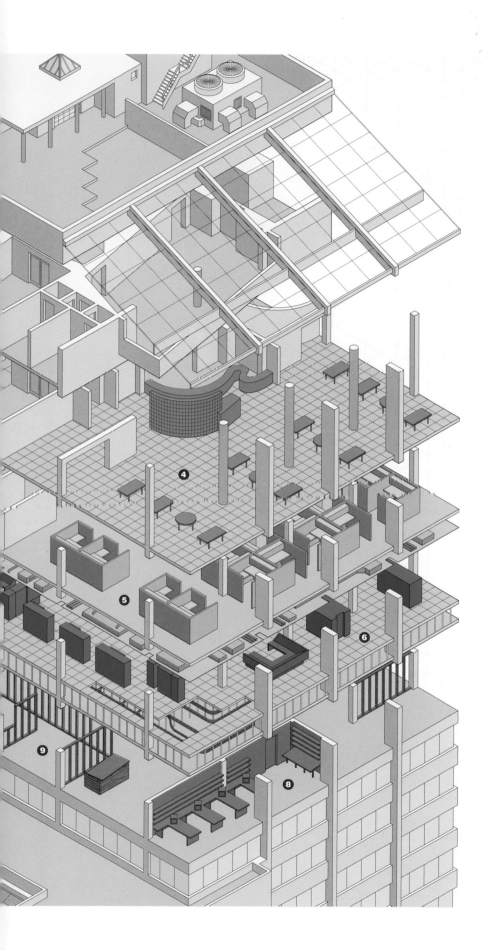

Construction Options

DESIGN: David Feinberg, Collateral Plus, USA

PUBLISHER/CLIENT: Structure Tone

DATE OF 1ST PUBLICATION/USE: 1989

DESIGN RATIONALE: Diagram highlighting the services offered by an interior construction company for use in a promotional brochure. Through its scale, intricacy and use of colour, the work invites the viewer to explore the contents of the various floors. It clearly illustrates the range of construction options being offered.

CREDITS: Art director, Peter McGuggart, Collateral Plus; illustrators, Jared Schneidman, Ron Kopels.

Garden Grove Temple

DESIGN: Newman Huh, USA

PUBLISHER/CLIENT: The Orange County Register

DATE OF 1ST PUBLICATION/USE: 1992

DESIGN RATIONALE: To show the construction of a Vietnamese temple in southern California.

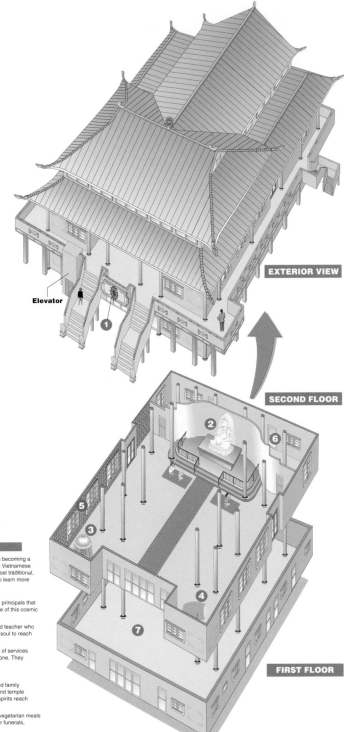

Elevator

EXTERIOR VIEW

SECOND FLOOR

FIRST FLOOR

A TEMPLE RISES

Chua Viet Nam, under construction in Garden Grove, is becoming a landmark in the area. When completed, the $1.1 million Vietnamese Buddhist temple will be Orange County's largest and most traditional, attracting tourists, students and other visitors seeking to learn more about Vietnamese culture.

A few highlights:

1 The darma wheel represents the natural and moral principals that apply to all things and beings and the dutiful observance of this cosmic law in one's life.

2 The image of Buddha, the religious philosopher and teacher who taught that self-denial and right-thinking will enable the soul to reach nirvana, a divine state of release from the mortal world.

3 4 Pounding of the drum and bell at the beginning of services serves to clear the mind and set a serious, meditative tone. They symbolize wisdom and intuition.

5 5,000 lighted Buddhas will decorate the interior.

6 Shrine is where members house icons for deceased family members. Photographs of the dead rest on the walls, and temple members' prayers and devotions help their ancestors' spirits reach nirvana.

7 Meeting room includes a full kitchen for preparing vegetarian meals and reception area for about 400 people. To be used for funerals, weddings and special events.

Source: The Register

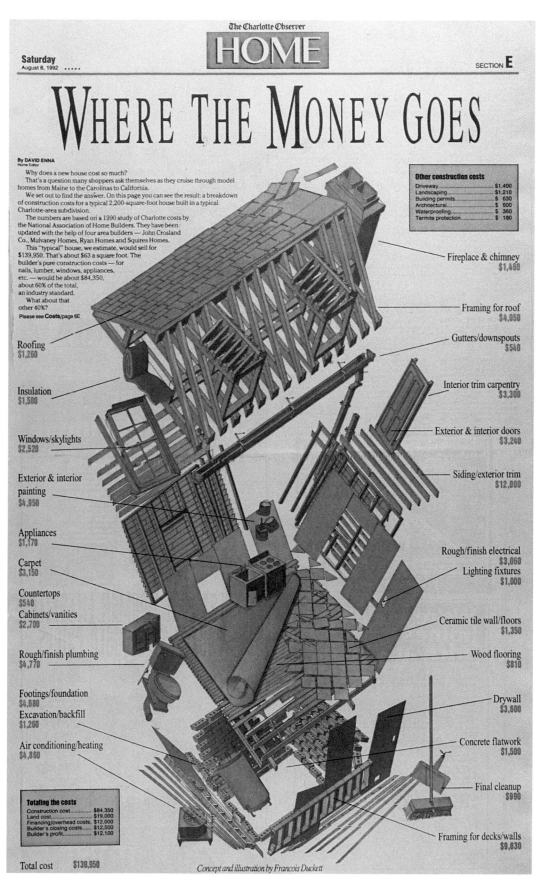

Where the Money Goes

DESIGN: François Duckett, Canada

PUBLISHER/CLIENT: *The Charlotte Observer*, USA

DATE OF 1ST PUBLICATION/USE: 8 August 1992

DESIGN RATIONALE: A simplified one-room house, exploded to show the components. A different way of showing something that is commonly represented as a cross-section.

CREDITS: Illustrator, François Duckett; writer, David Enna; type selected by Sarah Blaydon.

Other projects

In this chapter you will find large posters and graphics that do not fit neatly into other categories. In some cases, they contain elements of all the categories in this book.

The screen icons that guide the designer through the operation of a computer graphics program are a very important part of the efficient operation of the program. The design of the icons themselves is therefore an important field, and one that is represented here. While these icons are not strictly diagrammatic graphics, they can stand for the importance of the role that the computer plays in the production of information design.

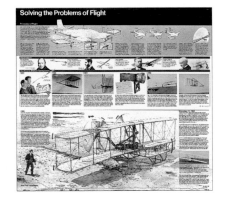

Non-advertising posters have been an efficient method of communication from the early days of printing, when publishing often meant pinning up the printed work outside the printshop to be read in public. In some developing countries today, walls of official "news" broadsheets are the only way for people to read

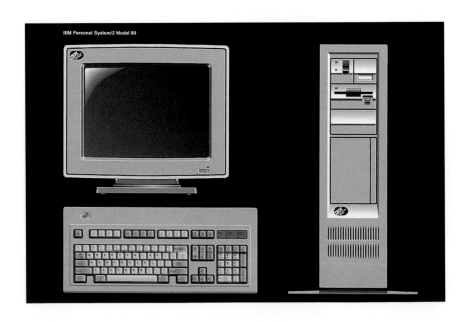

about the world, even if it is filtered through government censors. In the 1920s, Otto Neurath, an Austrian social scientist and philosopher, developed a style of teaching through large chart-posters at the Vienna Museum of Social and Economic Studies. He wanted to communicate ideas and information about the world to all classes of people, in fact to anyone who might go to his museum, regardless of their reading ability. The principles he used are still relevant, and his description of his own work is as good a definition of diagrammatic graphics as one could find today: "If the immense power of statistical truth is to be turned to full account, the prime necessity is the pictorial representation of statistical data. Our museum, with its carefully evolved method, is able, graphically, to represent social and economic problems. Meaningless columns of figures spring to life. Logic wedded to clarity is effective and convincing."

The graphics in this chapter, along with the many others in this book, aspire to be both effective and convincing.

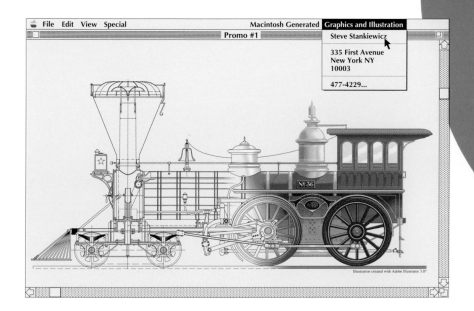

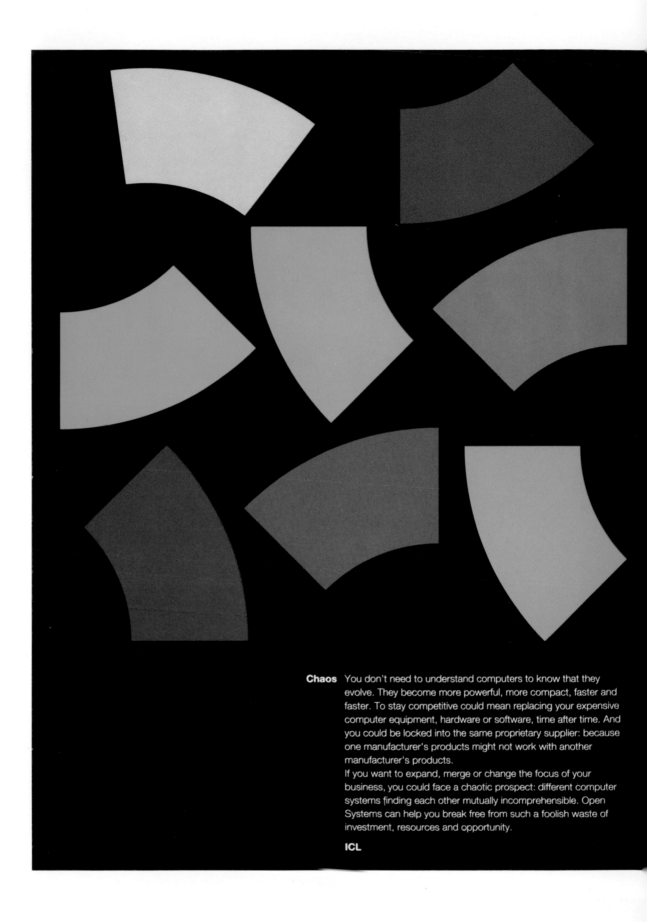

Chaos You don't need to understand computers to know that they evolve. They become more powerful, more compact, faster and faster. To stay competitive could mean replacing your expensive computer equipment, hardware or software, time after time. And you could be locked into the same proprietary supplier: because one manufacturer's products might not work with another manufacturer's products.

If you want to expand, merge or change the focus of your business, you could face a chaotic prospect: different computer systems finding each other mutually incomprehensible. Open Systems can help you break free from such a foolish waste of investment, resources and opportunity.

ICL

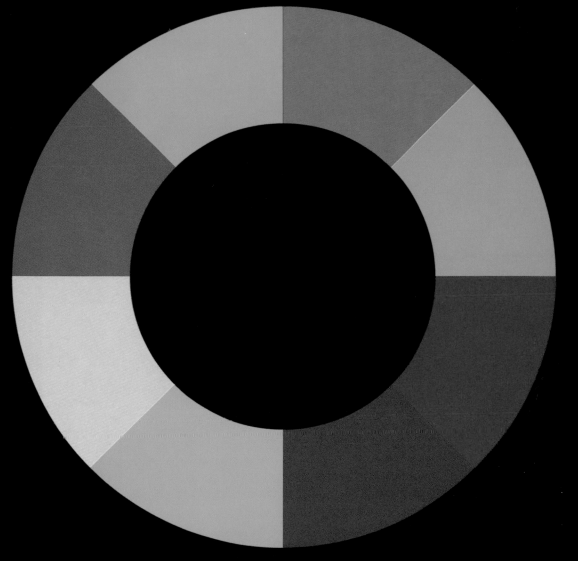

Open Systems

DESIGN: Williams and Phoa (Jo Shackleton, Sarah Jane Mackenzie), UK

PUBLISHER/CLIENT: ICL

DATE OF 1ST PUBLICATION/USE: 1991 (various publications)

DESIGN RATIONALE: Intended to promote ICL's services to the business sector. The target audience was top executives with little or no previous knowledge of open systems. Because it was distributed in 13 countries, the design had to be instantly striking, the copy very simple and the images international in order to cross cultural barriers.

CREDITS: Art director, Phoa Kia Boon.

Order Yet there's no such thing as an Open System: that is, it's not something you buy in a box. It's a far more orderly approach to the management, transmission, access and presentation of information. Open Systems are simply a set of internationally agreed standards, independent of any single supplier, to which all components of a system of information technology must conform. Any product manufactured to Open Systems standards will work with any other product manufactured to those standards by any supplier, anywhere. This used to be a theory. Now it's a fact. Throughout the international community, all kinds of major businesses and governments will deal only with companies whose information technology conforms to Open Systems standards. There is no real alternative any longer.
If anyone tells you Open Systems are a waste of time, ask yourself: does this person have my company's best interests at heart? Let's take a closer look at the real business benefits.

ICL

Congaree Swamp

River, Floodplain, and Forest

The Congaree River is formed in South Carolina's Richland County with the confluence of the Saluda and Broad Rivers. Some 60 miles downstream the Congaree loses its identity as it joins with the Wateree River to form the Santee River. With its characteristic flooding currents, the meandering Congaree River can gradually cut off one of its many meanders, or river turns, to form an oxbow such as Weston Lake.

The Saluda and Broad Rivers drain 8,032 square miles of northwest South Carolina and western North Carolina. The extent of a flooding episode in the Congaree Swamp is determined by the amount of rainfall upstream in these rivers' watersheds. Flooding occurs on an average of 10 times per year in the park. Initially, inundations of the Congaree floodplain come via its network of creeks, guts, and sloughs, some of which were former riverbeds. Recurrent floodwaters deposit rich soils whose nutrients support the diverse mixture of giant trees that makes Congaree Swamp so significant.

Within most of the park the elevation of the Congaree floodplain ranges from 100 feet above sea level on the west side to 80 feet on the east. Only several levees and some elevated points known as cattle mounds can slow down the floodwaters that surge through the park. Animals survive these flooding episodes by reaching higher ground or by swimming to the bluff lines on either side of the river. (See the diagram, Cross-section of the Congaree River.) A park ranger once saw three pigs riding out floodwaters on a floating log. Deer can swim the river to higher ground. Bobcats and salamanders may climb trees and wait out a flood.

Shallow, disk-shaped root systems make Congaree Swamp trees particularly prone to toppling. When a big tree falls, its crown may leave a half-acre opening in the forest canopy. Hikers beware: brambles grow in these openings left by treefalls, and in summer and fall wasps frequent canebrakes, the boardwalk, and footbridges. Despite treefalls, some areas of the forest have huge open understories, and the large, silent trees may well remind one of a cathedral.

Baldcypress
Congaree Swamp forests are healthy and vigorous. Baldcypress trees reproduce readily here despite exacting seedbed requirements. Because of their extensive root systems, baldcypresses rarely are blown down, as are hardwoods. The largest baldcypress here boasts a circumference of 27 feet and 5 inches. Buttressed bases and knees make this tree, a relative of the gigantic redwood, easy to identify. Knees up to 7½ feet high have been found in Congaree Swamp.

A Forest's Profile
Like most plant communities, including your lawn, forests grow in layers. Attaining a height of more than 150 feet, the forest profile at Congaree Swamp may reach from the ground to the top of a record-class loblolly pine. Poison ivy and wild grape vines may climb all the way into the canopy layers of the forest profile.

To the right of the diagram are brief descriptions of various forest layers and the emergent trees that rise above the canopy. Variations in amounts of sunlight and moisture make different levels of the forest profile quite different microclimates.

Floodplain Forests
Dramatic changes in soil conditions caused by slight elevation changes produce diverse associations of tree species. Sycamores, whose roots tolerate periodic inundation, dominate stream banks. Baldcypress or tupelo dominate low areas of standing water. Overcup oak forest associations dominate slightly drier flats.

Elevation
Changes of only a few feet in elevation can result in entirely different types of trees. Dense stands of cherrybark oak, sweetgum, and holly thrive on higher, drier soils. On lower areas stands of water tupelo, baldcypress, and water ash grow. Loblolly pines and canebrakes are indicators of slightly higher ground.

Sweetgum/Mixed Hardwoods
Most common in f[?] park, the sweetgu[?] mixed hardwoods[?] ciation occurs thr[?] out the floodplain[?] Sweetgum domin[?] along with swamp[?] chestnut, laurel o[?] and green ash. Ir[?] wood, holly, and s[?] times pawpaws d[?] nate its understor[?]

Paintings by John Dawson   Consultant L.L. Gaddy

Osprey

Great b[?]

Congaree River

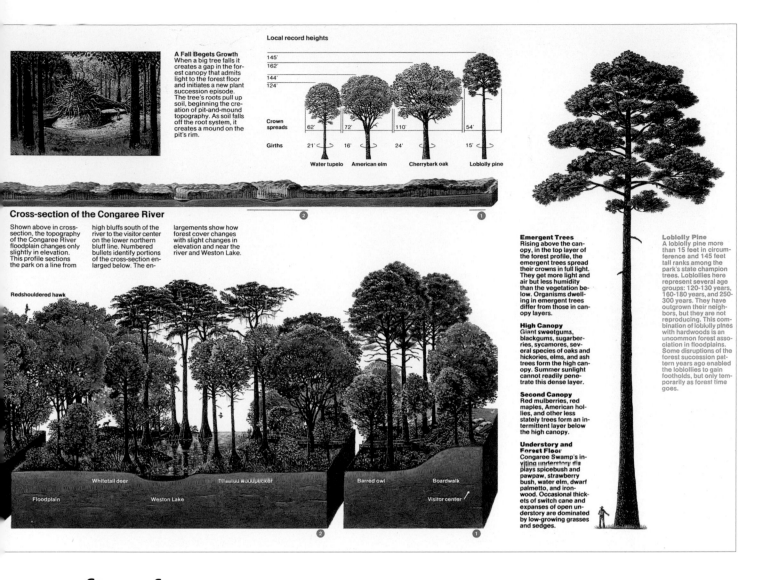

A Fall Begets Growth
When a big tree falls it creates a gap in the forest canopy that admits light to the forest floor and initiates a new plant succession episode. The tree's roots pull up soil, beginning the creation of pit-and-mound topography. As soil falls off the root system, it creates a mound on the pit's rim.

Local record heights

145'			
162'			
144'			
124'			

Crown spreads: 62'   72'   110'   54'

Girths: 21'   16'   24'   15'

Water tupelo   American elm   Cherrybark oak   Loblolly pine

Cross-section of the Congaree River

Shown above in cross-section, the topography of the Congaree River floodplain changes only slightly in elevation. This profile sections the park on a line from high bluffs south of the river to the visitor center on the lower northern bluff line. Numbered bullets identify portions of the cross-section enlarged below. The enlargements show how forest cover changes with slight changes in elevation and near the river and Weston Lake.

Redshouldered hawk

Whitetail deer   Pileated woodpecker   Barred owl   Boardwalk

Floodplain   Weston Lake   Visitor center

Emergent Trees
Rising above the canopy, in the top layer of the forest profile, the emergent trees spread their crowns in full light. They get more light and air but less humidity than the vegetation below. Organisms dwelling in emergent trees differ from those in canopy layers.

High Canopy
Giant sweetgums, blackgums, sugarberries, sycamores, several species of oaks and hickories, elms, and ash trees form the high canopy. Summer sunlight cannot readily penetrate this dense layer.

Second Canopy
Red mulberries, red maples, American hollies, and other less stately trees form an intermittent layer below the high canopy.

Understory and Forest Floor
Congaree Swamp's inviting understory displays spicebush and pawpaw, strawberry bush, water elm, dwarf palmetto, and ironwood. Occasional thickets of switch cane and expanses of open understory are dominated by low-growing grasses and sedges.

Loblolly Pine
A loblolly pine more than 15 feet in circumference and 145 feet tall ranks among the park's state champion trees. Loblollies here represent several age groups: 120-130 years, 160-180 years, and 250-300 years. They have outgrown their neighbors, but they are not reproducing. This combination of loblolly pines with hardwoods is an uncommon forest association in floodplains. Some disruptions of the forest succession pattern years ago enabled the loblollies to gain footholds, but only temporarily as forest time goes.

Congaree Swamp

DESIGN: Bruce Geyman, USA

PUBLISHER/CLIENT: US National Park Service

DATE OF 1ST PUBLICATION/USE: 1988

DESIGN RATIONALE: A profile of the Congaree Swamp Forest and cross-section of the Congaree River in South Carolina.

CREDITS: Art director, Vincent Gleason; illustrator, John Dawson; writer, Edward Zahniser.

The World Below

Moonmilk, dripstone, boxwork, cave "ghosts." Strange names for a strange place that seems out-of-this-world. Oregon Caves, though, is clearly of this world, being linked directly to powerful forces shaping the Earth inside and out. Violent geologic events spanning millions of years have created a cave nestled within all six of the world's major rock types.

Creation of the cave began 220 million years ago when continent and ocean rock sideswiped, tearing open an ocean basin. Sea creatures lived and died in the basin, their remains forming calcite-rich muds that hardened into limestone and silica-rich muck that solidified as chert. Unable to sink out of the way, the ocean rock smashed into the continent head-on, obliterating the basin. Land debris and rock melted and crystallized as (1) a lightweight, granite-like rock that "fried" (2) and "baked" (3) limestone into marble. As it rose, the molten mass broke and pushed aside rock along faults, slowly lifting marble into mountains above dense ocean rock.

Oregon Caves area

Another collision tore the Siskiyous from the Sierras and twirled them to point east and west. In faults and between angled rock layers, water, acidified by carbon dioxide, followed weaknesses to dissolve out a crazy mix of tilted rooms and twisting passages. Rock sliding under the Cascades melted and rose forming volcanoes that dumped ash (4) into the cave. By about 10,000 years ago, erosion had opened a cave entrance. The resulting loss of carbon dioxide in the cave air allowed seeping water to lose its acid as well and to deposit limestone (5) and cemented gravels (6), completing the group of six major rock types.

The large cutaway diagram of the cave (right) is not of any specific portion but shows a composite of formations and conditions to be found throughout. As you tour the cave look for the formations shown here: boxwork, clay worms, cave popcorn, and cave ghosts. You may also see roots of trees growing above the cave. These roots are a connection between sunlight and darkness, for they provide fluids for cave creatures while the roots are searching for nutrients for the tree above. Finally note the keyhole-like shape of the cave formed by the roundish chamber and the notch caused by the downcutting of the stream. The numbers in parentheses in the text (left) refer to the six major rock types that are described beneath the diagram of the cave (right).

The block diagrams (left) show two phases in a geological process that have taken more than 200 million years. The top diagram shows the ocean basin torn open by sideswiping continental and oceanic rock. The bottom diagram shows the uplifted marble mountains—the Siskiyous—torn into their east-west orientation. The colors depict the different types of rock: gray denotes basalt, pink is the quartz diorite, and white is the marble in which the cave formed.

1 Molten, plutonic matter oozed from inside the Earth, filling faults and solidifying into this quartz diorite dike.

2 When the quartz diorite dike intruded, the great heat of the molten mass "fried" the adjacent calcite, changing it—metamorphosing it—into a contact metamorphic rock.

3 Heat from tremendous bodies of molten plutonic matter "baked" limestone into marble, making it a regional metamorphic rock.

4 Volcanic a eruptions cave and in fine ho

The World Above

The surface world at Oregon Caves mirrors the diversity found underground, for the variety of rocks and soils have created a varied landscape. Serpentine rock serves as a refuge to some plant species and at the same time is intolerant of, even poisonous to, many others. The cave itself drains water away from the marble-based soils making them more suited to shrubs than to trees. The result is a mosaic of habitats that in turn supports a diversity of animals.

Yet climate overshadows the role of rocks and soils. Low elevations and south-facing slopes support fire- and drought-resistant oaks, while firs reign on cold, damp slopes high above the park. Late snowpacks, flood scour, and fire create meadows amidst virgin forest. In these age-old mountains limited glaciation has preserved one of the most ancient plant communities west of the Mississippi River where several plant zones meet just south of an Ice Age Purge. There is also a wealth of wildlife, the greatest diversity of birds and amphibians in Oregon. Steller's jays, deer, squirrels, and chipmunks are often seen. Other more secretive species call the park home including the northern spotted owl, mountain beaver, Pacific giant salamander, and a host of butterflies.

The Big Tree (left) is old, even for a Douglas-fir. A spring near its base may have shielded it from centuries of fires that killed its siblings. But even monarchs die. Its broken top attests to strong winter storms that may someday topple this forest giant.

The Madrone is the park's most easily recognized tree. Its adaptations may be endless. The peeling bark pops off burning embers during a fire, protecting the living tissue beneath. If the tree is burned to the ground,

sprouts soon rise up. Thick wax protects the leaves from drought, enabling the tree to survive on the dry and thin-soiled marble. Madrone even uses chemical warfare. Its leaves contain a growth inhibitor that prevents most other seedlings from sprouting nearby.

The Pacific giant salamander (above) barks when in danger, one of the few amphibians known to vocalize. Like a canary in a mine, a salamander warns us of changes in our environment. Today its cry tells of a mysterious worldwide decline in amphibians.

The northern spotted owl (above) prefers the dense stands found in old growth forests. It feeds on flying squirrels and red-backed voles. The Takelma Indians believed that the owl brought good news. Hunters prayed to the bird, promising the fat and blood of as many deer as they needed to catch the next day.

Since a mountain beaver's primitive kidneys need ample water, a decrease in rainfall over 30 million years has confined this living fossil to the wet Pacific Northwest.

For a rodent, the flying squirrel (above) has a huge brain, the better to enable it to escape the outstretched talons of its chief predator, the spotted owl.

Illustrations by Dorothy Michele Novick

Moonmilk

Cave ghosts

Cave popcorn

Rimstone dams

stant to the ited yers.

5 Fragment sedimentary rock is created from old, worn-down rock fragments, which are cemented together by calcite.

6 Chemical sedimentary rock is formed from rock materials dissolved by water and deposited in fine-grained layers, gradually hardening into rock.

Oregon Caves

DESIGN: Melissa Cronyn, USA

PUBLISHER/CLIENT: US National Park Service

DATE OF 1ST PUBLICATION/USE: 1992

DESIGN RATIONALE: To illustrate a composite of formations and conditions found throughout the caves.

CREDITS: Art director, Vincent Gleason; illustrator, Dorothy Michele Novick; writer, Robert Grogg.

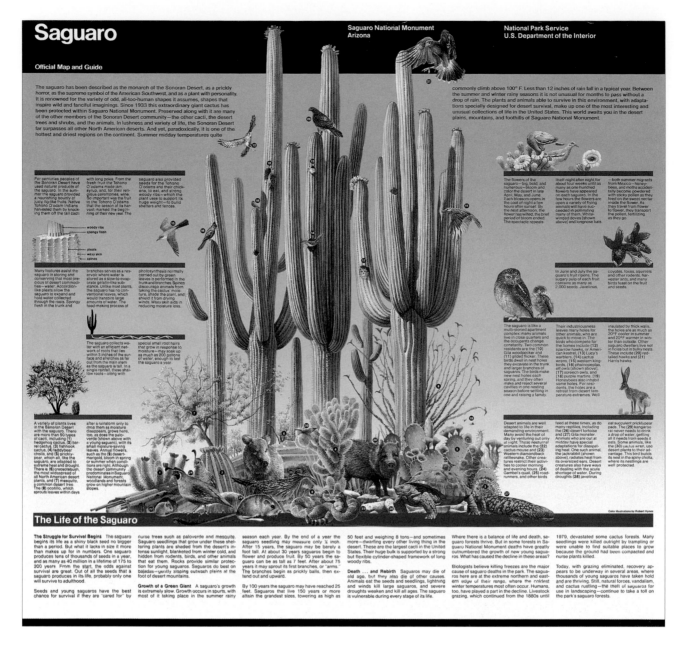

Saguaro

DESIGN: Melissa Cronyn, USA

PUBLISHER/CLIENT: US National Park Service

DATE OF 1ST PUBLICATION/USE: 1986

DESIGN RATIONALE: Illustrates the variety of life in the Sonokran Desert community, the unique adaptations to extreme conditions and the interrelationships among plant and animal life.

CREDITS: Art director, Vincent Gleason; illustrator, Robert Hynes; writer, Carolyn de Raismes.

Saguaro : A Park Guide

Saguaro National Monument
Arizona

National Park Service
U.S. Department of the Interior

Planning Your Visit
Saguaro National Monument is divided into 2 districts—Saguaro West, to the west of Tucson, and Saguaro East, to the east. Each has places to obtain park information, scenic drives, trails, and picnic areas. Neither has lodges nor campgrounds. For detailed descriptions of what to see and do in each district, see "Touring Saguaro West" and "Touring Saguaro East" below. For more information write: Saguaro National Monument, 3693 South Old Spanish Trail, Tucson, AZ 85730-5699, or call (602) 883-6366 (Saguaro West) or (602) 296-8576 (Saguaro East).

Saguaro's Desert Climate
Many people feel the best desert season is from October through April, when high temperatures are in the 60s and 70s°F. Nighttime temperatures during this time can fall below freezing. The hottest period is from May through September, when highs average in the 100s°F. Still, at night, temperatures drop by as much as 30°F, and high in the Rincon Mountains it is cooler, too. Rainy seasons occur twice a year—in short but violent thunderstorms from July through September and in gentle rains from January to March. Otherwise, sunshine prevails.

For Your Safety
Hiking and other strenuous activities in extreme heat can be hazardous. Pace yourself and rest often. Carry water (at least 1 gallon per person per day is recommended) and drink even when you don't feel thirsty. There is no water available at picnic areas or along most trails. ● Beware of painful encounters with cacti and other prickly plants. Be especially careful near cholla cactus spines that, with just the slightest touch, can become embedded in your skin. If a cactus joint attaches itself, use two sticks, a pocket comb, or other object as a lever to flip it away. ● The park is a sanctuary for living things. Leave plants and animals undisturbed. To avoid encountering poisonous rattlesnakes, scorpions, or Gila monsters, carry a flashlight at night and avoid putting your hands and feet under rocks or in other hidden places. All types of weapons are prohibited. ● During thunderstorms both lightning and flash floods pose threats. Avoid open and low-lying areas. ● Park roads are designed for sightseeing. Obey speed limits. Driving off the road is prohibited. Remember to always wear your seat belt. ● Pets must be leashed at all times. They are not allowed on trails. In an emergency, contact a ranger or call 911.

The Park
Saguaro National Monument consists of 2 districts, Saguaro West and Saguaro East. The 2 areas, separated by the city of Tucson, are about 30 miles apart. Together Saguaro West and the much larger Saguaro East (both shown below in more detail) preserve 87,114 acres of the life and landscape of the Sonoran Desert, including the park's namesake, the saguaro.

Saguaro West

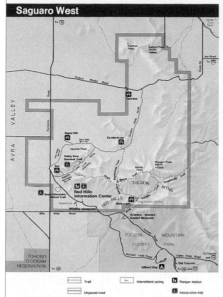

Saguaro East

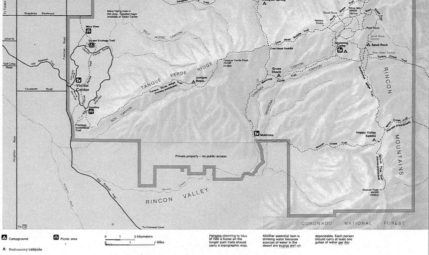

| | Trail | | Intermittent spring | | Ranger station |
| | Unpaved road | | | | Interpretive trail |

| ▲ | Campground | | Picnic area |
| ▲ | Backcountry campsite | | |

0 1 2 Kilometers
0 1 2 Miles

Persons planning to hike or ride a horse on the longer park trails should carry a topographic map.

Another essential item is drinking water because sources of water in the desert are scarce and undependable. Each person should carry at least one gallon of water per day.

Touring Saguaro West
Saguaro West, also known as the Tucson Mountain unit, offers a wide variety of Sonoran Desert life against the backdrop of the rugged Tucson Mountains. It is open 24 hours a day.

Information Center The Red Hills Information Center has brochures, books, maps, trail and drive guides, exhibits, and rangers who can discuss plans and interests with you. Schedules of park activities, which include guided hikes, nature walks, and talks, are posted. Most activities are conducted from December through April.

Scenic Drive The 6-mile Bajada Loop Drive passes through dense saguaro forests. This graded dirt road begins 1.5 miles from the information center. A guidebook is available. Persons with motorhomes or trailers should check road conditions before starting the drive.

Trails A hike in Saguaro West can be a stroll on a nature trail or a day-long wilderness trek. Within 1 mile of the information center are 2 nature trails. The Cactus Garden Trail, located at the center, follows a level paved walkway through a collection of desert plants. The Desert Discovery Nature Trail loops 0.5 mile along the gently sloping bajadas at the foot of the Tucson Mountains. Another short trail, the Valley View Overlook Trail, is a 1.5-mile roundtrip with spectacular views of mountains and desert scenery and extensive saguaro forests. Longer trails penetrate the wild country of the Tucson Mountains and their foothills. Because these trails intersect one another, you can make your hike as long or as short as desired. Horseback riding is permitted on all trails. It is recommended that you stay on trails; abandoned mine shafts make off-trail exploration hazardous. Camping is not permitted.

Picnic Areas Four picnic areas are located along park roads. A fifth, in the backcountry, can be reached only by trail. All trash must be packed out of this site. Each area has tables, grills, shade ramadas, and pit toilets.

Nearby Places of Interest Located south of Saguaro West, the Arizona-Sonora Desert Museum has a live collection of about 200 desert animals and 300 kinds of plants. Also to the south is Tucson Mountain County Park, which has hiking and horse trails and a campground.

Touring Saguaro East
Saguaro East, also called Rincon Mountain District, encompasses an aging saguaro forest at the foot of the majestic Rincon Mountains, as well as an exceptional variety of other desert communities. The park is open daily.

Visitor Center At the visitor center, you will find books, brochures, maps, trail and drive guides, exhibits, and a slide program about the saguaro and the Sonoran Desert. Rangers are available if you have questions about what to see and do. Schedules of ranger-guided walks and other park activities that are offered in the winter are posted. The center is open daily.

Scenic Drive The 8-mile Cactus Forest Drive winds through the heart of an extensive saguaro forest and offers a close leisurely look at a variety of Sonoran Desert life. This one-way road, which begins at the visitor center, is paved.

Trails About 128 miles of trails wind through the desert and mountain country of Saguaro East. Short hikes will introduce you to the plant and animal life of the Sonoran Desert. The 0.25-mile paved Desert Ecology Trail, located along Cactus Forest Drive, provides a brief explanation of water's role in the desert. This self-guiding trail is accessible to the disabled. Many other trails along the scenic drive are suitable for short hikes into the nearby pristine desert environment of this area. For information on these trails, stop at the visitor center. Several longer hiking trails penetrate the vast wilderness of the Rincon Mountains and their foothills. This is part of the park few people experience because it is it accessible only by foot or on horseback. It is quite unlike the lowland cactus deserts. In the Rincon Mountains, woodlands of scrub oak and pine and forests of ponderosa pine and Douglas-fir similar to those of the northern United States and southern Canada prevail.

Desert Plant Communities
In Saguaro National Monument several desert plant communities grow from the hot, dry desert lowlands to the cooler, moister mountain peaks. In Saguaro West, lowland communities of desert scrub—where the saguaro appears in exceptionally fine stands—and desert grasslands occur. Saguaro East, with its wider range of elevations, has all the communities shown here. This area has one of the most diverse assortments of plants in the Southwest.

Because many of the trails of Saguaro East intersect one another, trips of varying length can be planned. Horseback riding is permitted on all trails except the Tanque Verde Ridge Trail, Miller Creek Trail, and the Rincon Peak Trail. Before hiking or horseback riding into the Rincon Mountains, check with a park ranger on trail conditions.

Backcountry camping is allowed but only at designated sites. Backcountry use permits must be obtained at the visitor center in advance of an overnight trip.

Picnic Areas There are 2 picnic areas in Saguaro East, both located along the Cactus Forest Drive. Each has picnic tables, fire grills, and pit toilets. They do not have drinking water.

Nearby Places of Interest Coronado National Forest, which surrounds Saguaro East on the north, east, and south, has campgrounds, hiking trails, and picnic areas.

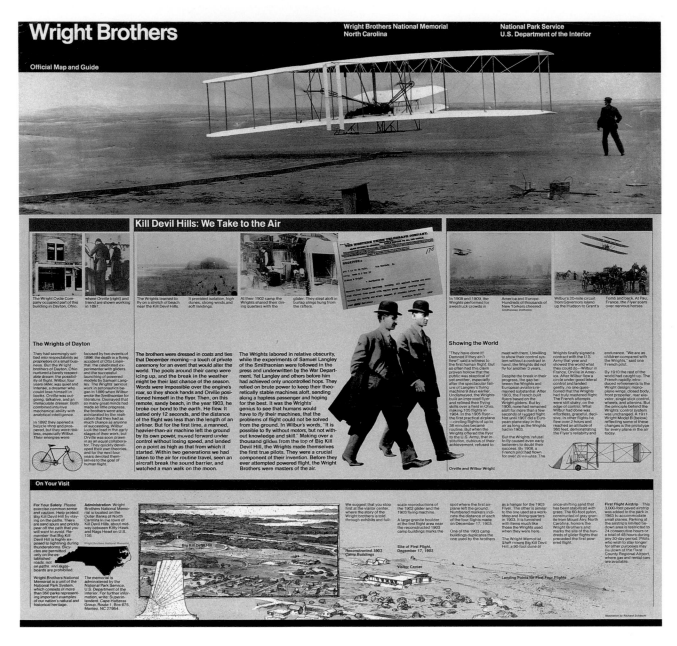

Wright Brothers

DESIGN: Bruce Geyman, Betsy Ehrlich, USA

PUBLISHER/CLIENT: US National Park Service

DATE OF 1ST PUBLICATION/USE: 1990

DESIGN RATIONALE: Illustrates the principles of flight and the constuction of the Wright brothers' first plane.

CREDITS: Art director, Vincent Gleason; illustrator, Richard Schlecht; writer, William Gordon.

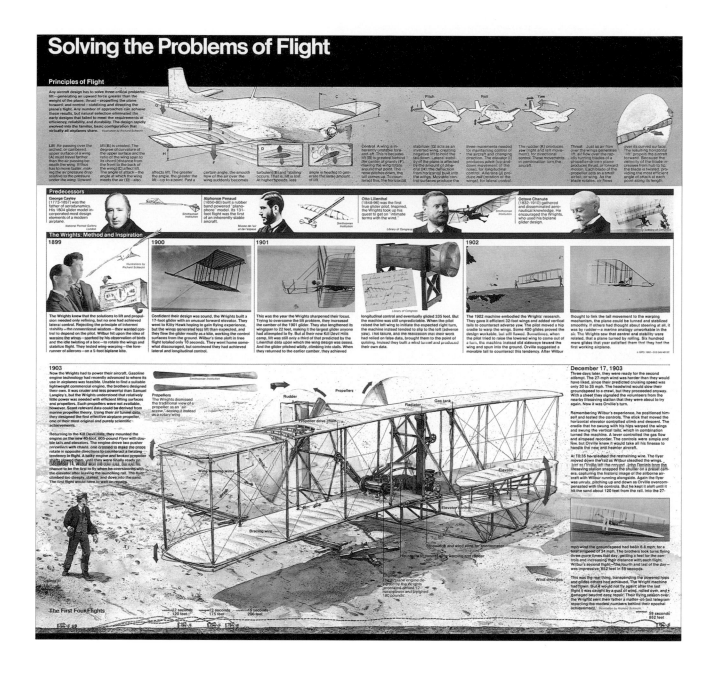

Solving the Problems of Flight

Principles of Flight

Any aircraft design has to solve three critical problems: lift—generating an upward force greater than the weight of the plane; thrust—propelling the plane forward; and control—stabilizing and directing the plane's flight. Any number of approaches can achieve these results, but natural selection eliminated the early designs that failed to meet the requirements of efficiency, reliability, and durability. The design rapidly evolved into the familiar, basic configuration that virtually all airplanes share. Illustration by Richard Schlecht

Pitch   Roll   Yaw

Lift Air passing over the arched, or cambered, upper surface of a wing (A) must travel farther than the air passing beneath the wing. If thus has to move faster, making the air pressure drop relative to the pressure under the wing. Upward lift (B) is created. The degree of curvature of the upper surface and the ratio of the wing span to its chord (distance from the front to the back of the wing) (C) affect lift. The angle of attack—the angle at which the wing meets the air (D)—also affects lift. The greater the angle, the greater the lift—up to a point. Past a certain angle, the smooth flow of the air over the wing suddenly becomes turbulent (E) and "stalling" occurs. That is, lift is lost. At higher speeds, less angle is needed to generate the same amount of lift.

Control A wing is inherently unstable fore-and-aft. This is because lift (B) is greatest behind the center of gravity (F), making the wing rotate around that point. The nose pitches down, the tail comes up. To counteract this, the horizontal stabilizer (G) acts as an inverted wing, creating negative lift to hold the tail down. Lateral stability of the plane is affected by the amount of dihedral (H): the deflection from horizontal built into the wings. Movable control surfaces produce the three movements needed for maintaining control of the aircraft and changing direction. The elevator (I) produces pitch (up-and-down movement of the nose), for longitudinal control. Ailerons (J) produce roll (rotation of the wings), for lateral control. The rudder (K) produces yaw (right and left movement), for directional control. These movements in combination turn the aircraft. **Thrust** Just as air flow over the wings generates lift, air flow over the rapidly turning blades of a propeller-driven plane produces thrust, or forward motion. Each blade of the propeller acts as a small airfoil, or wing. As the blade rotates, air flows over its curved surface. The resulting horizontal "lift" propels the aircraft forward. Because the velocity of the blade increases from hub to tip, the blade is twisted, providing the most efficient angle of attack at each point along its length.

Predecessors

George Cayley (1773-1857) was the father of aerodynamics. His 1804 glider model incorporated most design elements of a modern airplane. *National Portrait Gallery, London*

Alphonse Penaud (1850-80) built a rubber band powered "planophone" model. Its 131-foot flight was the first of an inherently stable aircraft. *Musée de l'air et de l'espace*

Otto Lilienthal (1849-96) was the first true glider pilot. Inspired, the Wrights took up his quest to get on "intimate terms with the wind." *Library of Congress*

Octave Chanute (1832-1910) gathered and disseminated aeronautical knowledge. He encouraged the Wrights, who used his biplane glider design. *Archives of Chicago*

The Wrights: Method and Inspiration

Illustrations by Richard Schlecht

1899

The Wrights knew that the solutions to lift and propulsion needed only refining, but no one had achieved lateral control. Rejecting the principle of inherent stability—the conventional wisdom—they wanted control to depend on the pilot. Wilbur hit upon the idea of warping the wings—sparked by his observation of birds and the idle twisting of a box—to rotate the wings and stabilize flight. They tested wing-warping—the forerunner of ailerons—on a 5-foot biplane kite.

1900

Confident their design was sound, the Wrights built a 17-foot glider with an unusual forward elevator. They went to Kitty Hawk hoping to gain flying experience, but the wings generated less lift than expected, and they flew the glider mostly as a kite, working the control surfaces from the ground. Wilbur's time aloft in free flight totaled only 10 seconds. They went home somewhat discouraged, but convinced they had achieved lateral and longitudinal control.

1901

This was the year the Wrights sharpened their focus. Trying to overcome the lift problem, they increased the camber of the 1901 glider. They also lengthened its wingspan to 22 feet, making it the largest glider anyone had attempted to fly. But at their new Kill Devil Hills camp, lift was still only a third of that predicted by the Lilienthal data upon which the wing design was based. And the glider pitched wildly, climbing into stalls. When they returned to the earlier camber, they achieved longitudinal control and eventually glided 335 feet. But the machine was still unpredictable. When the pilot raised the left wing to initiate the expected right turn, the machine instead tended to slip to the left (adverse yaw). This failure, and the realization that their work had relied on false data, brought them to the point of quitting. Instead they built a wind tunnel and produced their own data.

1902

The 1902 machine embodied the Wrights' research. They gave it efficient 32-foot wings and added vertical tails to counteract adverse yaw. The pilot moved a hip cradle to warp the wings. Some 400 glides proved the design workable, but still flawed. Sometimes, when the pilot tried to raise the lowered wing to come out of a turn, the machine instead slid sideways toward the wing and spun into the ground. Orville suggested a movable tail to counteract this tendency. After Wilbur thought to link the tail movement to the warping mechanism, the plane could be turned and stabilized smoothly. If others had thought about steering at all, it was by rudder—a marine analogy unworkable in the air. The Wrights saw that control and stability were related, that a plane turned by rolling. Six hundred more glides that year satisfied them that they had the first working airplane.

© GPO 1992 · 312-240-NB157

1903

Now the Wrights had to power their aircraft. Gasoline engine technology had recently advanced to where its use in airplanes was feasible. Unable to find a suitable lightweight commercial engine, the brothers designed their own. It was cruder and less powerful than Samuel Langley's, but the Wrights understood that relatively little power was needed with efficient lifting surfaces and propellers. Such propellers were not available, however. Scant relevant data could be derived from marine propeller theory. Using their air tunnel data, they designed the first effective airplane propeller, one of their most original and purely scientific achievements.

Returning to the Kill Devil Hills, they mounted the engine on the new 40-foot, 605-pound *Flyer* with double tails and elevators. The engine drove two pusher propellers with chains, one crossed to make the props rotate in opposite directions to counteract a twisting tendency in flight. A balky engine and broken propeller shafts delayed them until they were finally ready on December 14. Wilbur won the coin toss, but lost his chance to be the first to fly when he oversteered with the elevator after leaving the launching rail. The flyer climbed too steeply, stalled, and dove into the sand. The first flight would have to wait on repairs.

Propellers The Wrights dismissed the traditional view of a propeller as an "air screw," seeing it instead as a rotating wing.

Engine The airplane engine designed by the Wrights generated almost 12 horsepower and weighed 180 pounds.

December 17, 1903

Three days later, they were ready for the second attempt. The 27-mph wind was harder than they would have liked, since their predicted cruising speed was only 30 to 35 mph. The headwind would slow their groundspeed to a crawl, but they proceeded anyway. With a sheet they signaled the volunteers from the nearby lifesaving station that they were about to try again. Now it was Orville's turn.

Remembering Wilbur's experience, he positioned himself and tested the controls. The stick that moved the horizontal elevator controlled climb and descent. The cradle that he swung with his hips warped the wings and swung the vertical tails, which in combination turned the machine. A lever controlled the gas flow and airspeed recorder. The controls were simple and few, but Orville knew it would take all his finesse to handle the new and heavier aircraft.

At 10:35 he released the restraining wire. The flyer moved down the rail as Wilbur steadied the wings. Just as Orville left the rail, John Daniels from the lifesaving station snapped the shutter on a preset camera, capturing the historic image of the airborne aircraft with Wilbur running alongside. Again the flyer was unruly, pitching up and down as Orville overcompensated with the controls. But he kept it aloft until it hit the sand about 120 feet from the rail. Into the 27-mph wind the groundspeed had been 6.8 mph; for a total airspeed of 34 mph. The brothers took turns flying three more times that day, getting a feel for the controls and increasing their distance with each flight. Wilbur's second flight—the fourth and last of the day—was impressive: 852 feet in 59 seconds.

This was the real thing, transcending the powered hops and glides others had achieved. The Wright machine had flown. But it would not fly again: after the last flight it was caught by a gust of wind, rolled over, and damaged beyond easy repair. Their flying season over, the Wrights sent their father a matter-of-fact telegram reporting the modest numbers behind their epochal achievement. Illustration by Richard Schlecht

Labels on illustration: Propellers · Rudder · Radiator · Gas tank · Propeller drive chain · Wing warping wires · Elevator · Elevator control · Bracing wire · Hip cradle to control wing warping and rudder · Slipwatch and wind vane for anemometer · Wind direction

The First Four Flights

12 seconds 120 feet · 12 seconds 175 feet · 15 seconds 200 feet · 59 seconds 852 feet

House Management

DESIGN: Ronnie Peters, USA

PUBLISHER/CLIENT: Dynamic Diagrams

DATE OF 1ST PUBLICATION/USE: 1991

DESIGN RATIONALE: This in-house study analyses the design of a symbol consisting of two distinct levels of information (one layer contained within another).

CREDITS: Art director, Kris Lenk.

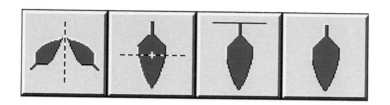

Computer Software Icons

DESIGN: Ronnie Peters, USA

PUBLISHER/CLIENT: Athena Design Systems, Inc.

DATE OF 1ST PUBLICATION/USE: 1993

DESIGN RATIONALE: The design of the icons for a painting software uses the image of a single object (a tree) and manipulates it to create representations of the different rendering options.

CREDITS: Art directors, Paul Kahn, Kris Lenk.

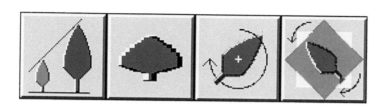

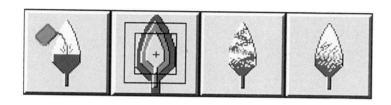

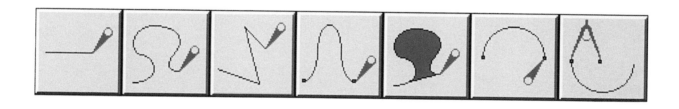

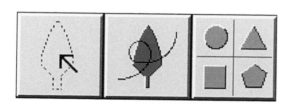

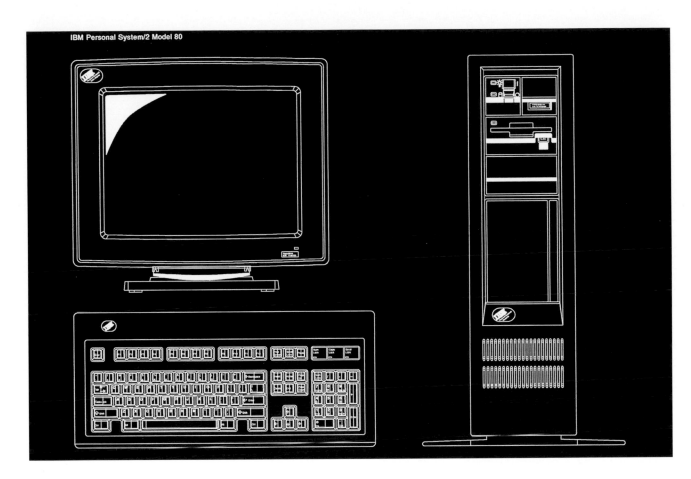

IBM Personal System/2 Model 80

Three Studies of a Computer-Generated Image of the IBM Computer

DESIGN: Ronnie Peters, USA

PUBLISHER/CLIENT: Dynamic Graphics, Inc. – An In-house Study

DATE OF 1ST PUBLICATION/USE: 1992

DESIGN RATIONALE: The following three studies were designed to be used as illustrations in IBM computer manuals. The renderings were created on a Macintosh 2cI computer with Freehand 3.1 software.

CREDIT: Art director, Ronnie Peters.

Study of a Computer-Generated Image of the IBM Computer

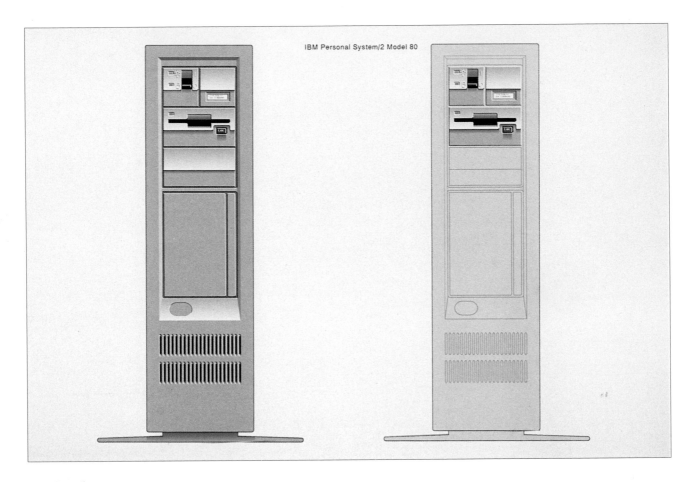

IBM Personal System/2 Model 80

**Study of a Computer-
Generated Image of the IBM
Computer**

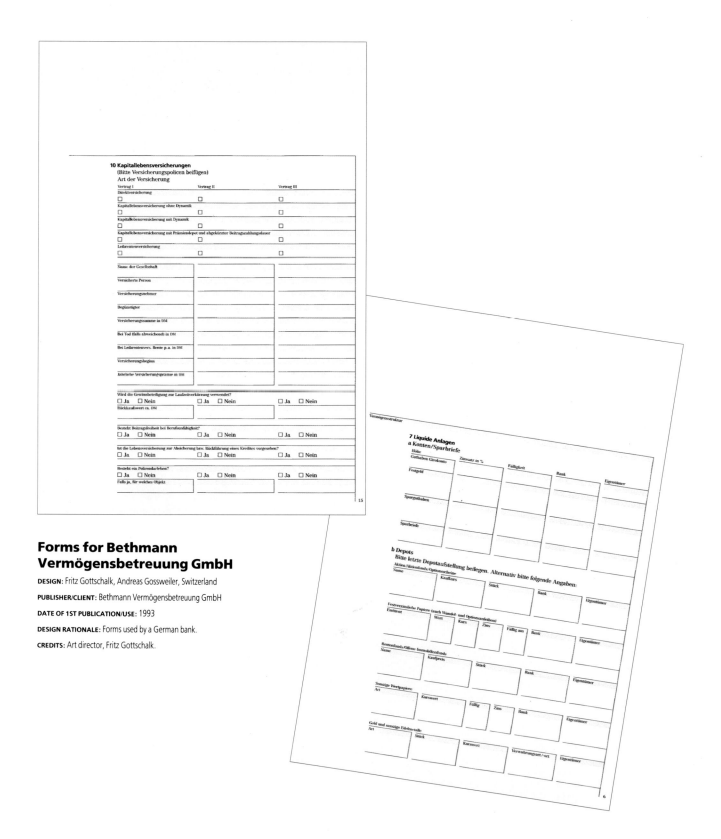

Forms for Bethmann
Vermögensbetreuung GmbH

DESIGN: Fritz Gottschalk, Andreas Gossweiler, Switzerland

PUBLISHER/CLIENT: Bethmann Vermögensbetreuung GmbH

DATE OF 1ST PUBLICATION/USE: 1993

DESIGN RATIONALE: Forms used by a German bank.

CREDITS: Art director, Fritz Gottschalk.

The British Land Company Educational Broadsheet Series

DESIGN: Ian Chilvers, UK

PUBLISHER/CLIENT: The British Land Company plc

DATE OF 1ST PUBLICATION/USE: December 1991

DESIGN RATIONALE: These educational broadsheets are part of a continuing series designed to stimulate greater interest in our environment by focusing on the everyday buildings around us. The broadsheets use architecture to explore design, social history, science, geography and even politics. Distributed to some 16,000 schools nationwide, they are useful teaching aids around which teachers can base lessons and develop topics for discussion.

CREDITS: Art director, Mike Dempsey; illustrator, Brian Craker; writer/researcher, Tim Shakleton.

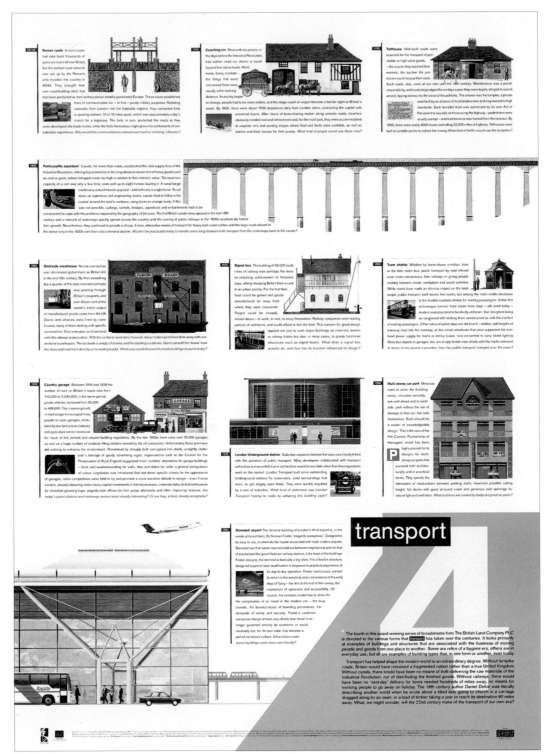

writers' houses

**The British
Land Company
Educational
Broadsheet
Series**

Train Promotional

DESIGN: Steven Stankiewicz, USA

PUBLISHER/CLIENT: Self-promotion

DATE OF 1ST PUBLICATION/USE: March 1991

DESIGN RATIONALE: An illustration of a 19th-century locomotive gradually metamorphosing from blueprint to three-dimensional rendering as it is read from left to right. As a self-promotional piece, this drawing suggests the ability to take a project from concept to finish.

CREDITS: Illustrator, Steven Stankiewicz.

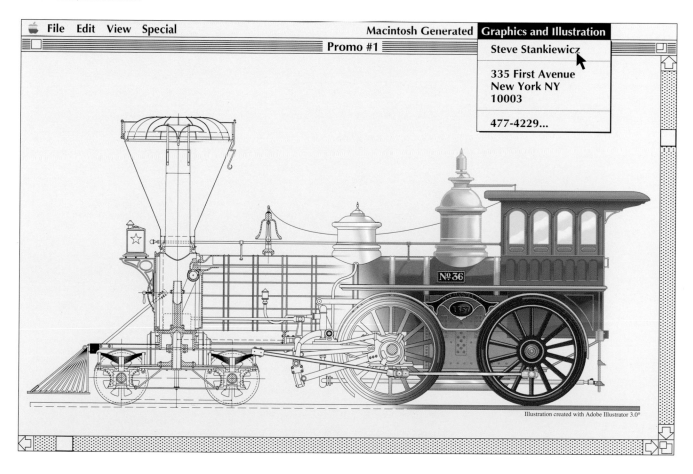

Index of Projects

Directory of Practising Designers

This directory lists the addresses of designers in current practice. While every effort has been made to ensure that this list was correct at the time of going to press, subsequent changes in address or status are beyond the publishers' remit.

Andersen, Nanna Guldborg
Illustreret Videnskab, Strandboulevarden 130, 2100 Copenhagen Ø   Denmark
PROJECT: Quantum Mechanics

Associated Press
50 Rockefeller Plaza, New York,
NY 10020   USA
PROJECT: Olympic Archery, Olympic Yachting, Diving on Montjuic

Baxter, John
Acme Design Co., 215 N St Francis Apt 4, Wichita, KS 67202   USA
PROJECT: Sand/Glass Molecular Structure

Berger, Nevin
Mac Week, 301 Howard Street, San Francisco, CA 94105   USA
PROJECT: Configuration 3: Moving on to Video
Editing, Document Management in a Mixed Environment

Bergman, Eliot
Eliot Bergman Inc., 362 West 20th Street, New York, NY 10011   USA
PROJECT: Water Saver, Gee, If Only I Had Known

Boon, Phoa Kia
Williams and Phoa, 2A Pear Tree Court, London EC1R 0DS   England
PROJECT: American Depository Receipts, Open Systems

Bounford, Trevor
Chapman Bounford & Associates, 115A Cleveland Street, London W1P 5PN   England
PROJECT: Le Shuttle Terminal Maps

Braddock, Paige
The Atlanta Journal – Constitution, 72 Marietta Street, Atlanta, GA   USA 30303
PROJECT: Around the World in 20 days

Bradford, Peter
Peter Bradford and Associates, 11 East 22 Street, New York, NY 10010   USA

PROJECT: *Medical Access* (surgical section), *American Health* magazine, Fordrea Community School, Camden Map, Sturgis administration model

Burg, Donald W
Shapiro Design Associates Inc., 10 East 40th Street, Suite 4102, New York, NY 10016   USA
PROJECT: Electro Biology, Inc. Annual Report 1985

Calver Lew
Newsweek, 444 Madison Avenue, New York, NY 10022   USA
PROJECT: Important Functions of the Brain

Carroll, Allen T
National Geographic Magazine, NGM Art Department, 1145 17th Street, Washington DC 20036   USA
PROJECT: History of Earth

Chengsos, Steve
Chicago Tribune, 435 North Michigan Avenue, Chicago IL 60611   USA
PROJECT: Aging in the Cell

Chilvers, Ian; Carroll
Dempsey & Thirkell Ltd, 21 Brownlow Mews, London WC1N 2LA   England
PROJECT: The British Land Company Educational Broadsheet Series

Chodel, Peter
Michael Peters Limited, 49 Princes Place, London W11 4QA   England
PROJECT: Tesco Plc Annual Report 1989

Cocks, Alison
The Dallas Morning News, 508 Young Street, Dallas, Texas 75202   USA
PROJECT: Cholesterol

Cook, Gary
The Sunday Times; 1 Pennington Street, London, E1   England
PROJECT: The Sarajevo Battleground, History in Flames

Cronin, Anne
The New York Times, 229 West 43rd Street, New York City 10036–3959   USA
PROJECT: Loops and Whorls into Bits and Bytes: How One System Matches Prints, The Negros' Burial Ground, Under the Gun

Cronyn, Melissa
National Park Service, USA, Division of Publications, Harpers Ferry Center, PO Box 50, Harpers Ferry, West Virginia 25425   USA
PROJECT: Oregon Caves, Saguaro

Cross, James
Siegel & Gale/Cross, 3465 W. 6th Street, Los Angeles, CA 90020   USA
PROJECT: Dimensions: The Design of the Earth

Davis, Jonathan
Michael Peters Ltd, 49 Princes Place, London W11 4QA   England
PROJECT: Lynton Annual Report 1988

Davis, Paul L
Paul Davis Studio, 14 East 4th Street, New York, NY 10012   USA
PROJECT: History of the United States, Family Tree of Cars, Family Tree of Great American Thoroughbreds, Family Tree of Paul Brown's NFL, Family Tree of Superheroes

Dominguez, Robert
see Associated Press

Duckett, Francois
The Charlotte Observer, PO Box 32188, Charlotte, NC 28232   USA
PROJECT: Where the Money Goes

Edotsune, Nobuko
4–24–17–202 Kamimeguro Meguro-ku, Tokyo   Japan
PROJECT: The Corruption of Italy, Inequality in the value of "one vote" throughout Japan

Ehrlich, Betsy
National Park Service, USA, Division of Publications, Harpers Ferry Center, PO Box 50, Harpers Ferry, West Virginia 25425   USA
PROJECT: Wright Brothers

Elsworth, Peter CT
The New York Times, 229 West 43 Street, New York City, NY 10036   USA
PROJECT: Tracking a Baseball

Feeney, Nick
2D3D, Mauritskade 1, 2514 HC Den Haag   Holland
PROJECT: Het Groenere Boekje (The Green Book)

Feinberg, David
Collaterol Plus, Jared Schneidman Design,

280 Park Avenue South, No. 20L, New York,
NY 10010   USA
PROJECT: Construction Options, Structure
Tone

Frankeny, Kelly
San Francisco Examiner, 110 Fifth Street San
Francisco CA 94103   USA
PROJECT: Hockey!, Dream to Reality –
The Bay Area Dream House, City Hall:
A Close Up

Geis, Irving
The Geis Archives, 4700 Broadway, Apt 4B,
New York NY 10040   USA
PROJECT: Three-dimensional Structure of
Cytochrome-c

Geyman, Bruce
National Park Service, USA, Division of
Publications, Harpers Ferry Center, PO Box 50,
Harpers Ferry, West Virginia 25425   USA
PROJECT: Congaree Swamp, Wright Brothers

Gleason, Vincent
National Park Service, USA, Division of
Publications, Harpers Ferry Center, PO Box 50,
Harpers Ferry, West Virginia 25425   USA
PROJECT: Greater Yellowstone

Goertzen, Jeff
see Associated Press

Gossweiler, Andreas
Gottschalk + Ash International,
Böcklinstrasse 26, Postfach 268, 8032
Zurich   Switzerland
PROJECT: Forms for Bethmann
Vermögensbetreuung GmbH, Self-promotion
Brochure for the Neue Bank

Gottschalk, Fritz
Gottschalk + Ash International,
Böcklinstrasse 26, Postfach 268,
8032 Zurich   Switzerland
PROJECT: Self-promotion for the Neue Bank
AG, Forms for Bethmann
Vermögensbetreuung GmbH

Green, Phil
The Sunday Times, 1 Pennington Street,
London E1   England
PROJECT: IRA Attack on No 10, The Last
Assault
on Mount Carmel Ranch, How 11.1 Million
Voters Changed Their Minds

Grimwade, John
Condé Nast Publications, 360 Madison Ave
(10th floor) New York, NY 10017   USA
PROJECT: Pit Stop, Football Punt, Counterfeit
Aircraft Parts, Jerusalem, Hitler's
Berlin 1963, Serengeti

Grundy, Peter
Thames Wharf Studios, Rainville Road,
London W6 9HA   England
PROJECT: Council Estate Signage, Cardiff in
Europe, Doughnut London

Guarnaccia, Steven
430 W 14th Street, Apt. 508, New York,
NY 10014   USA
PROJECT: 53rd Street Map

Gude, Karl
see Associated Press

Hagiwara, Sachiko
Tube Graphics Apt 204 Shuwa Akasaka
Residence, 19–40, Akasaka 6, Minato-ku,
Tokyo   Japan
PROJECT: Fencing, Judo, Sumitomo Bank,
Japanese Government, The Lavatory,
Kamikochi, Alaska, New Zealand Outfitting
Map, Sagawa Suspicion, Japanese
Government, Philosophy

Hamilton, Meredith
Newsweek, 444 Madison Avenue, New York,
NY 10022   USA
PROJECT: The Crooner Connection, Important
Functions of the Brain

Handsford, Tim
Michael Peters Ltd, 49 Princes Place, London
W11 4QA   England
PROJECT: Community Hospitals Annual
Report 1992

Hart, Steve
Time Inc, 1271 Avenue of the Americas,
New York, NY 10020   USA
PROJECT: Oil Fire Fighting Methods, HSCT Jet,
Moon Chart, Sleep, Former Soviet
Union Republics

Hofman, René
2D3D, Mauritskade 1,
2514 HC Den Haag   Holland
PROJECT: Het Groenere Boekje
(The Green Book)

Holmes, Mark
National Geographic Magazine, NGM Art
Department, 1145 17th Street,
Washington, DC 20036   USA
PROJECT: Macon Cutaway

Holmes, Nigel
Time Magazine, 1271 Avenue of the
Americas, New York,
NY 10020, Room 24–40   USA
PROJECT: 1,000 Years at a Glance,
The Golden State

Hurty, Arne
Macworld Communications Inc.,
501 2nd Street, San Francisco, CA 94107   USA
PROJECT: How Pointing Devices Work, Health
Risk Assessment, Inside the Macintosh L C,
Using a Mouse

Hutchison, Bob
Financial Times, 1 Southwark Bridge,
London SE1 9HL   England
PROJECT: Map of Yorkshire and Humberside,
Map of India

Jungerman, Eric
San Francisco Chronicle, 901 Mission Street,
San Francisco, CA 94103   USA
PROJECT: Gymnastics

Katz, Joel
Paradigm: design, 1309 Noble Street,
7th Floor, Philadelphia,
Pennsylvania, 19123   USA
PROJECT: Interstate 676 Guide, Interstate 476
Guide, Urban Icons (London,
Rome, Philadelphia)

Kealy, Megan
National Park Service, USA, Division of
Publications, Harpers Ferry Center, PO Box 50,
Harpers Ferry, West Virginia 25425   USA
PROJECT: Everglades

Kearsley, Steve
San Francisco Chronicle, 901 Mission Street,
San Francisco, California, CA 94103   USA
PROJECT: Rebuilding the Oakland Hills, A Tour
through San Francisco's Magnetic Fields

Kimura, Hiroyuki
Tube Graphics Apt 204 Shuwa Akasaka
Residence, 19–40 Akasaka 6, Minato-ku,
Tokyo   Japan
PROJECT: Judo, Fencing, Japanese
Government, Sumitomo Bank, Japanese

Pratt, Bob
National Geographic Magazine, NGM Art
Department, 1145 17th Street,
Washington, DC 20036   USA
PROJECT: North America in the Age
of Dinosaurs

Pugliese, Paul
Time Inc, 1271 Avenue of Americas,
New York, NY 10020   USA
PROJECT: Former Soviet Union Republics,
The Golden State

Radovic, Branislav
Financial Times, 1 Southwark Bridge,
London SE1 9HL   England
PROJECT: Oil Share Prices (Oil L709)

Ramsay, Viki
Reuter News Graphics Service, 85 Fleet Street,
London, EC4P 4AJ   England
PROJECT: Euro Disney Resort

Redfern, Stuart
Michael Peters Ltd, 49 Princes Place,
London W11 4QA   England
PROJECT: Albert Fisher Group plc
Annual Report

Robinson, Michael
Michael Robinson Design, 71 Park Avenue
South, London N8 8LX   England
PROJECT: Cost of Eating Out, Pride and
Productivity, Corporate Cutback, Broadgate,
IBM Building Plan

Rohr, Dixon
Newsweek, 444 Madison Avenue, New York,
NY 10022   USA
PROJECT: Countdown to Disaster

Sargent, Chris
The Sunday Times, 1 Pennington Street,
London E1   England
PROJECT: Assassination of Moussawi

Schakleton, Jo
Williams and Phoa, 2A Pear Tree Court,
London EC1R 0DS   England
PROJECT: Open Systems

Snook, Liza
2D3D, Mauritskade 1, 2514 HC Den
Haag   Holland
PROJECT: Inflow and Outflow Secondary
Education, Duration of
Registration Diagrams

Stankiewicz, Steven
317 East 18th Street Apt 3A, New York   USA
PROJECT: The Sinking of the *Titanic,*
Train Promotional

Stanton, Laura;
The Dallas Morning News, 508 Young Street,
Dallas, Texas 75202   USA
PROJECT: The Zoo & U2

Strawser, Kristine
San Francisco Chronicle
PROJECT: Electromagnetic Fields Walking Tour

Sullivan, Peter
Uplands Bush Ruff, Dover,
Kent CT16 3EE   England
PROJECT: Submarine Cutaway, Submarine
Control, Submarine Operations 1943, The
Attack on Sydney Harbour

Sweat, Stacy
Chicago Tribune, 435 North Michigan
Avenue, Chicago, IL 60611   USA
PROJECT: Triangle Offense

Tascón, Mario
see Associated Press

Teringo, J Robert
National Geographic Society, NGM Art
Department, 1145 17th Street,
Washington DC 20036   USA
PROJECT: Peruvian Tomb

Tsunemi, Misako
Sankei Shinbun Co Ltd, 1–7–2 Ohtemachi
Chiyoda-ku, Tokyo   Japan
PROJECT: Space Shuttle, Wind and Fire,
Comparison of Building Heights, Guide Map
to European Airports

Van Dam, Stephen
VanDam Inc., 430 West 14th Street, New York,
NY 10014   USA
PROJECT: New York City UNFOLDS®

Vicary, Jackie
Michael Peters Ltd, 49 Princes Place,
London, W11 4QA   England
PROJECT: Community Hospitals Annual Report
1992, Argyll Group plc Annual Report 1990

Wisenbaugh, Jean
43 Jacobson Street, Huntington NY
11743   USA
PROJECT: 1990 New York City Marathon

Journey of an Image, How Paper is Made

Yeend, Richard
International Herald Tribune, 181 Avenue
Charles de Gaulle, Nevilly-sur-Seine   France
PROJECT: Hydrogen as Fossil Fuel Alternative

Zakaria, Farah
Dynamic Diagrams, Inc., 12 Bassett Street,
Providence, RI 02903   USA
PROJECT: Tenses of the English Language

Zang, Matt
US News and World Report, 2400 N St NW
Washington DC   USA
PROJECT: Life in Space

**Every effort has been made to credit
designers. Quarto Publishing apologizes
should any omission have been made.**

The Pro Art Library of Architecture & Design

The Best in Contemporary Jewellery
David Watkins

The Best in Point-of-Sale Design
Stafford Cliff

The Best in Specialist Packaging Design
Stafford Cliff

The Best in Trade & Exhibition Stand Design
Stafford Cliff

The Best in Restaurant Corporate Identity
Stafford Cliff

The Best in Leisure & Public Architecture
Alan Phillips

The Best in Industrial Architecture
Alan Phillips

The Best in Science, Office and
Business Park Design
Alan Phillips

The Best in Lobby Design:
Hotels and Offices
Alan Phillips

The Best in Office Interior Design
Alan Phillips